NADER

Also by Justin Martin

Greenspan: The Man Behind Money

NADER

Crusader ❖ Spoiler ❖ Icon

JUSTIN MARTIN

A Merloyd Lawrence Book
BASIC BOOKS
A Member of the Perseus Books Group
New York

Published by Basic Books, a member of the Perseus Books Group.

Cataloging-in-Publication Data is available from the Library of Congress
ISBN 0-7382-0563-X (hardcover); 0-7382-0857-4 (paperback)

Basic Books is a member of the Perseus Books Group.
Find us on the World Wide Web at http://www.basicbooks.com

Text design by *Jeff Williams*
Set in 11-point New Caledonia by the Perseus Books Group

1 2 3 4 5 6 7 8 9 10—05 04 03

To my father, REX MARTIN,

and my brother, ANDREW MARTIN,

two men who chose the higher, harder road

CONTENTS

ACKNOWLEDGMENTS

I want to thank Merloyd Lawrence, my editor, for her careful readings, penetrating questions, superb suggestions, and most of all for lending this undertaking an air of excitement and discovery. This book's publisher, Perseus, is among the last of the indies, a haven for people who truly love literature. I am indebted to many on the Perseus staff, including Elizabeth Carduff and Jennifer Johnson in marketing; art director Alex Camlin and designer Jeff Williams; Marco Pavia in production and copy editor Chrisona Schmidt. Publicist Lissa Warren deserves high praise and much gratitude for continually finding ways to make sure books get their due. Thanks to Jacque Murphy for acquiring this project in the first place.

My agent, Lisa Swayne of the Swayne Agency, was a source of constant support. Thanks to her assistant, Monica Gray, for chasing down photo permissions. It was a true luxury to work with not one but two excellent research assistants, Steve Bujalski and Angela Graven. Both proved expert at searching out those telling little details that bring an anecdote to life. My friend John von Brachel located some obscure articles, which is much appreciated.

I want to give special thanks to the Nader family. A life as large as Ralph Nader's begs a lot of questions; he was extremely generous in setting aside ample time to answer all of mine. I especially enjoyed our lengthy Amtrak interview, New York City to Washington, D.C., with a stopover in Philadelphia. Claire Nader literally took me back in time, providing a tour of Winsted, Connecticut. Rose Nader welcomed me into her home and fortified me for the drive back to New York with some excellent homemade cookies. Laura Nader was a fascinating interview subject, a source of vivid and illuminating details about family life Nader-style.

Of course, Ralph Nader has come in contact with literally thousands of people in the course of his life. It was my great fortune to interview a pretty good percentage of them. Listing everyone would be impossible, but among the many who helped me along the way were the following: Theresa Amato, John Bushnell, Joan Claybrook, Frederick Condon, Phil Donahue, Joe Tom Easley, Andrew Egendorf, Robert Fellmeth, Mark Green, Richard Grossman, Greg and Jason Kafoury, Winona LaDuke, Ed Levin, Joan Levin, Lallie Lloyd, Mark McDougal, Saul Miller, Tarek Milleron, Morton Mintz, Alan Morrison, Mary Nix, Michael Pertschuk, Joseph Page, Peter Petkas, Anthony Roisman, Donald Ross, Victor Schwartz, Gary Sellers, Fred Silverio, Jerome Sonosky, Robert Wager, Harrison Wellford, and Sidney Wolfe.

Special thanks to Daniel Taubman for sharing with me his Congress Project diary and other materials and to Kirsten Hund at Project 55 for arranging interviews with some of Ralph Nader's Princeton classmates.

Some of the work on this book was done in a recreational vehicle, parked in the driveway of my mother-in-law's house in Rochester, New York. A phone line was run in and there was a good heater, fortunately. Thanks to Sylvia Charlesworth and Gerald Kressman for setting up this unique work space, roomier and with better natural light than my home office in New York City. Once again, Eric Charlesworth created an excellent web site for the book. Thanks to Jacqueline Charlesworth for input on some of the legal issues discussed in the text. Greg Schafer continues to do a great job in his informal capacity as West Coast sales rep.

As always, my wife, Liza Charlesworth, kept things in perspective, helping me with the book but also helping me get away from the book. She provided a monumental and joyous diversion when she gave birth to twins this past autumn. Thanks to Pema Norzom, our babysitter, for helping make it possible to finish this book by taking great care of little Tsepe and Jigmey—her Tibetan names for the twins.

And I want to thank my Mom—for her love and for her example.

"The only true aging is the erosion of one's ideals."

Ralph Nader

❖ ❖ ❖

"God spare me the purists."

Senator Joseph Biden

PREFACE

Ralph Nader has led a gigantic life. When he first came to public attention, the year was 1966, Lyndon Johnson was president, the Internet was not yet a gleam in anyone's eye, and the Beatles were still together. I saw him speak when I was in college in 1985, and it was the best speech I've ever attended. When I began this book in the year 2000, he was still a formidable force, still playing his unique and controversial role in American life. Over the years, he has done everything from conducting a full-bore investigation of the U.S. Congress to taking on the nuclear power industry, and he has worked on various causes alongside everyone from Alan Greenspan to Al Sharpton.

Never content with half measures, Nader has always taken everything to the extreme: even at the age of sixty-eight, he tries to read a half dozen publications a day, speaks four foreign languages with varying degrees of fluency, churns out countless books and articles on an old Underwood, and maintains several spares for the inevitable day when his typewriter breaks down. When he delivers a speech, it is usually three hours plus; when he sleeps, it is often four hours or less; and when he wages his various battles, it is with an intensity that tends to leave opponents stunned and confused.

At times during the 2000 election campaign, the rancor between Nader and the Democrats verged on the preposterous. Cursed in the halls of Congress, pilloried in numerous op-eds, urged by countless petitions to drop out, Nader responded instead—among other things—by actively campaigning in Florida, that most closely contested of states. The pressure should have been unbearable, but Nader seemed unfazed, which drove the Democrats to turn up the heat even more. Still, he did not flinch. During thirty-five years of public life, he has faced more than his share of opprobrium.

Nader's very first fight, and perhaps his most famous, was with General Motors. At the time, people pegged him for an auto safety crusader, exclusively. But Nader worked hard to wriggle out of that pigeonhole. He went on to address a vast litany of issues: unsanitary food preparation, flammable clothing, avaricious sports franchises, the limits of standardized testing. He also founded a number of organizations, many of which—notably Public Citizen and the Public Interest Research Groups (PIRGs)—are still in operation today. Others have fallen by the wayside. For a while, one of the Nader outfits offered a guided tour of Washington, D.C. Rather than visit monuments or the Smithsonian, participants got the opportunity to attend congressional committee hearings and the like.

When considering whether to take up an issue, Nader has always subscribed to the pasta school: throw it against the wall and see if it sticks. For each of his efforts that has failed, another has succeeded splendidly. If you get bumped from a plane and the airline provides you a voucher and reassigns you to a different flight, thank Nader. The policy grows out of a lawsuit he filed in 1972. When you get an X ray and the technician covers you with a lead apron—again Nader deserves thanks.

The net result of all Nader's frenetic activity was a full-blown movement, consumerism. The name is a bit misleading: consumerism is not just about the price of a cup of sugar, at least not at its core. It is more of a political and economic theory, born out of Nader's distinct observations about the ongoing struggle between corporations and individual citizens, producers and consumers. Still, Nader was never content to be a mere theorist. Through his efforts, dozens of safety laws have passed, and at times he has shown himself to be as skilled a legislator as any duly elected U.S. senator. At other times, he has demonstrated a media savvy that would do Madonna proud. Whenever a door has been closed on him, he has simply pushed open another—constantly adapting—gathering support at the grass roots when necessary, or getting his message out by running for president—three times now.

The consummate public figure, Nader has led an idiosyncratic private life. He has never married or had children, asserting that his battles require total commitment. He is a fierce proponent of openness on the part of government and corporations—in fact, he is the primary architect of the Freedom of Information Act. When it comes to his own life, however, Nader has always been inordinately secretive. He has even resorted to a little embellishment here, a bit of myth crafting there.

Nader has always been an immensely polarizing figure. With the passage of the years, the Nader faithful and Nader haters have only been pushed further apart. Because he has been involved in so many issues, it is not unusual for the same individual to hold a variety of disparate opinions about him. This is nothing so simple as ambivalence: it might better be described as violent mixed emotions. For example, there are those who feel a huge debt of gratitude for the model of advocacy he created, but at the same time are furious about his role in the 2000 election. Others support his presidential aspirations, but are confounded by the unshakable faith he places in lawsuits and all things lawyerly.

Among those stricken with the most violently mixed emotions are ex-Nader employees. Over the years, he has hired literally thousands of people to participate in his various projects. But he is also an inveterate bridge burner. "He gave me my start and helped shape the values I hold still," recalls James Cubie, who worked for Nader during the 1970s. "But he isn't in the personal loyalty business. Virtually everybody who has ever worked with him, he took a shot at later. I know he took a shot at me."

For a biographer, locating candid sources is always a challenge, but my job was made infinitely easier by the fact that Nader has ticked off so many people. The 2000 election, in particular, succeeded in prompting many close Nader associates—who in the past would have been guarded—to open up and go on record. Meanwhile, Nader himself was extremely generous with his time and I had the opportunity to speak extensively with his sisters, Claire and Laura. I also talked with a number of friends from his youth who had never before been interviewed. It is very rare that you get what might be termed access to all areas.

In the course of researching this book, I had the opportunity to speak with several hundred people. It was not unusual for an interview to last two hours, sometimes three. Nader's sprawling life inspires expansiveness in everyone who has ever known him. Very quickly I started to detect another pattern as well. Often an interview subject would describe Nader in the most glowing terms. Then, in the very next breath, the same person would rage about a conflict the two had experienced. My job became easy. All I really had to do was say, "I understand you know Ralph Nader" and then sit back and listen. What I gleaned most of all from these interviews was that in speaking so expansively, so candidly, so fervently, people were working to deliver up whole the complex story of someone who had played an incredibly important role in their lives and in the country's history. They wanted to do justice to a true original.

When a U.S. president's term ends another one is elected. Even when a center fielder for the New York Yankees retires, there is always another one waiting in the wings. But there has only ever been one Ralph Nader.

— 1 —

Winsted, Connecticut

RALPH NADER WAS BORN DURING A BLIZZARD on February 27, 1934. His three older siblings had been delivered at home and this time his mother was intent on giving birth at the hospital. The hospital, she figured, would give her a chance to rest. But the snow made it impossible and thus Ralph also was born at home. Shafeek was then eight years old, and the only Nader child with an Arabic name. Sisters Claire and Laura were five and two.

Nathra Nader—Ralph's father—had come to the United States from Lebanon in 1912. At the time, he had $20 and a sixth-grade education, and knew nary a word of English. He worked a series of jobs—at the Maxwell Auto Works in Detroit, a machine shop in Newark, a shoe factory in Lawrence, Massachusetts—until he saved up enough money to be a proper provider. Then he returned to Lebanon briefly to find a bride.

Rose Bouziane—Ralph's mother—was part of a sprawling family of eight daughters, two nephews, and two nieces raised under a single sod roof in Zahle, Lebanon. The family farmed and tended sheep. It was an arranged marriage, but Nathra and Rose were well suited. Nathra was an extreme personality: obstreperous, deeply moved by perceived injustice, and given to bursts of untamed idealism. He was tall and lean with something of the ascetic about him, as if all that restless mental energy were burning off calories. Like Nathra, Rose had had a variety of experiences by a very young age: she had grown up in a Christian family surrounded by Muslims in Lebanon under the French mandate. She was a natural teacher. When she and Nathra met, she was teaching French and Arabic. She was small and striking, with coal-black eyes and light, light skin. It is from Rose that Ralph and his siblings got their complexion, and their practical sense.

Rose married Nathra in 1925 and returned with him to America. The couple lived in Danbury for a year before moving to the town of Winsted, Connecticut.

Winsted is an old industrial town that dates to 1771. It is located in northwestern Connecticut, thirty-five miles from Hartford. During its earliest years—jokingly referred to by residents as the Iron Age—Winsted was known for forges that churned out tongs and pitchforks and carriage axles. The town sits at the intersection of the Still River and the Mad River, named for its propensity to flood. The rivers powered grain mills and textile mills that were the lifeblood of the town. When Nathra and Rose moved to Winsted, the largest single employer was the Gilbert Clock Company. Founded in 1805, it was once known the world over for its wooden mantle clocks; during the 1920s it still had sales offices in London, Montreal, and Rio de Janeiro.

Upon moving to Winsted, Nathra opened the Highland Sweet Shop, a bakery that over the years would expand into a full restaurant. The Naders also bought a house on a hill near downtown. It had two stories and ten rooms, and was built in 1917; there the four Nader children were born, quite literally, and raised.

Even as a small child, Ralph was astonishingly precocious. For example, his three older siblings might be learning a song in Arabic. Little Ralph was simply present in the room. Suddenly he would announce that he knew the song, and, to prove the point, he would then sing it from beginning to end. No one even expected him to pay attention, let alone learn the song faster than his brother and sisters.

Another time, when Ralph was nearly three, his mother was chatting with a visitor in the living room. Suddenly Rose realized that she had not gotten around to preparing lunch. "What time is it?" she asked the guest.

Ralph toddled into the kitchen and checked the clock. Then he returned and announced that it was ten minutes to noon. Rose was dumbfounded. She took the clock down off the wall and turned the hands to various settings. Ralph knew them all. When Nathra and the other kids arrived home, Rose still had not gotten around to preparing lunch.

Ralph learned quickly and seemingly by osmosis. By the time he was three, his mother was teaching him to read. "He simply absorbed," recalls his sister Claire. "He had this amazing way of absorbing a lot of facts, a huge amount of information."

When Ralph was three, he went to Lebanon for a year. The trip was the fulfillment of a promise Nathra had made to Rose's family: During the first fifteen years of marriage she would return at least once to Zahle for a visit. Nathra remained behind in Winsted.

During the trip Ralph began to exhibit certain personality quirks the equal of his precocity. On the boat ride to Lebanon, a steward took a liking to five-year-old Laura. It was nothing untoward; he simply found her a very charming little girl. One evening Laura was not feeling well, so she decided to skip dinner and stay in her cabin. The steward inquired after her and when he learned she was ill, announced that he was going to check in on her.

Ralph jumped up from the dinner table and raced to Laura's room. When the steward arrived, Ralph was barring the door with his spindly arms and legs. "You cannot go in there," he announced. "My sister is in there."

The family was puzzled by the ferocity of Ralph's reaction. Ralph even surprised himself. But in years ahead, the motivation behind the action would become clearer. Barring a steward from Laura's room was simply the earliest manifestation of one of Ralph's strongest and most idiosyncratic traits: he placed an extreme value on privacy.

In Zahle, Lebanon, the Nader children enjoyed being surrounded by Rose's hyperextended family. Besides Rose's seven sisters, two nephews, and two nieces, there were scores of cousins of varying ages. One cousin—certain that the visitors missed American-style Christmas—looked up Santa Claus in an encyclopedia and did her best to dress the part. An aunt who knew English taught the older Nader children so they would not fall behind in their schooling. They picked figs in the Bouzaine family orchard and took long walks in the lush Bekaa Valley.

A high point of the trip was a visit to Arsoun, the tiny village where Nathra had grown up. The kids got a thrill out of the bullet holes in the ceiling of Nathra's boyhood home. The holes were the remnants of a Lebanese wedding custom. When Nathra and Rose were married, well-wishers fired off a salute as they entered the house. The children could not help noticing another of the oddities of their father's old home: all the houses in Arsoun were arranged in rings facing toward the center of the village; Nathra's was the only one in the entire village that faced outward, toward a mountain.

When Nathra was just three years old, his father went to Brazil hoping to make a fortune but died of sunstroke instead. Nathra helped support his mother and two siblings in part by playing marbles for money. At age nineteen, he left Lebanon, also seeking opportunity, but in his case had gone to

America. The symbolism of Nathra's outward-facing house was lost on the Nader children during their trip to Lebanon. Once again, they were too young to understand. But in years ahead it would become a kind of touchstone, a symbol of the Nader family's separateness.

During the year in Lebanon, an archbishop called on the Bouziane household. He wanted to meet the visitors from America and offer them blessings. One by one, various relatives went up and kissed the archbishop's ring. When it was Ralph's turn he refused, saying: "I don't have to kiss your ring. I'm an American."

Everyone laughed. The archbishop tousled Ralph's hair.

"Who knows what led a four-year-old boy to do that?" recalls Nader. "It wasn't anything about the archbishop. It was more that I didn't want to defer like that. I probably would have agreed to sit in his lap and let him tell me a story. But there was something about the ring."

UPON RETURNING FROM LEBANON, the family was confronted with the question of whether Ralph was ready to start elementary school. He spoke English but had also picked up a fair amount of Arabic, and he mixed the two languages with abandon. Rose descended on the staff of the grade school near the Nader home, insisting that Ralph be allowed to attend. In 1939 he began going to the Fourth School, a classic brick schoolhouse nicknamed "Big Red."

As Rose had suspected, Ralph was not exactly daunted by the curriculum. Rather, he found it not nearly advanced enough. He was troubled that the math exercises focused entirely on addition and subtraction. His mother had already taught him the basics, using a pointed stick in the snow. So Ralph went to his first-grade teacher, Blanche Root Perol, and asked if he could borrow a book that explained multiplication and division. Ms. Perol was stunned but complied. While his fellow students departed Big Red empty-handed or tossing around a ball, Ralph always carried home a load of books.

Nancy Morgan grew up near the Nader family and went to school with Ralph from first grade on. "Well, he was pretty much always a student," she recalls. "I don't think he was ever too involved in social activities. I think he was about the only boy in the whole town who carried a book bag down Main Street, swinging it as he walked." It is an indelible image, a kind of Norman Rockwell in overdrive. And it captures something crucial about who Ralph Nader was and who he would become.

From an early age, he received a double dose of civics. He got it at home from his parents, who were sober—to the point of high earnestness—about the values of America. Equality, representative democracy, freedom of expression: these were not simply pieties to be tossed about by vote-hungry politicians. These were the promises of the Naders' adopted land. "When I passed the Statue of Liberty I took it seriously," Nathra was fond of saying. He was forever on the lookout for fresh examples of democracy in action and was shocked anew each time he detected hypocrisy or injustice. Ralph got a second jolt of civics from the town of Winsted itself. Many immigrant families settle in large cities, but long before Ralph was born, Nathra had his fill of Newarks and Detroits. He and Rose decided to raise a family in small-town New England.

Young Ralph's world was characterized by a remarkable degree of immediateness and accessibility. Sometimes lying in bed at night he could hear the cows mooing in the fields just outside of town. When he awoke in the morning, there would be fresh milk, delivered in glass bottles. All of Winsted's institutions—civic and otherwise—were within easy walking distance. "The library was right around the corner," he recalls. "The schools, the post office, the city hall, the town center—everything was within fifteen minutes."

When Ralph was about eight, Nathra began taking him to the county courthouse to watch lawyers argue cases. Under his father's tutelage, Ralph came to view penny-ante property disputes and the like as epic battles between the strong and weak, rich and poor, just and unjust. Early on, he vowed that he would also be a lawyer when he grew up, and not just any lawyer: he would represent underdogs, in keeping with the most sacred principles of democracy.

At a tender age, Ralph was introduced to town meetings, New England–style. This is a peculiar and regionally specific form of governance, developed by colonial-era settlers itching to escape the tight grip of the British monarchy. Long after the American Revolution, certainly well into the twentieth century, town meetings remained a vital democratic institution in New England. As of the 1930s, Winsted had a mayor and a board of selectmen. But their decisions had to meet with the approval of the townspeople. According to Winsted's charter, as amended in 1915, a quorum of just 10 percent of residents was required to alter ordinances, shoot down a statute, and so forth.

All of Winsted would show up for the meetings. This was bare-fisted democracy; often people got into heated personal arguments or were hooted into submission. "Value that person," Nathra would say to his children, whenever someone took a particularly unpopular stand. Certainly

Nathra was not afraid to go it alone. He waged a long and solitary battle to improve Winsted's sewers. As the Nader children got older, they were also urged to add their voices to the clamor at the ever fractious Winsted town meetings.

NATHRA'S RESTAURANT WAS ON Main Street and was called the Highland Arms. Winsted sits in the Berkshire hills, and Nathra liked the idea of "arms" reaching out to the community. By the time Ralph reached school age, the Highland Arms had grown into a substantial and prosperous business: patrons could choose between seats arranged along a lunch counter, booths set up in a dining area, or drinks in the so-called Pine Room. Nathra—hard-driving and innovative with his business—was the first in town to own a radar range and even brought in a chef from Maine. The menu included everything from meatloaf to fried belly clams. Growing up, Ralph and his siblings all worked in the restaurant at various times. As for clientele, the Highland Arms served mill workers on lunch break and traveling salesmen passing through. This was the era before fast food, when families generally ate at home.

For Nathra Nader, running a restaurant was a boisterous occupation. At every opportunity, he drew his customers into fevered political discussion. There was a standing joke in Winsted about the Highland Arms: "For a nickel you get a cup of coffee and an hour's conversation." People who could not stand the rhetorical heat usually chose to dine at one of the town's other two restaurants. Apparently plenty of people made this decision.

Sometimes local politicians would visit the Highland Arms, glad-handing their way along the lunch counter. Invariably, Nathra would try to persuade them to stick around, try the fish special, explain their platform plank by plank. He wanted to hear more than just a slogan. Any politician who accepted—whether Democrat or Republican—was certain to get an earful from Nathra, who had followed the dictates of his personality and registered as an independent. "He joshed them and pushed them and tried to stir them up," recalls Claire. "The only time he believed the Republicans was when they were talking about the Democrats, and vice versa."

Nathra was Winsted's version of Kierkegaard, the Danish philosopher who never strayed from his tiny village, preferring instead for the world to come to him. Parked behind his lunch counter, Nathra waited for the denizens of northwest Connecticut to lay bare their worldviews. Between forkfuls, visitors to the Highland Arms had better be prepared to defend themselves. Nathra just kept questioning and cajoling and hectoring and berating.

Worn down by the onslaught, a customer was once reduced to yelling: "I hate you, Nathra!"

"You don't know what you are missing," retorted Nathra. "I love you."

THE NADERS WERE OF Winsted, but also strangely set apart. New England town meetings represented participatory democracy in all its messy glory, yet the Naders' participation was always just a tinch too vocal. Nathra was proprietor of a small-town diner, the kind of place that is often a hotbed of political discussion, yet he was simply too outspoken for many people's tastes. As Joseph O'Brien, a longtime town resident, observes: "He was always interested in town governance, but he became so much of a gadfly that it irritated the powers that be."

The Naders were also set apart by where they lived, up on a hill, among the town's successful merchants and bankers. But Nathra also tried to imbue his children with his unique brand of egalitarianism. One time, Claire expressed disdain at the notion of working as a street cleaner. Nathra asked if she liked clean streets. Of course, she did. Well, then, that is a person to be respected, he admonished. "We weren't raised to look down on the workers," Laura recalls, "even though economically we were better off than the workers. We were raised that these people were building this country. It's on the backs of people like that that this country is built."

Winsted may have been a small place, but it had its social divisions and subdivisions. Many of the residents were of either Polish, Irish, or Italian descent. People tended to stick with their own kind, to the point that it mattered whether one's forebears hailed from northern or southern Italy. Besides the Naders, there were only a few other Lebanese families in Winsted, and assuredly there was no Eastern Orthodox church. There was a Methodist church close to home. Nathra and Rose were not especially religious, but they sent the children to Sunday school anyway. It was important, in their view, to make up one's own mind on such matters.

"The Naders were freestanding," recalls John Bushnell, a neighborhood friend of Ralph's. "They were a family that was not part of something else. They were in the mold of frontier families that you read about, very strong and self-sufficient."

Fred Silverio, another boyhood friend of Ralph's, has a similar impression: "As neighborhood kids, we saw the bond between the parents and all the children. They were a very cohesive family. And 'communication' is the word. They communicated with one another about everything."

WHILE NATHRA WAS BLUNT, Rose preferred a more indirect style. She liked to teach by means of folktales and aphorisms. Each day when the children came home from school for lunch, she would read them a ten-minute installment of an Arabic saga. Often she told Jeha stories, Jeha being a mythical Lebanese bumpkin whose misadventures always carry with them a moral. "Father was basically all about the issues of democratic justice, power, civic responsibility," recalls Ralph Nader. "Mother forged personal qualities in us like stamina, resiliency, and the need for no excuses."

Self-reliance was Rose's primary lesson. Whenever Ralph or any of the children complained about a conflict with a friend or a teacher, she had a favorite saying, "I believe it's you." What this meant was: examine your own role in a problem instead of trying to place blame on others. Rose kept Ralph in short pants until he was eight, and one day he came home complaining that the other boys were teasing him. They had all graduated to trousers. Rose had no sympathy for this kind of problem. Growing up in Lebanon, she had once been laughed at for wearing a makeshift garment stitched together from a variety of her sisters' hand-me-downs. "Are you a follower or a leader," she chided Ralph.

Rose was very health conscious. Her own mother had acted as a kind of neighborhood folk doctor, recommending various herbal remedies. As a consequence, Rose was very attuned to the spiritual and medicinal properties of food. Although the Highland Arms served hot dogs, Rose would brook no canned or processed foods in her kitchen. The Nader children grew up eating baba ghanoogh and fava beans and lamb kaftas and tabouli. She made laban—the Lebanese version of yogurt—and just about everything else from scratch. One of Rose's firmest nutritional beliefs was that giving kids sugar showed a lack of parental discipline. Whenever the Nader children invited someone over for a birthday party, Rose would dutifully prepare a perfect cake—chocolate frosting, candles, the works. But it was only for display. Before anyone could take a bite, she would strip away all the frosting, asking, "You don't really want that, do you?"

In a household that disdained sugar, not surprisingly, the smallest indulgences loomed large. The Naders' house in Winsted—like Nathra's boyhood home in Lebanon—looked out at a nearby hill, at the top of which stood a Civil War monument. Winters Ralph went sledding on the hill, summers he flew kites there. Sometimes Rose would let the children go off all by themselves, taking a picnic lunch up to the monument. "She made the simplest enjoyments seem like great things, so as a child you felt you were being given a lot," recalls Claire. "She made it seem like the most wonderful thing you could be allowed to do—to go and eat a sandwich. We didn't usually eat sandwiches, by the way; Mother thought that was just too much bread. But when you went on a picnic you couldn't very well have stew. You had to have a sandwich."

For the Nader family, Winsted was where old-world parsimony met New England thrift, creating in the process a formidable combination. The Nader children did not receive an allowance. Rose and Nathra did not want to encourage prodigal spending habits. If the children needed money for something specific, they were to ask their parents. Every Friday, Nathra gave each of the children a dime. They would march down to the Winsted Savings Bank and deposit the money. The few stray coins Ralph was able to scrape together from other sources, he kept in a little ceramic bank in the shape of a book.

THERE WAS NEVER A casual moment. In the Nader household, every waking instant was reserved for serious purpose. At no time was this more evident than during family dinners. Here, Nathra set the tempo. Following a typically long day at the Highland Arms, he came home refreshed and ready for more heated discussion. "He was interested in people and we happened to be the nearest people in his life," recalls Claire. "He didn't leave anybody alone—not his customers, his siblings, his wife, his children. He wanted to talk and he wanted to talk about the problems of the day."

Dinnertime discussions were like a daily newspaper, civics textbook, and political oratory rolled into one. The topics ranged freely: European colonialism, organized religion, taxation, social justice, FDR's New Deal. Often Nathra would talk about large corporations, about their mistreatment of workers and endless capacity for connivance.

He saved plenty of venom for Maxwell Auto Works, his first employer in America. Maxwell was founded in 1904 in Tarrytown, New York, and its cars quickly became popular for low cost (under $1,000) and durability. One model—the 1909 Model LD Runabout—was nicknamed "Doctor Maxwell" due to its widespread use by country doctors making house calls. The company moved to Detroit in 1912; that same year Nathra came to America and took a job at the factory doing piecework. When Maxwell ran into financial trouble in the 1920s, it was taken over by Walter Chrysler. Eventually he rechristened Maxwell as Chrysler.

That Nathra's first job was with an automaker is intriguing in light of the fact that the auto industry was the subject of his son's first consumer crusade. Then again, Nathra did not approve of any of the large businesses that had employed him; all had served to put a crimp in his independence. "He always wanted his own business," recalls Ralph Nader. "He used to tell us about the tricks big businesses used. He told us about how large grocery stores would shave one ounce off each five-pound bag of potatoes."

At dinner, Nathra always had plenty to say, but he always wanted plenty of feedback, too. Even as grade-schoolers, his children were expected to weigh in with well-formed and provocative opinions. These he would question and dispute. Soon the air would be thick with vigorous interfamilial debate, and dinner took on the flavor of a town meeting. Occasionally, very occasionally, after getting his brood stirred up, Nathra would actually desire some peace. Even this he turned into a kind of challenge, saying, "I will give ten cents to the child who can remain silent the longest."

As Claire recalls: "We were never allowed to run under fire. You know how you can get mad or frustrated and just want to run out of the room crying? We were never allowed to do that. You had to stand your ground and talk it out."

And as Laura says: "By the time I got to my Ph.D. orals I'd been through so many orals at the dinner table that it was a piece of cake."

Minus the frosting.

RALPH HAD A SPECIAL relationship with Shafeek, his older brother. In fact, Shaf occupied a unique position in the Nader household. As the first-born child of immigrant parents, he played the role of cultural translator. Because Shaf was born in America, he was able to absorb and accept its customs much more readily than his parents.

As the oldest, Shafeek put in the most time at the Highland Arms. "He wanted Ralph to have all the things he could not have," recalls Claire. "Shaf wanted to make the way easier for him. He wanted Ralph to have a bike; Ralph got a bike. He wanted Ralph to play sports; he introduced Ralph to sports."

For the fifth through eighth grades, Ralph attended Winsted's Central School, where he continued to range far beyond the prescribed curriculum. With Shaf as his guide, he was developing into a voracious reader. Nearly all of the books that Nathra and Rose owned were written in Arabic.

Shaf took it upon himself to introduce Ralph to various English-language authors. He even made a reading list, which Claire typed up and posted on the door of the closet in Ralph's bedroom. He dutifully worked his way through the list: *Moby Dick* and *The Mind in the Making,* by James Robinson. He enjoyed everything from Zane Grey novels to ancient Chinese history texts to Helen Keller's autobiography. "She was someone who overcame disabilities to lead not only a normal life, but an exceptional one," he recalls. "It emphasized to me the huge variations in people's use of time. Some frittered it away, some achieved enormous productivity."

Ralph also found that he was drawn to the *Congressional Record,* deadly dry fare by the standards of his classmates. It was relegated to the dustiest corner of the library stacks. But Ralph discovered that the orderly columns of seven-point print, unbroken by photos or illustrations, yielded up a world equally as vital as anything to be found on the pages of *Boys' Life*. He was fascinated by differences among the members of Congress: their varied political stances, issues, and oratorical styles.

Most of all, Ralph enjoyed reading the works of muckrakers such as Ida Tarbell, Lincoln Steffens, and Upton Sinclair. He was drawn to their sense of mission, undertaken in the slums and slaughter houses of gritty industrial-age cities such as Chicago, Cleveland, and New York. Compared to Winsted, it was all so very urban and exotic. "I read them trembling, literally trembling, with excitement, as I also read the Hardy Boys," he recalls. "I couldn't put them down. My mother would call on me to go out and mow the grass. I'd be in the middle of a four-hundred-page book."

Shaf also introduced Ralph to baseball. In keeping with a classic American boyhood, he quickly became passionate about the sport. If Winsted had its subdivisions between people of varying ethnic backgrounds, baseball loyalties created a roaring chasm in the town, between Yankees fans and Red Sox fans. Nader threw in his lot with the Yankees. In his youthful naïveté, he thought of the team as underdogs. Soon enough, he realized that the Yankees were only the most enduring dynasty in all of sports. By that time he was hooked. "I followed every game, knew all the stats," he says. "It was radio then, you could let your imagination roam. Sometimes I would listen in my room, holding a bat, making believe that I was Tommy Henrich or Johnny Lindell. Life was very simple."

Often Ralph would play pickup ball with other boys in the neighborhood. If eight or ten of them could be rounded up—good enough—that was a game. Often the number included David Halberstam. Halberstam spent part of his youth in Winsted and went to school with Ralph from the fourth through eighth grades. One of the most notable among his many works is *Summer of '49*, an account of a legendary pennant race between the Yankees and Red Sox.

On the ball field, Ralph modeled himself after Lou Gehrig, one of his heroes. Gehrig retired in 1939 when Ralph was five, but Ralph read and learned plenty about him. He was awed by Gehrig's stamina, by the fact that he had played in 2,130 straight games, then a record. And he respected the quiet dignity of Gehrig, forced to play in Babe Ruth's flamboyant shadow and later felled by a mysterious disease. If Ralph was going to be a Yankees fan, at least he was going to find affinity with a Yankee underdog.

Ralph played first base, and with that the similarity between Nader and Gehrig ends. During middle school, Ralph was lanky and uncoordinated. "Well, it seemed to me that there was a clear division between the good athletes and the good students," recalls David Halberstam. "I classified Ralph as someone who was always getting lots of As. But I didn't think of him as an athlete."

In order to graduate from Central School, all students were required to deliver a ten-minute speech. As his subject, Ralph chose John Muir, the naturalist and first president of the Sierra Club. The day of his speech Ralph was terribly nervous. He was sitting in the living room of his house, feeling like he was about to throw up. Shaf came walking in and asked, "Have you ever heard of Igor Stravinsky?"

Ralph shook his head.

"Have you ever heard of the *Rite of Spring*?"

Again Ralph shook his head.

"Stravinsky was not exactly on my mind at the time," he recalls. "I was thinking, 'What is this about?'"

Shaf proceeded to paint Ralph a vivid portrait of the controversial debut of Stravinsky's *Rite of Spring* in Paris in 1913. As the orchestra played the symphony's first bold notes, in Shaf's telling, a murmur rose among the audience. Soon there was booing and derisive laughter. Eventually most everyone stood up and walked out. Shaf concluded: "You're going to be speaking before a Central School audience. There will be people you know, friends of the family, classmates. No matter how you do, no one will be murmuring or booing. No one will walk out."

Shaf's story did the trick. "It really calmed me down," recalls Ralph Nader. "I never was nervous again, no matter how large the audience."

He graduated from Central School and it was on to high school.

THE GILBERT SCHOOL WAS named after the clockmaker who had founded Winsted's largest business. When Gilbert died, he left behind a considerable endowment. The result was a rather unusual school relying partly on public funds, partly on private. There were a few hundred students in Ralph's year, the class of '51. They were divided among various curriculums, "college," "commercial," and "mechanical arts." Ralph was among the youngest, one of just two students with a 1934 birth date. He was decidedly college-bound.

During high school, Nader mostly hung around with three other boys: John Bushnell, Saul Miller, and Fred Silverio. He had known them for years. All had grown up in the same neighborhood and all had played baseball together, poorly. By all accounts, Nader and his friends were their own little social island at the Gilbert School. Drive and focus—traits crucial to each boy's later life successes—mostly registered as egg-headedness and served to set the four apart from their peers.

Saul Miller remembers that Nader would periodically ask, "Who is Eck?" It was a running joke between them, Eck being a sixteenth-century German theologian they had learned about in Mr. Nichol's history class. Meanwhile, Bushnell recalls that he and Nader would spend hours on the phone, studying while a Yankees game played in the background. Each kept a scratch pad close at hand. If a player got a hit, they would race to recalculate his batting average.

While students in the mechanical arts curriculum were learning to operate a lathe, Nader and his crew were learning Latin from Ms. Mutch. This was a studious group, and competitive. "Believe me, there was a bit of a rivalry amongst us for high honors," recalls Silverio. "We were all hard-studying kids, all out to do the best we could for ourselves and to make our families proud. We just knew we were all going to college."

Nader—in the recollection of his friends—was also quite vocal in the classroom, no surprise. Here, the lessons of his upbringing conflicted. Certainly he had been urged to speak his mind freely, but his mother in particular had also taught him to respect teachers. He tried to split the difference. "When there was class discussion," recalls Bushnell, "Ralph would have arguments and would make points strongly, but not in a way that was antagonistic toward teachers." As Silverio recalls: "One thing, you could be assured that if the teacher asked a question, Ralph's hand would go up. He'd have the right answer. But there were times when he could expound on his answers a little more than might be necessary."

Mary Nix was one of the popular girls at Gilbert School. Because seating was alphabetical, she sat beside Nader in trigonometry. For Nix, high school was a smooth social whirl: the right clothing, the most desirable friends, the perfect steady date—with the star of the Gilbert Yellow Jackets football team. Outside of trig, she had little contact with Ralph. "If we had a party, Ralph was not there," she says. "If we had a dance, Ralph was not there. Because of how he was raised, his interests were not the same as ours. He did not stick out like a sore thumb or anything. He stayed pretty much neutral and kept his nose to the grindstone."

One of Nix's favorite high school activities was drama, in which she was often the star of various productions. The drama club was Nader's only extracurricular activity at Gilbert School. One of the plays the class of '51 put on was *A Connecticut Yankee in King Arthur's Court*, Mark Twain's tale about cultural collision. Nix played Elaine, a lead role. At one performance, she slipped and fell backward through a cardboard fireplace. This was greeted with warm laughter. Nader was behind the scenes; he had helped construct the set that Mary Nix fell through.

Nader and his friends spent a considerable amount of time playing chess. Going back to middle school, this had been one of their favorite activities, kind of an indoor sport to complement baseball. They were actually good. Often the four of them would convene at the Naders' house to play round robin tournaments. From early on, Nader showed a grasp of advanced strategies such as castling. One time, in the middle of a game, he suddenly declared "j'adoube" and to the surprise of his friends, he reached out and tinkered with one of his pieces. In chess terminology, "j'adoube" means a player can adjust a piece on the board without any penalty. "Our jaws dropped," recalls Silverio. "He was way ahead of us in his knowledge of the game and his repertoire."

Nader may have had all the right chess moves. During high school, however, there were other areas in which he was not even in the game. He was completely disinterested in dating. In this regard, he was set apart even from his three closest friends, who pursued girls to the best of their ability. Not Nader. "I don't recall Ralph ever dating," says Bushnell. "He never showed any interest. I think the girls in the class saw him as sort of different."

The motto under Nader's picture in the senior-class yearbook reads: "Anything for peace: quiet, smart, can be found either at home or at the restaurant—woman hater." According to Mary Nix, this last part, jarring though it is, should not be taken out of context. Yearbook mottoes are supposed to be provocative. "He had no interest in girls," says Nix. "But to say 'woman hater' seems extreme." Still, among the class of '51, in which Nader was truly known only by a select few, disinterest in girls wound up being one of his defining characteristics. In the Class Will, Nader's briefcase was bequeathed to Nancy Bronson. The joke was simple: Bronson was female.

Bushnell graduated first in the class and went to Yale. Nader was graduated with honors and chose Princeton. Miller went to Purdue, Silverio to the University of Connecticut.

For Nader, the decision had been between Princeton, Harvard, Haverford College, and Swarthmore. "I chose Princeton because it was strong in Oriental Studies and because of its beautiful open-stack library," Nader recalls. "The campus was irresistible, not too large or too small. Swarthmore seemed too small."

Nader's grades were good enough that he probably could have received a scholarship. He did not even apply. Nathra wanted to pay full tuition; it was his belief that people should not take financial aid unless it was absolutely necessary. Nathra had strong beliefs.

— 2 —

Tangling with the Ivies

On his very first day at Princeton, Nader slept through his very first class. The night before he had stayed up reading until 4:30. When he emerged from his dorm, he walked past a sundial and felt chastised by the short mid-morning shadow. "What a way to start Princeton," he thought. But that would be about his only academic transgression; Nader would work exceptionally hard over the next four years.

Nevertheless, he found himself strangely unprepared for Princeton: once again his studiousness served to set him apart from his peers. Such attitudes were understandable in a small mill town, but encountering them at an Ivy League university was something of a rude awakening. "The model was the Princeton Charlie who gets a gentleman's C," recalls Nader. "There was this supposedly casual attitude. If you studied hard, it was not 'cool,' though no one used that word back then."

Many of his fellow students were the sons of prominent fathers. (And only the sons: Princeton in this era was all male.) Nader sensed a bit of professional manifest destiny on the part of his classmates; careers in banking or insurance or real estate awaited them. His own father may have been successful by Winsted standards, but the family business was a diner, not a brokerage. Nader knew he could not afford simply to coast.

To Nader's dismay, he found that in some ways Princeton was simply the big Gilbert School in the sky, right down to the preeminence accorded to sports. "At Princeton, the athlete was king," recalls Nader. "Donald Rumsfeld was on the wresting team and he would swagger around campus."

Nader's response was to rebel, though in a rather subtle fashion. At the Gilbert School, Nader had simply stayed focused, woefully and willfully unaware of what others thought of him. At Princeton, away from home for the very first time, he chose—in typical collegiate fashion—to make a social statement. His statement was to study flamboyantly. He could be found at the Firestone Memorial Library right up until closing time. Spotting him through the windows, fellow students would sometimes hiss at him or call him a "greasy grind."

He regularly crept into one of the campus buildings after hours, intending to use the study carrels. Upon seeing a lone light burning, a professor entered the building to investigate and was surprised to encounter Nader. So impressed was the professor, according to Nader, that he gave him a key. When Nader's dorm mates learned about the key, they asked to borrow it, figuring that an empty building was an ideal place to take dates. Nader refused.

Nader also rejected Princeton's unofficial dress code. Many of Nader's classmates cultivated a sartorial nonchalance to match their study habits, acquired at prep schools such as Groton and Exeter and Lawrenceville, which fed into Princeton like so many tributaries. Staples of the favored look included pressed khaki slacks, but not too pressed, and white buck shoes, artfully scuffed.

Ralph could often be seen around campus in a pea coat, a gift from his brother, Shaf, who had served in the navy during World War II. This was not like wearing a T-shirt to a black-tie formal. Rather, it was simply odd—a subtle deviation in a place, Princeton, and at a time, the Eisenhower era, when any deviation was notable. The popular hairstyle was something called "short but combable." Nader's hair was short, Nader's hair was combable, nevertheless it did not qualify for the style "short but combable." At the same time, Nader did not fit into any known category of rebellion; he was not a beatnik or a communist.

Bill Shafer is one of a handful of people who number among Nader's Princeton friends. The two bonded autumn of freshman year, following Bobby Thomson's famous home run on October 3, 1951, probably the most dramatic event in baseball history. "We massaged that event endlessly," says Shafer. One time, they traveled to New York to see a production of *South Pacific,* strange fare for Nader, who favored gritty urban realism.

But mostly the two studied. Shafer had grown up in Cincinnati and had gone to public school. He also felt that he could not afford to coast. "We just seemed to click," says Shafer. "I came to Princeton not steeped in the traditions and the same went for Ralph."

Come sophomore year, it was time for an annual rite called "the bicker." This was kind of like a fraternity rush, only the goal was to gain entry into one of Princeton's seventeen eating clubs. The most esteemed were Ivy and Cannon. But there were also two so-called open eating clubs, Prospect and Court, where one did not have to be invited. While the exclusive clubs featured professional wait staffs—typically black people wearing uniforms and white gloves—the open clubs were cooperatives, where students did all the work. Nader joined Prospect Club. "Prospect was different," says Chet Safian, another in Nader's limited circle of friends. "They got people who were more renegades. Still, Ralph was not a rabble-rouser. He was not a wild man, or an angry young man. The thing I would stress about Nader is he did not seem to care about fitting into any social mold. He was just Ralph Nader."

Even in Prospect, the club for Princeton's social irregulars, Ralph was an outsider.

THERE WAS MUCH ABOUT Princeton—particularly Princeton in the 1950s—that Nader viewed with scorn. But he had chosen the school based on its curriculum, and in many ways it was a perfect fit for him, academically. Princeton has a tradition of preparing students for posts in government. Woodrow Wilson—class of 1879, thirteenth president of the university, twenty-eighth president of the United States—delivered a couple of speeches that carried the theme "Princeton in the nation's service." This was a notion that appealed deeply to Nader, one that resonated with the values of his family and his upbringing. While he was at the university, its graduates were making their mark on U.S. policy. John Foster Dulles (class of 1908) was secretary of state; George Kennan ('25) was a noted diplomat and a primary author of the U.S. policy of Soviet containment. Though Nader never would have suspected it, Rumsfeld ('56), the smug wrestler, was destined for a long career in government, including stints as secretary of defense for two different administrations.

Nader's freshman year grades were good enough that sophomore year he was able to get into the Woodrow Wilson School of Public and International Affairs, known as "Woody Wood." This was the only major at Princeton that one could not simply declare. It was necessary to apply and be accepted. The curriculum blended elements of history, political science, economics, and sociology, always with an emphasis on real-world policy making.

At Woody Wood, Nader specialized in Far Eastern Studies and economics. While pursuing the degree, he took a course load that also had a heavy Middle Eastern emphasis. Here again, Princeton had a rich tradition, fostered in large part by the Dodge family. The Dodges were descended from the founder of Phelps Dodge, the copper mining company. By the 1950s, several generations of Dodges had graduated from Princeton and had gone on to be active in the Middle East in various philanthropic and educational endeavors. From 1923 to 1948, Bayard Dodge served as president of the American University in Beirut. His twin brother, Cleveland Dodge, was the longtime president of the trustees of Robert College in Istanbul.

The Princeton-Middle East connection was a real draw for Nader. In the process of getting his degree, he traveled to Lebanon again. The trip was the basis for a 208-page thesis entitled "Some of the Problems in the Economic Development of Lebanon."

Nader's favorite professor at Princeton was Harper Hubert Wilson. Better known as H. H. Wilson, he was a self-described "anarchist," perfect for a greasy grind from Prospect Club. Wilson taught political science and specialized in the protection of civil liberties against encroachment by the government, corporations, anyone. This led naturally to an interest in what is now known as consumerism, though the term did not exist in the 1950s. One day, Wilson brought a can of hair spray to class. The particular brand was supposed to have been discontinued due to its flammability. But it was readily available at a pharmacy right near campus. Wilson reached into his pocket, withdrew a cigarette lighter, and produced a very graphic demonstration. It impressed Nader mightily. The only way to convey more clearly the danger posed by the product would have been to actually light someone's short-but-combable hair on fire.

Another class Nader enjoyed was twentieth-century history, taught by Eric Goldman. The course focused on Upton Sinclair and other muckrakers that Nader had idolized while growing up. Junior year, he tried to do a bit of muckraking of his own. Nader had noticed that every spring there were dead birds littered about the campus at the same time that the pesticide DDT was sprayed to kill mosquitoes. To Nader, it did not seem like a coincidence. He found himself wondering: if DDT was having such an effect on birds, what was it doing to Princeton students? He wrote several letters to the school paper, but to no avail. Finally he carried a dead bird into the offices of the *Daily Princetonian* and showed it to an editor. The gesture was met with indifference. "We have some of the smartest chemists in the world here," said the editor. "If there was any problem they'd let us know."

Nader was off the map and ahead of his time. He was trying to arouse the Silent Generation eight years before Rachel Carson's classic *Silent Spring*, which documented the harm caused by pesticides. It was a decade before the campus demonstrations of the 1960s. During Nader's time at Princeton, being an activist generally meant shouting "riot, riot" out the dorm windows before embarking on a panty raid of nearby Westminster Choir College. Of course, Princeton was not a monolith; there were programs like Woody Wood and professors like H. H. Wilson. Still, Nader sensed a pervasive complacency. Princeton simply was not receptive to reformist impulses, even from its own. When Adlai Stevenson, class of '22 and a liberal Democrat, ran against Dwight D. Eisenhower in 1952, a poll in the *Daily Princetonian* found that the student body overwhelmingly supported Ike.

While at Princeton, Nader had a brush with a titanic and decidedly reformist figure out of the university's past. Norman Thomas, class of '05, came to speak at his alma mater. Between 1928 and 1948, Thomas ran for president six times as the Socialist candidate. He was a fierce critic of both Republicans and Democrats. But he was particularly unsparing in his attacks on Roosevelt's handling of the Depression, arguing that the president emphasized economic solutions without regard for human consequences. As a politician, Thomas was a perennial also-ran, garnering just 140,000 votes during his final run. But he succeeded in getting FDR and others to adopt a number of his causes, including unemployment insurance and a minimum wage. He was also a cofounder of the American Civil Liberties Union. Thomas was a tall and imposing man, noted for his eloquent speeches. In later years, he would often limp to the podium with a cane. Arriving at the lectern, he would describe his slow progress as "creeping socialism" and the audience would be his. "He was a great debater, a fighter for social justice," says Nader. "So here was a radical Princeton grad, right?"

After Thomas's speech, Nader walked Thomas back to his hotel. Earnest, never one for small talk, Nader asked him to describe his greatest achievement. Without hesitating, Thomas said: "Having the Democrats steal my agenda."

Near the end of Nader's time at Princeton he had another brush with greatness—a brief but harrowing experience that may have played a small role in the future course of his life. During the school year, students were not allowed to have cars. The F. Scott Fitzgerald strain that runs through Princeton's history had simply produced too many gin benders in nearby

New York City, followed by horrific crashes along Route 1. As a consequence, students were allowed to drive their cars onto campus at the beginning and end of a school year, but only for the purposes of transporting their personal effects.

Nader, who owned a 1949 Studebaker, was all packed up and was leaving for the summer. He was near Holder Hall, headed toward Nassau Street. Suddenly a man with a shock of white hair wandered into the road in front of Nader. In that instant, Nader remembers mostly being struck by how oddly ethereal and abstracted the man seemed. Nader brought the car to a quick halt. Standing in front of him was Albert Einstein. All Nader could think was: "Imagine if the brakes had failed." (Einstein conducted research at Princeton's Institute for Advanced Study from 1942 until his natural death in 1955, the year Nader graduated.)

Nader ended his time at Princeton as he had started, by oversleeping. When his parents arrived at his dorm, they found him still in bed. Nader insisted that he did not want to bother attending the graduation ceremony. But Nathra set him straight, saying: "The ceremony is for us, not for you." So Nader raced down to the administration building to pick up his gown and mortarboard and found that because he was quite late nothing in his size remained.

Nader graduated magna cum laude. While specializing in Far Eastern studies and economics at Woody Wood, he had learned varying amounts of Chinese, Russian, and Spanish to complement the Arabic he had been taught as a child. Several of Nader's professors felt that he was a natural academic and suggested that he pursue a Ph.D. But Nader was dead set on law school. He had applied to Harvard and had been accepted, so it was off to Cambridge. Just one final step remained: with Nathra and Rose looking on proudly, Nader strode onto the stage to receive his Princeton diploma in an ill-fitting gown, several sizes too small for his 6'–3" frame.

DURING THE SUMMER OF 1955, as Nader recalls, he wanted to get as far as possible from both his past (Princeton) and his future (Harvard). He had the luxury of three months that were set aside, outside of time. His sister Laura, who was studying anthropology at Harvard, suggested that he take a trip out West. So Nader accompanied a medical student who had been hired to drive to Los Angeles and deliver a car to a buyer. "I'd finished four years," he recalls, "and I was going on to law school. I wanted a real change of pace, a change of scene. Everything was short-term, so it didn't matter what I did as long as there was variety."

Nader and his friend took a leisurely route. Along the way, they stopped at some Navajo and Hopi Indian reservations in Arizona. From L.A., Nader made his way north and got work as a day laborer in an apricot grove. Nader had never been averse to hard work, whether of the mental or physical variety. Growing up, he had the largest paper route in town; during college, he worked one summer at a factory in Winsted that made typewriter boxes. But an apricot grove had special cachet. Nathra had always shown a talent for engaging the mill workers and railroad brakemen who came into the Highland Arms, and his son thrilled at the romance of living in barracks among migrant workers.

Then it was on to San Francisco, where he found the summer job market fully saturated. His efforts to get work as a dishwasher or a store clerk were to no avail. Good jobs were available in Yosemite National Park, someone told him, and following that tip, he made a quick jog back east. "By the time I reached Yosemite I was broke and absolutely overwhelmed by the beauty of the place," says Nader. "I had no money to pay for a hotel. There were some houses with big porches in the Yosemite Valley. So I walked up to the door of one and asked if I could sleep on the porch."

The man who answered was Ansel Adams. Nader stayed on his porch for the night and the next morning, they ate breakfast together. Nader expressed awe over Adams's famous photograph of El Capitan, inquiring about his camera settings and technique.

In Yosemite, Nader found work at a grocery store. He lived in a tent at a ranger's station for a while before graduating to a dormitory. During his off-hours, he got to know the park, hiking along its paths, talking to locals, and soaking up the lore. It was a summer of adventure, certainly a departure from an after-hours study carrel. It sparked a wanderlust in Nader that would grow in the years ahead.

ON AUGUST 19, 1955, Nader was abruptly jolted out of his Western reverie. In the space of a few hours, more than a foot of rain fell over parts of New England, the aftermath of two separate hurricanes, Connie and Diane, that had battered the coastline. Winsted was particularly hard hit; the Mad River jumped its bank and three people were killed. Nader learned about the event from a newspaper; he was stunned to see images of his hometown in utter disarray. The phone lines in Winsted were all down, so he simply headed east and got all the way to Chicago before he was able to reach his family, who filled him in on the details.

Flooding had wiped out one entire side of Main Street. The Highland Arms was on the other side, but it had sustained serious damage. Prescott Bush—father of George Herbert Walker, grandfather of George W.—took a tour of the state to survey the damage. When he visited Winsted, Rose Nader grabbed his hand and said, "Senator Bush, Winsted needs your support in getting the Army Corps of Engineers to build a dry dam." He smiled and tried to move on. But she held onto his hand and repeated, "We need a dam."

Winsted got its dam, got two of them, in fact. The Highland Arms was rebuilt with a disaster loan and lived on for many more years. For Nathra, the occurrence provided a great conversation starter: "Which would you rather lose, your home or your business?" People who were asked this question had best be prepared because he had a detailed answer (he believed it was worse to lose one's home, but he could draw out the point endlessly).

AUTUMN OF 1955 FOUND Nader transported far from apricot groves and Yosemite and very much back into the orderly flow of his own life—at Harvard law following Princeton, following the Gilbert School. But his response was not what one might have expected. Nader's mode of rebellion was starting to take shape, fueled by his innate obdurateness. Getting into Harvard law was a goal he had vigorously pursued; he had actually taken the entry exam a second time, even after he was accepted, simply to improve his score. Once there, he found himself repelled.

"I was contemptuous of the narrow-gauge educational pedagogy that enveloped the students," he recalls. "To me, the law was an instrument of justice. They were preparing students for corporate law and occasional government service. And that turned me off. I was not going to become sharp by becoming narrow, which is the way they taught."

At Princeton, he had made a gaudy show of studying amid widespread disaffection and buckshoe-ism. At Harvard, thrown into an academic culture that encouraged striving—for high grades, law review, an assured future—Nader became almost willfully lax. Yet at Harvard, as at Princeton, Nader found subjects that gripped him, such as auto safety, and activities that engaged him, such as journalism. He would be set apart from, yet strangely of, Harvard, a relationship quite similar to the one the Nader family had always maintained with the town of Winsted. Despite his many protestations, the school's elitism also exercised its own queasy secret pull. There is a simple test for this: he never even considered dropping out.

DURING FIRST YEAR, Ed Levin was Nader's roommate at Hastings Hall. One of the main things he remembers was that Nader favored a certain sparseness in his surroundings. The two shared a common living area, but each had his own separate room. Levin put posters on his wall, *Great Thoughts of Eastern Man* and *Great Thoughts of Western Man.* Nader did not even bother to unpack his boxes from Princeton. When Levin played music on a radio, Nader seemed puzzled that anyone would want or require such a diversion.

Nader remained a late sleeper and often Levin smuggled him fruit for breakfast from the cafeteria. This was doubly necessary because Nader was short on money and had purchased only a partial meal ticket. The flood had hurt Nathra financially, and his son was forced to take student loans. Nader skimped wherever he could, though that could be a challenge because he was a prodigious eater in those days. Often he would leave campus in search of restaurants that offered generous helpings for very little money. A favorite was Durgin-Park, though he was careful to get there before 3:00 P.M., when the prices changed. Nader considered it a worthy challenge to eat an entire Yankee pot roast followed by one of the restaurant's monstrous strawberry shortcakes. Sometimes Nader would even make bets that he could eat additional shortcakes. Levin often accompanied Nader on his epic eating quests at various restaurants. "If I went with Ralph I was almost embarrassed," he says. "I thought they should be shuddering when he walked in. He had an extraordinary appetite and he never gained any weight."

Nader made money through a variety of part-time jobs. He was the afternoon manager at a duckpin bowling alley on Harvard Square. His ability to type roughly ninety words a minute also provided a stream of income. This was the era before computers, and typing was considered a clerical task, beneath the dignity of many law students. They wrote their papers in longhand and turned them over to Nader, who was happy to pound them out on his Smith Corona. "It was durable as the Rock of Gibraltar," he says. "And just one assignment paid its whole price."

The future consumer advocate also showed a distinct mercantile flair. On his trip to Lebanon, while he was still at Princeton, he had met some craftsmen who produced little inlaid metal boxes. While at Harvard, Nader began importing them. Meanwhile, Laura Nader spent some time in Mexico doing anthropology fieldwork and through this connection he imported handmade shawls directly from weavers. People recall that Nader would lope around campus hawking these goods like an old-time peddler.

Presto, just like that, Nader had set himself apart. But what truly distinguished him was the contempt he cultivated for the way law was taught at Harvard.

Nader has a distinct memory of walking through the campus and suddenly seeing a rain of pages fluttering down around him. When he looked up, he saw a student standing in a dorm window, ripping apart a case book. Nader stooped down, picked up one of the pages, and examined it. At first, he found himself puzzling over the question: Why this case? What was it about this particular case that had driven his fellow student to distraction? But then he drew back and asked himself the broader question, Why had someone gone verge-psycho while studying for a law-school exam? There was a sameness to the Harvard striver ethos, he found, that was as stultifying as anything he had encountered at Princeton. In years ahead, he would often refer to the school as a "high-priced tool factory."

He skipped countless courses. Or if he did not like the way a class was being taught, he would simply start attending the same course under a different professor. Where Nader had always been inquiring but docile in the presence of teachers, he became argumentative. He challenged the professor who taught landlord-tenant law, asking why the class learned everything about a landlord's rights but nothing about a tenant's rights. But in his greatest departure of all, he let his grades slide. Nader was on his way to graduating in the bottom half of his class. A lesser mortal—brainpower-wise—surely would have flunked out all together. "He was extremely good at cramming," recalls his friend Frederick Condon. "He had this amazing power of concentration, this incredible ability to soak up information, and that enabled him to survive."

At the beginning of each new term, grade cards could be picked up at a table in Langdell Hall. They were arranged in alphabetical order, and students generally snatched them up the instant they became available. Several weeks into second term, as Levin recalls, only one card—filed under *N*—remained. "He didn't see the point," says Levin. "Unlike the rest of us rote automatons, who would go to class and learn what we could learn, he was very perceptive and critical of what was happening at law school. He was a real free spirit. I was very impressed."

Yet there was also something perverse about Nader's mode of critique. He was willing to set duckpins, type papers, and hawk Mexican scarves, all in a bid to remain at Harvard law. Then he seemed intent on barely scraping by academically.

From late in his first year onward, Nader lived off campus and became increasingly secretive. Often he would disappear for long stretches. Friends would receive postcards from Putney, Vermont, or Ithaca, New York. A typical postcard was covered in writing, with appendages for each fresh thought, running up and down the sides, jutting off into the margins. One time, when Laura fell ill with malaria, he flew down to Mexico to visit her. She was living in Rincón, a remote mountainous area, accessed by a long jeep ride followed by a strenuous hike. Nader got as far as Oaxaca, where he came down with severe dysentery coupled with malaria–a relapse, in his case, since he first caught the disease as a young child while visiting Naples, Italy. Laura ended up traveling to Oaxaca to minister to him instead. From wherever he had sojourned, for however long, he would invariably return right before an exam. He would borrow notes from his friends and cram, cram, cram.

"HE DIDN'T TALK MUCH about his comings and goings," recalls Joe Page, one of Nader's best friends from Harvard law. "Nobody knew where he lived. Even back then, he always acted in mysterious ways. I don't know whether it's a Lebanese thing, might be a family thing, but it's been a constant throughout his whole life."

Obviously, Nader's yen for privacy has deep roots. The basis for it—according to him—is a kind of proof that he began working out even as a young man. He became fascinated by the question of why people were inhibited from speaking their minds. At first he decided that it must have to do with a fear of being laughed at or gaveled down. But that did not exactly jibe. "It began to occur to me," he says, "that people did not want to speak out because it might spark disclosure of information that was irrelevant, but nevertheless very touchy to them. Let's say someone has a relative who is mentally retarded and in an institution. They don't want anyone to know. They speak out at a city council meeting on some matter and then a local politician leaks it to the press. Now everyone says, 'Gee, you know, it must be the family.'"

Privacy and free speech are intimately linked, at least in the QED of Nader's proof. Basically, he was convinced that the more that was known about someone's private life, the more biases others would hold when that person tried to communicate various ideas. This begs the question: What was he hiding? But Nader's privacy premise inverted that question from the outset: What right did anyone have to muck around in areas that he had deemed irrelevant? Long before he had any reason to worry about protecting his privacy, it was one of his gravest concerns.

Also worth noting is the fact that during his time at both Princeton and Harvard Nader received a thorough indoctrination into all things Brandeis. Louis Brandeis was a monumental figure: a Supreme Court justice, liberal champion of the rights of workers and the poor, early advocate for a Jewish homeland in the Middle East, and coiner of the phrase "other people's money." At Princeton, Nader took a constitutional law course from Alpheus Thomas Mason, still considered Brandeis's most authoritative biographer. At Harvard law, Nader found that Brandeis (valedictorian, class of 1877) had assumed patron saint stature and that the case books runneth over with his decisions. One of Nader's assigned readings was the landmark 1890 *Harvard Law Review* article "The Right to Privacy," written by Brandeis and his law partner, Samuel Warren. "When I read Brandeis and Warren's article," says Nader, "it connected with the train of thought that I already had."

For Nader, however, there was a set-in-amber quality to the celebration of Brandeis, who had died in 1941. He preferred a different Harvard law eminence, someone who was very much alive, though quite old, and somewhat forgotten: Roscoe Pound. When Nader was at Harvard, Pound was in his eighties and held an emeritus post at the law school.

Pound is often called the father of sociological jurisprudence. He began his long and distinguished career as a botanist and earned his Ph.D. from the University of Nebraska in Lincoln, the town of his birth. Studying law was something he did to appease his father; he went to Harvard for just one year. Pound's dissertation, "A Phytogeography of Nebraska," is often considered the first ecological study published in the English language. As a botanist, he worked closely with Charles Bessey, a noted disciple of Darwin. He is also credited with discovering a rare type of lichen, dubbed *Roscopoundia*.

After his father fell ill, Pound took over the family firm without the benefit of a law degree. He passed the bar, though, and in 1903 became dean of the University of Nebraska law school and later joined the faculty at Northwestern. Applying the Darwinist theory of his early training, Pound revolutionized the practice of law. The notion of the law as a kind of immutable code handed down from on high struck him as hopelessly outdated, the remnant of an earlier Puritan age. He felt that the law must adapt to the changing values of a society that was increasingly urban and industrialized. "Law must be stable and yet it cannot stand still," was one of Pound's adages. He joined the faculty at Harvard law in 1910 and served as dean from 1916 until 1936. Phrases such as "social justice" and "law in action" are courtesy of Roscoe Pound, who never did get around to completing his degree.

As Nader recalls, he noticed Pound walking through Langdell Hall one day and followed him back to his small office, where he worked quietly, wearing a green eyeshade. "He was almost entirely ignored by the student body," says Nader, "because he was almost entirely ignored by the dean and faculty. They thought he was an anachronism."

Nader struck up an acquaintance with Pound. Often he would ask him for reprints of his various articles. Working his way through the mass of Pound's output, Nader was struck by his polyglot approach. "He was not a technician," says Nader. "He brought in all kinds of data from all the social sciences. The law writ large, that was the province of Roscoe Pound, and it was not in favor at Harvard when I was there. The law writ small was in favor—very technical, deep analyses of securities regulation X-10-B5 from the SEC and so forth."

During his youth, Pound had been known for his ability to hew to a punishing work schedule. And he had an encyclopedic memory; as a kind of parlor game, students would try to stump him with obscure legal citations. At age seventy-seven, Pound decided to learn Chinese and Nader recalls that Pound was still pretty vital, even in his eighties: "I once told him, 'you have remarkable balance,' meaning for his age. He said, 'I learned balance by riding a bicycle in 1890.' Remember those huge bicycles? That's where he learned his balance. And he told me how he'd learned how to fall, because he once fell while I was at law school and he didn't hurt himself. He said, 'I've learned how to fall.' He was a very methodical person."

Nader even asked Pound if he could write his biography. "Kindly no," was the old man's reply. He thought he might get around to writing it himself, though he never did.

GIVEN HIS SUBPAR ACADEMIC performance, Nader was hardly a candidate for law review. But he did join the staff of the *Harvard Law School Record*. An editorial arguing against capital punishment, which ran on October 27, 1955, was the first piece of journalism Nader produced. He followed this with a long article on the plight of American Indians, drawing on the trip he had made out West, his own extensive research, and consultation with Clyde Kluckhohn, Laura's Ph.D. adviser in anthropology.

Pieces on social issues such as capital punishment and the treatment of Indians were jarringly out of place in the *Record*, which was the law school's weekly paper. Typically, the *Record* reported on guest speakers, upcoming events, and the like. It was often just four pages long. The story on Indians ran roughly six thousand words, the length of a midsize *New Yorker* article in the heyday of the magazine's verbosity. But it also drew considerable attention. The Department of Interior purchased two thousand reprints.

During his second year, Nader became president of the *Record*, the last elective post he would seek for quite some time. Immediately he set about trying to transform the *Record* into a muckraking journal. He argued, unsuccessfully, that cheaper paper stock should be used so that the articles could be longer. He took the lead, writing a vast tract on Puerto Rico that dwarfed his story on Indians. This article was not nearly so well received, and in short order Nader faced a kind of insurrection among his staff. He was replaced as president by Robert Oliver. "He wanted the paper to be more aggressive," recalls Oliver. "It wasn't enough to publish an occasional article on a social issue. He wanted the general concept of the publication to be oriented that way. Essentially, he had the same personality [as today]. He was never really a person who was inclined to make a practical compromise. He could rationalize issues easily to suit his own view."

After the coup, Nader stayed on as a senior editor and continued to contribute periodic muckraking dispatches, though shorter in length, which appeared alongside the standard book reviews and faculty-retirement announcements.

Nader did not write any pieces on auto safety for the *Record*, at least while he was in law school. (Following graduation, he did contribute an article entitled "The American Automobile—Designed for Death?") But it was an issue that was already drawing his attention, for a variety of reasons. While at Harvard, Nader got rid of his 1949 Studebaker, not so much for safety's sake but more because he was tired of the upkeep. Unburdened of car ownership, he became a frequent hitchhiker. In those days, it was a safe way to travel and he enjoyed the company. "You met all kinds of people," he once told the writer Robert Buckhorn. "Executives would pick me up, tree surgeons, bricklayers, doctors, truck drivers. Not only did I learn a lot—outside of my father's restaurant it was the greatest education in the world—but you had to adapt to all kinds of personalities, and, remember, you were helping people too. Some of the drivers would pick you up because they were sleepy and you would keep them awake just by talking to them."

When Nader disappeared for days from Harvard, generally he was off hitchhiking. In the course of his travels, he received a kind of survey course on auto accidents. Truckers in particular were founts of information about common types of accidents and makes of cars that were disproportionately involved. Nader saw plenty firsthand as well, including a grisly incident while hitchhiking from Winsted back to Boston, the result of a pileup on the highway ahead of him. He got out of the car and walked to the scene to see if anyone was injured and spotted an infant girl. She had been killed by a glove compartment door that had sprung open on impact, nearly decapitating her.

While at Harvard, Nader closely followed the congressional hearings on highway safety conducted by Alabama Congressman Kenneth Roberts, finding the proceedings nearly as exciting as a ninth-inning Yankees rally. He showed transcripts to friends, who were thoroughly unmoved. He also read a 1956 *Harvard Law Review* article by Harold Katz suggesting that automakers might be liable in cases of unsafe auto design. Katz was one of the first people to make this argument. Nader wanted to learn more so he telephoned the author. "I got a call from this fellow, I'd never heard of him, but he was quite ecstatic," recalls Katz. "He told me that he was utterly astonished and absolutely delighted by my article. He didn't have any prior notion of using tort law to reform the auto industry. The idea captivated him." Nader also asked Katz if he would contribute an article on the subject to the *Record*, but that never came to pass.

In his third year at Harvard, Nader took a medical/legal seminar from William Curran. It was a unique course, designed to explore issues of confluence between law and medicine. When it came time to do a paper, Nader decided to delve into Katz's territory: auto safety liability. He researched furiously, chasing down obscure studies such as one from Cornell medical school that looked into engineering innovations that might cut down on car injuries. Nader's paper was entitled "Automotive Design Safety and Legal Liability." His heart was in this one and he received an A.

— 3 —

A Small World

NADER HAD SPENT THE PAST SEVEN YEARS—first at Princeton, then at Harvard—cultivating a sense of otherness. Even the brushes with Einstein and Ansel Adams seemed to Nader to be oddly freighted with meaning, hints perhaps that a unique fate was reserved for him—grander, more glorious, or at least different. Yet he could not figure out how to claim it. Over the next four years, until he turned twenty-nine, Nader would travel extensively, write periodically, try out teaching, dabble in law. Whatever he did, wherever he went, Nader would always find himself pulled inexorably back to Winsted.

Often he entertained notions of heading off to Alaska. One summer during Harvard law, Nader had worked in Washington, lobbying members of Congress, trying to persuade them to support statehood for Alaska and Hawaii. Nader did not do this in conjunction with a lobbying firm; rather he did it unpaid and on his own initiative. To make ends meet, he drew on his meager savings. Upon graduation, he was offered a job clerking for a judge in Alaska. Instead, he chose to go into the army.

In 1958 the draft was in effect, and a man either joined or ran the risk of being conscripted. It was better, in terms of duties and length of service, to go in as a volunteer. Nader spent six months in the Army Reserve at Fort Dix in New Jersey. He went through basic training, where he got into excellent physical shape, bivouacked outdoors, and actually learned how to fire an M-1 rifle. When his superiors learned that he was a graduate of Harvard law, they had him type up personnel files. But Nader's main experience in the army was as a cook. "You had to deal with huge quantities," he recalls. "I helped make banana bread for about forty thousand troops. I made soup for thousands. If you fell into that, and you didn't know how to swim, you were minestrone."

At the end of his Fort Dix stint, Nader went to the PX and bought a dozen pairs of boots for six dollars each and four dozen pairs of socks for thirty-five cents apiece. His discharge papers listed his comparable civilian occupation as "chef."

New Year's Day 1959, Fidel Castro marched his victorious rebel forces into Havana. That would be Nader's next stop. He tagged along with David Binder, an acquaintance a year behind him at Harvard law, who was editor of the *Record* and had been promised an interview with Castro. Nader planned a short freelance piece for the *Christian Science Monitor.* The trip was arranged by Charles Porter, a congressman from Oregon and Harvard law alum. Nader and Binder drove down to Key West and took a puddle jumper across to Havana, arriving shortly after Castro seized power.

They stayed at the Havana Hilton, as guests of Castro and the Cuban government. At one point, a mere teenager in fatigues got onto their hotel elevator and began twirling a gun. He dropped it and everyone jumped in fright. "Pardone, pardone," said the embarrassed teenager. It was a wild time, and all kinds of strange people were converging on Havana. Errol Flynn was staying at the Hotel Nacional and one night, apparently in a drunken haze, he managed to set his room on fire. Nader and Binder went over to the Nacional and poked around aimlessly, hoping to encounter Flynn or at least to get an account of the incident. They also paid a visit to the Tropicana, Havana's famous supper club. But they simply people-watched, lacking the money for a drink, let alone supper. Mostly they bought their meals from street vendors.

On the third day and final day of their visit, it was time for the big interview with Castro. Because Nader spoke decent Spanish, he was the designated inquisitor. It wound up being a press conference with several other journalists present. As it turned out, Castro's English was pretty good. Nader managed to shoehorn in a few questions about agrarian reform and U.S.-Cuban relations. "Castro was a nonstop talker, as everyone now knows," says Nader.

But mostly the trip was a lark. "Who wouldn't want to go," he says. "It was the revolution, the Bearded One, a period of waiting and hoping for Cuba."

Fresh from Cuba, trained at Fort Dix, Nader returned to Winsted and took a job in nearby Hartford. He went to work at a law firm that was the sole proprietorship of a man named George Athanson. The office at 54 Church Street was tiny, just a single room. Every day, Nader would hitch-hike to and from work. Both Winsted and Hartford had "bumming corners" and Nader would simply stand at one along Route 44 waiting to be picked up, even in the rain. Andrew Grinvalsky, a high school classmate who ran a pharmacy in New Hartford, sometimes gave Nader rides. "He did not have a car; it was as simple as that," says Grinvalsky. "Ralph was an eccentric genius. As you get older, you can categorize genius. At the time, he was just different."

Athanson, the future mayor of Hartford, was an avuncular man and people felt extremely at ease in his presence. They would come to him with their problems, which in turn became the firm's case load: divorces, trusts, bankruptcy, personal injury. Nader was drawn to the practice, he told law school friends, because this was not some high-flown, overly intellectualized approach to the law. This was real people seeking genuine justice. But friends such as Chet Safian, who attended both Princeton and Harvard with Nader, found the explanation unconvincing: "I thought it was a little strange for Ralph to be working in Hartford, in this little walkup, representing people like Mrs. DeTamaso, the nice Italian lady who slipped and fell. I did not expect him to go to a big Wall Street firm. But it seemed unusual. Maybe he was trying to distance himself from Harvard."

Apparently Nader also felt the need for some intellectual stimulation outside the Athanson firm. With his boss's help, he landed a teaching post at the University of Hartford, where he lectured evenings on government and history. He also wrote a profile of Roscoe Pound that appeared in *Reader's Digest*, entitled "The Grand Old Man of Law" and for the *Nation* he wrote a piece, "The Safe Car You Can't Buy."

Nader's interest in auto safety continued. Working at Athanson's firm, he handled some accident claim cases. As a sideline, he testified on auto safety before the state legislatures in Connecticut, Massachusetts, and New York. He also delivered speeches on the subject before assorted local chambers of commerce and women's auxiliary groups. At his urging, some of these organizations even adopted resolutions calling for safer auto design, but this had little impact.

Meanwhile, Ed Levin—Nader's first and only roommate at Harvard law—had moved to Chicago. In 1961 Levin became a bill drafter for the Illinois General Assembly. One of the bills being considered before the state legislature at this time would require cars sold in Illinois to have an attachment for seat belts, giving people the option to buy and install them.

Levin mentioned this to Nader, who responded by writing a series of impassioned letters urging him to take an active role in pushing the legislation. Levin resisted; it was not his cause. "At one point," he recalls, "Ralph wrote me this scathing letter. 'Did I want to be responsible for 50,000 lost lives?' He kind of held me personally to blame."

Levin found his old friend's letter odd and unusually harsh. He showed it to his wife, asking, "Is this fair?"

To his surprise, she said: "He's right. Somebody should be doing this."

So Joan Levin took up the cause, and with Nader's guidance formed a group called Illinois Citizens for Automobile Safety. She lobbied the state legislature, helping push the bill through the house. But it was killed in the senate by the auto lobby. "Here he was working in this little law firm in Connecticut," recalls Joan Levin. "I knew something was really burning in his soul."

DURING THE SUMMER OF 1961, Nader took a trip to Scandinavia. It had the character of many of his trips both past and future in that one of his primary goals was educational. Nader favored what might be described as pedagogic vacations. When he headed out west during the summer of 1955, he stopped at several Indian reservations and used the accrued knowledge to write an article for the *Record*. For his trip to Scandinavia, his intention was to learn more about ombudsmen, and he set up interviews with some ombudsmen and their staffs in Stockholm and Copenhagen.

From Helsinki, Nader traveled to Moscow. While there, he met up with Harold Berman, a Harvard law professor who was an expert in the Soviet judicial system. During his third year of law school, Nader worked for Berman as a research assistant. Once, during his tenure at the *Record*, Nader sent a letter to Nikita Khrushchev, asking him some questions about reform of the Soviet penal code. It was a bold gesture, but while at Harvard, Nader had already carried on a brief correspondence with Supreme Court Justice Felix Frankfurter over an article he had written for the *Record*. Nader also received a response to his Khrushchev letter, but apparently the Soviet premier had delegated the task to D. S. Karev, dean of the Moscow University law school. To Berman fell the task of verifying that the letter was authentic and translating it. The letter appeared in the May 1, 1958, issue of the *Record*.

"Ralph Nader was a very interesting young man, full of life, full of ideas, full of vision," recalls Professor Berman. "He realized that American-

Russian relations were very important—in those days, crucial. Russian lawyers constitute a group that was moving toward more humane practices. Lawyers tended to be more progressive, and Ralph Nader went to Moscow hoping to make contact with them."

Thus Berman arranged for Nader to meet with some lawyers during his visit. But this was not exactly a landmark encounter; it did little to thaw the Cold War. So it was back to Connecticut and George Athanson's law practice. Upon his return, Nader pushed the state legislature to introduce a bill that would establish an ombudsman. This effort also went nowhere.

FROM MAY TO EARLY September of 1963, Nader took yet another trip, this time an extended pedagogic sojourn through Latin America. His traveling companion was Joe Page, a friend from Harvard law. To defray costs, the two arranged to write dispatches for the *Atlantic Monthly* and *Christian Science Monitor*, which paid roughly $30 a pop. Nader was able to grind them out at a phenomenal rate, often two or three per week. "I've always been able to do that," says Nader. "I could go into a country and very quickly, I'd have a real grasp of the situation. I knew exactly what to look for, the variety of people you need to talk to. I knew how to cross-examine. And I knew how to filter out what was relevant and what wasn't."

Typically, he would compose his stories on a portable typewriter while sitting in an airport waiting for the flight to his next destination.

Page and Nader met up in Caracas and from there traveled to Recife in northeastern Brazil. In the early 1960s, Recife was a political hot spot due to unrest among the sugar farmers. The farmers were being organized into leagues by a charismatic lawyer named Francisco Julião. There was some speculation that Julião would be the next Castro.

Nader and Page hung around the Hotel Guararapes in Recife, where they got to know the various key players in the unfolding drama. They interviewed Catholic priests, communist party leaders, and union organizers. But Julião proved to be a holdout. Then one day, Nader received word through an aide-de-camp that Julião's car had broken down in the countryside. Here was the deal: if Nader would arrange for a jeep to tow Julião's car, he could have the interview. Nader would also need to pony up the $20 towing fee. So Nader and Page hired a jeep and headed out into the sugarcane fields, where they met up with Julião. "Ralph was always very prepared," says Page. "When it came to interviews, the way he saw it, the longer the better. He was not afraid of asking tough questions."

Their efforts resulted in a piece called "The Shadow City of Recife" which appeared, unsigned, in the *Atlantic Monthly*. Nader also produced a monster ten-thousand-word version that he submitted to the *New Yorker*, where he thought he might have a connection—a college roommate of his sister Laura had taken a job at the magazine. But the *New Yorker* said kindly no.

From Recife, Nader and Page traveled to Rio and then on to Brasilia, the country's modern capital, which was finished in 1960. Nader split off then and went on to Montevideo, Uruguay, where he had some friends. The two reconvened in Buenos Aires and from there they traveled to Chile. Upon arriving in Santiago, Page recalls that Nader had a small accident. "One of Ralph's characteristics is that he's a pack rat. On a trip he collects all this stuff—documents, reports, newspaper articles—that he wants to take back with him. He was accumulating these items in a plastic shopping bag that had gradually torn throughout the trip. We got out of the cab in front of our hotel and before Ralph could do anything, the bellhop grabbed his bag, and it basically disintegrated."

In 1963 Salvador Allende was getting geared up to make a bid for the presidency of Chile. He was relatively unknown to Americans, the perfect subject for a dispatch from Santiago, so Nader decided to see if he could land an interview. He called up the headquarters of Allende's party, the FRAP. Come down tomorrow at 3:30 P.M., he was instructed, and Allende will meet with you. As he hung up the phone, Nader and Page exchanged a glance: this just seemed too easy.

The next day Nader and Page showed up at the appointed time. Out strode Allende and the his first words were, "I'm not going to talk to American journalists. They distort everything I say." From here, he launched into fifteen minutes worth of very spicy Spanish. Allende was a small man, and throughout the tirade he was forced to look up at Nader and Page, his face growing progressively redder with rage. Then he stopped abruptly, turned on his heel, and walked away. Apparently the interview was over. Allende's assistant apologized, explaining that he had just conducted an interview with the *New York Times* and had been very displeased with the outcome. It seemed that Allende had simply decided to give a piece of his mind to the next American journalists he encountered. The assistant offered to arrange a second interview, suggesting that they might find Allende in better spirits.

For the encore interview, Allende picked up Nader and Page at their hotel. Nothing was said about the previous day's carryings-on. They repaired to Allende's house to have lunch. As promised, Allende was in a better mood—in fact, at home, surrounded by his family, he was downright giddy. Servants were bustling in and out setting out various dishes and Allende kept making jokes with his daughters. Nader was seated directly beside him. Every time Nader attempted to ask an interview question, though, Allende would simply ignore him, cheerfully saying "comer, comer!" (eat, eat!). The dispatch from Santiago contained precious few details about Chile's future president.

BACK IN WINSTED, NADER had dinner with David Halberstam. Halberstam had just returned from Saigon, where he had been stationed as a correspondent for the *New York Times*. When Nader started describing his own extensive travels, Halberstam was shocked. To the best of his knowledge, Nader worked at a small law firm in Hartford. Of course, Nader was cagey as always and would not reveal certain details about his trips or explain why he had been where he had been. He did not even bother to tell Halberstam that he, too, had been doing some journalism. Halberstam's brother Michael was present for the dinner and after Nader left he leaned over and said, "I think he's working for the CIA."

In 1964 Halberstam's foreign correspondence earned him a Pulitzer Prize. To celebrate, his mother threw him a party in Winsted and it was there that Halberstam had another off-kilter encounter with a member of the Nader family, this time Nathra. Nathra button-holed him and proceeded to hold forth with great enthusiasm: "You and Ralph are going to change this country. It's young people like you and Ralph."

Halberstam thought to himself: "What in the hell does Ralph have to do with it? I mean, I love you, Nathra, you're great—but Ralph? What has he ever done?"

The answer, as it happened, was that Nader had done a whole lot and not too much: He had been to Moscow, Montevideo, Cuba, and Copenhagen, had crossed paths, however briefly, with Castro, Allende, and god knows who else. And he had also worked in a small Hartford law firm, helping prepare divorce papers and bankruptcy filings.

Frequently Nader would call up old friends from college, floating the idea, "Come on, let's pick up and move to Alaska."

Invariably, they would protest; they had a wife or kids or were just starting a new job.

"It's the last frontier, the land of opportunity."

But what would we do, where would we stay?

"Just think about it," Nader would urge.

— 4 —
Unsafe

Modern-day car commercials are abrim with images of flailing crash-test dummies and shock-absorbing front ends crumpling in orderly cinematic slow motion. There have been umpteen variations on the advertisement in which a near-miss on a rainy road culminates in the driver glancing in the rearview mirror and letting out a sigh of relief upon seeing the baby still snoozing peacefully in the backseat. In short, safety sells. A time when it was otherwise is virtually inconceivable.

But as recently as the mid–1960s, safety was considered a rather ho-hum issue. Ample opportunity existed for styling and performance innovations, but when it came to auto safety, many experts maintained that the outer limits had been pretty well plumbed. Cars were as crashworthy as they could possibly be. Any further refinements in safety would have to come from driver behavior.

Harry Barr, General Motor's vice president of engineering, was quoted in the *New York Times* as follows: "The driver is most important, we feel. If the drivers do everything they should, there wouldn't be accidents, would there?"

Around the same time, an article in *Car and Driver* asserted that cars are "about as safe as can be" before concluding that "the principal cause of accidents is homo sapiens, few of whom ever really learn to drive well."

Fatal auto accidents were pushing fifty thousand a year by the mid–1960s and injuries had hit the 4 million mark. The toll had been rising each year going back to 1899, when a man with the unfortunate name of H. H. Bliss, in the course of helping a female passenger step down from a New York City trolley, was struck and killed by a horseless carriage, becoming victim number one. From the very outset, the safety issue was tossed into the driver's lap. The key was driver's ed—lots of it—coupled with strict enforcement by the police of traffic laws regarding speeding, drunken driving, and the like. Given that auto companies and engineers had done their part, about the only other recourse was to improve the quality of streets and highways. One cutting-edge safety expert called for a nationwide campaign to clear roadsides of obstacles—trees, boulders, lampposts—thereby removing them from the path of slovenly drivers. The fact was plain and there was no getting around it: cars don't kill people, people do.

OF COURSE, NADER DID not subscribe to this notion. He was part of a small group of people who held a fringe view, namely, that design and engineering innovations could play a substantial role in auto safety. And he was part of an even smaller subset—Nader exclusively—that believed in something called "body rights." It was a term that he had dreamed up but kept to himself. The first half of the 1960s had seen an explosion of civil rights advocacy, with people fighting for racial justice and gender equality. In Nader's estimation, insufficient attention had been paid to people's basic physical rights: against being maimed or killed. Quite often auto companies were the perpetrators of great carnage, in Nader's view, and yet the violence was met by the public with a strange complacency. In 1963 many idealistic young people set off to Selma and Birmingham and other points south, looking to be involved in the civil rights struggle. Nader moved to Washington intent, as he saw it, on becoming an advocate for body rights.

He hitchhiked down from Hartford and spent his first night at a YMCA. "I had watched years go by and nothing happened," he once said. "Before that, decades had gone by. I decided that it took total combat."

Nader was now twenty-nine years old and had so far failed to make his mark in any notable way. But neither was he the ultimate outsider, as he has often been portrayed. Degrees from Princeton and Harvard promised to open plenty of doors. He had some experience trying to get bills through various state legislatures, and he had helped found an organization, Illinois Citizens for Automobile Safety. He had worked briefly in Washington, lobbying for Alaskan and Hawaiian statehood. This was a glamorous and relatively uncomplicated topic. Getting people interested in auto safety engineering was going to be a considerably greater challenge. It would require a flawless alignment of disparate variables. Yet, bizarrely, that is exactly what happened. Nader was about to become part of a complex web of corporate gumshoes, congressional gamesmanship, and media frenzy—a potent mix that would transform his fringe view, giving it the force of revolution.

Nader took a job with Daniel Patrick Moynihan. It happened that Moynihan—while working as an aide to New York Governor Averill Harriman—had written a landmark article called "Epidemic on the Highways." It was published in 1959 in a magazine called *The Reporter*. A friend had sent the article to Nader during his stint in the army at Fort Dix. Nader—pleased to discover a fellow auto safety proponent—contacted Moynihan, and the two had corresponded on and off ever since.

By 1963 Moynihan had become assistant labor secretary. Although auto safety was not exactly prime Labor Department territory, it remained an area of personal interest to Moynihan. So he handed Nader a job as a part-time consultant, paying $50 a day.

From the beginning, Nader kept erratic hours, often arriving for work after midnight. His desk overflowed with papers and reports. Moynihan and other office mates found him unusually cagey, especially for such a lowly government functionary. "Ralph was a very suspicious man," Moynihan told Charles McCarry, author of a 1971 book on Nader. "He used to warn me that the phones at the Labor Department might be tapped. I'd say, 'Fine! They'll learn that the unemployment rate for March is 5.3 percent, that's what they'll learn.' But he kept warning me."

While at Labor, Nader's assignment was to write a report on highway safety. He amassed nearly one hundred pages of notes, which he left in a cab and was forced to reconstruct. But eventually he managed to write a 235-page report entitled *Context, Condition and Recommended Direction of Federal Activity in Highway Safety*. Meant for background use only, the report failed to make a ripple, let alone a splash.

Meanwhile, Elizabeth Moynihan hosted a series of dinner parties and invited the young members of her husband's staff. She made a few efforts to pair Nader with eligible young women but soon gave up. Auto safety, design defects, engineering snafus—he seemed to have a one-track mind.

DURING THE SUMMER OF 1964, Nader was presented with an opportunity that played to his singularity. Publisher Richard Grossman was casting about for an author to write a book on auto safety. Grossman was a former vice president at Simon & Schuster, which he had left in 1962 to start his own small house, dedicated to quality books on serious subjects. Grossman Publishers was a lean little operation that issued roughly eight books a year. His titles included a memoir by the French ethnographer Michel Leiris and *Instead of Violence*, a collection of essays by pacifists.

Grossman had first become interested in a book on auto safety when he read an article in the *New Republic* by James Ridgeway entitled "The Corvair Tragedy." Grossman contacted Ridgeway, who declined the offer, pleading that he was already mired in writing commitments. "Besides," Ridgeway explained to Grossman, "one of the key sources for my *New Republic* article, somebody with trunk loads of information on auto safety, is this guy, Ralph Nader."

It took some time for Grossman to track down the secretive Nader. There was no phone listing for him in the D.C. directory. As it turned out, Nader lived in a rooming house at 1719 19 Street, NW. There was a telephone in the hallway that Nader shared with three other boarders.

When Grossman finally located him, Nader immediately agreed. In September 1964, the two met to hammer out the project's terms at the offices of Grossman Publishers—a basement apartment at 19th and Irving Place in New York City. Nader was to receive a $1,500 advance for a work known simply as "untitled book on auto safety." As Nader read over the contract, there was a loud commotion outside. "We heard the crash of metal and we both rushed out," recalls Grossman. "The first thing I remember is Ralph saying, 'the kid will be all right.' There had been a child in the car. But it was just a fender-bender."

Nader set to work on his book. An adage holds that a person can learn just about anything by visiting the nearest public library or, these days, by going on the Internet. Nader followed a similar tack in his research. The role of engineering in auto safety may have been an arcane topic. But he had already amassed a huge amount of information, and more was available for the asking, much of it in the public domain.

For example, Nader found that for fifty cents a piece he could obtain patent filings, many of which proved extremely illuminating. Depositions of auto executives involved in lawsuits proved a rich vein, as did articles in technical publications such as the *GM Engineering Journal*. He was also able to obtain confidential documents, such as a California Highway Department circular that identified cars that in the experience of the police, had an unusually high propensity for accidents.

One of the very best sources, Nader soon discovered, was disillusioned auto-industry employees. In Nader's estimation, the upper echelons of management tended to be the province of compromise-happy strivers. That left the middle ranks full of people who wanted only to make cars that were better and safer. But often these employees found that their best ideas and innovations were stifled. Nader was able to persuade a number of long-stymied career engineers to talk, though often only on background. One source told him that "a square foot of chrome sells ten times more cars than the best safety door latch."

Although Nader conducted abundant original research, he also developed his book as a work of synthesis. After all, he was a lawyer by training, not an engineer. As much as anything, he drew on the existing work of a handful of auto safety pioneers, such as Hugh DeHaven and William Haddon Jr.

DeHaven holds the inelegant title "father of crashworthiness research." In 1917, while serving in the Canadian Royal Flying Corps, he was involved in a collision between two airplanes. He was the only one of four airmen to survive. It did not escape his notice that he was also the only one fortunate enough to have the portion of cockpit surrounding him remain intact during the accident.

The experience led DeHaven to speculate that humans could withstand crashes if they were properly "packaged." Others were not quick to embrace the notion, and consequently he was forced to finance his own research for the next twenty years. One of his main areas of interest was falling victims. He was particularly intrigued by a woman who survived a suicide leap from the balcony of her eleventh-story apartment in New York City. She landed on moist soil rather than concrete, leaving a pristine body print, which DeHaven studied assiduously. He concluded that the soil had acted to absorb the energy of her impact. Soon DeHaven was conducting experiments on eggs, dropping them onto various materials that served as cushions.

The world eventually took some notice of DeHaven. His research findings were incorporated into the design of certain World War II-era Navy planes, which featured padding in their cockpits. He was also an early advocate of shoulder harnesses in small planes, to protect people involved in crashes from hitting their heads on the instrument panels. DeHaven culminated his career by helping to found a crash injury research project at Cornell University, where he began to apply to automobiles some of the lessons learned from airplanes and eggs.

William Haddon Jr. was trained in both medicine and engineering, lending him an unusual perspective on auto safety. His major contribution to the field was the application of an epidemiological model that drew a parallel between auto accidents and infectious diseases.

Resolutely a realist, Haddon felt that there was precious little utility in trying to alter human behavior. Better to control what is controllable. In combating a flu epidemic, doctors tend to see more benefit in developing a vaccine than in telling people to wash their hands and get adequate sleep. Extending the analogy to auto safety, Haddon argued that engineering innovations could save more lives than driver's ed. Of course, this placed him in opposition to the prevailing views of the day. It is also worth noting that Moynihan's "Epidemic on the Highways" was meant to amplify and popularize Haddon's ideas.

COME EARLY 1965, NADER was deep into auto safety, feverishly researching his book and moonlighting—literally moonlighting—for Moynihan. He also found time to organize a protest outside an auto show held at the Coliseum in New York City. He was joined by Ted Jacobs, a friend from Harvard; Seymour Charles, founder of a group called Physicians for Automotive Safety; and his mother. Rose Nader carried a hand-lettered sign bearing a none-too-snappy slogan: "The people in the cars may cause accidents, but it is the vehicles that injure them. Back the drive to build safety in our automobiles."

But something much larger than any of this was afoot. Nader was about to be drawn into a series of events that would transform him—at eye-blink speed—from an anonymous wonk into a figure of national renown.

Abraham Ribicoff, Democratic senator from Connecticut, was casting about for an issue on which to hold hearings. Ribicoff was chairman of the Subcommittee on Executive Reorganization of the Committee on Government Operations, an extremely unwieldy title which meant, in a nutshell, that he was charged with identifying issues that might interest his fellow senators.

Ribicoff was a self-made man. The son of impoverished Polish immigrants, he had grown up on the wrong side of New London, Connecticut, and had paid his way through college by working in a zipper factory. Thereupon, he scrapped his way up the Connecticut political hierarchy—serving as a court judge and member of the state legislature—before being elected governor for two terms. Ribicoff was widely praised for his tough stance on drunken drivers and also for his handling of the 1955 Mad River flood, the one that damaged the Nader family's restaurant.

As a politician, Ribicoff was a blend of the progressive and the pragmatic. One of his favorite phrases was "the integrity of compromise." He became a strong ally of John F. Kennedy; in fact, Ribicoff was the first person JFK appointed to his cabinet, tapping him to become secretary of Health, Education, and Welfare.

Early 1965 found Senator Ribicoff looking for an issue that would engage his liberal leanings, but also one on which—per his pragmatic streak—he and his fellow senators could make a difference. He drew up a list of possible topics. One in particular grabbed him. "Let's get into the car," he said repeatedly to his staff as he began to warm to the idea. Ribicoff was well aware of the mounting automobile death toll, and he was also quite aware that Detroit remained free of regulation, in stark contrast to the manufacturers of trains, planes, and passenger ships.

Jerome Sonosky was staff director and general counsel of Ribicoff's Senate subcommittee. If auto regulation was to be next on the agenda, a friend kept telling Sonosky, he had to meet this guy, Ralph Nader. So Sonosky arranged a meeting at his office, Room 168 of the Old Senate Building. "Nader walked in," Sonosky recalls, "looking then as he looks now, sallow-faced, wearing his long overcoat, carrying a thousand pieces of paper under his arm. His message was that the auto industry has no right to produce unsafe cars. We talked for three hours about various aspects of the issue, and where we should go with it."

Immediately following the meeting Sonosky phoned Ribicoff.

"We just struck gold," he said.

"What do you mean?" asked Ribicoff.

"I just met somebody who knows more about auto safety than anybody I've ever come across. I don't have to run around town gathering up various experts. I just found him."

Nader became an unpaid adviser to Ribicoff's subcommittee. He didn't actually meet the senator at this juncture, but Nader met frequently with Sonosky, feeding him documents and helping map strategy. In the summer of 1965, Ribicoff officially announced hearings to look into the "fantastic carnage" on the highways.

MEANWHILE, NADER—PULLED IN a number of directions—was making scant progress on his book. The original plan had been to publish right before either Memorial Day or Labor Day, weekends notorious for their highway fatality tallies. But Nader missed both deadlines.

Finally Grossman simply traveled to Washington and checked into the Gramercy Motor Inn. He summoned Nader, who showed up bearing suitcases full of reports and legal briefs and other auto safety bric-a-brac. Grossman set up two typewriters side by side. Nader would type up a page, then hand it to Grossman for instant editing. After twenty-two days and nights of intensive collaboration, the book was completed.

Nader wanted to call it *Detroit Iron*. But in the course of reading a book called *The Insolent Chariots*, by *New Yorker* writer John Keats, one particular line jumped out at Grossman: "unsafe at any speed." That became the title, and the first printing was eleven thousand; the official publication date, November 30, 1965. The next day Grossman's wife and his business partner drove around New York City in a station wagon, hand delivering copies to bookstores.

In many ways, *Unsafe at Any Speed: The Designed-in Dangers of the American Automobile* is a blueprint for Nader's approach to virtually every issue he tackled in years to come. Foremost, the book is a criticism of how large, unaccountable forces—the auto industry in this case—make decisions that affect the lives of individual citizens.

In the book, Nader argues that financial considerations lead Detroit to choose style over safety nearly ever time. He lays out his case by cataloging engineering decisions ranging from where to place windshield wiper controls to whether to provide seat belts. This is contrasted with ample discussion of the "second collision," an idea advanced by Hugh DeHaven. The notion is that the real damage doesn't occur on impact. It happens during a second collision when poorly packaged passengers collide with unpadded dashes, unyielding steering columns, and an assortment of sharp, jutting control panel knobs and gewgaws.

The book also questions the objectivity of universities, the press, and other supposedly unbiased institutions. Circa 1965, the practice was not to identify the makes of automobiles involved in accidents. In conducting a study of car crashes, for example, a university might simply assemble aggregate statistics. Nader points out the inherent conflict of interest in cases in which colleges receive funding from the auto industry or newspapers depend on car companies for advertising revenue. A central theme of the book is that the failure of universities and the press to single out individual hazard-prone models did a terrible disservice to consumers.

By contrast and in protest, Nader devoted an entire chapter to the design flaws of a single model, the Chevrolet Corvair. In fact, his focus was even narrower, specifically those vehicles built between 1960 and 1963. Corvairs were the first American car to feature a swing-axle independent rear suspension system and an air-cooled, rear-mounted engine. This made the Corvair accident prone, liable to flip over even at slow speeds—at least that was the contention in a number of lawsuits involving General Motors.

Nader drew on various pieces of evidence to make a case that the Corvair had been foisted on an unsuspecting public, despite being the product of faulty, even negligent engineering.

Unsafe at Any Speed is vintage Nader, combining eye-glazing charts with visceral anecdotes, such as a boy racing to catch a baseball only to be fatally gored by the tail fin of a stationary Cadillac. It also contains plenty of Nader's trademark invective. In speculating on GM's decision to keep the Corvair on the market, Nader writes that "the absence of any corrective action year after year can only be explained by bureaucratic rigidities and the abject worship of that bitch-goddess, cost reduction."

GROSSMAN FELT CERTAIN THAT Nader had produced an important work. But drumming up publicity was going to be a challenge, and Grossman feared that the book might be overlooked due to the very conflict of interest Nader had identified, between the press and the auto companies that serve as major advertisers.

Grossman decided to travel around the country, personally visiting select book review editors. As he expected, a number of major publications such as *Life* magazine demurred, often without giving a reason. He received a rather more telling answer from the book review editor of the *Houston Chronicle*. "Are you out of your fucking mind?" was the man's response. "I wouldn't touch that book with a ten-foot pole."

Nevertheless, *Unsafe at Any Speed* did manage to get some press attention. The *San Francisco Chronicle* called the book "a searing document that may become the *Silent Spring* of the automotive industry." *Scientific American* praised it for pointing "an accusing finger at the automobile manufacturers charging them with indifference, callousness and arrogance in the face of genuine possibilities for safer automobile design." Prophetically, *Book Week* called Nader's work a "straight-out indictment" that "will be a hard book for the industry to ignore."

Despite a few glowing endorsements, sales remained modest. Urged on by a veteran Broadway flack named Eddie Jaffee, Grossman opted for a good old-fashioned publicity stunt. He called a press conference at Detroit's Sheraton Cadillac Hotel, a venue chosen strictly for the sake of irony. He sent telegraphs inviting the heads of the four major U.S. auto manufacturers.

The press conference was held on January 6, 1966. No auto chieftains showed, but plenty of reporters crowded into the single hotel room Grossman had rented for the event. Many were what Nader called "two hatters," members of the auto trade press. It was a hostile crowd, by and large.

"That day, Ralph was so skillful that I suddenly realized his genius for handling the media," says Grossman. "There was nothing in his background that indicated he was going to have this kind of skill. Number one, he was unflappable. Number two, he was a couple questions ahead of the reporters the whole time. He knew exactly how their minds worked."

Still, book sales did not exactly skyrocket.

But authorship had its perks. Now that Nader had written a book, he was valuable to Ribicoff as an expert, not merely as a behind-the-scenes adviser. Nader was invited to testify for the first time before the senator's subcommittee on February 10, 1966.

In the meantime, Nader had gone to Iowa to testify on auto safety. He was invited by Lawrence Scalise, the state's attorney general. "He managed to really energize a number of the attendees," recalls Scalise. "Initially some people thought it was crazy, to package people in a way that injuries could be minimized. It seemed radical. But not only did he have the supporting data, he was passionate about it."

Nader spent the night of January 10, 1966, at the Kirkwood Hotel in Des Moines. On several occasions he noticed a man in the lobby. "I began to get an uneasy sense that something was going on," he recalls.

To Scalise, and to a number of others, Nader confided that he thought he was being followed.

"I can't believe it," Grossman replied. "Ralph, your paranoia has grown to new extremes."

Sonosky told him simply, "C'mon Ralph. Get a grip."

There were more strange happenings in the days leading up to Nader's congressional testimony. He started to receive anonymous calls on his rooming house telephone, a number he had disclosed to precious few people. "Why don't you change your field of interest," urged one caller. Another time it was: "You are fighting a losing battle, friend. You can't win. You can only lose."

By Nader's count, he received six calls the night before he was scheduled to go before the Ribicoff subcommittee. Mostly the callers either hung up or made inexplicable comments like, "Mr. Nader, please pick up a parcel at Railway Express." He got the feeling that the calls were meant to check up on him, monitor his whereabouts. The last one came at 4:00 A.M.: "Why don't you go back to Connecticut, buddy boy."

THE FEBRUARY 10, 1966, hearing marks the first time Nader testified before Congress, something he would do hundreds of times in the years to come. He appeared in Room 1318 of the Dirksen Senate Office Building before a group of senators that included Ribicoff, Robert Kennedy, Carl Curtis (a Nebraska Republican), and Gaylord Nelson (a Democrat from Wisconsin).

Nader was surprisingly self-assured. As he had in *Unsafe at Any Speed*, he interwove dry statistics with bursts of vivid phraseology. He spoke at length, laying down lawyerly verbal constructions that piled dependent clause upon dependent clause, but right beneath the surface of his testimony there hummed a finely calibrated sense of outrage.

"The annual model change ritual is not a meaningful innovation for the public safety and welfare," he asserted. "Its purpose is to 'stir the animal' in the car buyer. It is aimed not at the reason of men but at their ids and hypogastria." At another point he catalogued the violent imagery evoked by the names of cars: "Ford continues to name its cars with such aggressive and ferocious titles as Comet, Meteor, Thunderbird, Cobra, Mustang (Mustang means 'a wild, unbreakable horse'), and Marauder (which means literally 'one who pillages and lays waste to the countryside'). There is also the Plymouth Fury and Barracuda, the Oldsmobile Cutlass, and the Buick Wildcat—to name a few. And coming soon to join the menagerie on the highways are the Mercury Cougar and Chevrolet Panther."

Onlookers from that day were struck by the fact that Nader was a natural. Congressional testimony is a form of theater, first and foremost, and Nader proved to be an ideal witness. As had become clear during his first brush with the press at the Sheraton Cadillac, he simply had a knack for it. "He was powerful, very powerful," recalls Sonosky of the February 10, 1966, hearing. "You could say then of Ralph—you could always say—he had the facts. He had a great delivery, which he would occasionally punctuate with this little chuckle that basically meant, 'how stupid those other people are!' The strength of his convictions shone through, as did his sincerity. He was convincing, very convincing, and I come back to everything he said was supported by facts."

Nader was back at the Dirksen Senate Office Building the next day for a television interview with NBC. Afterward, he got on an elevator, pressed the up button, changed his mind, decided he wanted to get a sandwich from the basement cafeteria, and hit the down button. Unbeknownst to Nader, two men were following him. This little elevator button gambit managed to throw them off his trail.

The two men approached a security guard named Marshall Speake and asked him about Nader's whereabouts. When Speake said that he had no idea, the two men decided to hang around, waiting. Speake grew suspicious and called a capitol police lieutenant, who threw the men out of the building.

Bryce Nelson, a reporter for the *Washington Post*, was completely unaware of the spy-jinks then in progress. He just happened to be in the Dirksen Building covering a story. Dark-haired and on the tall side, he happened to bear a slight, very slight, physical resemblance to Nader. A capitol policeman—mistaking Nelson for Nader—stopped him to deliver the following word of caution: "A couple of detectives are tailing you."

Nelson was confounded.

"I wondered if LBJ's gestapo was after me for something I'd written," he says.

Nelson asked a few questions and learned that the detectives were tailing someone who had written a book on auto safety. This meant nothing to Nelson. Still, he decided to relate the episode to his editor at the *Post*, Laurence Stern. "In case I wound up in the Anacosta River," says Nelson, "I thought somebody should know something strange was happening."

Meanwhile, Nader showed up unannounced at the offices of the *Post*. He remained unaware of the two detectives. But he had been party to a number of recent and inexplicable events—the uneasy feeling in Iowa, the late-night phone calls—and had decided the time was right to alert the press. He sought out Morton Mintz, a reporter he had never met, but whom he thought might be sympathetic. Mintz had won a Pulitzer Prize for his stories on the scandal surrounding thalidomide, a morning-sickness drug that wound up causing birth defects.

"Something in my gut said he was telling the truth," recalls Mintz. "I thought there was a potentially big story here. At the same time, as a responsible reporter you can't write a piece in the *Washington Post* saying someone was followed. Where's the evidence? Then I got that astonishing piece of confirmation. It was absolutely astonishing to me, still is."

The astonishing confirmation came from the fact that Mintz's editor was also Laurence Stern. Nelson had told Stern about two detectives tailing a guy who had written a book on auto safety. Then, along comes Mintz, telling Stern that Nader had shown up at the *Post* offices claiming that he was being followed. The story ran in the February 13, 1966, edition: "Car Safety Critic Nader Reports Being 'Tailed.'"

But a bit of press scrutiny did not scare off the gumshoes. To the contrary, the investigation went into overdrive during the days that followed, and events began to take a surreal turn. Nader was about to become the ultimate exemplar of the saying: "Just because you're paranoid doesn't mean that somebody isn't truly out to get you."

Thomas Lambert Jr. was editor of the *American Trial Lawyers Association* journal, a publication that had featured several auto safety articles by Nader. Lambert sent Nader a letter congratulating him on his new job. Around the same time, Nader received a call from Harold Berman, one of his professors at Harvard law.

"Congratulations," said Berman. "I understand that you are being considered for a job."

"I knew something was fishy," Nader recalls, "but I couldn't figure it out."

This was followed by an odd episode that occurred while Nader was in a store, leafing through an auto buff magazine. A good-looking woman—young and a brunette—approached him. "Pardon me," she said. "I know this sounds a little forward. I hope you don't mind, but can I talk to you?"

The woman explained that she and some friends were part of a group that met to discuss foreign-affairs issues. They were looking for someone new who could bring a fresh perspective to the group. Would Nader care to join them? Nader declined, saying that he was from out of town. But the woman was very persistent. She said they were meeting that very night. Finally Nader simply turned his back on her.

On another occasion, Nader stopped off at a Safeway near his rooming house to buy a package of cookies. Another attractive woman—this one blond and wearing slacks—approached him. "Excuse me," she said. "I need some help. I've got to move something heavy in my apartment. There's no one to help me. I wonder if you could lend me a hand."

Nader declined, telling her he was running late. But she was also persistent, pleading that it wouldn't take much time. Nader steadfastly refused and finally the woman turned and walked away. Nader couldn't help noticing that there was something extremely suspicious about her manner of exit. The Safeway was crowded, other men were present, some of them clearly by themselves, yet the woman left directly without asking anyone else to help move this supposed heavy object.

Then, on February 22, 1966, Frederick Condon—a Harvard friend—received a call from a man who identified himself as "Mr. Warren." Condon was assistant counsel for the United Life and Accident Insurance Company of Concord, New Hampshire. In 1961 he had fallen asleep while driving his Plymouth station wagon and had an accident that left him a paraplegic, confined to a wheelchair. Nader dedicated *Unsafe at Any Speed* to

Condon. "I think Ralph was really touched by what happened to his friend," says Laura Nader. "That's how he mourns. Ralph mourns by doing something. He mourned Condon's terrible situation by finding out more about cars."

The mysterious Mr. Warren told Condon that he represented a client who planned to hire Nader to do some research. But first a thorough background check was required, and Warren explained that he hoped to ask Condon a series of questions regarding Nader's employment history, sex life, whether he was involved in left-wing politics or was otherwise an "oddball," and whether he was capable of doing work in fields other than auto safety.

Something here was very akilter, Condon sensed, and he asked Warren to identify the client he represented. Warren answered that he was not at liberty to reveal this information. So Condon asked Warren to identify himself instead. Warren answered that he worked with a "Mr. Gillen," a New York attorney who specialized in this kind of background investigation.

Now Condon's suspicions were aroused. "This guy calls up," Condon recalls, "and I was on to him right away." He asked Warren to drop by his office that afternoon. Condon also resolved to pay extremely close attention during the meeting to see if he could figure out just what exactly was going on.

On arriving at Condon's office, "Mr. Warren" inexplicably switched identities and now referred to himself as "Mr. Gillen." Condon was sure that "Warren" and "Gillen" were one and the same—he recognized the man's voice. Beefy and barrel-chested, Gillen wore thick black-framed glasses and had slicked-back gray hair. Condon put him in his mid-fifties. Gillen also seemed very nervous. He sat there with his attaché case on his lap, and Condon suspected he was probably recording their conversation.

At the outset, Gillen seemed especially interested in Nader's driving record. He went at it from a variety of different angles. Did Nader have a driver's license? If so, issued by which state? Did he own a car while at Harvard? Had Condon ever seen Nader drive? Did he currently own a car? Condon answered where he could, but explained that he had not seen his friend in several years.

Abruptly, Gillen switched the subject to Nader's marital status, hinting that an unmarried man in his thirties was unusual.

"Are you asking me if he is a homosexual?" asked Condon.

"Well, we have to inquire about these things. I've seen him on TV and he certainly doesn't look . . . but we have to be sure."

Gillen also delved into whether Nader was involved in any radical political causes. In an effort to put Condon at ease, now that the discussion had taken an unseemly turn, Gillen attempted a joke about "going to Harvard and turning left."

Gillen pressed on clumsily, inquiring about Nader's "Syrian" ancestry. Condon corrected him, explaining that Nader was of Lebanese descent.

"Well, it's about the same thing," replied Gillen. "We just want to know if there is any anti-Semitic feeling there."

Gillen also inquired about Nader's association with Ribicoff. Had the two of them met? Was there some kind of Connecticut connection? Again Condon explained that—having not seen Nader in several years—he didn't know the specifics.

Gillen wound up the interview with a flurry of pleasantries and irrelevant questions. Given the touchy subjects raised earlier, Condon viewed this as nothing more than a transparent attempt to conclude their discussion on a congenial note. After Gillen left, Condon wrote up his recollections of the meeting—in order to keep the details straight—and gave Nader a call.

Now it was clear to Nader that someone was investigating him, as if he needed further proof. Nader contacted Jim Ridgeway at the *New Republic*. He furnished him with information about how to reach Condon, Lambert, Berman, and others who apparently had brushes with the investigator, or investigators.

Digging by Ridgeway soon turned up a Vincent Gillen of Vincent Gillen Associates, a detective agency located in Garden City, New York. When reached on the phone by a reporter, Gillen was flustered. "We've made inquiries about Nader," he allowed. But he refused to disclose his client.

"A lot of people were mentioned adversely in that book," he added. "I am a private investigator. We have hundreds of clients. We write thousands of reports . . . "

Suddenly Gillen switched tacks, asserting that the investigation was a preemployment background check.

"I was asked by a client to make an investigation of Ralph Nader," he continued. "I understand he is an intelligent, articulate fellow. And my client told me he was considering him for an important job, to research on something, I don't know what."

Gillen concluded the interview by insisting, "All I can say is, it is good for Nader."

Ridgeway's story appeared in the issue of the *New Republic* that hit the stands on March 4, 1966. The media firestorm was instantaneous. Within hours, major metropolitan dailies were all over the story. One after another, the big auto companies—Ford, Chrysler, American Motors—issued official denials, stating that they had not been involved in any way. A *New York Times* article concluded with an unnamed auto company representative asserting that the very sloppiness of the investigation removed Detroit from the suspect list: "You can bet that if one of us was doing it, it would be a lot smoother. If we were checking up on Nader he'd never know about it."

But what about General Motors? The company's Corvair had been singled out in *Unsafe at Any Speed*, yet GM had remained suspiciously silent about the whole matter. Consequently, the company headquarters was besieged with calls as the press narrowed in on GM.

Late on the evening of March 9, 1966, GM issued a press release that read in part: "the office of [GM's] general counsel initiated a routine investigation through a reputable law firm to determine whether Ralph Nader was acting on behalf of litigants or their attorneys in Corvair design cases pending against General Motors."

Senator Ribicoff was livid. General Motors could claim the investigation was routine, but the fact remained that Nader was now a congressional witness. Harassing a congressional witness is a federal crime; at the time, the maximum penalty was $5,000 or five years in prison.

Ribicoff called a hearing, set for March 22. Nader was asked to be present, as was James Roche, CEO of GM, along with the company's general counsel, other key members of the legal department, and Vincent Gillen. Prior to the hearing, Ribicoff also demanded that GM and Gillen turn over various documents related to the investigation.

— 5 —

Nader Versus Goliath

IN TEMPER AND TONE, NADER'S SECOND congressional hearing was a complete departure from his first. A capacity crowd had squeezed into the Caucus Room of the Old Senate Office Building, and the press had set up klieg lights and TV cameras. This was a bona fide event. People were hoping to witness some real drama, perhaps even a confrontation.

Arrayed along a rostrum, with an expanse of marble wall serving as a backdrop, sat Senators Ribicoff and Kennedy as well as Fred Harris of Oklahoma and Henry Jackson of Washington. The General Motors president, James Roche, detective Gillen, and others involved in the scandal were relegated to considerably lower elevation and sat facing their inquisitors. Roche was accompanied by Theodore Sorensen, a partner with the New York law firm Paul, Weiss, Rifkind, Wharton and Garrison.

More than anything, Sorensen was present to provide a kind of moral support to Roche. General Motors had retained him only one day before the hearings. During the entire proceeding, he would not utter one word publicly. Yet his mere presence would prove another gaffe for GM and would backfire terribly.

Sorensen had been part of JFK's inner circle, serving as counsel, speechwriter, and friend to the president. Among the senators present, there was a perception that GM had brought along Sorensen to lend the proceedings a clubby air. But the presence of so much media made this a very public forum. The senators did not appreciate GM's attempt to cozy up, and they were intent on not giving any appearance of impropriety. "Now we've really got to be tough," Ribicoff confided privately.

Nader was scheduled to be the first witness. But when the proceedings were called to order, there was no sign of him anywhere. The subcommittee recessed for fifteen minutes—still no Nader. So they decided to start without him, calling Roche instead. Moments after Roche had sworn in under oath, Nader showed up. Because the subcommittee wanted to question the various GM witnesses in sequence, Nader's testimony was rescheduled for later in the day.

Roche was sixty and the embodiment of the GM company man, having worked his way from statistician to president in the course of thirty-nine years with the firm. White-haired and grandfatherly, he conveyed a midwestern probity—the legacy of his youth in Elgin, Illinois. First, last, and always he was unflappable. He took pride in his ability to manage the 745,000 employees of a far-flung enterprise without ever raising his voice.

"To the extent that General Motors bears responsibility," Roche began, "I want to apologize here and now to the members of this subcommittee and Mr. Nader. I sincerely hope that these apologies will be accepted. Certainly I bear Mr. Nader no ill will."

Having struck a proper note of contrition, Roche sought to clarify a couple of matters at the outset. He had not been personally aware of the investigation. And the investigation was not prompted by Nader's role as a congressional witness on auto safety. Instead, Roche maintained, GM's sole intent had been to learn whether Nader was secretly representing clients involved in Corvair litigation while at the same time writing books and articles critical of the vehicle.

If so, it would be a violation of Canon 20 of the Canons of Professional Ethics of the American Bar Association. Lawyers are not supposed to covertly drum up sensational and adverse publicity in an effort to bias juries against their opponents. A Supreme Court decision had laid it out succinctly: "It is impermissible to litigate by day and castigate by night."

The Corvair had been singled out for criticism in *Unsafe at Any Speed*. If Nader was secretly representing litigants in Corvair cases, charges could be filed against him with the bar for a breach of legal ethics.

Despite heated questioning, Roche remained unbowed. Throughout his testimony, he maintained that GM's only aim was to establish whether Nader was engaged in unethical practices. If other issues had been touched on during the investigation, they were not at GM's behest: "I personally have no interest whatsoever in knowing Mr. Nader's political beliefs, his religious beliefs and attitudes, his credit rating or his personal habits regarding sex, alcohol, or any other subject."

But the subcommittee had in its possession various documents turned over by GM and Gillen. In the course of calling a series of witnesses, the senators effectively worked their way down GM's chain of command: from Roche to the company's general counsel, Aloysius Power, to Louis Bridenstine, the assistant general counsel. A very different picture of the intent of the investigation began to emerge.

Power testified that he had long suspected that Nader might be the "mystery man" behind the various Corvair lawsuits. In fact, he had ordered an investigation on November 18, 1965, two weeks before *Unsafe at Any Speed* was published. But Power explained that his suspicions had already been raised by articles Nader had written in the *American Trial Lawyers Association* journal and other publications.

At the outset, GM had hired a detective named William O'Neill, who had poked around Nader's hometown of Winsted, Connecticut, to very little effect. The detective report he had submitted to Power was chock full of banality, characterizing Nader as a "swell kid" who had "carried papers for the *Winsted Evening Citizen* in 1949."

With the publication of *Unsafe at Any Speed*, GM's suspicions were raised to a new level. Eileen Murphy, the company's law librarian, flew to Washington on January 11, 1966. There she met with Richard Danner, a former FBI agent. Murphy explained to Danner that she wanted to investigate Nader. Danner subcontracted the job to Vincent Gillen, who ran the New York area franchise for a nationwide private eye outfit called Fidelifacts. There were twenty-six former FBI agents in Gillen's employ.

According to the detective report—a copy of which had been turned over to the subcommittee—Nader had been placed under intense surveillance, beginning on February 4, 1966. Detectives followed him around Washington as he went into restaurants, mailed letters, visited his bank, and attended to other mundane matters such as purchasing paper at an office supply store in Georgetown. They wrote down the license plate numbers of cars in which he rode. All told, they questioned nearly sixty of his friends, family, and other acquaintances. It was all assembled in thick blue binders; the total cost of the investigation was $6,700.

Even faced with increasingly damning evidence, the various GM witnesses stuck to their story. The investigation was "routine," meant only to determine whether Nader was litigating by day, castigating by night. Anything else that was uncovered was strictly incidental.

Senator Robert Kennedy in particular chipped away at the notion with special fervor. General Motors had received detective reports on a weekly basis. If the company was after information on Corvair litigation, why was there so little of relevance in the reports? Why was there so much information about Nader's personal life?

Meanwhile, Ribicoff read into the record a memo containing Gillen's instructions to his own detectives: "Our job is to check his life, and current activities to determine 'what makes him tick,' such as his real interest in safety, his supporters, if any, his politics, his marital status, his friends, his women, boys, etc., drinking, dope, jobs—in fact all facets of his life. This may entail surveillance, which will be undertaken only upon OK of Vincent Gillen."

Next to testify was Gillen himself: working its way down the chain of command, the Ribicoff subcommittee had finally gotten to the detective to whom GM had contracted the job. Finally it was time to hear his story.

Gillen proved to be spectacularly buffoonish—a character straight out of *The Bank Dick* by W. C. Fields. More than anything, he appeared to be caught up in the glamour and excitement of the proceedings. He opened his testimony with an exhaustive account of his detective career, one during which—to his great pride—he had refused to do divorce work such as spying on errant spouses to document their affairs. Also with evident pride, he recited his firm's motto: "There is no substitute for quality and integrity." He even pulled out a miniature spy camera and proceeded to snap pictures of the senators.

By now, the congressional hearing had pretty well established the purpose of the investigation. But Gillen perversely stuck to the claim that the sole intent was to uncover possible breaches of legal ethics by Nader. To obtain such information, he explained, a suitable pretext was needed. He and his detectives could not simply ask Condon, Berman, and others whether Nader was secretly involved in Corvair litigation. It was necessary to invent a cover. In this case, the ruse was that Nader was being offered a job.

Gillen laid it all out quite matter-of-factly, at one point telling Ribicoff: "If you wish every investigator to conduct everything openly and honestly I don't think they would get much information, sir."

The senators were dumbfounded. They could even accept that Gillen required a pretext to carry out the investigation—the wages of a seamy trade. But what had he uncovered relating to Corvair litigation? And how could he possibly explain his own memo, instructing his agents to mostly muck around in Nader's personal life?

Of course, the irrepressible Gillen had an explanation, a suitably bizarre one related to his own supposed professional code of ethics. The investigation's pretext—he pointed out—was that Nader was going to be offered a job. That required the detectives to raise certain touchy questions. Once raised, explained Gillen, they couldn't simply let the questions drop unanswered. In "fairness to Ralph" it became necessary to conduct a thorough investigation of his personal life.

"What is fairness to Ralph?" Kennedy shot back. "You have to keep proving he's not anti-Semitic and he is not queer. In fairness to Ralph? Ralph is doing all right. You were just a public-spirited citizen rushing around the country in fairness to Ralph?"

Gillen remained strangely nonplussed. He told Kennedy at one point that he admired him greatly and identified himself as a constituent.

"I just hope my next election is not decided by one vote," responded Kennedy.

WHILE GILLEN PROVIDED COMIC relief, when Nader's turn to testify came, he delivered the drama the packed Caucus Room was awaiting. It was only his second appearance before Congress. But this time he was not present merely as an auto safety expert. He was an aggrieved party—wronged by GM and a bumbling gumshoe—and righteous indignation was his for the taking. This had the potential to be a defining moment, and Nader was in top form, save for the fact that he had been late to the hearings.

He began his testimony with an explanation: "Mr. Chairman, members of the subcommittee, I owe you a deep apology for being late this morning. I ought to explain it briefly to you and to anyone else in this room. I usually take no more than twelve minutes to come down from my residence to the Capitol by cab. In this instance I gave myself twenty minutes. And I waited and waited and waited and waited to get a cab, and as my frustration mounted, I almost felt like going out and buying a Chevrolet. But that is the simple reason I am late."

With that out of the way, Nader got down to the serious business of addressing any doubts that might still exist regarding his motives in writing *Unsafe at Any Speed*. He assured the senators that he was not covertly involved in any Corvair litigation. Sure, he subscribed passionately to the notion of treating as a tort any injuries or deaths that resulted from faulty auto engineering. But he was not pursuing any cases himself. That GM suspected otherwise was not his problem. Rather, it served as commentary on the company's askew worldview: "General Motors executives continue to be blinded by their own corporate mirror-image that it's 'the buck' that moves the man. They simply cannot understand that the prevention of cruelty to humans can be a sufficient motivation for one endeavoring to obtain the manufacture of safer cars."

Nader also sought a parallel between the bungled spy job and poorly engineered cars. GM's executives were haughty and out of touch, he asserted, leading to a situation in which "people sitting in executive suites can make remote decisions which will someday result in tremendous carnage, and because they are remote in time and space between their decision and the consequences of that decision, there is no accountability."

Nader suggested that executives ought to be criminally prosecuted in cases where substandard cars were carelessly foisted on the buying public. He also called for legislation and regulation aimed at the industry. And he pledged to devote any royalties from *Unsafe at Any Speed* to the cause of auto safety. It was a bravura piece of testimony.

The assembled senators praised Nader for his courage and integrity. Ribicoff told him: "While you have suffered as a result of this, for whatever it is worth, you do have the satisfaction of knowing that the detective agencies, at the rate of $6,700, haven't been able to find a thing on you."

The hearing lasted six hours, devoted to everything from procedural fine points to grandstanding to the loopy discursions of Detective Gillen. But a single indelible image emerged: GM's CEO apologizing to Ralph Nader.

The contrast was irresistible. Roche had arrived by chauffeured limo, Nader by taxi. Roche was CEO of the world's largest company, with $20 billion in sales in 1966, while Nader rented a room in a boarding house for $80 a month. GM had tried to sully Nader's character, but he had spun matters around, tarnishing theirs instead. It was a perfect David-and-Goliath story.

That evening Nader was on all the network news shows. The next morning he was featured in front-page stories all over the country. Nader had been transformed into a public figure.

ALTHOUGH THE MARCH 22 HEARING centered around whether GM had spied on Nader, it had the effect of galvanizing public opinion on the once obscure topic of engineering safe cars. A window of opportunity was now open, legislatively, and congressmen raced to introduce competing bills. President Johnson proclaimed the week of May 15, 1966, as National

Transportation Week. "We can hardly tolerate such anarchy on wheels," he said. "We can no longer tolerate unsafe automobiles."

Meanwhile, Detroit prepared to defang this nascent movement. The Big Four wielded tremendous power and were responsible for more revenues, more jobs, a greater slice of GDP than any other industry in America. Auto executives descended on Washington, meeting with members of Congress and trotting out the classic arguments. Henry Ford II—for one—favored a claim that as much as 98 percent of the onus for safety fell on drivers and law enforcement.

The industry hoped to simply wait this one out. There was a sense that such a specialized issue would fail to hold the attention of Congress and the American people for long. Such sentiments were clearly evident during a May 13, 1966, meeting of the Business Council, a group that considers the impact of government policies on industry. W. B. Murphy—chairman of the Business Council and president of Campbell Soup Company—described the current "auto safety kick" as "on the same order as the hula hoop—a fad. Six months from now, we'll probably be on another kick."

Nader managed to insert himself into the battle to pass an auto safety law even as it took shape. He was hardly an established power broker. But in this—his very first brush with the legislative process—he showed a precocious grasp of how things truly worked. The March 22 hearing had raised awareness, but that was far from adequate. Nader sensed that anything of substance was going to be accomplished through protracted and relentless hammering of the details. "We saw him every day, sometimes every hour," recalls Robert Wager, one of Ribicoff's committee staffers. "He would be talking to us, pushing his views—a very intense, very committed guy."

Nader delivered a key piece of intelligence to the Ribicoff subcommittee. If they wanted to back the auto companies into a corner, obtain information on the number of defects. Ribicoff sent telegrams to the presidents of the Big Four, demanding that they list recall campaigns year by year going back to 1960. When the numbers came in, they were astounding.

Ribicoff held a press conference to announce that, between 1960 and 1966, there had been 426 recall campaigns involving 8.7 million cars. That was one out of five. Beyond the sheer numbers, the truly shocking finding was Detroit's casual attitude toward defects. Often, a so-called recall campaign consisted of an auto company quietly informing dealers of a defect and suggesting they fix it when customers dropped by for a routine tune-up. The public—it turned out—was rarely informed about defects, even grave ones involving brakes or steering.

"There is another and equally important lesson in this data," said Ribicoff during the press conference. "It shatters once and for all the myth that accidents are invariably caused by bad driving. From now on we must be concerned, not just with the 'nut behind the wheel' but with the nut in the wheel itself, with all parts of the car and its design."

The momentum for legislation was now in place. Detroit shifted into damage-control mode. The industry retained Lloyd Cutler, a lawyer and lobbyist with a deep well of Washington contacts. Cutler had represented the pharmaceutical industry during a federal-regulation showdown in 1962, and he was precisely what Nader had railed against at Harvard: a lawyer who was ever ready to help the powerful out of jams so long as they met his steep fee. Many years hence, as the Whitewater scandal heated up, Clinton would say privately that he needed a "Lloyd Cutler-type." Clinton wound up retaining the man himself.

Nader remained vigilant as auto safety legislation wended its way through Congress. The day the Senate voted on the bill, Nader parked himself in one anteroom, while Cutler was in another. Aides shuttled back and forth between them, and Nader fought to keep the bill intact. Nader kept up pressure on other fronts as well. Whenever anyone—Cutler or a member of Congress sympathetic to Detroit's perspective—threatened to pare down the bill, Nader would leak the news to journalists such as Drew Pearson, a syndicated columnist who wrote "Washington Merry-Go-Round."

On August 25, 1966, Senate-House conferees reached final agreement on an auto safety bill. It lacked the criminal provision favored by Nader, the one that made auto executives liable for egregious errors of safety engineering. Nevertheless Nader pronounced it a "significant step forward." It had been a mere five months since the March 22 hearing, light speed in legislative time.

President Johnson signed the bill on September 9, 1966. It required the auto industry to adopt certain safety features. The features were to be selected by a newly created National Highway Safety Bureau, and Johnson also announced that William Haddon Jr.—pioneer of the epidemiological approach to accidents—would head up the agency.

From the outset, Detroit fought each individual standard. But over time, a number of safety features became mandatory: shoulder straps for front seat passengers, limits on glare-producing chrome, shatter-proof windshields, energy-absorbing steering columns, flashing hazard lights, and dual braking systems, which include a backup set in case the first fails.

Even before the first set of mandatory standards took effect, Detroit began to make voluntary adjustments. Ever attuned to public sentiment, the auto companies concluded that now safety would sell. Certain features began to be touted as early as the autumn of 1966, only weeks after the bill was signed.

A television ad for the 1967 Buick Special featured Sho Onodera, a black belt in karate. After a deep bow, Onodera climbs into the car. He then explodes in a series of chops and kicks meant to demonstrate the abundant padding in the new model. A voice-over concludes that the Buick Special features padding on "everything but the price."

After a few years, it became possible to better gauge the impact of the safety legislation. A 1970 University of Michigan study found that mandatory standards were resulting in 5 percent fewer fatalities, which translated into twenty-five hundred lives saved annually. That was one of the first conclusive studies, but there were thousands to come. Over time, the notion that better engineering could cut down on auto deaths and injuries would become the accepted wisdom.

There are several other postscripts to the 1966 auto safety bill. The hearings and hoopla gave a lift to *Unsafe at Any Speed*; the book reached number five on one national best-seller list, and ultimately sold nearly half a million copies. Nader earned $53,000 in royalties before taxes, and, per his promise, he plowed the money back into his work.

The Corvair—subject of numerous lawsuits and Nader's target in both his book and congressional testimony—remained on the market. But bad PR caused sales to slump, from 304,000 in 1962 to 15,000 in 1968. That year, GM voluntarily discontinued the model.

Finally, nobody was prosecuted for harassing a congressional witness, and so Nader filed suit against GM on November 14, 1966. He used what was then a relatively untested charge, invasion of privacy. Ironically, this tort had been dreamed up by Louis Brandeis in his landmark 1890 *Harvard Law Review* article. There had only been a dozen previous invasion-of-privacy cases in which damages were awarded, with $12,500 as the highest amount. Nader asked for $26 million.

It was going to be a tough battle. GM continued to maintain that the investigation was routine and on certain issues—such as whether it hired the sex lure in the Safeway cookie aisle—the company was adamant in its denials.

Meanwhile, Detective Gillen was thoroughly enjoying his notoriety, milking it for all it was worth. During an interview with a reporter for the

Detroit Free Press, he took issue with Nader's account of the investigation. "I would refer him to a psychiatrist," said Gillen. "He was followed, but not at the times he claimed."

So Nader sued Gillen for defamation, asking for $100,000 in damages.

It proved a serendipitous move. The lawsuit allowed Nader's lawyers to take a deposition from Gillen. As it turned out, Gillen had in his possession a number of documents and recordings—sixty-nine in all—some of which the Ribicoff subcommittee had failed to obtain. One exhibit settled some lingering questions: Had GM, as it always maintained, truly wanted to confine the investigation to whether Nader was secretly involved in Corvair lawsuits? Had Gillen—an overeager detective—expanded the investigation into Nader's personal life without GM's blessing?

As it turned out, the gadget-happy Gillen had made surreptitious recordings of the instructions he received directly from GM. One contained the following smoking gun: "get something, somewhere on this guy . . . shut him up."

Even so, the case would drag on for years. GM was a giant corporation. Ralph Nader was just one man.

— 6 —

One-Man Army

NADER'S SHOWDOWN WITH GM GAVE HIM instant visibility. But his time as a public figure also threatened to be fleeting. Absolutely no one—including Nader—knew what he would do for an encore, or whether there would even be an encore. Ralph Nader, tireless advocate, permanent champion of consumer interests, would come only later, the result of relentless effort.

Flash back to the period immediately following the 1966 hearings. Among the public, the press, and members of Congress, Nader appeared to be a single-issue expert. He had proved highly effective if oddly fervent on the technical topic of auto safety.

But Nader was not content to be a historical footnote. He was busy casting about, searching for a follow-up issue, one that was a fitting vessel for his own sense of outrage and would also seize the public's attention.

ENTER NEAL SMITH—LAWYER BY training, farmer in practice, and also a Democratic congressman from Iowa. Smith was dedicated to toughening up meat inspection standards.

The law on the books in 1966 was a direct result of Upton Sinclair's 1906 muckraking masterpiece, *The Jungle*, which documented such grotesqueries as rats ground into sausage and pork loins laden with tubercular spittle. Sinclair's exposé rated front-page coverage around the country and even drew the attention of President Theodore Roosevelt, who summoned Sinclair to the White House to discuss possible remedies. The upshot was the Meat Inspection Act of 1906, designed to put an end to the gruesome practices at processing plants.

Smith—when wearing his farmer's hat—became aware that the original act was prone to abuse. At livestock auctions, he noticed that the same buyers were in the habit of purchasing diseased cattle and pigs. He learned that the meat from these animals was not subject to federal inspection so long as it was not slated for transport across state lines. This was a loophole in the 1906 act.

Smith—in his role as congressman—had been trying since 1960 to amend the act. But his efforts were undercut by ingrained and well-financed special interests such as the American Meat Institute and the National Independent Meat Packers Association. Furthermore, meat inspection—like auto safety—was a rarified issue. It required a burst of concerted public interest à la Sinclair's *The Jungle*. "The process doesn't move by osmosis," recalls Edward Mezvinsky, Smith's legislative assistant during the mid–1960s. "Just because you're right doesn't mean the political process will move. The weapon to push along the process is public exposure."

It so happened that Mezvinsky was friendly with Ralph Nader. Mezvinksy had met him through Lawrence Scalise, the Iowa attorney general who had organized an auto safety conference at which Nader was a featured speaker.

Mezvinsky had grown up on a farm near Ames, Iowa. His parents—like Nader's—were immigrants. In Mezvinsky's case they were one-time fruit peddlers from Eastern Europe. After law school, Mezvinksy went to Washington, bursting with ideas about how to make life better for the farmers and factory workers who made up Congressman Smith's constituency. For his part, Nader was impressed by Mezvinsky's dedication.

In 1966—as in later years—precious few people were in possession of Nader's unlisted number. Only a handful ever got as far as the foyer directly outside his room at the boarding house. The foyer—according to a sprinkling of firsthand accounts—featured a red velvet chair, a few fake plants, a Deco-esque statuette of a woman, and a telephone that was shared by Nader and three other boarders. Nader paid $80 a month in rent. The boarding house had once been the residence of the Japanese ambassador, pre–World War II, and Nader's landlady, Dorothy Remington, was a piano teacher and one-time opera singer.

Nader gave Mezvinsky his unlisted number. Mezvinsky was also one of the select few to ever earn an invitation beyond the foyer, into the spare little sanctum that was Nader's room. Mostly, Mezvinksy remembers what was not there—no TV, no appliances. Tall, lanky Nader had even removed the foot board from his bed so that he could stretch out. "The room was antiseptic," recalls Mezvinsky. "It fit Ralph. He was leading an unusual life and it made an impression. His lifestyle gave him credibility."

Of course, Nader and Mezvinsky mostly talked shop. A close relationship, Nader-style, still tended to stick closely to the issues. Mezvinsky filled Nader in on the details—the gory details—of uninspected meat. It was a topic with which Nader had a measure of familiarity, since he had worked at the Highland Arms growing up and had sometimes helped his father purchase meat from wholesalers. There was also his six-month army stint, spent as a cook. The topic spoke to Nader.

"It quickly became clear that he wasn't just a one-issue guy," recalls Mezvinsky. "He had an uncanny ability to see the moving edge, to see how people were affected on the consumer side. That's how he came out of nowhere. It wasn't that he had a one-track mind on auto safety. Frankly, he had a one-track mind on special interests. He had an uncanny ability to go to the heart of an issue, and expose it."

For his part, Nader once said: "Every time I see something terrible, it's like I see it at age nineteen. I keep a freshness that way."

NADER SEIZED ON THE topic and immediately took ownership. He wrote a couple of articles, "We're Still in the Jungle" and "Watch That Hamburger," which appeared in the *New Republic* during the summer of 1967. They served up such details as the fifteen thousand meat processing plants in the United States that did not sell their products across state lines. This meant fully a quarter of the nation's supply of meat—8 billion pounds annually, enough to feed 30 million people—fell outside of federal jurisdiction.

The articles also discussed the practice observed by Congressman Smith, namely, unscrupulous intrastate operators who sought out inexpensive livestock known as "4-D meat"—dead, dying, diseased, and disabled animals. Meanwhile, sulfite—federally banned as an additive—was frequently used to give meat a deceptively healthy pink hue. When it hit the grocery store shelves, the meat's real condition would be masked. Basically, intrastate meat-processing practices were nauseating and no one was doing anything about it. While federal inspection standards were rigorous, state standards tended to be lax or, in some cases, nonexistent.

Nader did not flinch from the subject. His *New Republic* pieces mixed dry statistics and stomach-churning anecdotes with abandon. "Contaminated meat, horsemeat and meat from sick animals originally intended for dog and cat food has ended up in hamburger and processed meat," he wrote. "Eyeballs, lungs, hog blood and chopped hides and other indelicate carcass portions are blended skillfully into baloney and hot dogs."

The articles received a great deal of attention. As with *Unsafe at Any Speed*, Nader proved as much a popularizer as an original researcher. In this case, he drew on the groundbreaking work of Nick Kotz, a regular handball opponent of Mezvinsky and a Washington-based investigative reporter who contributed stories to the *Des Moines Register* and *Minneapolis Tribune*. Kotz would win a Pulitzer Prize for his 1967 series on intrastate meat processing. "I broke the stories," recalls Kotz. "They got a much greater reach through Nader, who would take these issues and publicize them via all the routes he could dream up. In terms of digging up the material, I turned up most of it. Nader was the megaphone that got a much larger audience."

In this—his second turn on the public stage—Nader proved once again to be energetic, opportunistic, and surprisingly savvy in the ways of Congress and the media.

Nader took raw data obtained by Kotz from the Department of Agriculture and broke it down state by state. He then sent press releases to newspapers located near the worst plants. This resulted in a flood of local stories about unsavory practices at intrastate plants, many of them operated by major companies such as Armour and Swift. Nader also set off on a ten-city tour and traveled from Boston to Los Angeles publicizing the issue. At every opportunity, he urged people to write letters to members of Congress and also to Betty Furness, President Johnson's consumer adviser.

"You wouldn't believe the letters," Furness told *Newsweek*. "They were from meat inspectors themselves, their wives, ordinary consumers—everybody—demanding tough action."

Public attention was starting to focus on the esoteric issue of intrastate meat processing. Neal Smith introduced yet another bill, which was designed to close the loophole in the original act. As the bill wended its way along, Nader worked to build support in Congress.

He showed superb instincts regarding who would be receptive. One of his most enduring observations: The way to a congressman's heart is through his legislative assistants. Long before Nader met Senator Ribicoff, he had worked closely with his staffers, Jerome Sonosky and Robert Wager. The lesson was not lost on Nader.

The fact is, approaching a member of Congress directly can be a losing proposition. Senators and representatives are consumed by here-and-now issues such as voting on bills, meeting with constituents, getting reelected. Often they can scarcely focus on the welter of pending legislation, much of which will not come to a vote for years, if ever.

Congressional staffs can attend to a bill far earlier in the legislative process. It's part of their job. If they encounter a bill on a compelling issue, they may bring it to their boss's attention. Staffers, more than members of Congress, get involved in the nitty-gritty details of legislation, the procedures and mechanics. As a bonus, staffers tend to be young and idealistic and they were therefore receptive to Nader's points of view.

In 1967 Richard Falknor was a legislative assistant to Tom Foley, a Democrat from Washington state. As Falknor recalls: "Nader had a tractor beam for young Washington staffers who wanted to do something, who wanted to leave a footprint. I plead guilty. He's able to put a legend on an issue. Ralph can give staffers the feeling that if a particular issue doesn't take up all his spare time, he's failed society."

Falknor arranged a Saturday meeting between Nader and Foley at the Old Ebbit Grill in Washington. Nader showed up wearing jeans. But there was nothing casual about his approach. He held forth on the topic of tainted meat at length and with near-messianic fervor. Of course, Foley had been aware of the issue. But in the way typical for members of Congress, it had never commanded his full attention. Nader's performance was instrumental in convincing Foley to join forces with Smith in sponsoring the legislation. Intrastate meat inspection would be the first major issue for the freshman representative from Washington state.

Nader also became a regular witness before the House and Senate agricultural subcommittees. Many of these sessions were closed to the press, so he distributed the prepared portion of his testimony to reporters beforehand. Such tactics grew out of another of Nader's quick-study observations: to keep a bill alive in Congress you need to keep the issue alive in the press. "Thanks to all the dirty-meat stories written by me and peddled by Nader, Congress responded very quickly," says Kotz. "They were responding to what they perceived to be public opinion."

NEVERTHELESS, THE HOUSE INITIALLY passed weak legislation. Intense pressure from various meat-packing lobbies succeeded in defanging the original Smith-Foley bill. Instead, the House adopted a measure that called for federal aid to upgrade state inspection systems where they existed. States that lacked an inspection system would be required to develop one of their own devising. Bottom line: The federal government would not step in and impose its more rigorous standards on intrastate plants.

At this point, Kotz broke a crucial story. He learned that an industry group called the Western Meat Packers Association had mailed its membership a fund-solicitation letter. The association was building a war chest. As it turned out, the moneys were earmarked for the campaigns of select members of Congress, those who opposed subjecting all slaughterhouses to federal standards. Nader played his megaphone role, amplifying Kotz's story. The White House—which had taken a soft line on the issue—started to feel the pressure.

On November 20, 1967, Johnson made a plea to Congress: "We need the strongest possible meat inspection bill. Nobody in this country ought ever to take a chance of eating filthy meat from filthy packing houses. It doesn't make any difference how powerful the meat lobby is."

Over in the Senate, Johnson's call was heeded by Walter Mondale, then a freshman Democrat from Minnesota. Mondale had been pressing for a stronger measure. In turn, Nader had been busy pressuring him. In fact, Nader had taken to calling the senator as late as 4:00 A.M. to talk tainted meat legislation. When the phone rang at an ungodly hour, Mondale would pick it up and answer, simply, "Hello, Ralph."

Mondale's bill was tougher, but it also contained an element of compromise, designed to maintain a line between federal and state jurisdictions. The bill gave states three years to develop standards of their own that were commensurate with federal standards. It also set aside some grant money to help states get up to speed. Only states that proved unable or unwilling would face the imposition of federal standards.

The bill passed the Senate on December 6, 1967. It later passed the House, and both chambers adopted the same bill in conference. Speaking on the floor, Mondale singled out Nader for his role: "I commend those selfless private citizens who worked courageously and creatively in this field. I would name Ralph Nader as one of these. I am proud, as a lawyer, that we have some people's lawyers, who seek no profit, but who, guided only by the motive of public service, are digging out the facts, and leading such blameless lives that they can stand up as examples of the finest of our profession."

A few days later, at a White House signing ceremony, President Johnson elected to read the most repugnant passages from an Agriculture Department study—this one dug up by Nader rather than Kotz—that catalogued abuses in intrastate plants. LBJ was infamous for the pleasure he derived from shocking people. He delighted in showing off his scars and reputedly once stripped naked in front of a congressman who was visiting his Texas ranch and dove into a pool.

The report provided ideal fodder. "A man was wrapping pork shoulders," Johnson drawled. "He dropped one in the sawdust, picked it up, and wiped if off with a dirty, sour rag." This met with groans all around. So Johnson continued: "Beef was being broken on an open dock by a dirt road in ninety-five-degree weather. There were flies on the meat. Drums of bones and meat scraps were covered with maggots . . . "

Nader was present for the signing ceremony, as was Upton Sinclair. The prospect of meeting his boyhood hero was exciting: an encounter between two muckrakers from different eras. Now eighty-nine years old, Sinclair was confined to a wheelchair and accompanied by a nurse.

Leaning down close, Nader said, "We're continuing your work, Mr. Sinclair."

"I see that you are," replied Sinclair. He added, "Keep watching them."

ACT TWO ON THE public stage had shown Nader to be something quite rare, what might be termed a pragmatic idealist—clearly a mix of traits from his mother and father. He had a keen eye for abuses against consumers and in speaking about the subject, or writing about it, he could summon considerable outrage. But he was not content to stop there. Nader was also demonstrating himself to be a student of power, with a grasp of how things get accomplished in America. Nader the idealist showed a very pragmatic willingness to see the process through, teaming with journalists, stirring public interest, identifying congressional allies, and even worrying about the details of which bill to back, and in what form.

He described his approach as follows: "I try to figure out how to use what I have, the best form to put it in. A speech? A magazine article? A congressman? A letter to a corporation? There's no formula."

Nader was also emerging as a consummate issue entrepreneur. His lifeblood was ideas, and he required a constant stream of new ones, both to be effective and to remain in the public eye. As for identifying suitable issues, Nader was promiscuous. Sometimes he generated an issue himself, but he was equally likely to popularize the research of a scientist or to latch onto a piece of consumer legislation introduced by a congressman. The years ahead would find Nader on high alert: perpetually receptive to new ideas and issues, from whatever source they might hail.

Alan Morrison—a longtime friend and colleague of Nader's—has the following observation: "I have never known anybody who has more ideas about more things than Ralph. He's not interested in two or three or five or ten things. He's interested in a million. He sees things differently from everybody else. He just sees injustices, unfairnesses, and improper ways of handling situations that everyone else just accepts. He has a cosmic view of these things, very broad, but at the same time, he is a person who pays enormous attention to details. I never met anybody who can think so big and think so small at the same time."

DURING THE PERIOD IMMEDIATELY following passage of the Wholesale Meat Act of 1967, Nader had a hand in three other pieces of legislation: the Natural Gas Pipeline Safety Act, the Wholesale Poultry Products Act, and the Radiation Control for Health and Safety Act.

The circumstances surrounding passage of the radiation law—its journey from embryonic idea to legislative act—are especially illustrative of what was emerging as Nader's standard operating procedure.

Nader was introduced to the issue of the dangers of X rays by Karl Morgan, a scientist at the Oak Ridge National Laboratory, where Nader's sister, Claire, was then working. Nader proceeded to write an article entitled "X Ray Exposures" for the *New Republic*. He also drummed up a concerned congressman and potential legislative sponsor in E. L. Bartlett, a Democrat from Alaska. Bartlett was an outspoken opponent of nuclear weapons testing and the resulting radioactive fallout. The issue of radiation overexposure struck Nader as a natural corollary.

Testifying before the Senate Commerce Committee, Nader asserted that blacks receiving X rays were routinely exposed to as much as 50 percent more radiation than whites. This was based on the spurious notion that it required a stronger dose to penetrate blacks' darker skin. The American Dental Association issued a statement in response, saying that Nader "continues to make undocumented and inflammatory statements that needlessly frighten the public."

Nader enlisted the aid of Morton Mintz, the *Washington Post* investigative reporter who had broken the story that Nader was being tailed. With some digging, Mintz succeeded in turning up an instruction manual from General Electric—the largest manufacturer of X-ray equipment—that did in fact recommend higher dosages for blacks. Mintz's subsequent story effectively exonerated Nader and further amplified the question of whether the public was being exposed to dangerous levels of radiation. And so it went—articles, congressional testimony, challenges from industry groups, rebuttals by Nader and cohorts—culminating in passage of the Radiation Control for Health and Safety Act.

The law and attendant public interest led to a variety of reforms. Technicians who took X rays began routinely using "fast" film that exposed people for around a quarter of a second instead of "slow" film that required an exposure of up to four seconds. The American Dental Association—lax to this point—officially recommended that all dentists begin using lead aprons to guard against overexposure to X rays. Meanwhile, the Federal Trade Commission urged viewers to sit at least six feet away from color television sets.

IT SEEMS REMARKABLE IN hindsight that Nader was involved in the passage of four different laws in roughly a year. But he was also the beneficiary of excellent timing.

Lyndon Johnson had assumed the presidency in 1963 following John Kennedy's assassination. During the first years of his tenure, LBJ rode a crest of social activism, the legacy of the youthfulness and zeal that characterized the Camelot era. Johnson had a legislative Midas touch and was able to convince Congress to pass virtually everything on his wish list. Among LBJ's Great Society initiatives were Medicare, Medicaid, two major civil rights laws, and federal aid to schools.

But by 1966, Johnson was in retreat. Democrats in Congress took a beating during the midterm election. Meanwhile, it was becoming increasingly clear that the United States could not afford the exorbitant cost of a war overseas and generous new social programs at home. The only substantial piece of social legislation Johnson was able to push through during the second half of his second term was a 1968 civil rights bill that dealt with fair housing.

Against this backdrop, consumer legislation proved a remarkably easy sell. While social programs were costly, consumer bills were surprisingly cheap to enact. A good example is the Wholesale Meat Inspection Act, which provided modest grants for states to improve their inspection processes, and from a cost standpoint, nothing more.

Consumer legislation was not as divisive as social programs. The country was increasingly fractured over Vietnam and there was a backlash brewing against the civil rights movement. But almost everyone—liberals and conservatives, northerners and southerners, rich and poor—could get behind efforts to legislate cleaner meat, safer X rays, and pipelines that would not spontaneously combust.

Johnson needed Nader, and Nader certainly benefited from the legislative climate that prevailed during the latter part of Johnson's presidency. Even so, the two men exchanged nothing beyond a few pleasantries, mostly as Johnson handed Nader commemorative pens at a series of bill-signing ceremonies. But Johnson still managed to pay a small and inimitable tribute to Nader.

One time LBJ was driving across his Texas ranch in a big new Chrysler. He noticed a splotch on the windshield. He reached for the wiper control, only to wind up groping about blindly. Turned out the car was fitted with the type of nonprotruding controls called for by the National Traffic and Motor Vehicle Safety Act of 1966. "That goddamned Nader," muttered LBJ to his passenger.

BY NOW, IT WAS becoming abundantly clear that Nader was not, as his friend Ed Mezvinsky had noted, simply a "one-issue guy." The flurry of legislative efforts in which he was involved landed him on the cover of *Newsweek* on January 22, 1968. The magazine featured an image of Nader in a suit of armor, meant to cast him as a knight errant to consumers in peril. The story was entitled, "Meet Ralph Nader."

As for who Ralph Nader was exactly—vocationally speaking—that remained something of a mystery. His public image was yet to congeal.

The *Newsweek* article deemed him a "self-appointed lobbyist." Of course, he was also a lawyer by training. While paying tribute to Nader's role in the meat act, Senator Mondale had claimed him as such. At the same time, Nader had burst onto the scene due to a book he had authored. And he continued to write feature articles for publications such as the *New Republic*. Numerous newspaper articles from this period identify Nader as a "journalist" or even an "investigative reporter."

Certainly, there was some sense that Nader was a modern incarnation of the Progressive Era muckrakers. In the early years of the twentieth century, Upton Sinclair, Ida Tarbell, and Lincoln Steffens had written numerous investigative pieces for magazines such as *McClure's* and *Harper's*, exposing Standard Oil's monopolistic practices, graft in high places, and assorted other malefactions.

Nader even became a consulting editor to a new magazine called *Mayday*. It was the project of an all-star cast of latter-day muckrakers: Andrew Kopkind and James Ridgeway, both recent departees from the *New Republic*, and Robert Sherrill, a correspondent for the *Nation*.

The magazine was a four-page weekly that featured no photographs, no illustrations, and, for that matter, no advertisements. It was started on $20,000 in seed money. Half the sum came from Lou Wolfson, a shifty Jacksonville, Florida, scrap iron dealer who owned a Kentucky Derby horse and later wound up in trouble with the SEC. *Mayday* cost twenty-five cents an issue and was distributed by Richard Grossman, publisher of *Unsafe at Any Speed*.

"We started on a shoestring, and wound up on half a shoestring," recalls Sherrill. "It was a pathetic little publication we put out. Nader contributed very little, if anything. But you could say he gave some cachet to it. It certainly needed all the cachet it could get from anybody."

After a few issues, a West Coast magazine surfaced with a prior claim on the name "Mayday." The muckraking journal changed its name to *Hard Times* and staggered on.

Around this time, Nader became friendly with a man named Anthony Mazzochi. Mazzochi was a union organizer. The two met due to their mutual involvement on the issue of exploding pipelines. Nader would ply Mazzochi with endless questions about union organizing: how do you pick leaders, how do you put together an effective team, how do you inspire people to fight for various causes?

"I don't think he held with a Lone Ranger concept," recalls Mazzochi. "You can't accomplish so much as one individual riding into the sunset. You need an organization."

Nader also put out word via the *Newsweek* cover story. The very last paragraph contains the revelation that Nader was "looking for help." It went on to explain that he was searching for young lawyers who were interested in working with him.

Nader was a lawyer, a muckraking journalist, and a self-appointed lobbyist—he did it all, he did it in the public interest, and so far he had done it alone. But he was about to get some help.

— 7 —

Nader's Raiders

SPRING TERM 1968, ROBERT FELLMETH AND Andrew Egendorf were attending Harvard law and Harvard business school, respectively. They happened to see the *Newsweek* cover story about Nader and were intrigued by the mention that he was looking for young people to do public interest work.

On January 29, 1968, they wrote a joint letter to Nader that included the following: "We hear that you are establishing a unique organization in Washington to intensify your judicious jihad. Your work is most appealing to two disgusted Harvard graduate students who must endure endless years of drivel in order to mechanically defend the guilty and profitably screw the consumer. We want to work with you this summer."

Fellmeth and Egendorf had no idea how to reach Nader. Both his address and phone number were unlisted, of course. The article did furnish one clue: Nader had grown up in Winsted, Connecticut. So they took a chance and sent the letter to his boyhood home in care of his father, Nathra Nader.

A few days later, Egendorf was studying in his dorm room at Harvard's Gallatin Hall, sometime after midnight, when the phone rang. He picked up and was shocked when the caller identified himself as Ralph Nader. As Egendorf recalls, the two talked about the potential for harnessing student power. Nader said he had been intrigued by Fellmeth and Egendorf's letter, and yes, it was true: he hoped to enlist a small group of volunteers for a summer project.

"It was an absolute fluke," says Egendorf. "The phone rings and it's Ralph Nader. To this day, I'm convinced that because I answered on the first ring at 1:00 A.M., he figured I must be right for the job."

Besides Egendorf and Fellmeth, Nader managed to locate five other people—or vice versa—for the summer of '68 project.

William Howard Taft IV was in his second year at Harvard law. He was the great-grandson of President William Howard Taft. Edward Finch Cox was in his final year at Princeton, where he had taken a seminar on government from Nader. (While riding herd on four laws, Nader had also tried teaching.) Cox was scion of an established eastern family that numbered among its forebears Robert Livingston, one of the drafters of the Declaration of Independence. A few years hence, in 1971, he would marry Tricia Nixon, the president's daughter.

Peter Bradford was Yale '64, Yale law '68. Judy Areen—the only female in the group—was in her third year at Yale law and was the daughter of Gordon Areen, a high-ranking Chrysler executive. "It's a matter entirely within her own province and hasn't got anything to do with me or Chrysler, for that matter," the elder Areen told the *Wall Street Journal*. "These young people have a very definite crusading spirit. If they didn't, this country might be in pretty sad shape."

Nader tapped John Schulz to lead the group. At twenty-nine, Schulz was several years older than the others and had spent his post-Yale years teaching law at the University of Southern California.

In terms of social background and educational attainment, this was an almost comically elite collection of people. It numbered the great-grandson of a former president, the future son-in-law of a future president, and between the seven, not one solitary credit hour had been earned outside the Ivy League. This owed partly to the fact that Nader's own alma maters were Princeton and Harvard. He had chosen people from institutions where he had a connection. Nader may have felt ambivalent about the two schools, but he knew that their graduates would have no trouble doing the work.

Drawing heavily on Ivy Leaguers had another practical side effect. The late sixties were a time of extreme intergenerational tension. It was an era that featured LSD and the Apollo space program, George Wallace and Baba Ram Das, "Mrs. Robinson" and Mr. Rogers, and on either side of age thirty, a mutual and growing mistrust. Nader's seven volunteers were anything but wild-haired radicals. To the contrary, they were eminently presentable young citizens who would not appear out of place poking around the power centers of official Washington.

"None of us was a hippie," says Egendorf. "No one was running around with flowers and beads, and there was no pot smoking that I can remember. We were all serious grad students, not dropouts. We were looking to fix the system, not destroy the system." Or as Fellmeth puts it: "We were radicals, but we weren't irresponsible radicals. We were hardworking radicals."

Politically, the seven were actually a rather diverse lot. Fellmeth had supported the presidential aspirations of ultraconservative Barry Goldwater in 1964. Early in 1968, before their summer stint with Nader, both Taft and Schulz traveled to New Hampshire to help with the campaign of the avowedly liberal Eugene McCarthy. McCarthy volunteers tended to be sober-minded and dedicated types. They favored jackets, ties, and regular haircuts—a look that came to be known as "Clean for Gene."

The volunteers who went to work for Nader adopted a similar comportment and style. "We made a point of being well dressed, suits and ties," recalls William Howard Taft IV. "Certainly our hair was not as long as some people's in those days. We were a little more 'professional-looking' you might say."

THE PROJECT THAT NADER selected for his summer crew was an investigation of the Federal Trade Commission. This was supposed to be the U.S. government's primary consumer protection agency. When it was founded in 1914, the FTC was charged with regulating corporate mergers with an eye toward unfair competitive practices. During the 1930s, the agency was handed the additional responsibility of protecting consumers from shady methods of interstate commerce, such as deceptive advertising.

But the FTC had long been considered a laggard among the various government agencies. It had even been the target of a previous investigation, a 1949 study by a commission headed by former president Herbert Hoover, which concluded that the FTC's performance was "disappointing." Nader was especially galled by the widespread perception that the agency was a patsy for big business. Ample evidence suggested that the FTC was extremely deferential to the corporations it was supposed to police. Regarding the agency's supposed conflicts of interest, Nader was in the habit of saying: "The wolf's been hired by the sheep."

When the volunteers arrived in Washington, Nader met with them at a cafeteria near his boardinghouse. He filled them in on the FTC's spotty history. Chairman Paul Rand Dixon—aware of Nader's reputation and fearful of his contacts in Congress—had agreed to give the student team relatively unrestricted access to his agency's records and personnel. But Nader also provided his investigators with the names of some disaffected FTC employees, people who might be willing to really spill. "He seemed to have his own set of contacts, behind the scenes," says Egendorf. "He played it close to the vest, on a need-to-know basis, like a spy."

Nader's initial instructions to his charges had a suitably covert flavor: "You have to really watch yourselves. Be careful what you do. Remember, we're battling huge forces here. Look out, because if you make a mistake, they'll come after us."

He urged them especially to be careful about minor details: "I'm after substance, but they'll get us on the little stuff."

The summer volunteers fanned out and, true to the billing, discovered an agency in deep decline. The FTC's own records showed that in recent years it had brought progressively fewer cases against companies. Nader's team determined that only one in 125 consumer complaints resulted in action of any sort. On average, it took the FTC four years to investigate a case. About the only sanctions the agency ever handed down were voluntary cease-and-desist orders, easy enough for a violator to simply ignore.

Taking on a major corporation of any stripe was an extreme rarity. Mostly the FTC went after pipsqueaks. For example, the agency demanded that a tiny milliner in Fall River, Massachusetts, stop using the word "Milan" to describe hats manufactured in the United States. In another case, the FTC devoted six years to proving that Carter's Little Liver Pills would not benefit a person's liver. The FTC's case docket for the first quarter of 1968 included pending actions against thirty-three companies, twenty-nine of which were too small to appear in any kind of corporate directory.

When it came to policing deceptive ads, the FTC was an abysmal failure. At one point during the 1960s, it had dreamed up the novel approach of simply hiring a group of middle-aged women to watch TV all day. They tuned in to soap operas mostly, and during the commercials either talked or got snacks. What they did not do was identify deceptive ads, and the program was discontinued.

Rifling through the agency's personnel records, Nader's team discovered that the FTC was sinecure central for civil servants who hailed from the South. The practice dated to the Great Depression when—according to agency lore—Boss Crump of the Memphis Machine gained inroads into the FTC patronage system and began installing his cronies.

Little had changed by the late 1960s. Commissioner Dixon was from Nashville and the majority of the staff were also from Tennessee or elsewhere in the South. The FTC had even opened a field office in Oak Ridge,

Tennessee. As of 1968, it was yet to open offices in such major cities as Detroit and Philadelphia. Of five hundred lawyers in the FTC, the students learned that only about forty were Republicans, the balance being Democrats, mostly Southern Democrats.

Not surprisingly, the FTC's cozy culture was quite amenable to leisurely, martini-drenched lunches. The students identified Stevie's and Saxony as favorite watering holes. On arriving to interview one high-ranking official, a member of Nader's team discovered him asleep on a couch in his office, the *Washington Post* sports page draped across his face.

Commissioner Dixon's forbearance toward the student sleuths—northerners and Ivy Leaguers to boot—wore out in a hurry. One day, team leader Schulz was interviewing Dixon in his office. Their discussion began to take on an inquisitional tone. Dixon stood up, walked around his desk, seized Schulz by the arm, and bodily escorted him out the door. "When Dixon threw Schulz out of his office, we knew we were on the right track," recalls Ed Cox. "That provided the hook Nader needed, and he used his contacts to leverage it into a big story."

Nader had chosen his target well. The FTC was a proverbial fish in a barrel, a government agency that was laughably ineffectual and corrupt. The students were holding up their end, doing impeccable research. The story proved irresistible to the press.

This was 1968, after all, a cataclysmic year in American history, one that ranks right up there with 1776, 1861, 1941, and 2001. The country was in the midst of a nervous breakdown.

Assorted women's liberation groups organized a picket of the 1968 Miss America Pageant in Atlantic City, and some of the participants tossed their bras into a symbolic "freedom ash can." Abbie Hoffman disrupted the trading floor of the New York Stock Exchange on one occasion and on another unveiled the Yippie presidential candidate, a pig named Pigasus.

During 1968, the number of Americans in Vietnam hit a high-water mark, 541,000. Meanwhile, the domestic front was wracked with astonishing violence. Clashes between police and demonstrators at the Democratic National Convention in Chicago sent more than one hundred people to emergency rooms. Martin Luther King Jr. was assassinated, Robert Kennedy was assassinated, Andy Warhol was shot, though not fatally. Race riots in cities including Baltimore, Newark, and Detroit did millions of dollars in property damage and left forty-six people dead.

Against this backdrop, Nader assembled a group of well-groomed, supremely educated, and altogether serious young people. They burned neither bras nor draft cards, certainly did not demonstrate, riot, loot, or worse. They didn't even smoke pot. Instead, they were in the midst of a meticulous investigation of a specialized government agency that had abdicated its responsibility to consumers. It made for great copy, especially in the context of—and by contrast to—everything else that seemed to be going on in the country. *Time* magazine dubbed the summer volunteers "Nader's Neophytes." But the name that stuck was coined by William Greider in an article in the *Washington Post*. He called them "Nader's Raiders."

THE RAIDERS WRAPPED UP their summer project by writing a report on the corrupt FTC. It wound up being 185 pages long and, here and there, managed to deliver a pretty good facsimile of Nader's unique purple-passioned invective. The report describes the FTC as a "self-parody of bureaucracy, fat with cronyism, torpid through inbreeding unusual even for Washington, manipulated by the agents of commercial predators, impervious to governmental or citizen monitoring." Another barb: "Alcoholism, spectacular lassitude, and office absenteeism, incompetence by the most modest standards, and a lack of commitment to the regulatory mission are rampant." The report concluded that the FTC ought be reformed, and Commissioner Dixon dismissed.

The team made 150 copies and careened around Washington in Cox's Volkswagen Beetle, hand delivering them to members of the press.

The Raiders also got a chance to testify before Congress. Through Ribicoff, Nader was able to arrange for a group of college students to appear before the Senate Subcommittee on Administrative Practice and Procedure.

William Howard Taft IV would later serve as permament representative to NATO and a legal adviser to Secretary of State Colin Powell. He would become a veteran at testifying on the Hill. But Taft has fond memories of his very first appearance before Congress: "It was sort of an ego trip for us all. It's not often that people get to testify at the age of twenty-two or twenty-three."

Far from being nervous, Nader's team was remarkably cool in the spotlight. Once again, this has everything to do with the temper of the times. "Here you are a twenty-two-year-old kid in front of the United States Senate with the TV cameras on," recalls Fellmeth. "You have to understand that during this era there was a certain feeling that some of the people in control of the country really were screwed up. We'd learned our history and we were not too awed by adults. We thought adults were basically fucked up and desperately in need of a new approach. They needed the children to lead them. I don't think we were too far wrong."

NADER'S FTC RAID REALLY did accomplish something; his seven children really did manage to lead the adults. In 1969 Richard Nixon, newly elected as president, asked the American Bar Association to conduct an independent investigation of the FTC. When the ABA issued its own report, the findings were remarkably similar to the conclusions of Nader's Raiders, though couched in more temperate language. The ABA deemed the FTC a "failure on many counts," calling the cases it brought "trivial" and charging its staff with widespread "incompetence."

Under fire, Paul Rand Dixon stepped down. In January 1970, Nixon appointed Caspar Weinberger as his replacement. Weinberger was an activist chairman who reorganized the FTC staff, increasing its enforcement capabilities and expanding the field operations. By the early 1970s, the FTC would be a revitalized agency. It began undertaking significant cases: against Coca-Cola's Hi-C fruit drink for false nutritional claims and against McDonald's restaurants for offering a $500,000 sweepstakes but only awarding $13,000 in prize money.

Meanwhile, the 1968 FTC raid helped to further clarify Nader's image. He was a public interest gadabout: lawyer, lobbyist, and muckraking journalist. He was also a curious hybrid of Beltway insider/outsider. Nader worked closely with Congress and delved into auto legislation or the workings of the FTC in mind-numbing detail, yet he approached matters as a critic, solidly outside the system. As Nader was fond of saying, "I don't work in government, I work on government."

He was unique, a Washington fixture with no official position, elected or otherwise. One would simply have to be invented for him: "consumer advocate." It would become Nader's title, appended to his name in countless articles, even though "consumer advocate" did not exactly do him justice. The term has a kind of home ec flavor, evocative of a busybody complaining about the price of a dozen eggs. Nader was so much more. As the FTC raid made clear, Nader was concerned with the power exercised by corporations, and most especially with their ability to undercut the bodies meant to regulate them. He was staking out a grand territory: consumers versus producers. And he was forcing huge questions: How can freedoms be protected? How can injuries be prevented? How can balance between the two parties be restored? As Nader once famously stated, his goal was "nothing less than the qualitative reform of the industrial revolution." But "consumer advocate" it was; this was slightly more apt than being identified as a "crusading lawyer."

BECAUSE THE FTC RAID had been such a success, Nader decided to expand his ambitions considerably in the summer of 1969. He called for one hundred interns to poke around Washington, exposing various and sundry consumer effronteries. Nader put the word out in the press and in speeches he delivered at colleges. This time, he offered a small stipend, anywhere from $200 to $500 for the summer. In years to come, he would hire as many as a thousand Raiders. A number of them would subsequently sign on with him full-time to work on various crusades.

Directing an entire army of muckrakers-in-training requires at least some measure of organization. So Nader founded the Center for the Study of Responsive Law, the first of an array of nonprofit organizations in which he would be involved. In 1969 he set up headquarters in a decrepit Victorian-era mansion near DuPont Circle. Nader rented it from the transit authority, which had plans to eventually raze the building and create a metro stop.

Now Nader had an address. No longer would it be left to the sheer ingenuity of job seekers to track him down.

Nader's new nonprofit managed to attract a handful of grants. The Carnegie Foundation provided $55,000. He also received $5,000 from the Sierra Club and $10,000 from Speiser Shumate Geoghan, the law firm retained for his ongoing invasion-of-privacy lawsuit against General Motors. IRS filings show that the Center for the Study of Responsive Law received $173,117 in contributions for 1969. Nader supplemented the contributions from his own income: royalties from *Unsafe at Any Speed* and lecture fees. Nader did not mind. He lived frugally, saying he required just $5,000 a year for his personal needs.

The grants, coupled with Nader's personal contributions, made it possible to hire a modest permanent staff in 1969. More would sign on full-time in the years to come. The term "Raider" would blur, coming to denote not only a summer intern but anyone who worked for Nader.

The DuPont Circle headquarters was a shambles. A hand-lettered cardboard sign announced: Center for the Study of Responsive Law. There were books and files everywhere, stuffed in wooden fruit crates, piled in the old mansion's dormant fireplace. A handful of the Raiders had offices there. For the rest, the building served as a kind of nerve center, a sometime meeting place for legions of Naderites, living around Washington and working on assorted projects. "There was a political campaign-like slovenliness to the place. In terms of furniture, everything was begged, borrowed, or stolen," recalls Harrison Wellford, the Center's first executive director.

Nader did not even maintain an office at his own headquarters. He paid $97 a month to rent a cramped little warren at the National Press Building. He attempted to guard the location from all but his closest associates. At one point, Nader refused to reveal it to a *Life* magazine reporter, saying: "Too much of what I do has to remain confidential and secret. I must have my privacy."

An interesting side note about the Center for the Study of Responsive Law. Its initials—CSRL—appear to form a pattern (C equals Claire, S equals Shafeek, R equals Ralph, and L equals Laura). Nader says this is simply a coincidence. Undeniably, he remained extremely close to his siblings. In 1969 Laura was teaching anthropology at Berkeley. Claire—who had received a Ph.D. from Columbia in public law and government—was working at Oak Ridge National Laboratory in Tennessee. One of the areas she explored was whether water desalination could help foster peace in the Middle East.

Shaf had returned to Winsted, following graduation from the University of Toronto. He worked in the Highland Arms and was a highly vocal activist in Winsted. "He was to local democracy what I was on a national level," says Ralph Nader.

Like his famous younger brother, Shaf Nader had all kinds of ideas, some of which bore fruit, some of which foundered. When the Gilbert School moved to a new building in 1959, the old building was left vacant and Shaf suggested that it was an ideal space for a community college. Tiny Winsted as the site of a community college struck many of the townsfolk as bizarre. Shaf pushed hard for it, fighting as furiously in Winsted as ever Ralph did in Washington. He won his battle, and in 1965 Northwestern Connecticut Community College was established, making Winsted—for a time at least—the smallest American town with a community college. On another occasion, Shaf suggested that landlocked Winsted should have its own fishing boat out in the Atlantic, trolling and making money for the town. He fought for that one, too, but was nearly laughed out of the town meeting.

"He just looked at things differently," says Nader. "He was a huge idea man. He was really the fountainhead of so many ideas."

Shaf used to tell his younger brother that everything truly important was decided on the local level.

"It happens here, Ralph," he would say.

"But look at the bills I'm getting through," Ralph would protest.

"No, everything that really matters happens right here."

THE 1969 NADER'S RAIDERS—and subsequent crops as well—were fairly homogeneous. They were liberal-leaning for the most part, though a smattering fell elsewhere along the political spectrum.

Most Raiders were currently attending law school or were newly minted lawyers. This was not because the work required legal training. Much of what the Raiders did—investigating and writing reports—had more in common with journalism. The lawyer affinity was more the result of Nader's own background as a law school graduate. "Ralph has this kind of arrogant attitude that lawyers can do anything," says Joe Tom Easley, a 1969 summer Raider, who went on to work closely with Nader on a number of projects in the years to come. "He believes that lawyerly training has extremely broad application—maybe not to setting a broken leg, but to virtually everything else."

Another common denominator was that the Nader's Raiders tended to come from top-rated schools, with a heavy Ivy League slant. This was certainly true of the first crew—Cox, Taft, Egendorf et al.—who raided the FTC, and it would continue to hold for future groups. Some joked that it was harder to become a Raider than to get into Harvard. Applications in 1970 bore this out, when three thousand people jockeyed for two hundred summer slots.

"We were hard-working, obsessional, preprofessional types," recalls Michael Charney. "The Raiders tended to be extremely intelligent people with high standing at their universities. We were very taken with what Nader was doing, acting constructively, improving the system through hard work."

Charney—a Raider of 1969 vintage—attended Yale at the same time as George W. Bush. "When I was studying," he says, "Bush was getting drunk at the frat house across the street."

Nader's hiring methods were canny, if not exactly egalitarian. The fact was that Ivy Leaguers could be counted on to do good work. Nader was never much of an administrator. Confronted with a flood of job seekers, it was logical to tap the applicants from Ivy League schools. As a bonus, people who attended prestige schools often came from rich families. In many cases they had supplementary sources of income and did not have to actually try to live on the meager sums Nader paid.

IN THE SUMMER OF 1969, Nader's recruits—102 of them to be exact—looked into mine safety, water pollution, food additives, and the treatment of consumers by airlines, to name a select few projects.

What Nader was not involved in to a significant degree—circa 1969—was either of the big causes of the day, Vietnam and civil rights. This showed a degree of discipline on Nader's part or, at the very least, expediency. Nader was strictly a consumer advocate. He had limited resources and selected his projects with great care. He did not wish to be redundant or to compete with various groups that were committed to civil rights or ending the war. Nevertheless, the pressure on Nader to weigh in was intense.

In a *Playboy* interview, Nader was called on to account for his conspicuous inaction on both fronts. Per Vietnam, he responded by contrasting war fatalities with traffic deaths, pointing out that the cumulative number of Americans who had died in the conflict was equal to just twenty-seven weeks' worth of highway carnage. "I'm not saying this to minimize in any way the terrible human suffering the war has caused," he continued, "but to emphasize another kind of violence that is generally ignored by the public."

He explained his lack of concerted action on civil rights as follows: "The consumer movement, in both its immediate and long-range impacts, is intimately related to the problems of the poor and to the problem of the urban ghettos. I have not addressed myself to specific areas of the civil right struggle, because there are many people working in this area already, and with considerable political muscle."

Few blacks became Nader's Raiders. The issues he selected were not issues that enticed or inspired young blacks of an activist bent. Female Naderites would also remain a distinct minority. The gender mix of the first set of Raiders—six men, one woman—would pretty much hold as the ratio going forward. The reasons were simple. During this era, markedly fewer women attended law school, Nader's primary recruiting pool. Furthermore, consumerism had nothing on feminism as an issue that enticed and inspired young women of an activist bent. The upshot: women would play a relatively small role in Nader's various efforts over the years, with some very notable exceptions.

Nader held an orientation for his 1969 recruits. He urged them to take the task of writing reports extremely seriously. "Look, people will read these things," he said. "The president may read them."

He also counseled: "You should not allow yourself the luxuries of discouragement or despair. Bounce back immediately, and welcome adversity because it produces harder thinking and harder drive to get to the objective."

NADER PROVED TO BE an intensely demanding boss who led by example rather than fear. His own work schedule was brutal: twenty hours a day, seven days a week. Late sleeping was something he had given up after college, though occasionally he would sleep in on a Saturday to replenish himself.

Otherwise, he appeared to have few indulgences. He drank an occasional Dubonnet on the rocks. Once upon a time he had smoked, holding himself to exactly fifteen cigarettes a day, but he gave that up in 1961. To many who worked for him, Nader appeared to have a staggeringly low need for diversion. It was an image that he clearly relished and cultivated. "Relaxing is a subjective term," he once said. "To some people, it means lying on a beach, or getting drunk, or frugging in a discotheque, or sleeping twelve hours a day. But I don't create an artificial distinction between work and leisure. I find my work so imperative, so stimulating, so demanding of those qualities within me that I value, that it's really, in the deepest sense, fun."

Leading mostly by example—his own indefatigable example—Nader managed to push his charges into taking on volumes of work. As a young lawyer fresh out of Harvard, Mark Green got his start with Nader. Decades later, he would run a close race for mayor of New York City but lose to Michael Bloomberg. In Green's recollection: "I don't ever remember Nader saying, 'I can't believe you're not working harder.' But there was a certain expectation, not of hours but of performance, and it often required many hours. Ralph is something of a Calvinist."

Money was always a problem. Beginning in 1969, as the roster of ongoing raids grew, it became necessary to hire increasing numbers of full-time staff. Nader generally paid them around $5,000 a year, pretty paltry by the standards of the day. For someone who was older, around thirty say, he would sometimes spring for as much as $10,000. Nader was forever looking for ways to pare costs. Once a staffer received a message from Harvey Jester, Nader's accountant: "Ralph wants to know why you ordered the extra-long phone cord."

But tight money was its own kind of goad. Among those who worked for Nader, there was a sense of us versus them—"us" being noble but cash-strapped consumer advocates, "them" being well-heeled corporate interests and bloated government bureaucrats. "We were fanatics," recalls Beverly Moore. "We wanted to get the job done because this was a cause, and we knew that Ralph had very limited resources. If we didn't do it ourselves, nobody else would."

He (yes, Beverly is another male Raider) remembers that someone tacked a memo on the bulletin board in the DuPont Circle headquarters. It stated that henceforth people should not throw away carbon paper after a single use. The directive was signed "RN." A box was set out to collect used carbon papers. It turned out to be a practical joke. "A lot of people actually believed it," says Moore, "and they started putting carbons in the box to deliver them to Ralph."

The notion of time off bemused Nader—most certainly full vacations but also holidays, even weekends. He maintained that he did not require any of these respites, content in what he termed "laborious leisure."

His charges tried to adopt a similar work ethic. When they fell short, Nader was not one to yell or openly chastise them. He opted for a more effective technique, an offhand comment here, a sly jab there. To wit, a Raider named Reuben Robertson was working on a project that involved the company ITT. He took a weekend off to go to the beach and returned Monday morning to find a note on his chair: "I'll bet Geneen [ITT's CEO] didn't take the weekend off." It was signed "RN" and this time it was not a practical joke.

"I can remember several Memorial Day weekends and Easter weekends and July 4 weekends when we were working away," recalls Peter Petkas, a close associate of Nader's from this era. "Battle is the best metaphor. You're in a struggle, and you are fighting giants. The enemy is well-armed and bigger and heavier. You needed to work harder and smarter."

Nader held onto his army boots from his stint at Fort Dix. Per the martial analogy, he would occasionally wear them while testifying on the Hill—battling in Congress quite literally. Once he even showed up in combat boots at a Beverly Hills fund-raiser attended by Jack Benny and Carl Reiner.

And then there were the phone calls. Day bled into night fed into day according to Nader's idiosyncratic personal clock. When Nader needed to call someone, he needed to call. He showed no restraint, regardless of the hour. What trash-talking was to Muhammad Ali, late-night phone calls were to Nader. It was a cornerstone of his technique.

"Ralph was notorious for this," says Joe Tom Easley. "I can't tell you the number of times I was awakened at night by him. I did the same as every other person, I suspect. That is, I'd turn on the light, try to snap into alertness, and act as if it was the middle of the afternoon."

"Ralph's no fool," adds Easley. "I think this was a very conscious strategy. Ralph was saying, in effect: 'It's the middle of the night. I'm working on behalf of the people, and you should be, too.'"

Nader led an ascetic existence. He turned thirty-five in 1969 but remained unmarried. Around this time, while visiting his Harvard roommate Ed Levin in Chicago, Nader made some comments that shed light on his priorities and choices. "He said that he did not want to get married," recalls Levin. "He said he thought it was such a responsibility to be a husband and father and that he would not be able to pursue the work he wanted to do. It sounded as if it wasn't rehearsed; it sounded as if it was coming from the heart."

Nader may have chosen to remain unattached, giving him the luxury to work around the clock, but many of his employees found that their own choices put them in a bind. Harrison Wellford was twenty-nine when he began working for Nader. He was married and had a young daughter. "Ralph didn't have a lot of sympathy for the demands of family life," he recalls. "If you stood up to Ralph and made clear what your boundaries were, he would respect them. But a lot of people didn't, and he could totally consume you, and he did. He was utterly committed to what he was doing. If he felt you were not showing the same degree of commitment, he could make life very difficult."

Wellford managed to reach a comfortable accommodation with Nader. Wives of Raiders were often less than appreciative of the demands placed on their husbands and more than a few marriages broke under the strain.

Nader—friend of the consumer—could be a brutally tough boss. The work was grueling, the hours long, and to top it off, pay was a pittance. As one Raider said: "Here we were trying to save the world, and we were doing it on the back of a sweatshop."

BUT FOR THOSE WHO stuck it out, there was also abundant recompense. Few places of work handed such great responsibility to people so young. Peter Petkas remembers that on the day he was admitted to the D.C. bar, he was testifying before a congressional committee. In 1969 and in the years ahead, countless Raiders would also get the opportunity to write reports.

A report, Nader style, was not exactly an eye-glazing technical document bound up in gray. As with *Unsafe at Any Speed* and the FTC report, they tended to fairly vibrate with vitriol, handing down savage indictments of bureaucratic bumblers, raging against greed and folly and hypocrisy in all its myriad forms.

Reports bore titles like *Water Wasteland*, *Bitter Wages*, and *The Madness Establishment* (a report resulting from a raid on the National

Institute of Mental Health). In a nod to Nader's debut effort, there was one called *Small—On Safety: The Designed-in Dangers of the Volkswagen*. Many of the reports were published by Richard Grossman's press. The best of them were treated as hot new paperback exposés, earning attention from reviewers at major newspapers and selling in bookstores—hundreds of thousands of copies in certain cases. Royalties reverted to Nader, who would pour the money into still more raids. But the reports provided tremendous exposure to the authors, who were always given prominent bylines.

Michael Kinsley—who would go on to become editor of *Slate* magazine—spent a summer working for Nader. He recounted his experiences in an article called "My Life and Hard Times with Nader's Raiders," which appeared in *Seventeen* magazine. In the article, he describes a brief impromptu pep talk Nader gave him. "I want you to work as hard as you can," Nader urged. "Work day and night. Because remember: You're going to be very surprised how important what you're doing is going to turn out to be."

Kinsley was a bit skeptical. For his project, he had been assigned to delve into a stupefyingly obscure area of tax policy. At summer's end, he dutifully wrote up a report. As Nader predicted, it made a splash. His findings wound up on the front page of the *Baltimore Sun* and the *Washington Star*. Kinsley was just nineteen years old.

— 8 —

"Maiden Muckrakers"

NADER WAS LAUNCHING INTO HIS MOST productive period, what might be termed his golden age. It would last from 1969 through 1976.

When Nader first got started, he felt that four projects at once was the maximum he could handle. The period ahead would see him take on as many as a hundred a year, some solo, some with teams of Raiders. Nader would accelerate his already dervish-like pace and delve into a range of issues so broad as to baffle the mind: nursing homes, nukes, DuPont, Citibank, GM again, the FAA, the CAB, pension laws, land use policies in California, whistle-blowers, GM yet again, and on and on and on.

The key to this golden era was Nader's ability to maintain excellent relations with the press and Congress. Both the press and Congress were intertwined in certain ways. Both would eventually grow weary of Nader, but first he would manage quite a run.

FROM EARLY ON—GOING back to the auto safety press conference at the Cadillac Sheraton—Nader had shown a kind of preternatural media savvy. By the late 1960s, this had grown into outright mastery.

Nader was an avid student of the press. During this era he made a point of reading six papers a day: the *New York Times*, *Washington Post*, *Wall Street Journal*, *Congressional Record*, *Federal Register*, and *Journal of Commerce*. He kept tabs on a huge variety of other publications and had informed—if self-serving—opinions about their editorial policies and consumer coverage. He purported to be a big fan of the *Rochester Times Union*, not exactly a major market daily. And he once ripped into the

Philadelphia Inquirer, deeming it "the worst paper in the country for consumer news."

Nader was excellent at cultivating reporters. Along with Morton Mintz of the *Washington Post* and Nick Kotz—the man who broke a number of stories on intrastate meatpacking—Nader worked closely with Jack Morris of the *New York Times*, Pat Sloyan at United Press International, and Saul Friedman of the *Detroit Free Press*. He was a constant source of tips and ideas to Jack Anderson, who wrote "Washington Merry-Go-Round," a widely read syndicated column. (Nader had far less of a grasp of television and never fully appreciated the medium's power.)

With select newspapermen, Nader shared the phone number of his boarding house, 202-234-1978. In return, these reporters could expect to be the recipients of Nader's patented late-night calls, a practice that was as effective with the press as it was with his own employees. Senators did not call at 2:00 A.M., and neither did CEOs. But Nader would and did, frequently, and this went a long way toward convincing many journalists that he was the one person out there with a handle on the issues that really mattered to the public. "His story ideas virtually all dealt with health and safety and things that profoundly affect human life," says Mintz, who received more than his share of wee-hour calls.

For many press people, covering Nader provided the opportunity to be a kind of muckraker-by-association. It was a chance to exercise oft unrealized investigative aspirations. Back in the 1960s, newspapers tended to devote far less in the way of manpower and financial resources to investigative reporting. Journalists such as Mintz and Kotz were marked exceptions. Everything changed with Watergate, and papers began placing considerably more emphasis on exposing corporate and governmental misdeeds, telling the unofficial story, as it were.

Pre-Watergate, reporters often had trouble convincing their papers to let them tromp off to West Virginia for a month and look into abuses suffered by coal miners. But Nader was doing exactly this kind of work, dispatching teams of Raiders on large-scale investigations. During the summer of 1969, Nader had his 102 Raiders scrutinize the operations of the Department of Agriculture, the Food and Drug Administration, and the Interstate Commerce Commission, to name just few projects. Writing up a Nader raid made it possible for journalists to fulfill that investigative yearning without going off on a long and expensive assignment or even leaving town.

Of course, some reporters are merely lazy. For them, Nader made it possible to feel a sense of vital social mission, and without even leaving their desks. Among the lazy reporter set, Nader was a godsend.

During the late 1960s, there was a science reporter at a major metropolitan daily who had a reputation for being less than intrepid. Nader got into the habit of assembling ready-made stories for him. The reporter would receive regular packets that even included the phone numbers of additional sources who might be counted on to amplify and supplement Nader's own points of view on a given issue. "I learned one thing early and it was probably the most important lesson," Nader once said. "The press will cover the story much more readily if the issues are paraded and discussed than go out on its own and investigate."

Nader had by now established a high level of credibility on consumer issues. His every pronouncement was judged newsworthy. Numerous stories from this era are little more than dutiful recountings of Nader press conferences. Such stories cover the fact that Nader attacked this agency or took that special interest to task. For the sake of journalistic fair play, the last paragraphs contain a quote or two of rebuttal from the parties excoriated by Nader.

But Nader was flexible, relying on his careful observations of the needs and styles of various journalists and tailoring his approach accordingly. A veteran reporter like Jerry Landauer of the *Wall Street Journal* was unlikely to construct a story wholly from a Raiders report or the proceedings of a press conference. Nader regularly contacted him, knowing that Landauer would do his own independent reporting in order to check out a story fully. Often Landauer would even write a story about a corrupt agency that made only the briefest mention of the ongoing Nader raid.

Referring to Landauer's practice, Nader told a colleague: "If you want to be effective in Washington put your own ego aside. Feed other people's egos, leave your ego out of it. Stay focused on the goal and what it is you want to get done."

Nader was a great tactician. He made himself available to his press allies for weekend interviews. The reason: weekends tend to be slow, even at large metropolitan dailies. Sources are often unavailable. Nader knew that if he was reachable on Saturday and Sunday, the Sunday and Monday editions might be sprinkled with stories on his various projects.

He was also endlessly creative in figuring out new ways to get press attention. For example, the Rivers and Harbors Act of 1899 contained a water pollution clause that had long since fallen into disuse. Nader decided to publicize this fact. But he chose not to issue a stock press release. Instead, he sent letters to the governors of all fifty states lamenting the clause's underutilization. Copies of the governor's letters were sent to journalists in each state. As a result, Nader managed to drum up considerable press coverage on a little-known legislative clause.

Much of Nader's work dealt with just this kind of arcana. But in discussing obscure topics Nader showed a facility for crafting phrases that stuck in people's minds, and this also did wonders in holding the press's attention. In the estimation of one-time Nader Raider Daniel Guttman: "His phrase making may not have been up there with Bob Dylan, but he definitely had a distinct voice—it was quintessentially of the sixties and helped define the era."

A 1969 summer project involved looking into the ingredients of hamburgers and hot dogs. Raiders purchased assorted brands at grocery stores and shipped them off to a laboratory for analysis. The main finding was that labels often low-balled the fat content. Nader called a press conference and lambasted meat companies for producing "fatfurters" and "shamburgers." The memorable terms were picked up in places such as *Time* magazine, giving the story the kind of play that it otherwise would not have received.

Of course, Nader's stature with the media depended on his attacks being accurate as well as entertaining. The reports from this era are of remarkably consistent quality. Several factors are at work here.

Foremost, Nader benefited from the existence of some truly low-hanging fruit. At the outset, he had the entire vast field of consumer abuses to explore. Hot dog companies were mislabeling fat content; there were government agencies as preposterously corruption-riddled as the FTC—Nader had his pick. As time went on, it would become harder to find truly abhorrent targets for investigation. Nader gets some credit here for getting agencies and corporations to improve their practices.

Nader also benefited from a beneficent press. The idea, the mere idea of Ralph Nader, held great appeal. There was actually someone out there working tirelessly on behalf of consumers, someone who had unleashed an army of squeaky clean young people to take on vast and impersonal interests. No one wished to scratch away at this image. Unquestionably, the Raider reports are sprinkled with small errors, and even a howler here and there. But that story was a nonstarter in the late 1960s. During this era, an investigation of Ralph Nader's techniques would not have been a popular move.

To Nader's credit, he was able to get stellar work out of very young and inexperienced people. Nothing produced during this era contains an error so egregious that the press had no choice but to respond. And Nader was very meticulous. "I can't make any mistakes," he once said. "An institution can blur accountability. I can't."

As time went on, Nader would become sloppier in his methods and would pay the price. But for a while, at least, Nader managed to combine anger with accuracy.

"He had the facts," says Nick Kotz. "Here was someone who was passionately talking about issues that affected people's lives, and he had solid information. He was a machine gun with the facts."

BEING A MEDIA DARLING put Nader in excellent standing with Congress. It guaranteed that Nader's calls would be returned, that he would be frequently tapped as a witness before committees, and that the issues he touted would be given serious consideration.

Nader worked closely with a number of members of Congress. There were Ribicoff and Mondale, of course, but any partial list should also include Phillip Burton and Warren Magnuson.

Burton—a Democrat from California—was considered one of the most effective tacticians in the House. Politically he was quite liberal, but he favored a hard-boiled manner that reflected his constituency, miners and longshoremen. Burton was famously described as a "good-doer" who had no patience with "do-gooders." His goal was to drive through legislation by whatever means available, and he did not mind roughing up a few congressional egos along the way. He and Nader would often team up on matters such as black lung disease and occupational health and safety. Nader once offered Burton what one can assume to be his highest praise for a pol: "You never see a politician who is nuts and bolts and supremely pragmatic, but then who uses his tactical and strategic brilliance for idealistic goals."

Magnuson, a veteran Democrat from Washington, had been in the Senate since 1952. During the first part of his career, he rose to be senior ranking member of the Appropriations Committee and was viewed as a business lackey, content to dole pork to his state's industries—logging, trucking, aerospace. During an election in 1962 he came within fifty thousand votes of losing to a political novice. Maggie—as he was known—decided it was time for an image overhaul. In keeping with the times, he recast himself as a consumer-friendly legislator. By 1968 he was able to claim credit for the passage of eight consumer laws. Nader and Magnuson worked together on a number of issues, including exploding pipelines.

Mike Pertschuk, staff director of the Senate Commerce Committee chaired by Magnuson, has the following observation: "Nader was able to appeal to the way members like to see themselves and be seen—as true public interest advocates. Ralph would reach in and pluck that chord of idealism. He had a great sense of psychology."

Nader was good at reading people, at picking up on their quirks and mannerisms. A little-known Nader talent is mimicry. It's not exactly a skill he ever trotted out in an interview, but people who worked closely with Nader remember that sometimes in recounting a conversation with a member of Congress, he got a kick out of playing both parts.

A favorite target was James Eastland of Mississippi, powerful chair of the Senate Judiciary Committee. Nader would let his face go slack, approximating Eastland's drooping jowls. He would then slide into a languid, syrupy drawl, stretching each syllable to the breaking point: "con-sti-tu-en-cy."

As a skilled social observer, Nader knew exactly how to approach various members of Congress. "Ralph knew how to play Congress like an orchestra," recalls one-time Raider Joe Tom Easley. "He knew which issues intrigued them. And he also had a good sense of the various egos. Ralph had an ability to know who to badger, who to defer to, who to fawn over, who to bully, and who would be receptive to intellectual arguments."

As already mentioned, Nader was also good at sorting out congressional power dynamics. In certain instances it made more sense to cultivate congressional staffs than members of Congress themselves. Staffers could afford to devote time to an issue, were willing to get mired in the details, and often played a major role in shaping the members' own legislative agendas.

"When you deal with somebody on the Hill, a lot of people think you want to go to the top," says Easley. "Ralph realized that power on the Hill is diffuse. It varies from committee to committee, and member to member. What you had to find out was, who has the power? If the power resided in an assistant legislative staff person who was in some little cramped office shared with six other people—if that was the key person—then that's who you wanted to work with. You would rather spend fifteen minutes with the assistant legislative director than spend an hour with Senator Full-of-Himself."

Sometimes Nader would even use his connection with a member of Congress to gain access to someone lower down in the nominal pecking order. He might ask a senator, "Is it all right if I call your legislative assistant?"

This approach would land him a valuable contact, one he could then use to exercise leverage on that very senator. Because they tended to share his passions for process and minutiae, Nader enjoyed working closely with staffers. He was in the habit of calling their attention to articles on product safety or nutrition in obscure journals—something one could never do with a senator. Staffers, in turn, would furnish Nader with legislative drafts that he would return vigorously annotated.

Nader continued to be much sought-after as a congressional witness. Good witnesses are hard to find. Academics and experts tend to have authority but often lack dynamism. Celebrity witnesses can provide dramatic testimony but are often not credible, and are unpredictable besides.

Tom Susman is a one-time staffer to Teddy Kennedy of Massachusetts. He once arranged for Paul Newman to testify, seemingly quite a coup. It did not go off as planned. "He was scared shitless," recalls Susman. "Here's someone you would kill to have provide testimony, but he was just not comfortable in the political arena."

By contrast, Nader was a dream witness. "At hearings the first audience is other senators," says Susman. "They are more likely to come if they think the testimony will be interesting and provocative. Nader always was. And then there were the cameras. Nothing gets a senator more geared up at hearings than the presence of cameras. When Nader spoke the rooms were packed. He got coverage. His effectiveness was due to the publicity he generated."

Nader was truly in fine form. Everything was working together in a kind of glorious symbiosis. Because he was provocative and made for rich copy, the media loved him. Because the media loved him, Congress could not afford to ignore him. Round and round it went, ratcheting Nader's public profile ever higher and resulting in . . . mail.

As of 1969, Nader had an actual headquarters with a listed address. The mail poured in by the satchelful. Of course, the Center for the Study of Responsive Law was not the most obvious name; it did not exactly trumpet its association with Nader. Some of the letters that made their way to the Center were addressed simply "Ralph Nader, Washington, D.C."

People also continued to try to reach Nader through his home in Winsted, Connecticut. His mother would screen the mail before forwarding it along, marking promising pieces of correspondence: "Read this, Ralph!"

But the simple fact was—whether properly addressed to his nonprofit organization or arriving via more tortured routes—Nader wound up getting mail, loads of mail. To sort through it all, he relied on his own idiosyncratic method. He tried to give every envelope at least a cursory glance in order to note the return address. If he was intrigued, he would open it. Otherwise, he would pass it along to his employees. Letters that bore return addresses from universities were must-opens. College professors, in Nader's experience, were prime sources of reliable and substantive information on health hazards and shoddy products.

Letters from corporations were also high priority. Nader continued to hew to a theory he had first hatched while working on *Unsafe at Any Speed*, namely, that the best informants were found at the midlevels of management and below. They often knew more than their superiors about what was really going on in a company. Certainly they were more likely to talk. It was rank-and-file engineers—rather than top executives—who had slipped Nader choice pieces of intelligence about auto safety. For Nader, this would be an enduring observation.

The mail was treated accordingly. Letters from CEOs certainly caught Nader's eye, and he received his share—inviting him to speak at conferences, questioning his methods, or simply trying to open a dialogue. But Nader was generally more intrigued by correspondence from people lower in the corporate hierarchy. Such letters might include tips. Nothing grabbed his attention like a letter that began: "Dear Mr. Nader, I work in quality control at the Gatlinburg, Tennessee, plant of . . . "

These were the only types of letters that Nader bothered to answer. As for the bulk of the mail, Nader passed it along to his staff to be sorted and classified. Many of the letters were from ordinary citizens, laying out grievances against various products and entreating Nader to take up their cause.

A Milwaukee landlord wrote to complain that tenants kept clogging his toilets with tampons: "It states on the box that they are to be disposed of by throwing them down the toilet, but they plug the toilet. This kind of advertising is a misrepresentation and should be stopped immediately."

A boy—identifying himself simply as "Mike"—wrote the following: "One day we walked into a little food mart and got a Popsicle and my friend Tom said his tasted funny. So I said lets (sic) get your money back. So we went back and said we wished to get our money back or we would write to Ralph Nader. So he said go ahead. So we are writing you."

Often people sent Nader samples of products that had disappointed them, shrapnel from blown-out tires or—in one case—a loaf of stale bread. A judge from California mailed Nader the handle from his car's emergency brake with a note: "It's come off twice—you keep it!"

Nader's employees did their best to organize the deluge. Unruly stacks of letters sprung up all over the DuPont Circle headquarters, labeled "appliances" and "cosmetics" and "fabrics" and "TVs." Viewed in aggregate, they provided a great snapshot of what ailed the populace. Noting the frequency of different kinds of complaints—insurance fraud, say, or bum toaster ovens—made it possible to identify patterns of consumer abuse.

In 1971 a couple of Raiders would even publish a book that drew on the remarkable number of letters—thirty thousand—that Nader had received from disgruntled auto owners. "I remember him telling me about this enormous amount of mail he got," says Phil Donahue. "People would send him diagrams explaining what happens to their car when they turn a corner. They'd employ these terms of physics—torque, centrifugal force, center of gravity, on and on. He was getting these huge letters, many, many pages, written in longhand by desperate people with cars that wouldn't work, cars that wouldn't start, cars that stalled, cars that this, and cars that that."

When Phil Donahue was just starting out, on WLWD in Dayton, Ohio, Nader was one of his first guests. Within a few years, he had been on the show a number of times. The title of the book culled from auto complaint letters was *What to Do with Your Bad Car: An Action Manual for Lemon Owners*.

Letters created a vital link between Nader and consumers. He was an issue entrepreneur, after all, requiring a constant stream of new ideas. The mail was essential. It helped identify targets for future raids.

The following is from a letter Nader received regarding the inhumane conditions in a nursing home: "One day while I was visiting my mother, a poor soul had evidently passed away. The undertaker (I question that) arrived with a canvas bag. I presume the old soul had nobody at all. He talked for a bit with the head nurse, then went to the back of the building to get the lady. I heard a funny dragging and looked up to see him pulling the bag (now full) down the home's at least 80 cement and wooden steps. I have never seen such a thing or ever want to again. The reaction on the faces of the old folks was rather shocking. They probably pictured themselves going like that."

It was a pretty graphic little missive. Nader made a mental note: maybe the plight of nursing home residents was a topic that warranted further investigation.

ON NOVEMBER 20, 1969, Nader delivered a speech at Miss Porter's School in Farmington, Connecticut. It was arranged by Robert Townsend, a former CEO of Avis Rent-A-Car. His daughter, Claire Townsend, was a student there.

Miss Porter's is an exclusive girls finishing school, founded in 1843, and steeped in white-glove tradition. Among its notable alumna—quaintly referred to as the "ancients"—are Jacqueline Onassis and Letitia Baldridge, the noted expert on etiquette.

As for Robert Townsend, he was a great admirer of Nader. Like Nader, Townsend was a dedicated corporate reformer, though as a one-time CEO, he approached the topic from a vastly different perspective. When Townsend took over Avis in 1962, it had not turned a profit in thirteen years. Townsend leveled old hierarchies and freed up communications among the employees. His management style was a timely mix of the industrial age and the Aquarian age, and it succeeded in reinvigorating the company. Townsend's 1970 book *Up the Organization* is a classic of contrarian management advice. He would also serve as a major financial backer for various Nader projects in years to come.

Nader's Miss Porter's School appearance was extremely successful. The school—like Avis and just about every other institution in America—was going through tremendous upheaval in 1969. Among the 230 girls present for Nader's speech were a number who had older brothers serving in Vietnam. Many were also starting to question the prescribed roles they were expected to play in the course of their lives: debutante, society wife, wealthy dowager perhaps. The wider world was sneaking across the manicured lawns of Miss Porter's School.

Lallie Lloyd was a student at the school in 1969. She attended Nader's speech and has the following recollection: "He's a very passionate speaker and he got us very stirred up. We became excited about the idea of what it was that we could accomplish, as consumers and as citizens. What Nader also brought was a sense of political empowerment for us as young women. It was the nascent stages of the women's movement, which was only beginning to seep into my consciousness."

Following the speech, girls flocked around Nader. He was besieged by questions: The girls wanted to know what they could do, how they could fix what ailed society? They wanted to be Raiders.

THAT NIGHT, CLAIRE TOWNSEND filled her diary with reactions to the big speech, interweaving impassioned notions about how to make the world a better place with assorted observations about Nader himself:

"First impression: tall, thin, gaunt
Second impression: shy, nervous
Third impression: funny and nice

Fourth impression: witty, intelligent, articulate, and concise."

Back in Washington, Nader mulled over his exuberant reception at Miss Porter's School. Was there a project, he wondered, that would be manageable and appropriate for teenage girls? How could he channel all that youthful energy and idealism? Then it hit him: nursing homes. Teenagers frequently worked as orderlies, and the subject matter—abuse of the elderly—was far less demanding than much Nader fare.

Nader selected five girls—Claire Townsend and Lallie Lloyd among them—to spend the summer in D.C., conducting an investigation of nursing homes. Margaret Quinn, a twenty-five-year-old teacher at Miss Porter's, would accompany the girls as a chaperone.

This was a strange new subspecies of Nader Raider: teenage and female, but also impossibly privileged. From the latter standpoint, they bore a marked resemblance to the initial seven—Cox, Taft IV, et al.—who had investigated the FTC.

Claire Townsend—besides being the daughter of a corporate chieftain—lived in exclusive Locust Valley, Long Island. Lallie Lloyd was from a tony Philadelphia suburb and had been born into an investment banking dynasty. Her father worked for Drexel Burnham Lambert, the firm her great-grandfather had founded.

A bemused press dubbed the five "The Maiden Muckrakers."

In an interview with the *New York Times Magazine*, Nader explained the logic in hiring a team of teenagers: "The nursing home project did not require the kind of specialized legal and accounting knowledge that investigating, say, First National City Bank does. There is also a great deal of suffering in nursing homes, and the industry is saturated with Government involvement. I feel a society is tested by compassion, by its treatment of the very young and the very old. So there was a tremendous symbolic reason I wanted young people on the project."

And why young people of such manifest privilege? "There have been all kinds of investigations of nursing homes and the problems of the aged, but they weren't really dramatic. With Claire and the girls it would be the very young reaching out to the very old, and here also were young, pretty, rich girls from Jackie Onassis's school and I felt that what these girls did would be noticed."

OFF WENT THE MAIDEN MUCKRAKERS—chaperone in tow—to spend the summer in Washington.

As a rule, Nader interns, even those who had family money, tended to choose suitably seedy accommodations for the summer. They might crash on a friend's couch or rent a vacant dorm room at one of the city's many colleges. Not this group. Instead, Robert Townsend purchased a townhouse in southwest Washington so they could live in the style to which they were accustomed. The girls set up house, divvied up cooking nights and cleaning duties, and bought a mongrel dog they named "Ralph."

First order of business was finding jobs as aides and orderlies. The plan was for the five to split up and work subrosa at various nursing homes. They would keep diaries of the atrocities they observed for use in a report.

Here's a choice excerpt from Claire Townsend's diary:

> The nurse I was assigned to, Ethel, was so kind to some patients and so mean to others; it was especially cruel when the two extremes happened in the same room with two patients. While Ethel and I were putting the favored patient to bed (doing a lot of extra fussing and smiling and taking a long time) the other patient, who was sitting in a chair in her own filth, kept saying, "Girlie, please put me to bed." But I didn't know how to do it. I'd been given no orientation and no training whatsoever, even though I'd said that I'd never done this type of work before. So I just stood there feeling helpless and horrible waiting for Ethel. Finally, Ethel came over, dragged the woman out of the chair, slammed her against the bed, and began to undress her roughly. The old woman kept saying that she was slipping and about to fall, but Ethel just told her to shut up. Then Ethel swung the old woman into the bed, threw the covers up over the woman's face, and left the room.

BESIDES NOSING AROUND NURSING homes and keeping diaries, Nader also wanted the girls to do some original research. He directed them to interview various experts in government and the elder-care industry in order to gain a deeper understanding of the issues. This aspect of the project proved daunting.

Lallie Lloyd interviewed a specialist on for-profit nursing homes at the Securities and Exchange Commission. "This guy knew perfectly well he could not resist an interview request from Ralph Nader," she recalls. "But he gave me nothing. I only got out of him what I knew enough to ask for, and I don't think I was as well-informed or well-prepared as I might have been."

On another occasion, the girls tried to infiltrate a meeting of the American Nursing Home Association. Dressed in appropriate business attire, the five filed into the auditorium and took their seats. They thought they were being discreet. But they were also, quite visibly, the only teenagers present. The next speaker to take the stage blew their cover. "I understand we have some visitors here," he said. "Will the young ladies who are working for Ralph Nader please stand up."

The girls arranged a strategy session with Nader to learn how they might get better results. He gave them some tips on how to play rough with sources. One of his suggestions was to tell the interviewee that someone from a competing organization had promised the same information: "I have a source who can have the information ready by next week, but I thought maybe you could give it to me now."

As an alternate approach, Nader suggested, the girls might try to shake these nursing home bureaucrats out of their complacency, really remind them of the true nature of their work. Nader suggested saying something along the lines of: "You seem to be caught up in quite a bit of paperwork here. Do you ever think about or even feel for the 1 million nursing home patients around the country?"

The girls tried Nader's hardball strategies but had limited success. What truly worked—at least in their case—was inviting sources over to the townhouse for dinner. They discovered that a home-cooked meal, enjoyed in the company of comely teenage girls, worked wonders at loosening people up. Dr. Robert Butler—a Washington psychiatrist who specialized in aged patients—stayed past midnight, a fount of tips and leads and other useful pieces of information.

The girls also tried to get Nader to come over for dinner. He was rather hesitant. Impropriety, the mere appearance of impropriety, had been a constant concern for him ever since the alleged GM sex-lure incident. In the intervening years, his list of enemies had only grown. He had no doubt that there were powerful interests out there who would love to get some dirt. Dining with teenage girls, he felt, had limitless potential to be twisted or misconstrued.

Nader told the girls that maybe he would accept their invitation. If so, he would give them exactly twenty-six hours' notice. The girls puzzled over this strange choice. Why twenty-six hours?

One day, late in the summer, Nader called the girls' house. Claire Townsend answered. It was 5:00 P.M. Nader said he had decided to accept their dinner offer. Expect him the next evening at seven o'clock (twenty-six hours).

The girls never did figure out the reason for this quirk. As one-time Raider Andrew Egendorf noted, Nader liked to conduct his life like a spy.

As for planning the menu, it proved quite a challenge. During their phone conversation, Claire asked Nader if he would like a chicken dish.

"No."

"Oh," she pursued. "Well, do you like any kind of meat?"

"No."

"Are you a vegetarian?"

"No. But just about to become one."

"I see. What do you like?"

"Tomatoes, onions, and squash."

"Uh-huh. What do you like to drink? Do you like wine?"

"No."

"Milk?"

"No."

"Water?"

"No. Neither would you, if you knew what was in it."

"Well, what do you like?"

"Grapefruit juice."

The girls pored over a Betty Crocker cookbook until they came across a recipe calling for tomatoes, onions, squash, eggplant, and green peppers. They also consulted with a Lebanese friend who helped fix tabouli.

Upon sitting down to dinner, Nader said grace in Arabic, a big hit. By all accounts, he quite enjoyed his home-cooked Middle Eastern meal prepared by five Connecticut prep-school girls. He did not stay past midnight.

AT THE CLOSE OF the summer, the Maiden Muckrakers participated in a rite already undertaken by a number of other Nader teams. They wrote a report entitled *Old-Age: The Last Segregation* that was 229 pages long. The bulk of it consisted of diary entries recounting the grisly episodes the team members had witnessed while working undercover in various nursing homes. Nader had predicted that the project would be dramatic and garner attention and it did.

Reviews were overwhelmingly favorable, though with some reservations. The consensus held that the passages from the diaries were the most effective part of the book. They provided a fresh-eyed look at the enormous human suffering that existed in nursing homes, an issue to which many supposed pundits had grown inured. Otherwise, it was agreed, the book broke little new ground. The public policy recommendations were unimaginative, merely rehashings of ideas in the existing literature. Then again, the authors were teenage girls.

The five also got a chance to testify before Congress. They appeared before the Senate Subcommittee on Long-Term Care's Special Committee on Aging, chaired by Frank Moss of Utah.

Before their testimony—while waiting around outside the Senate committee room—the girls started to get a bit giggly. Nader shushed them. "Above all," he cautioned, "you must be serious."

Two-year-old Ralph Nader with sister, Laura. The plan had been to take a photo only of Ralph, but he cried, insisting that Laura join him.
CREDIT: THE NADER FAMILY

Nader as a grade-schooler—in his hometown of Winsted, Connecticut—shows off some produce from the family garden. CREDIT: THE NADER FAMILY

Ralph was extremely close to his older brother, Shafeek. The picture is from around 1940. CREDIT: THE NADER FAMILY

The parents: Nathra and Rose Nader. CREDIT: THE NADER FAMILY

Circa 1967, on an overpass above I-495, the Beltway that surrounds Washington, D.C. Nader was about to become a consummate Beltway insider. CREDIT: AP/WIDE WORLD PHOTOS

A man, alone: During his early years in Washington, Nader was the one-man army behind a number of safety laws. CREDIT: THE NADER FAMILY

"I happen to know Ralph Nader's mother drives this model."

CREDIT: F.B. MODELL, CARTOONBANK.COM

Nader and Lyndon Johnson shake hands, commemorating the passage of a landmark auto safety bill in 1966. CREDIT: THE NADER FAMILY

First appearance on the *Phil Donahue Show,* March 27, 1968. Nader would become Donahue's most-frequent guest, appearing thirty-three times.

CREDIT: PHIL DONAHUE

Farewell dinner for the initial set of Nader's Raiders, August 1968. Among those present (left to right), John Schulz, Ed Cox, Robert Fellmeth, and Nader. Andrew Egendorf took the photo.

CREDIT: ANDREW EGENDORF

Nader has often described his work as "playing fifty chess games simultaneously." CREDIT: LOWELL DODGE

In the summer of 1969, Nader hired 102 Raiders to poke around Washington, uncovering malfeasance. His 1972 team was more than a thousand strong. CREDIT: JOHN ZIMMERMAN, TIMEPIX

— 9 —

GM Redux

NADER—AT THE HEIGHT OF HIS POWERS—was a multitasker nonpareil, capable of a formidable degree of involvement in a huge variety of issues. He directed scores of concurrent Raider projects, crisscrossed the country delivering speeches, even managed to write an occasional magazine article. In the year 1970 alone, Nader was sufficiently conversant to testify before Congress on topics ranging from mine safety to mercury pollution, unfair credit practices to the sanitary implications of passenger trains emptying their toilets onto the tracks.

But no matter how many topics Nader was exploring at a given time, he could not resist returning to the one that had given him his start. Acting on a kind of homing instinct, regardless of the number of current projects, regardless of ongoing commitments, Nader was forever looking for opportunities to pound on his old nemesis, General Motors.

Thus he was very receptive when he was approached by two young lawyers who had roomed together at Harvard, Geoffrey Cowan and Philip Moore. The pair had a novel idea about how to exercise leverage against GM on various issues such as pollution control and worker safety.

Cowan and Moore, though only in their twenties, were veterans of a growing shareholder rights movement. At Harvard, Cowan had been involved in an attempt, albeit an unsuccessful one, to get the university to divest its holdings of Mississippi Power & Light. He had also participated in an attempt by shareholders to pressure Dow Chemical to stop making napalm, also a losing battle.

But the notion was a sound one: an organized group of people who held stock in a public company might be able to influence that company's policies.

Say, for example, that Harvard and other large stakeholders had agreed to dump their holdings of Mississippi Power & Light, thereby threatening the financial health of the state's primary source of electricity. Money talks. To regain investment dollars, Mississippi might have had to improve its record on race relations. In this fashion, shareholder activism had the potential to advance the cause of civil rights. Had there been a massive and well-organized shareholder campaign aimed not only at Dow Chemical but at aerospace companies and assorted other defense contractors, it might have hastened America's withdrawal from Vietnam.

Nader met Cowan and Moore at the Peking Restaurant in Washington. Over tea, the two young lawyers laid out a raft of demands they hoped to press on GM at its next annual meeting, scheduled for May 22, 1970. Among other things, they wanted the company to make its factories safer for workers, improve employee health benefits, hire more minorities, manufacture cars that produced less pollution, and recall defective models more readily.

Cowan and Moore also wanted to force GM to expand its board of directors, adding three new members who represented a consumer perspective. Their proposed slate was Nader; John Kenneth Galbraith, the noted liberal economist from Harvard; and John Gardner, founder of Common Cause, a grassroots group involved in campaign finance reform and other issues of government accountability.

Nader declined, explaining that he could not possibly serve as a GM board member—not even a consumer-focused board member—due to his ongoing lawsuit against the company for invasion of privacy. (This was not the first time Nader had been proposed as a GM board member. During the company's 1966 annual meeting, a woman wearing a crash helmet and suit of armor had submitted his name from the floor. Her suggestion met with boos and hisses. Still, Nader received ten thousand share votes—out of 87.8 million cast.)

Although Nader refused this latest call to serve as a GM director, he loved the notion of organizing the company's own shareholders against it. He agreed to help Cowan and Moore by providing tactical advice and publicizing their efforts.

Cowan and Moore were flabbergasted. They had walked into the Peking Restaurant a couple of wet-pup lawyers with an interest in the then-rarefied topic of shareholder activism. They walked out with the imprimatur of the most powerful consumer advocate in the land. "Ralph said he would support us if we developed this project," recalls Cowan. "He obviously believed in the ability of young people to do terrific things. He had a kind of trust in youth, which was not necessarily common at the time."

Cowan and Moore began assembling a team for the project, which they called the Campaign to Make General Motors Responsible—Campaign GM for short. It would eventually number about a dozen people. Each team member purchased a single share of GM stock. That made them shareholders, with all the accompanying rights, including the right to attend the company's annual meetings. To formally launch Campaign GM, Nader held a widely attended news conference at the Mayflower Hotel in Washington. "The basic thrust of the campaign," he explained, "will be to alert and inform the public about their omnipresent neighbor, General Motors, and how it behaves."

He put the company on notice, hinting that its upcoming annual meeting would be very different from ones in the past: "General Motors may be the host to a great public debate on the giant corporation rather than a wooden recital of aggregate financial data."

In 1970 General Motors was among the world's most widely held stocks. The company had nearly 286 million shares outstanding, divided among more than a million different shareholders. During the press conference, Nader asserted that this vast constituency would be made aware of GM's record on issues such as safety and the environment, and would have a chance to do something about it: "The campaign will reach to the universities and their students and faculty, to the banks and their depositors and fiduciaries, to churches and their congregations, to insurance companies and their policyholders, to union and company pension funds and their membership and to other investors."

STEP ONE FOR CAMPAIGN GM was putting together a series of shareholder resolutions. Cowan and Moore came up with nine. One demanded that GM increase the number of minorities hired into management positions. Another called for GM to lobby in favor of taxpayer-financed studies aimed at improving mass transit. This was something that GM lobbied against, vigorously and at considerable expense. In essence, if the shareholder resolution were adopted, GM would be forced to promote transportation alternatives to the automobile.

Campaign GM submitted the resolutions to company management, demanding that they be included in the proxy statement. Proxies are mailed out in advance of a company's annual meeting. They list the various resolutions—some generated by management, some by shareholders, some merely procedural—that will be put to a vote. Shareholders who choose not to attend the annual meeting still have the option of voting their proxies and mailing them back to the company.

Not surprisingly, GM management adamantly refused to include the nine resolutions in its proxy.

So Campaign GM filed a complaint with the Securities and Exchange Commission, which oversees certain aspects of a public company's conduct toward its shareholders. The SEC threw out seven of the resolutions. As for the remaining two, it ruled that GM would have to include them in its proxy, thereby submitting them to shareholder vote.

One Campaign GM resolution upheld by the SEC was the slate of consumer-friendly board candidates. Galbraith and Gardner also declined to run. So a new ticket was assembled, consisting of Betty Furness, LBJ's onetime consumer affairs adviser; René Dubos, a Pulitzer Prize–winning biologist from Rockefeller University; and Channing Phillips, head of the Housing and Development Corporation and a prominent black leader.

The other proposal called on GM to establish a shareholders committee. It would be broadly representative of GM's investor pool, would include scientists, members of civil rights groups, United Auto Workers rank and file, and ordinary citizens. The shareholders committee could act as a watchdog. GM would be required to provide it full access to company files and other internal documents.

CAMPAIGN GM FACED STIFF odds. It had been a quarter century since a shareholder resolution had passed against management's objection. Typically, a shareholder-generated proposal that did not have support of GM leadership fared about as well as the 1966 Nader-for-director motion, supported by 0.0001 percent of the vote.

Because of Nader's association, Campaign GM received massive press attention, everything from local papers to *Time*, the *New Yorker*, and *Business Week*. As Nader had predicted, GM-as-corporate-citizen was of great interest to the company's broad community of shareholders. College students were especially gripped by the topic. After all, a number of universities held substantial blocks of GM stock.

At the University of Pennsylvania, a student referendum came out in support of Campaign GM. Under pressure, Penn's trustees agreed to vote the school's twenty-nine thousand shares in favor of the two resolutions.

GM launched a spirited counterattack. To each of its million-plus shareholders, the company mailed a twenty-one-page booklet extolling its record on plant safety, minority hiring, and the environment. There was an accompanying letter signed by CEO Edward Cole and James Roche—he of the famous apology to Nader—now company chairman. The letter accused Campaign GM of "using General Motors as a means through which it can challenge the entire system of corporate management in the United States." It concluded that the project's true aims were "harassment and publicity."

AS THE ANNUAL MEETING drew closer, it became evident that Campaign GM enjoyed an unusual level of support. Along with Penn, about thirty other universities announced that they planned to vote in favor of the two resolutions. Among them were Amherst (37,000 shares), Tufts (9,300 shares), and Brown (4,700 shares). Harvard and Princeton, Nader's alma maters, decided to vote with management. Harvard, for one, had made a policy of resisting the activist shareholder movement, going back to its first rumblings. In 1967 university president Nathan Pusey had spelled it out quite plainly: "We don't use our money for social purposes."

By far the largest stakeholder to come out in support of Campaign GM was the pension fund for New York City employees, which held 160,000 shares. Dreyfus Fund, First Pennsylvania Bank, and a scattering of other financial services firms also announced plans to vote for the resolutions.

And then there was Stewart Rawlings Mott. He was the son of Charles Stewart Mott, GM's senior director. As a Volkswagen owner and vocal antiwar protester, the junior Mott was someone who could only be described as a hippie heir. He agreed to vote his two thousand shares for Campaign GM. (He had another 700,000 tied up in a trust fund to which he did not yet have access.)

MAY 22, 1970, FOUND Detroit's Cobo Hall in pandemonium. Only seven hundred stockholders had attended the previous year's annual meeting, but this time more than three thousand were on hand. A whole battalion of security guards was also present. One month earlier, antiwar protesters had disrupted Honeywell's annual meeting in Minneapolis, and it had to be canceled after fourteen minutes.

Campaign GM held a premeeting rally in a conference room at Cobo Hall. Cowan, Moore, and various supporters wore buttons, red-and-white stop signs bearing the words "Tame GM." Robert Townsend—corporate gadfly and father of a Maiden Muckraker—delivered a brief impromptu speech. During his days as Avis's CEO, he asserted, he had never relished dealing with GM. "If I were making a profit of $5 million a day," he said, "I'd probably be arrogant, too. The only way you can have any effect on General Motors is not to buy any of their cars until they produce a clean one—and they could do it in three years."

Nader was not present, again due to the conflict posed by his ongoing lawsuit. His role with Campaign GM remained carefully undefined. On the one hand, the project's great visibility was due to Nader's association. He had launched Campaign GM at a press conference, had provided counsel to Cowan, Moore, and others. John Esposito, a sometime Nader employee, was a member of the Campaign GM team. It was a role aptly summed up in a *New Yorker* article that described Nader as Campaign GM's "guru."

Yet Nader had never formally joined the team and provided no financial backing. By a strict legal definition, he was not part of Campaign GM. This kind of hairsplitting would become a primary Nader characteristic in years to come. It would reach its apotheosis when Nader ran for president as a Green Party candidate but refused to join the party.

At 2:00 P.M., James Roche struck his gavel, calling GM's 1970 annual meeting to order. Chairman Roche, CEO Cole, and other top executives were seated facing the audience on a raised dais covered in blue bunting, the company color. It was the mirror image of the 1966 congressional hearing, when Roche and Sorenson were seated so that they had to look up at an imposing row of senators set against a white marble backdrop. This was GM's home field, and Roche was firmly in control.

The meeting kicked off with the standard procedural pirouettes and recitations of financial data. A twenty-five-minute film was shown highlighting GM's accomplishments on safety, diversity, and other issues. Throughout, the Campaign GM team groaned and sniggered.

Next came the part of the meeting where the floor was opened to shareholders. Roche called on a series of people who asked questions that sparked detailed discussions. He also called on a female shareholder who delivered a lengthy diatribe that accused Nader's Raiders of drug use (she clearly did not know the Raiders) and held them responsible for accidents because they were undercutting companies like GM that manufactured cars.

Roche was handling the meeting with great adroitness. He was calling only on people whom he knew would speak at length, criticize Nader, or both. He was creating a filibuster, in effect.

But finally, discussion of the two controversial resolutions could be delayed no longer. Nearly five hours into the meeting Roche finally recognized Campaign GM. The team answered with a strategic masterstroke of its own. Neither Cowan nor Moore—Campaign GM's leaders—elected to stand up and ask a question. Instead, the honor went to a black woman.

Barbara Williams, UCLA law student and member of the Campaign GM team, stepped to the microphone. Voice quavering, she asked: "Why are there no blacks on the board?"

"Because none of them have been elected," Roche replied.

"I expected better of you," shot back Williams. Then she repeated the question: "Why are there no blacks on the board?"

"No black has been nominated and no black has been elected."

She asked the same question again.

"I have answered the question," said Roche.

"You have failed not only the shareholders but the country," rejoined Williams.

Then she switched tack, asking why there were no women on the board.

"Our directors are selected on the basis of their ability to make a contribution to the success of General Motors," said Roche.

"You have not adequately answered the questions," concluded Williams. She sat down amid cheers and cries of "Right On!" from the Campaign GM team and its supporters.

The Q&A period staggered on for a few more minutes. And then it was time to announce the results of the balloting. Campaign GM's slate of consumer-oriented board members received more than 6 million votes from 61,794 different shareholders. Still, that added up to a mere 2.4 percent of votes, far less than what was needed for adoption. The proposal to create a watchdog shareholder's committee did slightly better, gaining support from 2.7 percent of voters.

Roche thanked the shareholder community for "a most gratifying expression of confidence." He added: "We leave this meeting more determined than ever to fulfill our responsibilities. . . . There is much more that pulls us together than pushes us apart. . . . Join us, help us, so that we may work constructively together."

With that, Roche banged his gavel, bringing the longest annual meeting in GM history to a close.

Although Campaign GM collected only a sliver of votes, the team played it as a moral victory.

"The measure of victory is not the votes," was the official statement, "but the kind of debate we can have between shareholders and the public, so we can explore new ways corporations can be made responsive to the public."

Adds Cowan: "My impression was that Ralph felt great about it."

In some sense, Campaign GM was far more than a moral victory. Within months of the 1970 annual meeting, GM named its first black director, Leon Sullivan.

Sullivan had once served as assistant pastor to Adam Clayton Powell at Harlem's Abyssinian Baptist Church. Throughout the 1960s, he had organized boycotts against companies with poor minority-hiring records. He was also the founder of the Opportunities Industrialization Center, a job-training program that had opened branches in ninety cities by 1970. "I know General Motors is going to use me as a symbol and sample of how liberal it has become," he said, "but I am going to use them."

During the 1980s, Sullivan would become a leading opponent of apartheid in South Africa. The so-called Sullivan Principles set parameters for direct investment in foreign countries by U.S. companies. Everything comes full circle. Campaign GM played a role, at least indirectly, in installing Sullivan as a GM board member. Sullivan himself became a leading proponent of using investor power to push for social change.

With the passage of time, Campaign GM has come to be viewed as something of a watershed. It was an early, failed, but highly visible effort at shareholder activism.

ON AUGUST 13, 1970, Nader's lawsuit against GM was finally resolved, having dragged on since 1966. Originally, Nader had asked for $26 million for invasion of privacy. He wound up settling the case for $425,000. GM was large enough and had sufficient resources to drag the case out indefinitely. Better to take what the company offered was Nader's conclusion, a point reiterated in a statement he released to announce the settlement: "There is every likelihood that General Motors could have delayed this case into the 1980s, when all the culpable officials would have been retired. Against such a background it was deemed wiser to settle the case and devote the proceeds, after deduction of legal fees and expenses, to the cause of consumer protection and corporate responsibility."

Nader may not have hit the punitive-damages jackpot. At the time, however, a $425,000 settlement ($280,000 after legal fees) was the largest amount ever collected in an invasion of privacy case. By suing GM, Nader also succeeded in dredging up all kinds of information about the company's investigation of him. The suit had played out over four-plus years and produced a steady stream of bizarre disclosures.

At the outset, General Motors had hoped to pin the blame on the detective, Vincent Gillen. The company attempted to establish that delving into Nader's personal life was an unauthorized decision by an overexuberant private investigator. What GM had not counted on was that Nader would also sue Gillen for defamation. That suit was eventually dropped but not before Gillen was deposed, bringing all kinds of sordid information to light.

It turned out that Gillen had conducted twenty-five previous investigations for GM, going back to 1959. In one case, he spied on a Harlem civil rights group that had questioned GM's minority-hiring practices. On other occasions, he was retained to look into the lives of various UAW officials. Gillen had even investigated Danny Kaye. Preliminary to offering the actor an endorsement deal, GM wanted to make sure he did not have any long-buried scandals or off-kilter political beliefs that might embarrass the company. Kaye checked out and was offered the endorsement deal.

Gillen was in the habit of surreptitiously recording conversations with people. The same cereal-box decoder-ring earnestness that made Gillen a comic figure also made him a tremendous resource for Nader's lawyers. Turned out, he had taped his instructions from GM. As already mentioned, Gillen furnished the notorious smoking gun regarding Nader: "get something on him . . . shut him up." Gillen's tape collection also included choice snippets such as: "Who is he laying? If it's girls, who are they? If not girls, maybe boys, who?"

Gillen also had in his possession some very revealing memos. One in particular was from Eileen Murphy, GM's law librarian and the company's unofficial point person on the investigation. Murphy was the recipient of Gillen's detective reports. Halfway through the investigation, she had become frustrated because Gillen was failing to turn up enough prurient detail. She wrote the following message: "It strikes me that everyone is going overboard trying to impress us with what a great, charming intellectual this human being is—Eagle Scout type. There are too many variances for this to be accurate. . . . What is his Army record? What did he do for six months in the Army? . . . He mentions an accident which happened a decade ago. He saw a child decapitated. See if this gem can be uncovered as to where, when or how he was involved. . . . Well, friend, have fun."

The letter was on plain white paper, sans GM letterhead, so that it could not be easily traced back to the company. It was signed simply, "Eileen." Obviously, this was a very damaging letter and GM knew it.

Under questioning from Nader's lawyers, Gillen revealed that GM's general counsel had demanded that he return the letter prior to the famous March 22, 1966, Roche apology hearing. The company did not want it to fall into Ribicoff's hands. Gillen complied, returning Eileen Murphy's letter to GM. What he did not tell the company was that he made a copy and kept it for himself.

In a sworn affidavit, Gillen revealed that GM had also asked him to alter certain key documents before turning them over to the Ribicoff subcommittee. Others he had been instructed to simply destroy. Again Gillen followed GM's orders, but not before making copies of the originals for his own files.

As Nader's lawyers worked their way through Gillen's collection of tapes and memos, one thing became manifestly clear: the investigation had nothing to do with establishing whether Nader was secretly representing clients in Corvair litigation, as GM had originally claimed. It had everything to do with getting dirt on Nader.

Despite the fact that his suit produced some spectacular revelations, Nader was not entirely pleased with the outcome. For one thing, the case failed to resolve the sex-lure question. Throughout four-plus years of testimony, GM had been resolute in denying that it had hired women to accost Nader on two occasions, in a Safeway and a drug store. Nothing contradictory emerged. While Gillen had provided answers to all kinds of lingering questions, none of his tapes or memos even touched on the issue of the alleged sex lures.

In light of all the other shady tactics GM employed against Nader, trying to entrap him with sexy women hardly seems a stretch. But the fact is, no evidence of GM's involvement was ever uncovered.

Years later, one of the Nader's Raiders, while attending an Alcoholics Anonymous meeting, happened across the son of someone who had been on GM's legal staff in 1966. For what it's worth, the son confided to the Nader Raider that his father had been aware of a scheme by GM to hire prostitutes to try to lure Nader.

As for Nader's other big disappointment with the lawsuit: He had hoped that in the course of the lawsuit evidence would surface showing that GM had lied to the Ribicoff subcommittee about the Corvair. Nothing surfaced.

Nader had long contended that not only was the 1960–1963 model Corvair the product of grossly negligent engineering, but the GM executives involved, in his estimation, deserved to be prosecuted like common street criminals. He had written about this in *Unsafe at Any Speed* and had hammered on it during his congressional testimony. While it was a compelling notion, once again, Nader did not possess incontrovertible proof.

Sure, Corvairs were involved in numerous lawsuits during the mid-1960s, but none of the plaintiffs ever managed to prove that company executives knowingly put a dangerous car on the market. Even the question of whether the Corvair was unsafe was not satisfactorily resolved. Tests done by various safety organizations and auto experts were maddeningly inconclusive. Some indicated the Corvair was defective, while others determined that nothing was inherently wrong with the car's design.

It's worth noting again that GM was never forced to recall the Corvair. No GM executives were ever brought up on charges in conjunction with the car's design. Instead, the Corvair line was voluntarily discontinued in 1968, following years of slumping sales.

This would remain a sore point with Nader. And GM—favorite target that it was—had certainly not heard the last from him regarding the Corvair.

IN 1970 NADER RELOCATED the headquarters of the Center for the Study of Responsive Law. He vacated the crumbling Victorian mansion—it would soon be demolished to build a metro stop—and moved into a modern building a few blocks away that had been headquarters for the Nixon-Lodge campaign back in 1960. Rent was $1,200 a month. Nader hired a new executive director, Ted Jacobs, a friend from Princeton and Harvard.

At the new headquarters, Nader decided to actually have an office of his own. The door featured a hand-painted "1" and was padlocked shut when Nader was not around. Inside the office, about the only decorative touch was a portrait of Thomas Jefferson. Nader maintained a notoriously messy desk, piled high with papers and mail. "I file by the Pompeiian method," he once quipped, meaning that to find something in his office required an excavation.

As a boss, Nader remained an original. He once claimed that his number-one criterion for hiring people was that they be thick-skinned. "People often ask me how I choose the people to work with me," he explained. "Well, you start off by saying they have to be bright, hard-working, the usual traits. But the one key probably is how willing they are not to be loved."

He added: "What would happen to me if I went out to Jim Roche's house to dinner, for instance? Well, pretty soon it's Ralph and Jim, and pretty soon there's a report coming out on GM and someone says, 'You know you can't do this to Jim. Remember those great dinners at his house? Not to good old Jim.' Well there it is—the most important quality for this kind of work is to have no anxiety to be loved."

Besides new headquarters and renewed hostilities toward GM, 1970 was notable for Nader in one other respect. The year saw the first real hints of dissonance regarding his public image. Up to this point, the Nader persona had been remarkably streamlined: he was committed, passionate, ascetic—a prime candidate for secular sainthood. But a couple of episodes in 1970 can be seen as distant seismic tremblings, as the first vague clues—for anyone not intimately familiar with his tactics—that there was another, more hard-bitten side to Ralph Nader.

The first episode was an attack by Nader on Edmund Muskie. Muskie was a very popular liberal senator from Maine who in 1968 had been the Democratic candidate for vice president, chosen to run alongside Hubert Humphrey. As chairman of the air and water pollution subcommittee, Muskie played a major role in the passage of the Air Quality Act of 1967. His commitment to fighting pollution had earned him the sobriquet "Mr. Clean."

A 1970 Raider report, *Vanishing Air*, cowritten by John Esposito and Larry Silverman, savaged Muskie at every opportunity. The report painted him as a phony, a political opportunist, and a friend of industry; those were just the warning salvos. "Muskie is, of course, the chief architect of the disastrous Air Quality Act of 1967," the report continued. "That fact alone would warrant his being stripped of his title as 'Mr. Pollution Control.' But the Senator's passivity since 1967 in the face of an ever worsening air pollution crisis compounds his earlier failure."

Nader signed off on *Vanishing Air*'s content. In a news conference to announce its publication, he renewed and amplified the attack. It struck people as an odd move. To this point, Nader had a well-defined list of targets: corporations, bloated bureaucracies, anticonsumerist members of Congress. That Nader would go after an avowed liberal and celebrated pollution fighter simply did not compute.

"It certainly surprised people who didn't know him well," says Mike Pertschuk, who as staff director of the Senate Commerce Committee worked very closely with Nader, "but I don't think it was out of character. There's always been a strong sense of righteousness in Ralph, and outrage. General outrage was his currency. What was new was that he had directed it at someone who was seen as an ally. In Washington, you don't do this. It was a surprise."

Harrison Wellford, a long-time Nader associate, also has an observation. "All alliances, in Ralph's view, were temporary, and purely tactical. If a congressman was helpful one day, but less useful the next, Ralph would drop him like a hot rock. That's not the way it's done in Washington. In Washington you develop relationships, you have networks, you do a favor, you get a favor. For the most part, he just refused to play the game."

On first exposure to this trait, most people were merely confounded. This was certainly the reaction of Senator Ribicoff, when he found himself the unexpected target of Nader's wrath.

One of Nader's most concerted drives was aimed at creating a Consumer Protection Agency. It would handle complaints, conduct research, and educate the public on consumer issues. He envisioned it as an independent agency with a status similar to the FTC or Federal Reserve. The agency would not be subject to supervision by the president or by various cabinet departments. It would answer only to consumers. This would be the one government body dedicated to their needs. Nader put enormous energy into lobbying Congress to create a Consumer Protection Agency. It took precedence over many of his other projects.

During a 1970 session, the Senate passed a bill by a 74–4 margin that would create just such an agency. Nader was present, sitting in the Senate gallery. A few days earlier, he had praised the bill for creating a vital new agency. But now he turned churlish. He started sending notes to various senators on the floor complaining that the bill had been gutted beyond recognition. Nothing had really changed about the bill except for Nader's attitude.

That evening he issued a statement calling the bill "unacceptable." He also accused Ribicoff of "intolerable erosions." The senator was serving as floor manager, responsible for helping to push the Consumer Protection Agency bill along.

Ribicoff was puzzled. He had worked closely with Nader to pass an auto safety bill in 1966. Now he was involved in another legislative drive in which he thought he could count on Nader as an ally.

"Ribicoff was very unhappy at this point," recalls Robert Wager, the senator's one-time staffer. "He was a very pragmatic guy. When the bill passed the Senate, only to have Nader denounce it, Ribicoff lost a great deal of regard for him."

Without Nader's backing, the bill lost momentum. After going through a few more convolutions, it died in committee. This was not the way things were done in Washington.

—10—

PIRG (Pronounced Purg)

NADER TOOK THE $280,000 FROM HIS GM lawsuit settlement and used it to start a law firm. If Nader had a knack for crafting media-friendly terms like "fatfurter," he showed a similar aptitude for founding organizations with blasé names, names that were willfully nondescriptive and seemed to seek anonymity. Dramatic raids of government agencies were done under the aegis of the Center for the Study of Responsive Law. When Nader opened a law firm, he called it the Public Interest Research Group, or PIRG.

The name belies the firm's outsized ambitions. Going back to his days at Harvard, it had been a dream of Nader's to start a law firm that fought against corporate power. The basic notion: cash-fat corporations can afford to hire platoons of lawyers to represent their interests. Why not a law firm dedicated to serving the interests of the public, at least as defined by Nader?

"The best lawyers should be spending their time on the great problems," he once told *Time*, "on water and air pollution, on racial justice, on poverty and juvenile delinquency, on the joke that ordinary rights have become. But they are not. They are spending their time defending Geritol, Rice Krispies, and the oil-import quota."

Of course, there were plenty of lawyers in 1970 who had chosen nontraditional routes. But generally they worked in areas such as legal aid, where it was common to get swallowed up in unending caseloads. Certainly upholding the rights of poor and indigent clients was a far cry from corporate law, but this kind of work could also become a grind and achieving visible results was often difficult. Setting a society-altering legal precedent was pretty much out of the question.

Nader had a different model in mind. He wanted to build a public interest practice that was the equal of the most influential and elite corporate law firms. On this score, the Washington firm of Covington & Burling was Nader's yardstick, and his nemesis. Its lead partner was a consummate insider, Dean Acheson, former secretary of state under Harry Truman. The firm had its pick of graduates from top law schools and also had its pick of clients, representing roughly two hundred of the nation's top five hundred companies in 1970.

Nader wanted the PIRG to be the mirror image of Covington & Burling. It was his aim to recruit similarly high-wattage legal talent. And he wanted to select cases that had dramatic, even landmark potential.

In certain respects, his idea was very Brandeisian. As already noted, there are similarities between Brandeis and Nader, though Nader—preferring to cast himself as a true original—has always played up the differences between the two.

Beginning in 1879, long before he sat on the Supreme Court, Brandeis and partner Samuel Warren built up a lucrative law practice. It served as a base for Brandeis to develop a rather more unremunerative sideline, taking on what he termed the "curse of bigness." Brandeis worked tirelessly to prevent corporations from taking away the rights of workers. Between 1907 and 1914, big business made a concerted effort to roll back state statutes regarding minimum wages and maximum hours. Brandeis stepped forward and fought to uphold a number of those statutes. He also challenged the life insurance industry on the issue of exorbitant rates. His intervention resulted in a new practice whereby affordable life insurance was offered over the counter by banks.

Brandeis even took on J. P. Morgan, paragon of corporate power and bigness. Morgan wanted to merge the New York, New Haven, and Hartford Railroad with the Boston and Maine Railroad. The proposed combination looked like a monopoly, detrimental to consumers in the Northeast. Brandeis played a prominent role in the ensuing battle with Morgan, one that was protracted but ultimately successful.

"The leading lawyers of the United States," Brandeis once said, "have, to a large extent, allowed themselves to become adjuncts of great corporations and have neglected their obligations to use their powers for protection of the people."

Brandeis's efforts at law in the public interest were undeniably high-profile, landmark even, and earned him the title "the people's attorney."

But Brandeis was hardly an ascetic in the Nader mold. He had more in common with the upper-crust reformers who were his contemporaries, such as Theodore Roosevelt. He maintained a summer home on Cape Cod and was an organizer of the Dedham Polo Club. This is the side that Nader has always chosen to highlight when faced with the inevitable comparisons. On one occasion, Nader dismissed Brandeis by saying that he "took a few briefs for child labor after he had made a million dollars and so became 'the people's lawyer.'"

In 1970 the *Harvard Law School Record* named Nader as the most distinguished graduate the school had ever produced. It was a grand honor, and somewhat surprising, given his ambivalent relationship with Harvard. No doubt, the accolade secretly pleased him. It meant that he had eclipsed Brandeis as the school's leading light. It also suggested that Nader's this-is-war approach to defending the public interest had a chance of supplanting the Brandeis gentleman's-sideline model.

As a speaker, Nader made frequent appearances at Harvard and other law schools. His speaking earned money for his causes and was a great recruiting device. He also enjoyed challenging and provoking audiences full of future lawyers, forcing them to question their assumptions. One of his favorite questions, circa 1970: "How many of you would do good in the world for $15,000 a year? How many for $10,000? How many for $5,000? How many for nothing?"

NADER MANAGED TO QUICKLY hire ten or so young lawyers for his PIRG firm at salaries of $4,500. To cut down on administrative hassle, they received two $2,250 paychecks a year.

As with so many Nader projects, the PIRG was overseen by a kind of den mother, an employee who was older and possessed a measure of professional seasoning. John Schulz, a twenty-nine-year-old assistant law professor at USC, had served as den mother on the FTC raid; Margaret Quinn, a twenty-five-year-old teacher at Miss Porter's School, had chaperoned the Maiden Muckrakers. At the PIRG, the task fell to Gary Sellers, aged thirty-two.

For his first job out of University of Michigan law school, Sellers had worked at Covington & Burling. He had also worked in the Bureau of the Budget during the Johnson administration and as a legal consultant to California Congressman Phillip Burton. He had even done a prior stint with Nader, overseeing a study on workplace safety that contributed to the passage of the Occupational Safety and Health Act of 1970.

Sellers was a tiny man, seemingly compacted by rage, with a pin-drop predilection for displays of extreme temper. Capable of fierce loyalty, he also prided himself on an ability to cut personal ties in an instant over matters of moral or political disagreement. He once described himself as "someone who would work for a minimal salary and be violent in my opinions."

Among the various Raiders over the years—and there have been thousands—Sellers has to be considered the truest believer. Nader was best man at Sellers's wedding.

Another key Nader associate also got her start at the PIRG firm, emphasis on "her." Joan Claybrook is one of the notable exceptions—a female who achieved prominence in Nader's male-heavy hierarchy. Claybrook was very similar to Nader, sharp-tongued, dogmatic, and capable of bruising tactics in pursuit of goals such as clean air and product safety. Like Nader, Claybrook grew up in a politically aware family. Her father was a member of the Baltimore city council who fought for issues such as desegregation and affordable legal services for the poor. As a child, Claybrook hoofed around town wearing a sandwich board supporting her father's reelection efforts. On another occasion, her family picketed Baltimore's Lyric Theater, which had refused to book performances by singer Marian Anderson, who was black.

After graduating from Goucher College in 1959, Claybrook went to work for the Social Security Administration. She was also involved in the 1966 auto safety legislation, working for James Mackay, a Democrat from Georgia. After the bill passed, she took a job with the National Highway Safety Bureau and worked closely with the head of NHSB, traffic-safety pioneer William Haddon. Heavy involvement in auto safety provided her first brush with Nader.

Claybrook's initial impression was that he was very shy. "He was very tall," she recalls, "but he slumped down in his seat like he was hiding." She found that he reminded her of John Wilkes. She had written a college thesis on Wilkes, an advocate for the poor in eighteenth-century England. In a letter to a former college professor, Claybrook described Nader in the following terms: "The most interesting thing has happened to me. I've met John Wilkes all over again, and his name is Ralph Nader. He has no resources, he just has an idea, and he lobbies everybody until the idea takes hold. It's a fascinating thing."

By 1970 Claybrook had earned a law degree from Georgetown, attending the school at night. By 1970 Nader was no longer without resources and did not have "just an idea." He had growing coffers and an endless stream of ideas, including the PIRG firm, for which he hired

Claybrook. In years to come, Claybrook would become Nader's right-hand woman.

TO LAUNCH THE PIRG FIRM, Nader gathered his team of young lawyers at the new offices at 1025 15th Street, NW. It was easy walking distance from many of Washington's most established firms. Attitudinally, it was light years removed. The furniture had not yet arrived, and for the inaugural meeting, the lawyers sat in a circle on the floor. A lone Earth Day poster on the wall was the only adornment.

Nader instructed his legal team to read voluminously, prescribing his standard six publications. "Ralph told us we should absolutely read everything. He said it was the only way to keep up," recalls Karen Ferguson, a charter member of the PIRG firm.

Nader also divvied up areas of expertise including health care, banking, pensions, tax policy, and the environment. The idea was that the PIRG lawyers would hunt down potential cases that fell within their bailiwick. Although they often took on cases on behalf of individual clients, Nader encouraged his charges to think in broader terms. Any case taken on by the PIRG needed to have the potential to benefit the broad public and consumers in general. This is what Nader claimed as the firm's constituency. The intent was to provide this broad constituency with the same level of representation that a corporation received when it hired a top-tier firm.

Within weeks of opening, the PIRG lawyers had a full roster of cases. The firm petitioned the FDA demanding better warnings on the packaging for birth control pills. It initiated a case with the FTC regarding an unsubstantiated claim being made by Bristol Meyers, manufacturer of Excedrin. Advertisements touted Excedrin as having twice the effectiveness of aspirin, when it simply contained a larger dosage of pain killer. Though the cases dragged out, the PIRG firm eventually won them both.

Nader was extremely involved from the outset, picking over expenses with care that was unusual even by his standards. After all, he was trying to provide white-shoe service on a shoestring budget. Nader cracked down on photocopying, asking his lawyers to do mimeographs whenever possible. They also did their own correspondence. Unlike most law firms, there were no secretaries, hence no dictation.

Nader also demanded monthly progress reports from each member of the firm. He would read them with great care. It peeved him to no end if a PIRG lawyer claimed to have helped—merely helped—with a particular cause.

"What do you mean *helped*," was his standard riposte. "What have you accomplished?"

Per the inverted Covington & Burling model, Nader was in the habit of measuring the PIRG firm's accomplishments according to a kind of reverse bottom line. Whenever possible, Nader liked the lawyers to calculate the financial impact of a successful case. How much money had they saved the public?

Thomas Stanton joined the PIRG firm at its inception. Almost immediately, he was thrown onto an esoteric case regarding the IRS and tax policy. The Nixon Administration had proposed an accelerated depreciation schedule that would reduce the tax bills of corporations by roughly $4 billion a year. In Nader's eyes, this showed favoritism for corporations over ordinary taxpayers. Stanton fought the measure assiduously. It passed anyway, but in a modified form as a slightly less accelerated depreciation schedule that would reduce corporate tax bills by more like $3 billion annually.

"How much have you saved taxpayers?" Stanton recalls Nader asking him.

And he had an answer: roughly $1 billion.

"Viewed in context, shaving off $1 billion is not a huge victory," says Stanton. "But you also have to consider the political imbalance, the PIRG firm versus the Nixon administration."

He adds: "Ralph was very pleased. He loved this kind of stuff. Accelerated depreciation is a very dull subject. But one of Ralph's big points was that when your eyes glaze over, that's where the money is."

THE FIRST PIRG FIRM had barely started up and the third-hand furniture had only just arrived, when Nader hurtled on to his next project. He decided he wanted to franchise PIRGs, kind of like Kentucky Fried Chicken or 7-Eleven. Firms could be set up in college towns all over the country and could work in conjunction with students. Among Nader's abundance of ideas, this would be one of his most idiosyncratic, and also one of his most enduring. It was based in part on a curious Nader observation: What if the My Lai massacre had happened during the summer?

Nader was well schooled in the tremendous vitality of college students; he hired them by the hundreds for his various projects. Throughout the 1960s and into the early 1970s, there was a climate of general activism, evident in everything from the organization of the first Earth Day to participation in the Peace Corps. Although it was not his area of focus, Nader had witnessed the anti-Vietnam movement, had seen the kind of vigorous protests students could mount in response to events such as the My Lai massacre.

On March 16, 1968, the U.S. Army's Eleventh Brigade—Charlie Company—entered the Vietnamese village of My Lai on a "search and destroy" mission. A number of the members of Charlie Company had recently been killed or seriously injured by land mines. The men—gripped by a mix of terror, fury, and raw nerves—rampaged through My Lai, guns blazing. No Vietcong soldiers were present in the village; there were only women, children, and old men. Charlie Company killed three hundred of them, often in unimaginably brutal ways. Terrified women, some kneeling in prayer, were shot in the back of the head. Lieutenant William Calley, the mission's commander, ordered a group of villagers into a ditch where they were mowed down by machine gun fire.

The story did not become known to the American public until November 1969, when a reporter, Seymour Hersh, spoke with a Vietnam veteran named Ron Ridenhour. Ridenhour had heard about My Lai through members of Charlie Company. When Hersh's story broke, on the Dispatch News Service, there was an immediate public outcry. As usual, some of the most visible and vocal protests occurred on university campuses. Nader could not help wondering what would have happened had the My Lai massacre story broken during summer vacation. Perhaps the response would have been less organized and vigorous.

This set Nader to thinking about the ephemeral nature of student power. After all, students are in school only nine months of the year and generally spend only four years in college. How, then, to capture all that energy? That's when the notion hit him: Have students work in conjunction with PIRG franchises set up near their universities. These would be offshoots of the original Washington PIRG firm, staffed mostly by lawyers but also scientists and other professionals.

Students would identify projects of interest. Say a group of students at a university decided they wanted to fight the construction of a dam that threatened to disrupt the migratory routes of salmon. They could work in conjunction with their local PIRG. When the students were on summer break, the PIRG lawyers and biologists would continue pursuing the issue. Maybe it would drag on for years, and whole generations of students would pass through the university. A PIRG could focus on an issue in perpetuity.

This model had an additional advantage, to Nader's thinking. College students are notorious for a breathless save-the-planet-at-2 A.M. sincerity.

Meanwhile, convention holds that people in the work world lose that exuberance while gaining the means to actually accomplish something. Nader—pragmatic idealist that he was—figured, Why not blend the passion of college students with the can-do of professionals?

The real stroke of inspiration was the funding mechanism. To make it possible for a group of students to hire a staff of lawyers required a unique model. Nader hit on the following: finance the PIRGs out of tuition payments, specifically the portion allotted to campus activities. Athletic facilities, literary magazines, guest speakers—all are paid for out of activity fees. Nader envisioned the PIRGs as a kind of campus civics team. At a given university, it would cost each student $2 or $3 extra per year to fund the operation of a PIRG.

Of course, students had to agree to the additional fee. Typically, something like this gets put to a vote by the entire student body. Here, Nader favored a unique model, known as a negative checkoff option. According to this model, if establishing a PIRG wins favor with the campus majority, every student is assessed the additional fee. Students who objected to the PIRG concept would have to take prescribed steps to get their money back.

The negative checkoff option is similar to the approach used by Columbia Record Club. If club members fail to return their cards in time, they automatically receive the month's selection.

The negative checkoff option was a cornerstone of the PIRG concept, as envisioned by Nader. Nader's argument was that individual students wind up paying for football teams and assorted other programs whether they support these programs or not. If a majority—even a slim 51 percent—agreed to start a PIRG, everyone would be assessed a fee. For students who objected, there would be a process in place for getting the fee refunded.

Nader had dreamed up a real platypus—franchised activist organizations staffed by lawyers and other professionals, directed by college students, and often funded by their parents, the party springing for tuition money.

PIRGs MAY HAVE BEEN odd, but Nader had the means for peddling his concept. As of 1970, he was represented by a speaker's agency called the American Program Bureau. He commanded the top rate at that time, $3,000 a speech, same as Jane Fonda and Dr. Benjamin Spock, the noted pediatrician. Nader was delivering scores of speeches a year—many to colleges—and this gave him a tremendous platform to promote his new idea.

Nader was a strangely affecting speaker, though he could scarcely match the celestial arc of a Martin Luther King sermon or the gritty glory of a Vince Lombardi locker-room tirade. Then as now, he did not rely on a prepared text. Instead, Nader ran logorrheic marathons, lining up anecdote after anecdote, not really building toward any defined climax; he would flag, get a second wind, flag, only to get a third wind. Yet by the time he was finished, typically after several hours, he would have succeeded in constructing something of undeniable weight—*so much wrong with the world, something must be done.*

During the autumn of 1970, Nader began pitching the PIRGs in his university speeches. He had always been a champion of civic involvement by students, but now he had a prototype. He would describe the PIRG model, explain the funding mechanism, and—more often than not—take a jab at the audience's apathy as well: "The average student spends $250 a year on soft drinks, tobacco, and movies. If you would each contribute only three dollars per year, you could recruit the toughest, finest lawyers to begin dealing with pollution and corruption."

Nader was publicizing the PIRGs far and wide. But to get the concept to take hold required some conspicuous successes. At least a handful of universities would need to start PIRGs. Nader concentrated his efforts in two states, Oregon and Minnesota. Oregon was an obvious choice, given the state's tradition of liberalism and activism, particularly on environmental issues. A strong populist strain runs through Minnesota's history, evident in politicians the state has produced such as Hubert Humphrey and Eugene McCarthy.

During the fall of 1970, Nader visited Oregon three times in the space of six weeks. On a single day—November 16, 1970—Nader spoke at eight different colleges, traveling from Lewis and Clark University near Portland to Willamette College in Salem to a community college in the town of Bend.

Nader also did a whirlwind ten-college tour in Minnesota, visiting St. Olaf College and Carleton College, among others. Jazzed by the idea of starting a PIRG, Karim Ahmed assembled a student welcoming committee to aid Nader in his travels around the state. Ahmed was pursuing a Ph.D. in biochemistry at the University of Minnesota in 1970. He had helped organize the first Earth Day, and had been jailed for protesting the war in Vietnam. Nader never drives, so Ahmed agreed to taxi him around.

A few days before he was to arrive in Minnesota, Nader called Ahmed with the following instructions: "Pick me up in a four-door sedan with four seat belts that have shoulder straps. Under no circumstances should you come in a Volkswagen."

The specifications were a challenge for Ahmed and the welcoming committee. Most drove Volkswagens—or rode bicycles. But as it turned out, the father of one member owned a Cadillac dealership.

When Nader arrived at the airport, Ahmed and the other students greeted him in a shiny black Caddy. Nader appeared unfazed. But as they approached the venue for his first speech, Nader said: "You know what you have to do. Please drop me three blocks away, give me directions, and I'll walk."

Nader explained that he had to be scrupulous. He told the students that he even removed the manufacturer's labels from the handful of suits he owned, thereby ensuring that no one could possibly view his choices in haberdashery as a kind of tacit endorsement. Certainly he could not afford to be seen in a Cadillac. He requested that the students return with a different car to pick him up following his speech.

They went back to the dealership and were able to procure a suitably nondescript Oldsmobile station wagon with the requisite shoulder harnesses. "He was very happy with it," recalls Ahmed, "and we traveled all over Minnesota."

NADER'S RELENTLESS CANVASSING PAID off. A petition drive was launched at the University of Minnesota, and a majority of students—thirty thousand out of fifty thousand—voted to pay $1 a quarter in additional fees to start a PIRG. The university's regents upheld the negative checkoff option, meaning that all fifty thousand students would be assessed the fee. Several other schools in the state also voted in favor of starting PIRGs. The schools agreed to pool their resources and hire a single professional staff for the entire state.

Minnesota PIRG had a first-year budget of $200,000, enough for operating expenses, four full-time attorneys, and a small administrative staff. Ahmed acted as a liaison between students at the University of Minnesota and the PIRG professionals. Other schools also chose student liaisons to work with the PIRG staff.

Petition drives were also successful at University of Oregon and a number of other colleges in that state. Once again, the schools chose to pool their resources. The Oregon state PIRG (OSPIRG) had a total budget of $150,000 during its first year and managed to hire a professional staff of six.

The projects the student PIRGs tackled were very basic, usually of a Consumerism 101 variety. They had to be. It was essential to choose projects that engaged both the interests of students and the abilities of the professional staffs.

For one of its initial projects, OSPIRG decided to expose a common deception practiced by auto repair shops. As a first step, a group of students had the steering alignment of their cars inspected by auto safety instructors at various community colleges. If the alignment was off, the safety instructors fixed it.

Thus all the students participating in the project had cars with pristine alignment. They then took them to auto repair shops in various college towns. Predictably, they were told that they needed to fix their alignment and were quoted various fees. The students publicized the findings in the manner of a Nader raid. The PIRG professional staff did its part, helping draft a state bill aimed at curbing deceptive practices by auto repair shops.

"Everybody went wild and ate it up," recalls Steve McCarthy, OSPIRG's first executive director. "The auto repair guys were not so clever. They walked right into it and got pasted in the face. This was a quintessential PIRG project because it was simple and involved kids at a number of different campuses."

OREGON AND MINNESOTA SERVED as Nader's two working PIRG prototypes. He continued to highlight the concept in speeches before various college audiences. Nader functioned almost like an advance man, introducing students to the PIRG concept and piquing their interest. Members of the original PIRG firm in Washington, D.C.—traveling in pairs—followed in Nader's wake and reinforced the message.

For example, PIRG lawyers Thomas Stanton and Jim Welch visited schools in Ohio, Illinois, and other midwestern states. The mere fact that they were associated with Nader drew students to hear their speeches. Routinely, Nader could pack an auditorium with a five-thousand-person capacity. Stanton and Welch might only fill a hundred-seat lecture hall. But they could also spend time with interested students, explaining the PIRG concept in detail.

Stanton has a vivid recollection of their visit to Northern Illinois University. "I still remember going to a local pub for a drink," he says. "It was like we were playing in a rock band, all the students were so excited to see us."

Not everyone met with such enthusiasm. Christian White and Sam Simon were assigned to travel through the American South. "As you can imagine, starting a PIRG was not the most popular idea in Tuscaloosa," White recalls. "A couple guys from D.C. coming down and telling everybody how to do things was not a popular notion at the time. We were looked upon as oddities, outsiders, and potential upsetters."

Of course, Nader was relying on just ten PIRG lawyers to blanket the country. In keeping with the notorious Nader work ethic, they were already monstrously overburdened with their caseloads, not to mention the mandate of reading six papers a day. To supplement their efforts, he hired a couple of full-time organizers. Nader paid them the standard minuscule salaries and provided $11 a day in expenses to travel from campus to campus. Per usual, there was method in Nader's frugality. The PIRG organizers were forced to forage for cheap food and accommodations. Typically, they ate in college cafeterias and slept in dorm rooms, the better to remain in close contact with the very students they were supposed to be organizing.

"I traveled nonstop," recalls Donald Ross, one of Nader's PIRG organizers. "My ability to survive on $4 a day in the Peace Corps in Africa enabled me to live on $11 in the U.S."

Ross adds: "Often Nader would go to a campus and draw a huge crowd of people who would be very enthused and wanting to do something. I would follow a day later or a week later, and pull these people together. My job, and the job of others who followed in his wake, was to find the natural leaders among the crowd. I would work to motivate them and energize them and instill in them a belief that they could make a difference."

Ross traveled to forty states as a PIRG organizer and visited hundreds of different schools. The model really caught on. By 1974 PIRGs were operating in twenty-two states, and 500,000 students were involved. As the number of PIRGs increased, they stuck closely to Nader's original vision. Prime PIRG territory continued to be basic civics projects that teamed students and professionals.

Students involved in Missouri PIRG (founded in 1971) looked into conditions in St. Louis jails; the professional staff worked to appoint a prison ombudsman. At Vermont PIRG, students conducted a 1973 study which determined that elementary school students were getting substandard dental care. In turn, the PIRG professionals helped draft Vermont state resolution H-321, the so-called Tooth Fairy Act, which is still in effect and provides free dental care for needy kids. PIRGs in Illinois, Texas, and North Carolina did surveys highlighting the huge variations in the prices of prescription drugs purchased in the same cities. Students and lawyers at Massachusetts PIRG teamed up to successfully fight a utility rate increase in 1972.

Over the years, various old-reliable projects have been taken up by various state PIRGs, one after another. For example, numerous PIRGs have joined in fights for bottle bills, which tack a nickel deposit onto various containers with the aim of cutting down on littering. Another PIRG standby: the Christmas toy safety report. Every year, a number of different PIRGs publish consumer alerts regarding dangerous toys. It is a popular public service and always receives ample press attention.

PIRGs HAVE BEEN SURPRISINGLY successful, and also quite controversial. One issue is Nader's own arm's-length relationship with them, similar to his approach to Campaign GM. Nader's assertion has always been that he merely helped set the PIRG movement in motion. Causes championed by individual PIRGs have nothing to do with him.

Often he has made the claim in response to the criticism that there is a decidedly liberal slant to the projects undertaken by PIRGs. Nader has always pointed out that PIRGs are free to do as they please. If a PIRG so chooses, it could take up a conservative cause, maybe fight to get an abortion clinic closed.

True enough. Nader is certainly not the PIRG puppet master. The genius of the model lies in its decentralization and the fact that the various PIRGs are self-sufficient and self-perpetuating.

At the same time, Nader's stance is more than a little disingenuous. After all, it is not as if PIRGs are the result of a casual offhand suggestion he made. He developed a rigorous model, worked vigorously to get the first ones started, and even hired full-time organizers throughout the 1970s. There is an annual national PIRG convention, which draws representatives from the various state PIRGs; over the years, Nader has been a frequent attendee. Nader and Donald Ross even coauthored a handbook on PIRG organizing, *Action for a Change*, published in 1971.

"Ralph is a very savvy guy," says Steve McCarthy, first executive director of OSPIRG. "When he personally takes on an issue, he can be very effective. But Ralph knew he could not take on every issue everywhere. So he came up with a device for magnifying his own abilities."

McCarthy adds: "Ralph was our spiritual leader. We watched Ralph and read about Ralph and tried to figure out everything we could about how he did it so we could do it, too. We soaked up everything we could."

THE OTHER ENDURING PIRG controversy is the funding mechanism. The original negative checkoff option has met with great resistance. After all, a university's entire student body (save for those who specifically request a refund) winds up paying for an organization that arguably pursues a liberal-leaning agenda. Students who are unaware that a portion of their fee is supporting a PIRG can wind up unwittingly financing something that undercuts their own political beliefs.

An amusing side note: an employee once sent Nader a memo that proposed a certain course of action and added: "Unless I hear from you otherwise, I'll assume this is OK."

Nader was furious and responded: "I do not and will not run my life by the Book-of-the-Month Club system."

Nader would not stand for it, and neither have a number of universities. The negative checkoff at Oregon was voted down in 1972. Consequently, OSPIRG had to lobby the student government directly each year for an allotment of operating funds. Students at Pennsylvania State approved a negative checkoff in 1975. But the school's board of regents overrode the action. A PIRG was still started at Penn State, but with a positive checkoff option that assessed a fee only from those students who gave their okay.

Had the negative checkoff stood, it would have generated an estimated $270,000 in revenues for Penn State's PIRG in 1975. A positive checkoff generated more like $30,000. In response, Nader called Penn State a "citadel of fascism" before adding: "If the board of trustees doesn't understand democracy, which I don't believe they do, those who don't understand it should resign."

Today, many PIRGs get their funding by canvassing. Students solicit funds over the phone or by going door-to-door in their communities. As for Nader, the PIRGs have been a tremendously effective means of "magnifying" his effectiveness, to use McCarthy's term. Many Nader crusades have been aimed at federal agencies and global corporations. But PIRGs act on a state and local level, where many battles must be fought.

Getting the PIRG model up and rolling also represents Nader's first foray into grassroots organizing. As such, it helped lay the foundation for subsequent grassroots initiatives, such as running for president.

NADER WAS FOREVER INTERESTED in developing systems. His idea for systematically combining the unique abilities of students and professionals resulted in the PIRGs. For his next project, Nader decided to try to open up channels for gathering intelligence about shady practices by corporations and government agencies.

"The price of liberty is eternal vigilance," Nader once said, quoting Thomas Jefferson, before adding, "and I believe eternal vigilance can be institutionalized."

Nader had abundant experience with informers. Without them, his work would have been infinitely more difficult. While researching *Unsafe at Any Speed*, it was a GM engineer who had first called his attention to alleged design defects in the Corvair. Frustrated agency personnel provided some of the most damning details about the FTC. The best knowledge of the worst practices often comes from people on the inside.

Over time, Nader developed a kind of corporate cosmology. It held that those who climb to the top often do so through steely ambition, shedding their principles along the way. That leaves the ranks below full of frustrated idealists. They know better but are forced to look on helplessly as their superiors set the agenda, churning out shoddy goods, perhaps polluting, or even subjecting their own employees to hazardous conditions. The conscience of an organization, in Nader's view, resides with those at the midlevel and below.

If only it were possible to tap into the knowledge of all those frustrated idealists. There was no shortage of malfeasance among corporations and government agencies—of this, Nader was convinced. It was simply a matter of getting employees to speak out more freely. If only there were a way to create a system or an institution that would make it easier for people to go public if their employer was engaged in some kind of transgression.

As erstwhile Raider Peter Petkas recalls: "One of the main sources of fuel for Ralph's machine—in terms of ideas and information—was insiders. They saw Ralph as a way they could get their concerns and gripes ventilated. People would crawl out of the woodwork and come to Ralph. Over time, Ralph said that we need to do something to institutionalize this process."

Nader's first step was to attempt a bit of semantic alchemy. There are a range of terms, mostly pejorative, to describe people who act as informants: "rat," "fink," "whistle-blower," "snitch," and "squealer." Among those, Nader noted that "whistle-blower" is a fairly neutral term. His idea—strange as it seems—was to invest this neutral term with positive associations such as honor, rectitude, and civic-mindedness.

Late in the autumn of 1970—as he was grappling with exactly how to institutionalize whistle-blowing—Nader met with Ernest Fitzgerald, who had been involved in a highly controversial whistle-blowing incident. He was celebrated in some quarters, reviled in others.

While working as a cost-control expert at the Department of Defense, Fitzgerald had become aware that the C-5A was $2 billion over budget. The C-5A was a cargo plane, being built for the Air Force by Lockheed. In 1968 Fitzgerald went before a Senate subcommittee chaired by William Proxmire to reveal his findings.

In the wake of his testimony, Fitzgerald was first demoted and later dismissed. This, despite the fact that his most recent job performance ratings had been stellar. He had even been nominated for a Distinguished Civil Servant Award. In fact, Fitzgerald was that rare person who actually had a framed copy of the Code of Ethics of the U.S. Government Service hanging on the wall of his office. The code reads in part: "Put loyalty to the highest moral principles and to country above loyalty to persons, party or Government department."

Following his dismissal, Fitzgerald faced a full-bore character-assassination campaign. The Pentagon questioned his loyalty, motives, and mental stability, and even accused him of leaking confidential documents. Fitzgerald also learned that his former employer had investigated his background and personal life, hoping to discredit him.

Working with Proxmire, Fitzgerald was able to obtain copies of the investigative files. He learned that the Department of Defense had tried to establish a pattern of "moral lapses" on his part, although nothing substantive was uncovered. The investigation had also explored whether Fitzgerald maintained financial ties to a previous employer while working at the Pentagon. This would have been a clear breach of conflict of interest guidelines. But it also proved a dead end.

Ultimately, the investigators were reduced to painting Fitzgerald in their report as a "penny pincher" because he drove an "old Rambler." It was a strange charge to level against a cost-control analyst. It also bore a striking resemblance to the kind of tactics GM had employed against Nader.

Fitzgerald and Nader had lunch at a French restaurant in Washington. "Ralph was sympathetic," recalls Fitzgerald. "He wanted to do something to help out truth tellers. It was very cheering. Ralph at that time was a big hero. I was extremely notorious; my adventures were all over the papers and television."

ON JANUARY 30, 1971, Nader held a conference on whistle-blowing at the Mayflower Hotel in Washington. The featured speaker was the controversial Fitzgerald. He was joined by a panel of fellow whistle-blowers that included Jacqueline Verrett, a scientist at the FDA who had revealed the danger of the artificial sweetener cyclamate, and Ralph Stein, an Army intelligence officer who had gone public and exposed the practice of putting civilians under surveillance. Another speaker was A. Dale Console, former medical director of E. R. Squibb. During testimony before Congress in 1960, Console had revealed various shady techniques by pharmaceutical companies—"research" grants to doctors, for example—that led to the overprescription of certain drugs.

Nader delivered a keynote address in which he laid out the fundamental quandary of the whistle-blower. "The key question is, at what point should an employee resolve that allegiance to society (e.g., the public safety) must supersede allegiance to the organization's policies (e.g., the corporate profit), and then act on that resolve by informing outsiders or legal authorities."

Nader suggested that potential whistle-blowers should first work their way up the chain of command within their organizations, similar to the exhaustion of remedies in a legal case. If no one proved receptive, then it was time to go outside. Nader spelled out techniques for getting the attention of investigative reporters. They tended to be harried folks, explained Nader, always weighing the merits of a variety of potential stories. It was important to truly grab their attention. But Nader cautioned that the burden of proof would lie with the whistle-blower. If the facts were not straight, the whole case would be undermined.

In a way, Nader was simply laying out his own professional tenets: intense attention to detail, a legalistic approach, a winning way with the media. Once again, he was seeking ways to push these practices into the society at large.

Certainly the conference served to publicize the issue of whistle-blowing. Anything Nader did in this era was newsworthy. There was talk afterward of an annual conference, perhaps featuring an awards ceremony, kind of an Oscars for whistle-blowers.

Nader's ultimate aim was to institutionalize whistle-blowing, and that required creating an institution. So Nader followed up the conference by founding the Clearinghouse for Professional Responsibility. To run it, he chose Peter Petkas, then twenty-five years old and fresh out of the University of Texas law school. The clearinghouse received funding from Robert Townsend—former Avis chief and father of a Maiden Muckraker—and Stewart Mott—the rebel General Motors heir who had supported Campaign GM.

The Clearinghouse's first step was jaw-gapingly simple. For a mere $24 a year, a mail drop was set up to receive tips. The address was P.O. Box 486, Benjamin Franklin Station, Washington, D.C. 20044. It was dubbed the "confessional box."

At every opportunity—in op-eds he wrote, during interviews with the press—Nader provided the address of the mail drop. "The idea was to generate a lot of publicity," says Petkas. "We wanted to let people know there was a place they could go. Nader knew he could be a magnet for people who were troubled ethically by conduct within their organization."

Soon the clearinghouse was receiving more than two hundred letters a month. During the week following an appearance by Nader on the *Dick Cavett Show,* four hundred came pouring in; some were signed but the majority were anonymous.

Nader and his Raiders would follow up on the various leads. A letter that arrived in a Ford Motor Company envelope, for example, detailed a design flaw in the Pinto engine that made it susceptible to catching on fire during hot weather. The claim bore scrutiny, first by Nader's minions, then by the National Highway Traffic Safety Administration, and thirty thousand Pintos wound up being recalled.

Besides setting up a "confession box," the clearinghouse undertook a variety of efforts on behalf of whistle-blowers. A major thrust was lobbying Congress and various government agencies, promoting measures that would protect whistle-blowers against retaliation by their employers. The Occupational Safety and Health Administration (OSHA), for one, agreed to adopt some of the whistle-blower protections suggested by the clearinghouse.

Nader even hired an employment counselor to work full-time at the clearinghouse, aiding whistle-blowers who had been dismissed from their jobs. This met with mixed success. Whistle-blowers proved to be tough placements. Often they had been blacklisted within their industries. But even when it was not possible to place them in new jobs, there were other ways to help. Sometimes the employment counselor was able to keep an out-of-work whistle-blower's creditors at bay, or stave off a mortgage foreclosure. The Clearinghouse for Professional Responsibility also assisted dismissed whistle-blowers in obtaining legal counsel—often on a pro bono basis—to help them either get reinstated in their old jobs or sue their ex-employers.

Predictably, the business community was less than thrilled at this latest Nader crusade. It was one thing for Nader to be a corporate gadfly, quite another for him to actively recruit whistle-blowers. Critics nicknamed Nader's clearinghouse the "fink tank."

James Roche of General Motors even weighed in during a 1971 speech before the Executive Club in Chicago: "Some of the enemies of business now encourage an employee to be disloyal to the enterprise. They want to create suspicion and disharmony and pry into the proprietary interests of the business. However this is labeled—industrial espionage, whistle-blowing, professional responsibility—it is another tactic for spreading disunity and creating conflict."

Roche did not mention his old adversary by name. Then again, he did not have to.

—11—

At a Zenith

NATHRA NADER ONCE TOLD his son Ralph: "No movement in history has ever succeeded unless it was described in one word."

The year 1971 brought a new entry to the *Webster's Third International Dictionary*: "Consumerism [kən-ˈsü-mə-ˌri-zəm]: the promotion of consumer's interests (as against false advertising or shoddy goods)."

Now Ralph Nader had his single word, and his movement was ascendant. By the early 1970s, the war in Vietnam was winding down and the civil rights movement had made gains sufficient to lose some of its urgency. But consumerism—nonpartisan, cutting across a broad swath of society—was a pluperfect issue for a time characterized by growing anxiety about inflation. Americans were spending more on everything from food to housing to gasoline, and people wanted to get their money's worth.

Consumer legislation became the rage. During the first years of the 1970s, hundreds of bills were passed, covering everything from warranties to fair credit to toys to tainted fish. States including New York, Maryland, and Arizona enacted laws providing "cooling-off periods" for consumers, during which they could cancel contracts made with pushy door-to-door salesmen. The practice of tampering with the odometers on used cars was outlawed in states such as Massachusetts, Florida, and Texas.

Nader played a role in only a select few laws. But it can safely be said that he was the animating force behind much of the era's consumer activism, the man behind a movement. By a margin of 80 percent to 7 percent, a Harris poll revealed that the public felt "it is good to have critics like Nader to keep industry on its toes." But perhaps the greatest bellwether of Nader's reach and influence, more significant than the inclusion of "consumerism" in *Webster's*, was the fact that he was lampooned in *Mad* magazine. He rated a two-page parody. It included a selection of made-up cranky Nader letters and an account of the contents of his wallet, including an identification card listing his occupation as "lawyer, consumer crusader, ecologist, recaller of cars, destroyer of detergents, busy-body."

In a sense, *Mad*'s satire was dead-on: Nader really was a busybody, tirelessly delving into an impossibly broad range of issues and concerns. By this time, Nader had founded an entire network of different organizations. There was the original PIRG law firm and its offshoot, the various student PIRGs. There was the Clearinghouse for Professional Responsibility, dedicated to cultivating whistle-blowers. But these represented a mere sliver of his burgeoning empire. At the same time that he was directing the Raiders, hectoring senators, cultivating reporters, and perusing his standard six publications daily, Nader somehow carved out time to sire still more organizations.

For Nader, the path from idea to institution was remarkably short. It occurred to him, for example, that the nation's 60 million recreational fishermen might have a special stake in fighting pollution in ponds and streams. Thus was the Fishermen's Clean Water Action Group born in the spring of 1971. He thought it high time for air travelers to band together to demand cheaper, safer service. Hence the Aviation Consumer Action Project was launched, also in 1971. During that year—1971—it's fair to say that Nader went on an organization-founding rampage, launching a number of groups that would have varying degrees of effectiveness and longevity.

Whenever possible, Nader sought to fund his various far-flung enterprises with grants. His flagship, the Center for the Study of Responsive Law, required $250,000 to meet its operating expenses in 1971. Financial support was forthcoming from a number of foundations, including the Carnegie Corporation and Philip M. Stern Family Fund as well as from Gordon Sherman, a liberal philanthropist who was heir to the fortune generated by Midas International, the muffler company.

The Midas money came with no strings attached. Nader reciprocated by making no promises: "I candidly told him [Gordon Sherman] I was hell-bent on getting rid of the internal combustion engine and mufflers, which could eventually eliminate a major part of his business."

When necessary, Nader dug into his personal coffers. Speeches alone were generating more than $100,000 annually for him during this era. He netted another $25,000 or so from writing articles in the *New Republic* and *Ladies Home Journal*, for which he produced a regular column. Add in royalties from the Raider reports, and Nader was earning roughly $250,000 annually. But he continued to maintain that he needed just $5,000 a year in living expenses. The balance was cycled back into his organizations.

Even so, Nader realized he needed yet another source of funding. In 1971, he founded Public Citizen, a nonprofit organization that solicited donations via direct mail and newspaper advertisements. "Ralph Nader urges you to become a Public Citizen," began a pitch that appeared in the *New York Times*, *Washington Post*, and other major publications. It ended by imploring: "Let it not be said by a future, forlorn generation that we wasted and lost our great potential because our despair was so deep we didn't even try, or because each of us thought someone else was worrying about our problems."

During its first year of operation, Public Citizen raised $1.1 million from sixty-two thousand donors. The majority of the contributions were fifteen dollars, the amount recommended in the advertisement.

With a fresh source of funds, Nader decided to found more organizations. His newest projects—including the Health Research Group and the Litigation Group—were placed under the umbrella of Public Citizen, which provided a direct source of funding.

The Health Research Group was headed up by Dr. Sidney Wolfe. Wolfe had attended medical school at Case Western University, where he studied under Benjamin Spock. He and Nader first met in 1968, and Wolfe had acted as a consultant on the topic of nursing homes to the Maiden Muckrakers. In years to come, the Health Research Group would be seen as one of Nader's most effective organizations. Wolfe would delve into a range of issues including quack doctors, faulty medical devices, unnecessary surgery, and famously the dangers of red dye No. 2.

To run the Litigation Group, Nader tapped Alan Morrison, an assistant U.S. attorney for the southern district of New York. Morrison and his colleagues would pursue a variety of high-profile cases on matters such as affordable legal services and lobbying restrictions. On several occasions, they would even argue before the Supreme Court. The original PIRG law firm would gradually be phased out and replaced by Public Citizen's Litigation Group.

Beyond the organizations discussed so far, a full roster of Nader groups circa the early 1970s must also include the Corporate Accountability Research Group, Center for Auto Safety, Professionals for Auto Safety, Center for Concerned Engineering, Tax Reform Research Group, Retired Professionals Action Group, and the Center for Women Policy Studies.

This was quite a fiefdom, especially for someone who only a few years before had operated alone. But Nader, pragmatist that he was, fully recognized the value of institutionalizing his personal approach. As he was fond of saying: "Nothing is possible without an individual. Nothing is perpetual without an institution."

Of course, overseeing a disparate collection of organizations was quite an administrative challenge, and Nader was not exactly a talented administrator. Whenever possible, he delegated paperwork and personnel hassles to others. But on the issue of costs, he remained a nano-manager. Nader well knew that his expanding empire was dependent on stretching a buck. And he continued personally to sign the paychecks of every employee who worked for him.

NADER WAS FAST ASSEMBLING a public interest conglomerate. He was now a perennial fixture on the cultural landscape. Inevitably, with his stratospheric profile came criticism, plenty of criticism, especially from the business community.

Walter Wriston was president of First National City Bank, an outfit that had been the subject of a Nader raid. Wriston struck back, saying that Nader "franchises himself like a fried chicken stand."

James Kemper Jr., president of Kemper Insurance Company, had the following to say while addressing a conference of business leaders: "The man who began his public career as a crusading author and publicist in a narrow field has become one of the most powerful men in America. His influence is enormous. He has the electronic and print media so much at his disposal that it is as if he owned them. Powerful legislators give him immediate audience. He now deals with the most corrupting of all devils, power. And he appears to have fallen heir to the same arrogance, prejudice, dishonesty, irresponsibility and shoddy performance of which he accuses his target. The hunter has acquired the characteristics of the prey."

Apparently GM's Roche was the most Nader-rattled of all. He was far too dignified and savvy to publicly strike out at his nemesis. But in the years following the gumshoe debacle, Roche supposedly fell into the habit of obtaining Raiders reports and reading them on the sly. Once, in an unguarded private moment, he deemed Nader one of the "bitter gypsies of dissent." To the end of his days, Roche would remember the precise date and time of their initial confrontation.

Versus Nader, versus the movement he had spawned—consumerism—business was truly on the defensive. A Harris poll found that only 47 percent of the public gave a positive reply when asked whether business was succeeding in "bringing better quality goods to people." This was down from 75 percent in 1967, shortly after Nader burst onto the scene. A survey by Daniel Yankelovich's outfit was particularly telling. It identified the second Eisenhower administration as a high-water mark for public acceptance of business practices. Assigning this period an index value of 100, the survey then found that the barometer had fallen to 29 by 1971.

David Sarnoff, president of RCA, addressed these concerns during a speech before the Poor Richard's Club in Philadelphia: "Lifestyles may differ, but a $5 lemon is just as sour as a $5,000 lemon, and double-talk is no more welcome in a Main Line home than in a Harlem flat or on a Kansas farm. Young or old, dove or hawk, square or hippie, one tie that binds us all is irritation at being had. . . . This is the age of the articulate consumer. The buyer is demanding a more active voice in determining the nature and quality of things available to him. Business will have to spend less time talking and more time listening—and responding to what it hears."

Respond business did. During the early 1970s, Chrysler and Pan American World Airways were among the companies that added a new position to the organization chart, vice president of consumer affairs. Chrysler ran ads publicizing its consumer affairs VP as "Your Man in Detroit." Whirlpool set up a dedicated toll-free phone number for consumer complaints, an innovation at the time. Once again, it would be a mistake to claim Nader was directly involved in urging these and other specific companies to become more consumer friendly. However, he was responsible for creating a climate in which such changes were possible, even necessary.

That business would alter its approach was quite a tribute to Nader. But imitation remains the sincerest form of flattery. The consumer field was now replete with advocates, experts, pundits, and assorted Nader knockoffs working in a wide variety of areas. For example, Robert Choate came to national attention in 1970 when he testified before Congress that breakfast cereals tended to be nutritionally deficient. To continue his work, he founded the Council on Children, Media, and Merchandising. Edward Swartz, a Boston lawyer, wrote a scathing critique called *Toys That Don't Care*. Meanwhile, Jeffrey O'Connell, a law professor at the University of Illinois, authored *Safety Last*, an auto industry critique that came out not long after *Unsafe at Any Speed* and was eclipsed by it. O'Connell continued his work on auto safety, concentrating during this era on auto insurance reform.

Foremost among the emulators was John Banzhaf III, a professor at George Washington University law school in Washington, D.C. He organized groups of his students to conduct various investigations. The students were dubbed Banzhaf's Bandits, a clear nod to Nader's Raiders. But where Nader was fond of obliquely named organizations such as the Center for Concerned Engineering, Banzhaf had a weakness for acronyms. He organized PUMP (Protesting Unfair Marketing Practices), in which students investigated claims that service stations were selling identical gas under a variety of brand names and octane ratings. Meanwhile, SOUP (Students Opposed to Unfair Practices) urged the FTC to ban a Campbell's Soup commercial in which marbles were allegedly used to push all the ingredients to the top of the bowl. Other examples of Banzhaf Banditry include LASH (Legislative Action on Smoking and Health) and CAP (Collection Agency Practices).

Representative Benjamin Rosenthal, a Democrat from Queens, hired a dozen interns for the summer of 1971 and charged them with poking around Washington to uncover corruption. He referred to his team as "Rosenthal's Roustabouts."

Then there is Jerry Brown, a Yale law grad who was deeply influenced by Nader. In 1971, freshly installed as California's secretary of state, Brown sought to cast himself as a consumer-friendly activist. A few years hence, he would be elected as the state's governor. But he would eschew the governor's mansion, choosing instead to live in a low-rent apartment à la Nader's famous rooming house. Other parts of the Nader formula proved harder to follow. As governor, Brown would also carry on a very public romance with singer Linda Ronstadt.

An abiding presence in America, Nader went global. It was his contention that if corporations were multinationals, well then, he should be too. In January 1971, at the invitation of the newspaper *Yomiuri Shimbun*, he traveled to Japan. Speaking before capacity crowds in Osaka, Kyoto, and Tokyo, Nader was highly critical of the preeminent role corporations played in Japanese life and society. He faced off against the vice president of New Japan Steel for a televised debate on pollution. He also called a press conference in which he challenged Japanese automakers to "produce at least as safe a vehicle for Japanese motorists as the companies are required to produce for export sale." In a bold move, Nader reiterated the challenge in a letter that he sent directly to Eisaku Sato, Japan's prime minister.

During a five-day stay, Nader sat on traditional straw tatami mats and impressed his hosts with his serviceable command of foreign languages but refused to eat sushi, fearing mercury poisoning. His visit was chronicled on the front pages of every major newspaper in the country. "Nader's arrival here has had the most extraordinary effect," said a Japanese journalist. "You know, we are governed by a very stupid consortium of politicians and industrialists, interested only in profits. As a result, our islands are being wrecked environmentally. Now Nader comes and talks about real problems. Shows us solutions. No foreigner has had such an impact on Japan since MacArthur."

Nader also visited Australia. No sooner had Nader disembarked from his flight than he called a press conference in which he was highly critical of the country's record on consumerism. He aimed a choice few barbs at William McMahon, the prime minister. Once again, Nader chose to razz the top official of a country he was visiting—apparently a winning formula. But in this case, Nader had a meeting scheduled with McMahon. Upon introduction, the prime minister said: "Well, Mr. Nader, you seem to be quite a pot stirrer."

Nader replied: "I regret that I am unable to return the compliment."

Consumerism continued to make inroads, even in countries that Nader did not visit during this era. To look after consumer interests, Sweden appointed a special ombudsman known as a *konsumentombudsman*. Meanwhile, a consumer magazine was started in Hungary, notwithstanding the country's status as a Soviet satellite. The new publication was called *Nagyito* (Magnifying Glass) and was devoted to examining everything from men's shirts to refrigerators. One issue compared soft drinks, including Coca-Cola, Pepsi, and Hungary's own Sztar-Cola. The highest rating went to Sztar-Cola.

Nader also spawned a French wanna-be. Having first written a pair of books on consumerism, Pierre-Francoise Divier used the royalties to found an organization called Le Centre de Recherches et d'Etudes pour la Defense du Consommateur Française. Divier received a grant to visit the United States in order to study Nader-esque methods of consumer organizing. In an interview with the *Washington Post*, he contrasted his approach and Nader's in typically Gallic terms: "To succeed in America, a nation of reformists, one has to be a revolutionary. To succeed in France, a nation of revolutionaries, one has to be a reformist."

NADER'S UBIQUITY MADE HIM ever more effective, but also conferred a status with which he was less than comfortable, celebrity. In many ways, Nader was not well suited to being a public figure. People who simply happened to recognize Nader—in an airport, say, or walking around Washington—were often shocked to find that America's number one consumer advocate could be extremely prickly.

As a champion of body rights (as opposed to civil rights), he had an aversion to the custom of shaking hands. Often he would refuse an outstretched hand. It was only a minor invasion of his physical self, not exactly a car crash, but Nader resented it nonetheless. He also blanched at the implied contract—*we've shaken hands so now we are communicating openly and honestly*. As for autograph seekers, he had a stock line: "What is this asking for an autograph? You should be asking what you can do."

Nader remained hypervigilant about guarding his privacy. This particular concern was deep-rooted, part of his makeup. At the same time, Nader was aware that there was a benefit to shrouding himself in mystery. One time, Nader and Bobby Fischer were scheduled as guests on the same episode of the *Dick Cavett Show*. While sitting in the greenroom, they got to talking. Nader had been a formidable chess player during high school and he was impressed by Fischer's ability to garner international attention for such a cerebral game. Fischer's matches with Russia's Boris Spassky had received front-page coverage.

Nader asked Fischer his secret. Fischer explained that there was calculation in many of his decisions, whether showing up late to matches, canceling interviews, even refusing an invitation to visit the White House. It made him seem like a temperamental genius, even more than he actually was, and the public ate it up. "If you want to get attention to the game, you have to manipulate the press," Fischer explained.

For Nader, this was confirmation of his own instincts. His aim was to draw attention to the cause of consumerism. During this era, he was a marionette master when it came to the press. At every opportunity, Nader cast himself as an indefatigable advocate, grave, selfless, working away while the innocent citizenry sleeps. This had the advantage of not being too far from the truth. But it was not the whole truth.

The fact is, Nader was a fan of country singer Tammy Wynette. People who worked with him during the early 1970s recall that he enjoyed the occasional Marx Brothers movie. What is notable is not that Nader sometimes liked to unwind with a piece of light fare. Rather, it is interesting that he tried so hard to hide this fact. In all his years as a public figure, tastes such as Tammy Wynette or the Marx Brothers were never once mentioned in a Ralph Nader profile. Instead, he has always chosen to stress his seriousness of purpose, even in leisure. He provided the following description of fun, Nader-style, to a *Newsweek* correspondent: "Oh, I like to sit down and talk about anthropology with an expert for a couple of hours."

On another occasion, a wire service photographer took a surreptitious snapshot of Nader on a visit back home to Winsted, Connecticut, tobogganing with some kids. Nader was furious and made quite a bit of noise about invasion of privacy. But close associates suspected that the real affront was that the photographer caught him in a lighthearted moment. And that did not jibe with his scrupulously honed public image. "Even something as humanizing as sliding downhill with some kids is an invasion to Ralph," a friend once said.

All this vigilance yielded impressive results. Profiles of Nader from the early 1970s cast him as a kind of superhero of asceticism, lacking in ordinary appetites, immune to ordinary vices. A profile in the *New York Times*, dated January 10, 1971, carried the headline "The Terrible Swift Sword" and described Nader as follows: "Ralph Nader, the incorruptible in the corrupting society . . . the fiery sword, the zealot breaking down the doors of the corporate state . . . with no mercy for his enemies, the manufacturer or public officials who he believes have lost sight of the public interest." A *Reader's Digest* profile concluded: "His work schedule is a Washington legend—18 hours a day, 365 days a year, no weekends, no holidays, no family, no girlfriends, no hobbies."

The centerpiece of Nader's public image was his $80-a-month, spare little room in a boardinghouse with a single communal telephone. Even though he was now making $250,000 a year, he continued to give his address as 1719 19th Street, NW.

Then a woman called the *New Republic* anonymously to claim that the rooming house was "1965 stuff." The caller said that Nader lived instead in a $100,000 house on Bancroft Place, a rather stylish neighborhood. This rumor circulated in official Washington, but nobody would touch it. Among Nader's press allies, there existed a kind of implicit deal: Don't dig into his private life, and he would remain a ready fount of scoops. "I never got into his personal life," recalls Morton Mintz of the *Washington Post*. "For years, we would be driving home and he would say, 'let me off at Florida and Connecticut.' And he'd walk somewhere, I don't know where."

Finally, the rumor was taken up by Maxine Cheshire, a gossip columnist for the *Post*. She asked Nader point-blank about the Bancroft Place house. "Nader still lives in his old boarding house," she reported. "He is angry he says because some anonymous 'snoop' keeps calling up newspapers and magazines to claim the Bancroft place actually belongs to him."

Cheshire reported that it was actually Nader's brother, Shafeek, who lived in the house. In the early 1970s, he had moved to Washington to work as an educational consultant. The two brothers remained close. Shaf also remained a bachelor. In fact, among the four Nader siblings, only Laura married.

David Sanford, an editor for the *New Republic*, followed up Cheshire's column by conducting a deed search. His finding: the house had been purchased on November 29, 1971, and the deed was in Shafeek's name. But records also showed that the down payment on the Bancroft Place house was $20,000, a substantial amount in the early 1970s. Shafeek Nader—new to Washington, just getting started as an educational consultant—was not thought to be exactly loaded. This set off a small round of speculation that Nader may have cosigned on the mortgage loan or even put up some of the purchase money.

Sanford's theory: Nader had bought the house, installed his brother in it, taken up residence there as well, but continued to claim that he lived in the rooming house. But now the story was getting complicated, full of deed searches and mortgage cosignings. It was impossible to prove anything. Besides, Nader had gone on record saying that he did not live there.

So that was that. For decades to come, even into the 1990s, journalists in search of the telling little detail that would sum up their subject dutifully reported that Nader lived in a spare little $80-dollar-a-month room in a boardinghouse at 1719 19th Street, NW. Once again, this may be partially true. But it does not appear to be the whole truth.

Several people who worked closely with Nader believe that—public denials notwithstanding—he actually lived at the house on Bancroft Place, at least part of the time. True enough, he continued to maintain his boardinghouse room, at a cost of roughly $80-a-month (one has to assume the rent had been raised since 1965). True enough, his brother Shafeek lived in the house full-time. His sisters, Claire and Laura, also stayed there when they were in Washington.

There is some feeling that this is more of Nader's careful lawyerly hairsplitting. "Ralph has a very strong family," explains former Nader Raider Jim Turner. "They are all very welded together as a unit. His argument was that the house was all of theirs. They all lived there."

For what it is worth, James Oglesby was a resident of the 2100 block of Bancroft Place during the early 1970s and he is quite certain that Nader also lived on his street. One evening, while he was out walking his dogs, he saw a car pull up with Nader as a passenger. The car just sat there for the longest time with the engine idling. "I am sure he knew me from the neighborhood," recalls Oglesby. "So I thought to myself 'Fine, I'm just going to play this waiting game.' Finally, he got out of the car, put a briefcase on the side of his face, and dashed past me into the house."

NADER COULD BE VERY CAGEY. If there was a topic that was truly off limits, it was his love life, or lack thereof. GM had delved into this topic with disastrous consequences—for the company and its reputation. As of 1971, with Nader at a zenith, reporters were generally afraid to even inquire where he lived or what he really did for fun. No one was about to make inquiries about possible partners.

Compounding matters, Nader himself remained incredibly cautious. The GM experience had taught him how treacherous an adversary could be. He did not want to give even the appearance of impropriety. Some believe that Nader was burned by the whole GM imbroglio and swore off romance. Then again, he did not really date during high school or college, either.

The upshot: Nader was the most public of figures, yet press accounts contained no hints, not even the vaguest innuendo, about romantic interests. Nader was a bachelor—end of story.

Even so, close associates had their suspicions. Many thought that Nader might be carrying on a secret interoffice romance with Joan Claybrook. Claybrook was a divorcée. It was noted that she blushed in his presence, echoed his manner of speaking, enthusiastically adopted his viewpoints. The two often traveled together.

But if some of the Nader's Raiders had their private suspicions, they were very protective of Nader. Literally thousands of articles on Nader were written during the early 1970s and there were a half dozen biographies—yet nary a one linked Nader to anyone. The silence would finally be broken in a *Washington Post Magazine* article dated July 23, 1989, in which a passing reference was made to "occasional rumors" of a relationship with Claybrook.

Most likely, the paucity of press accounts owes to the fact that the rumored relationship really was nothing more than a rumor. Speaking years later, in 2001, former Nader's Raiders found it easier to let their guard down. Beverly Moore allowed: "We always thought he was having sex with Joan Claybrook. But we never had any evidence whatsoever."

Far more intriguing than a minor-league sex scandal (Nader and Claybrook were unmarried, consenting adults, big deal) is what might be termed an antisex scandal. For every former Raider who thinks Claybrook and Nader were an item, two are convinced that Nader simply lacks the usual human appetites.

Lowell Dodge says: "Close as I was—and I was for four or five years—I never saw any signs of any personal interest in close relationships with other people, men or women. Ralph's thrill is taking the outrageous situation and translating it into an 'I gotcha.' That's as close as he comes to a sexual experience, I believe."

Peter Petkas concurs: "Here's a man so devoted to his work that some of the things that normally motivate people were sublimated. There are people like that in history—Joan of Arc, for one—whose normal human impulses are redirected."

Who knows? What is certain is that Nader was able to get considerable mileage out of an apparently moribund love life. It became another part of the Nader mystique. As Anne Zill, another former Raider, recalls: "He had very little private life, and he traded on that fact. It helped to preserve his image."

NADER'S PUBLIC IMAGE WAS truly enviable: hardworking, dedicated, brimming with integrity, a Washington insider, but also an effective outside critic, name recognition approaching 100 percent, and dogged by no scandals, sexual or otherwise. In short, he was the perfect political candidate.

Going back to 1968, people had been urging Nader to run for the Senate. When Christopher Dodd of Connecticut lost his reelection bid in 1970, many felt that the seat could have been Nader's for the asking. But Nader showed no interest.

Harrison Wellford, first executive director of Nader's Center for the Study of Responsive Law, has the following recollection: "At various times we talked about him running for the Senate from Connecticut. Ralph felt that having to respond to one constituency when he had the whole world at his doorstep was limiting. He felt at that time—which was true—that he was more important than any senator."

Come 1971, Nader was receiving his first calls to even higher office. There were some who believed that he would be an ideal challenger against Richard Nixon in 1972. Mike Royko was a writer for the *Chicago Daily News*. In one of his columns, he included a mail-in form with the names of five presidential possibilities: Ted Kennedy, George McGovern, Muskie, Humphrey, and Nader. A couple weeks later he wrote up the results. He had received 2,067 responses: 1,614 for Nader, 148 for Muskie, 42 for Kennedy, 41 for McGovern, and 11 for Humphrey. Another 211 voters had written in other names.

Royko marveled at the results: "I've never received that much mail about any political figure I've written about except when the readers suggested one of them be put behind bars. . . . Throughout the letters ran a common theme: Nader is honest; Nader cares about ordinary people; Nader won't sell out the people for the good of a political party."

NADER WAS EVEN OFFERED the candidacy by an upstart third party, fittingly known as the New Party. The New Party had been founded in 1968, the day after Eugene McCarthy's defeat in the Democratic primary. More than one thousand disillusioned Democrats had met at the University of Chicago to lay the groundwork for a new party that would "provide an alternative for those who were no longer willing to compromise their views or vote for the 'lesser of evils' candidates."

Over the July Fourth weekend in 1971, the New Party leadership convened at a left-wing political confab held near Albuquerque, New Mexico, on a homestead surrounding an adobe house. Sessions were held outdoors. Attendees arrived in VW minibuses and sat Indian-style listening to calls to abolish the CIA and institute a "thirty-hour workweek at forty-hour pay."

Benjamin Spock—the noted baby-book writer and antiwar activist—was the main speaker. He suggested that an alliance of progressive parties could provide an alternative to the Democrats and Republicans. "The two major parties haven't had the courage and forthrightness to get out of the abominable war in Vietnam," he said. "They have failed abysmally to represent the American people."

Gore Vidal—controversial author, distant cousin of Al Gore, and cochairman of the New Party—suggested Nader would be the perfect candidate in 1972. "He is ideal in that he presents a cold-blooded analysis of what's wrong and he offers solutions, which you can't say about the conventional politicians."

Vidal would continue to raise Nader's name while traveling around the country, building support for the New Party. Back at the party's DuPont Circle headquarters—a mere two blocks from Nader's own Center—operatives mailed out "Nader for President" bumper stickers. It was a strange medium, given Nader's aversion to the auto industry.

The New Party even crafted a rather lame campaign song, hoping to entice Nader.

> There's nothing wrong with the land; it's the best
> But I've taken it for granted like the rest
> So as a good-intentioned resident
> Who up to now has been hesitant

I say it's time we had the best man under the sun
For President.
Nader's the one!

BUT NADER REFUSED THE New Party's entreaties, even those set to music. Nader could not be swayed. Instead, the New Party had to settle for a ticket of Spock for president and, for vice president, Julius Hobson, a civil rights leader from Washington, D.C.

Mark Green—later a politician himself—spoke to Nader frequently about politics and the presidency during this time period. He has the following observation: "People frequently urged Ralph to run, first for the Senate, then president. I'm talking about the early '70s, when he could have easily had a Senate seat and could have been a competitor in the Democratic primaries if he chose to run.

"I believe, at the end of the day, he knew his skills and his limitations. He knew he had a historic role to play as an independent, brilliant national Jiminy Cricket. Seeking and holding political office would be a real straitjacket. It would require a level of fund-raising and compromise and insincerity that were really anathema to his natural gifts."

Marcus Raskin, a friend of Nader's, also happened to be a theoretician for the New Party. He spoke privately with Nader about the party's invitation: "I think Ralph Nader was not ready to change his persona in society at that time, his persona being a representative in Washington of citizens, and someone who was beyond politics."

In talking to his friend, Raskin learned of one other major concern. Nader certainly did not want to run for president in 1972 on a third-party ticket. He feared that if he drew enough votes, he might pull support away from the Democratic candidate. Thus might he unwittingly help throw the election to Nixon.

—12—

The Raid on Congress

As Nader was fond of saying, he preferred to work *on* government rather than *in* government. And so it was that a man often considered a senatorial shoo-in decided instead to conduct a full-on investigation of Congress. That was to be his next raid. It would be along the lines of other raids he had launched—versus the Federal Trade Commission, say, or the nursing home industry; in terms of scope, logistics, and cost, however, it would be vastly, wildly, absurdly more ambitious.

The time was right, Nader believed, to peer into the inner workings of Congress. It was his contention that the power of the legislative branch was in deep decline versus that of the executive. Nixon, nearing the end of his first term, had managed a massive power grab and had succeeded in transforming his office into a so-called imperial presidency.

When Congress voted appropriations for highways and such, Nixon was in the habit of impounding the funds on occasion, claiming that he had the authority not to spend federal money. He had even usurped war making, traditionally a congressional responsibility. By declaring the invasion of Cambodia an "incursion" rather than a "war," he had found a loophole, thereby avoiding the oversight of Congress. While this was going on, members busied themselves with such weighty issues as admission fees to national parks. It showed the country's legislators to be ineffectual and grossly out of touch.

Nader addressed these and other concerns in an article, "Making Congress Work," that appeared in the *New Republic* on August 21, 1971. Congress was overrun by lobbyists, enslaved to special interests, warped by lax campaign finance rules. It was an aristocracy, a plutocracy, a gerontocracy, and about any other negative "-acy" one could dream up. "Yet it is the only Congress we have," he concluded. "It has immense authority and it distributes over $220 billion a year. It can't be ignored. It can be improved and made more responsive to the people's needs."

While Nader made his case publicly in articles and speeches, close associates suspected that he also harbored more private gripes. Some pointed out that the liberal consensus in Congress that had been so receptive to him throughout the Johnson years was fast evaporating. Perhaps an investigation of Congress might help nudge the increasingly centrist Democrats back to the left.

Others thought this was revenge, pure and simple. Nader was the prime mover behind a number of pieces of legislation. Yet many of these laws had not been enforced to Nader's satisfaction; in his words, they were "no-law laws." Maybe a raid would punish Congress for scaling back some of the bills he favored and passing toothless legislation. He was also concerned about campaign financing. Corporations had the power to buy members of Congress, he felt, ultimately to the detriment of consumers.

Whatever his motive, it was a shocking move. Nader had worked so very effectively with Congress, and now he planned to investigate the entire institution.

Jim Turner remembers a dinner with a group of Raiders during which Nader expressed his frustration. "You know, when I first started," said Nader, "I thought if only I can get a paragraph in *Time* magazine, we can turn this whole thing around. Now I have a cover of *Time* and a cover of *Newsweek*. But they're still doing all the same bad things they have always done. Okay then, let's go after government in a big way."

On November 2, 1971, during a luncheon at the National Press Club, Nader announced his latest raid. Christened the Congress Project, it aimed to investigate every single representative or senator who was up for reelection the next term—484 of the 535 members. To allay any suspicions of partisanship or bias, Nader announced that he would neither take foundation money nor use charitable contributions to his Public Citizen organization. Rather, he would finance the entire endeavor out of his own pocket. Nader said that he planned to devote a whole year to the Congress Project. Findings would be released during the autumn of 1972, in time to help the electorate decide whom to keep in office and whom to vote out.

Robert Fellmeth—then twenty-six years old and one of the original seven Raiders—was named project director. Another dozen of Nader's associates signed on full-time, including Joan Claybrook. But the bulk of the work was to be saved for the summer of 1972. Nader planned to hire one thousand Raiders, where previously he had never hired more than one hundred or so. To accommodate this expanded workforce, Nader rented the entire top floor of a building at 2000 P Street. This was to be a massive undertaking made by a bunch of college students on summer break—a veritable "children's crusade," as one critic remarked.

Step one was preparatory work, tons of it. Quite a bit had to be in place before a battalion of summer Naderites could be unleashed on Congress. Several hundred volunteers were solicited—mostly housewives and retirees—in the far-flung districts of the 484 reelection seekers. The volunteers were charged with gathering census data and obtaining materials from local chambers of commerce that could be used to create portraits of each district.

Meanwhile, Fellmeth put together a questionnaire that will live in infamy. It was ninety-six pages long and featured 633 questions—actually closer to a thousand if one counted the "subquestions." Members of Congress would be asked to compose policy statements on thirty-seven topics ranging from abortion to drug abuse. "I had absolutely no clue," recalls Fellmeth with a chuckle. "I guess you could say I wasn't very sensitive about time demands or anything."

The plan was to assemble preliminary files on each of the 484 congressional quarries. When the summer Raiders arrived, they could dive into the thick of the project: interviewing members of Congress, writing and editing, and doing the extensive clerical work necessary to produce 484 individual profiles.

Grossman Publishers—the company that had issued *Unsafe at Any Speed* and many of the Nader reports—was slated to print the profiles. They would be available individually. Though it posed a distribution challenge, the goal was to make the appropriate profiles available in the appropriate districts. Say someone in Massachusetts wanted to learn more about Teddy Kennedy in advance of casting a vote in the 1972 election. Well, his profile—and that of other Massachusetts legislators—would be available in local bookstores. Grossman also planned to make bound volumes of all 484 profiles available to whoever might be interested.

APPLICATIONS FLOODED IN FOR the summer Raider slots. For the most demanding positions, such as profile writers, Fellmeth and company actually interviewed the candidates. As for the other, more pedestrian tasks, it was necessary only to reach into the ridiculously deep well of applicants and extract a résumé, any résumé: Harvard law student, recent history major from Princeton, senior at Berkeley.

Sarah Glazer, newly graduated from the University of Chicago, landed a plum job as a profile writer. During her interview, she remembers that Nader's associates emphasized the project's potential for grand historical impact: "It was going to be in bookstores and on newsstands. The project was going to make it possible for people to actually change government by voting based on real insider knowledge about the members of Congress. To a young person like me, it was a very inspiring idea."

Congress Project hirees were to receive roughly $500 for a summer's work. Because this was the largest crop of Raiders ever, hailing from all over the United States, accommodations were made available at George Washington University's dormitories. For those who selected this option, room and board were to be subtracted from their already meager paychecks. Whenever possible, people were encouraged to join the project on a volunteer basis. After all, Nader was stuck with the entire tab.

On June 3, 1972, Nader held an orientation for the Congress Project at a George Washington University dorm. He arrived in his typical state of mild dishevelment, wearing a dark blue suit, light-blue shirt, and a 1950s vintage skinny tie. But the atmosphere was electric. Very few of the young hires had actually met Nader, and this would be a first brush with a genuine American hero, the man who had inspired them to spend a summer in Washington.

Nader began by comparing the project to the Wright Brothers' first flight and asserting the project would exceed "everything we've ever done before." This was going to be hard work, Nader explained. He urged his charges to emulate him and to adopt a rigorous work ethic. "Many of you are too smart for the courses you're going through," he said, "but let me assure you, you'll be really sweating, literally and figuratively."

Nader warned against pot smoking. It was illegal and if anyone got busted it would reflect poorly on the project. He ended by stressing that the 484 profiles simply had to be completed by Labor Day. Granted, that was an extremely tight deadline. "If it's not met," he said, "there's no tomorrow."

Nader's Raiders, class of '72, dove into this stupendous new challenge. Many were shocked to find that they had been instantly invested with a great deal of power. "I was twenty-four and I didn't know anything," recalls John Immerwahr, who took time off from teaching at Oakland University in Michigan and enlisted as a volunteer. "But all I had to say was, 'I work for Ralph Nader.' Everybody would get nervous, like today if *60 Minutes* showed up at your door."

Even so, the project met with a mixed reception. Members of Congress may have quaked at the prospect of being investigated by Ralph Nader, but not all of them chose to cooperate. Previous Nader raids had mostly focused on federal agencies and the small-fry career bureaucrats who staffed them. They tended to be pretty easy marks compared to members of Congress, many of whom were polished, powerful, and schooled in techniques for keeping the Raiders at bay.

A case in point is what transpired when the Raider assigned to write a profile of B. Everett Jordan (D–North Carolina) called to set up an interview.

"The senator just doesn't have any time on his schedule between now and August," his secretary explained.

"Fine," said the Raider. "How about an appointment in August?"

"He hasn't started a schedule for August yet, so that's impossible."

Thus was Senator Jordan able to duck the interview.

Certain legislators granted interviews and dutifully answered every question. They were friendly, forthcoming, leisurely, verbose, erudite. Invariably, such performances left the summer interns dazzled—until they went back over their notes and realized that absolutely nothing had been revealed. Others simply stonewalled. "I'm not going to give you anything," a grinning Joe Waggonner (D–Louisiana) told the writer assigned to profile him.

Congressional liberals, oddly enough, tended to be hardest to crack. Many of them had worked closely with Nader on various projects over the years. Now they were the targets of a Nader raid. "The conservative members tended to be easier to deal with," recalls Fred Khedouri, who signed onto the project fresh out of University of Chicago. "Liberal Democrats perceived a betrayal. We were supposed to be on their side. They did not appreciate being scrutinized."

Meanwhile, the 633-question survey was winning few fans. It took about ten hours to complete and included such queries as No. 370: "Do you believe that Members of Congress should have to disclose publicly all aspects of their personal wealth or financial interests?" and No. 415: "If you were defeated in the next election, what occupation or activity would you take up?"

Joel Broyhill, a Republican congressman from Virginia, complained to the press that the questionnaire "borders on arrogance." He added that it "must be considered as an unwarranted intrusion on the duties and responsibilities that a congressman and his staff owes to the constituency he represents." Broyhill concluded: "This is a great imposition that will benefit only one person—Nader."

All told, sixty-three members of Congress refused to answer the questionnaire, submit to an interview, or both. In such cases, the profiles had to be drawn up from existing sources, such as press accounts. It is a tribute to Nader's power that the remaining 421 chose to cooperate. Of course, many of them only filled out partial questionnaires or prevaricated wildly during their interviews.

IN SOME WAYS, THIS was the least of the project's challenges. As Nader promised, the workload was onerous. Sarah Glazer recalls that the moment she arrived at her George Washington University dorm room, she had an inkling of what the summer held. It was eerily quiet, save for people typing away. There were no pranks or Frisbees flying down the hallways, and certainly no pot smoking. "You had so much work to get done that you worked around the clock," she recalls. "People were working these twelve-hour days, no weekends." The joke among the 1972 crew became "What congressman did you interview today?"

Only about fifty of the summer Raiders had been handed the most esteemed job, profile writer. Each of them was charged with writing nine profiles, approximately thirty pages apiece, double-spaced and typed (in the long-ago days before word processing). First drafts were to be rigorously footnoted, so that editors could see the sourcing. A typical profile was supposed to have between 150 and 200 footnotes, though one came in with 452. Summer interns with less glamorous tasks—production, research, clerical—had equally crushing workloads. It was not very far into the summer before people were falling desperately behind.

Joan Claybrook took on the task of whipping the writers into shape. She posted a notice that writers would be docked $50 for each profile they failed to produce. And she began placing late-night phone calls to laggards, a nod to one of Nader's most effective techniques.

The writers did not respond well. "It was apparent to me that Joan Claybrook had Ralph Nader's ear," says Anne Zill, a fledgling journalist in Philadelphia before she signed on to the project. "But she was guarded, and had a demeanor that was untrusting. The project had a kind of corporate attitude, a GM-like attitude, ironically. Her style was to keep cards close, not to be open or collaborative."

In turn, Claybrook, Fellmeth, and other more seasoned Nader associates who headed up the project were often surprised at the naïveté of the writing team. The writers, it was felt, should have come to the project with a better knowledge of the workings of Congress. Explaining elementary points of procedure to them was growing wearisome.

The project was quickly devolving. As Peter Schuck, a one-time Nader Raider, recalls: "It was a massive undertaking, understaffed and underresourced. It relied almost entirely on people who had very little experience on the Hill, whose knowledge of politics was mostly from textbooks, and who were given assignments that exceeded their levels of competence. Mostly, it was young people who had nothing to offer except their raw intelligence and boundless energy."

Frustrated, the profile writers decided to hold a beef session. It was to take place at a George Washington University dorm and was meant exclusively for them. But Claybrook learned about it and showed up. That got everyone present quite exercised.

One writer complained: "The word that people will be cut money really offends me. If people can only do six [profiles] and they've really been working, I think that's really unfair."

Another lamented: "Try to write thirty pages on Chalmers Wiley of Ohio. He hasn't done anything in his life."

Claybrook took it all in before concluding: "I'll just have to tell Ralph your feelings."

The writers were growing restless. To address their concerns, Nader called a meeting scheduled for July 19. He led off by inquiring whether any members of the media were present. Apparently none were, so he pressed forward.

"The study is now at a crossroads," he said. "There is always a dead point, a slump. . . . Do the best you can. But if you keep saying to yourself you can't do it, then you won't finish. You can only loosen the standards so much, otherwise it becomes meaningless. . . . I really think you can do it. Skeptical ones should be careful about contagioning others. If you have a problem try to keep it to yourself. It's [the project] like a fragile vase."

Nader did, however, agree to lower the number of profiles from nine to eight and tacked an extra week onto the deadline. He also announced that he would hire some additional profile writers on a freelance basis. Bolstered by a few choice words and a few small concessions from Nader himself, the project lurched into August.

AROUND MIDNIGHT, ON AUGUST 3, 1972, the telephone rang at the Congress Project's headquarters on P Street. It was answered by Andy Winer, just another of the legion of hires that summer.

"Hello, Congress Project," he said in a comical singsong voice.

"May I speak to Ralph Nader, please."

Winer explained that Nader was not around and asked who was calling.

"Well, this is George McGovern. . . "

This prompted Winer to put down the receiver and begin looking for Claybrook, Fellmeth, or any other adult who might be present.

Meanwhile, Jane Glickman, another summer Raider, picked up the receiver. "Senator, you don't know me," she said, "but I just wanted to say hi."

It was truly a children's crusade.

Winer returned, unable to find anyone who might know Nader's whereabouts. He took a message.

The next morning, Nader returned the call. As it turned out, McGovern wanted to offer Nader the vice president's slot on the 1972 Democratic ticket. Thomas Eagleton, McGovern's running mate, had recently dropped out of the campaign due to the revelation that he had sought electroshock therapy for depression.

Nader declined McGovern's invitation. He was registered in Connecticut as an independent, same as his father. To Nathra, he had given his solemn promise that he would remain an independent. "If Ralph ever allowed his name to be identified with one party or the other," Nathra once said, "it would be the biggest disappointment of my lifetime. Because both parties sell the country very cheap." Ultimately, McGovern tapped Sargent Shriver.

MCGOVERN ASKING NADER TO be his running mate was a nice little diversion. But presently another Raider revolt was brewing. In early August, Nader made a decision to put out a quickie paperback. It was meant as a teaser, designed to draw mass attention to the 484 profiles that composed the larger Congress Project. Three long-time Naderites—James Fallows, Mark Green, and David Zwick—were assigned to write the book, drawing on the research of everyone else involved.

This infuriated the summer Raiders. They were concerned that a quickie paperback would steal their thunder. Who then would want to buy data-laden profiles of individual members of Congress? There was also a feeling that this was a sellout on Nader's part. He seemed to be suggesting that people would not have the attention span for detailed individual profiles. But that was the project's original selling point: arm voters with reams of facts and figures.

Nader had managed to attract an army of idealistic young people to the project. Now that idealism was being focused inward, on Nader and his organization. "These were people who were purists," recalls project leader Fellmeth. "They wanted to stand on principle. If they found something they thought was wrong, by god, they were going to stand up. Obviously, the very organization they're part of is the first place they're going to examine with a purist's eye. I don't have a problem with that as long as they don't sabotage it."

Some of the profile writers now threatened to quit. A number of them vowed to withhold their research findings from Fallows, Green, and Zwick. "A lot of people felt frustrated," recalls Daniel Taubman, who joined the project after his first year of Harvard law. "People worried that their work was going to go for naught. We had to spend all summer doing grunt work. All the glory was going to go to a few people close to Nader."

On August 8 Nader called another meeting, hoping to quell the summer's second rebellion. This time, the tone was very different. People who were present recall that Nader made scant attempt to inspire the troops. Instead, he appeared merely to be irritated. He did not yell, barely raised his voice even. But his mood was palpable.

"Let's get it out in the open," Nader said, according to Taubman's detailed notes of the meeting. "I don't want you to be discomfited. If you want to leave, leave. If you don't want to leave, don't. But let's get on with it.

"Look, I'm not an innocent in this area. I know how to use the press. I know what I'm doing. This book will enhance the project. I have enough problems with a minuscule budget as it is—let alone a roomful of critical academic peers. The decision to print the book depends on my judgment. If you don't agree with my judgment, if you doubt it so deeply, don't cooperate! Look, this is the real issue. If this book doesn't come out, chances of publishing your stuff are almost zero. We have to create a market. We have to attempt to make Congress readable."

And that was that—there would be no concessions this time around.

Fallows, Green, and Zwick holed up in a basement at 1800 M Street and in six weeks, working virtually around the clock, they churned out the paperback, entitled *Who Runs Congress?* Reputedly, it was edited in a single day.

Meanwhile, the youth brigade assigned to the broader Congress Project scampered to meet its impending deadline. Completing 484 profiles was an exercise in uncontrolled chaos, and with each passing day, the workload grew more insurmountable. Morale—which had sank throughout the summer—hit new lows. "We knew we had an imperfect product," recalls Anne Zill.

CRITICS TENDED TO AGREE when at last they got a peek at both finished products. The first printing of the quickie paperback was an impressive 275,000, and the book actually made some national best-seller lists. But unlike previous Nader efforts, it was not popular with reviewers.

Time magazine slammed the book: "It is tendentious, hostile and superficial and contains nary a footnote to indicate its sources. Hastily edited, the book is flawed by a number of factual errors and incorrect data."

Another review, syndicated in the Knight Ridder newspapers, was equally harsh: "The average American is Nader's target, and the way the book will repel is by its totally combative approach. It starts from the basic activist bias that new is better and change is best."

As for the 484 individual profiles, merely completing them was a feat. Combined, they totaled 13,720 pages. "It was a very substantial work," says Claybrook, "and it was way ahead of its time." She points out that the project delved into campaign finance, a topic not nearly as in vogue back then. The project also provided a record of how members of Congress had voted on certain key issues, going back as far as twenty years in some cases. This, in the days before the widespread use of computer databases.

Unfortunately, the profiles did not become available to the public until October 22, 1972. That was much too close to election day and undercut the original plan of fostering an informed electorate. As feared, there were also distribution problems. Getting the correct profiles into the proper local bookstores and newsstands ended up being a real challenge.

To top it off, critics were underwhelmed. Where *Who Runs Congress?* had at least been provocative, the 484 profiles were viewed as a kind of bland civics exercise, and factually suspect to boot. "To the surprise of many persons who have followed Mr. Nader's numerous investigations of government and business conduct, the profiles contained no sensational revelations or charges," asserted the *New York Times* review.

Apparently, the members of Congress had succeeded where the FTC, FDA, ICC, GM, and ITT—a whole alphabet soup of federal agencies and corporations—had failed. They had succeed in stymieing the Raiders.

The *Denver Post* described the project as "hastily, frantically thrown-together writings that were rushed to the publisher for release in the peak interest of an election year." The paper also catalogued a few errors before asking: "How can the entire product—which has been lavishly described as the most authoritative study of its kind ever undertaken—be taken seriously as fact?"

A conservative-leaning publication called *Human Events* even alluded to Nader's original comparison of the Congress Project and the Wright Brothers' flight at Kitty Hawk. The reviewer concluded that the project was "under-powered, highly unstable, off course, barely got off the ground and after being up for only a few seconds has come crashing left-wing first back to earth."

Predictably, Nader's latest effort also met with a hostile reception from the legislators themselves. Launching a raid on Congress had been an act of supreme hubris. More than previous projects, this one had to be dead-on. In order to find favor with the press, the project really needed to feature research that was both bold and impeccable. When it came up short, legislators seized the opportunity to pick it apart: questioning the overall accuracy, dissecting Nader's motives, speculating about whether he had lost his touch.

Jonathan Bingham, a congressional Democrat who represented the Bronx, told the *New York Times*: "Mr. Nader's workmanship on a few of the factual details in the recent report on me isn't much better than he said General Motors was on the Corvair."

Representative William Minshall (R-Ohio) wrote to Nader: "While I have long respected your courageous fight on behalf of consumers, I must join your other critics who believe you have now spread yourself too thin and are relying upon too many eager, but untrained, youthful aides. They have done you a disservice on this project. Their work is too distorted to be susceptible to accurate correction."

G. William Whitehurst, a Republican representative from Virginia, declared: "My overall impression is that it was too hastily done, and from the basis of too many preconceptions. . . . My own feeling is that in the long run it is the credibility of Ralph Nader, not that of Congress, which is going to suffer as a result of this report."

The Congress Project was Nader's first real misstep. Earlier contretemps—such as the 1970 attacks on Senators Muskie and Ribicoff—had barely registered, but this would actually affect his public image. It damaged his reputation with two key constituencies, Congress and the press.

Looking back, Nader also admits that he may have put too much pressure on his young hires. "We expected them to do more than what was reasonably possible given their experience," he says. In addition, Nader took a direct hit to the pocketbook. The final price tag for the raid on Congress: $500,000. Forever after, Nader would refer to the project as "my C-5A"—a reference to the grossly over-budget transport plane on which Ernest Fitzgerald blew the whistle.

THERE IS ONE FINAL brief chapter to the tale of the ambitious but ill-starred Congress Project. Late in the autumn of 1972, Nader was attending a function at the Kennedy Center. Also present was one of the countless people who had worked for him during that past summer. This particular ex-Raider—like so many of the young people involved in the project—was frustrated by the working conditions and disappointed in the outcome. As he nursed a cognac, he became increasingly agitated. Finally, he picked up a glass of water. He walked over to the table where Nader was sitting and threw it in Nader's face. Then he walked away without saying a word.

THE CONGRESS PROJECT WILL go down as an example of Nader's capacity to spread himself too thin. Yet he was also given to bursts of near-demonic focus. These seem like contradictory impulses. But in a way, they are simply two facets of Nader, the pragmatic idealist.

Nader aimed to define his consumer agenda broadly, poking into every nook, touching on every aspect of American life. He was willing to delve into topics as diverse as airline safety and pension rights. If Congress was growing less responsive to the electorate, if it was passing fewer consumer-friendly laws—well then, he would simply have to investigate the entire institution. That was the idealist in him, capable of grandeur, ever at risk of overreaching.

But Nader also had a pragmatic bent and truly enjoyed getting mired in the details. In an effort to see a matter through, he possessed this impulse to keep revisiting and reevaluating, hammering away at the fine points until they were subatomic. Even into the early 1970s, he remained thoroughly preoccupied with his first adversary, General Motors.

It would seem that Nader had soundly trounced the company. He had received a public apology from CEO Roche; the Ribicoff hearings had spurred legislation that forced GM—and other auto companies—to install seat belts, padded dashes, and other safety features; the Corvair line had been dropped; he had helped organize the company's own shareholders against it; and Nader had beaten GM in a landmark invasion-of-privacy suit and had been awarded $425,000. Yet Nader continued to go after GM with a vengeance.

It had long been Nader's contention that Corvair was the product of not only faulty engineering but also criminally negligent engineering. Allegedly the GM brass was aware of design flaws and went ahead and sold dangerous vehicles to an unsuspecting public anyway. Nader claimed there were an array of sources—insiders, secret films, and GM proving-ground tests—that he could draw on to make his case. Perhaps this would prompt an investigation of GM.

From the instant the auto safety bill passed in 1966, Nader had worked tirelessly to find a receptive audience. He sent letters to the media, fellow consumer advocates, and officials at government agencies. And he continually dogged members of Congress, including Ribicoff. At one point he told the *Washington Post* that the senator had "literally closed shop on auto safety."

Ribicoff was not pleased. He had been puzzled the first time Nader had taken a jab at him, regarding the Consumer Protection Agency bill. When it came to auto safety, he felt he had impeccable credentials. As governor of Connecticut in the mid-1950s, he had cracked down on speeding and drunk driving, earning him the sobriquet "Mr. Auto Safety." Of course, he had worked closely with Nader on federal legislation in 1966.

Ribicoff was also keen on delving into a number of issues. In the years following the auto safety hearings, he had become heavily involved in foreign relations and health care reform. He was not about to be bullied into devoting the sum of his senatorial energy to the issue of auto safety, actually to the even narrower issue of GM.

But Nader kept after Ribicoff, sending him a barrage of lengthy letters. Often they were accompanied by page upon page of highly technical exhibits. In one letter, Nader asserted: "Now comes decisive evidence which reveals a labyrinthic and systematic intra-company collusion, involving high General Motors officials, to sequester and suppress company produced data and films proving the Corvair (1960–63 models) dangerously unstable."

What finally grabbed Ribicoff's attention was Nader's assertion that GM had lied about this matter during testimony before his subcommittee. This was a serious allegation. In essence, Nader was charging that GM execs not only knew that the Corvair was dangerous prior to putting it on the market (bad) but also lied about this fact during the 1966 hearings (doubly bad). Ribicoff assigned the task of investigating the matter to two of his staffers, Robert Wager and John Koskinen.

Over a two-year period, 1971–1973, Wager and Koskinen devoted a substantial portion of their time to this effort. Basically, they agreed to investigate any lead provided by Nader and his associate Gary Sellers. As was his wont, Nader often called in the middle of the night.

Wager and Koskinen dutifully followed up. They traveled all over the country and spent hundreds of hours interviewing sources. They pored over documents, at Nader's behest, and immersed themselves in the fine points of Corvair safety. But nothing panned out.

For example, Sellers suggested a meeting with Mauri Rose, a three-time Indianapolis 500 winner. Upon retirement from racing, Rose had gone to work test-driving Corvairs. He had since moved on from this job as well. Sellers promised that Rose would be an ideal insider source because he was an experienced driver, but also one that was not exactly wed to GM. No doubt, he would be able to provide some telling insight about proving-ground tests, and what GM executives knew in advance of marketing the Corvair. Wager and Koskinen traveled to Detroit to meet the one-time Indy driver. To their great surprise, Rose said he thought the Corvair handled extremely well. He had even bought one for his daughter.

Meanwhile, the secret films and suppressed test-drive documents never materialized. The deeper Ribicoff's staffers dug, the more convinced they became that there existed no "labyrinthic and systematic intra-company collusion." In fact, they grew to believe that while the Corvair might have handling problems under certain conditions, such as improperly inflated tires, it was not really defective. More to the point, they found no evidence that GM executives had thoughtlessly put a car on the market despite defects, handling problems, whatever—a conclusion that in turn foreclosed the possibility that executives had lied about the matter during congressional testimony. Predictably, this conclusion left Nader extremely galled. Soon the investigation took on an angels-on-pinheads aspect, as Nader sent Ribicoff's staffers scurrying after information on Corvair rebound camber angles and the like.

As a young congressional staffer during the 1966 hearings, Wager was awed by Nader. But he found this later experience quite disillusioning. "He could not let go of the Corvair issue," says Wager. "He was fixated. And if you didn't accept or believe the same things he did, you were either stupid or venal. Those were the only two reasons you could possibly disagree with him, because he had morality and righteousness on his side.

"Nader's greatest strength became a weakness," he adds. "His zealotry, his intensity, simply does not wear well."

Ultimately Wager wrote up a thirty-thousand-word account of the investigation. He filled it with lengthy technical discussions and charts, like a Raider report. Ribicoff entered the entire write-up into the *Congressional Record*, dated March 27, 1973. This was a way of showing faith in his staff. And it was also a subtle kiss-off to the pushiest of his Connecticut constituents.

—13—

Kingmaker

DONALD ETRA—A RAIDER DURING THE early 1970s—remembers being present when Nader learned that one of his projects had suffered a major setback. "For about a nanosecond, he had a look of disappointment," says Etra. "Then he went back to work."

This is a telling anecdote. It speaks to a certain quality of unflappability on Nader's part. He may have taken his first public stumble with the Congress Project. He had even managed to alienate Senator Ribicoff, a key figure in launching his career. But spiraling into self-doubt was just not Nader's way.

"I have a very stable set of purposes and convictions," he once told the writer Robert Buckhorn. "I know it is going to be a rocky road so I am not ruffled very easily. I am sort of programmed to anticipate all these things, and I try to do what I can to prepare myself. For example, I don't get all clutched up or nervous if things go wrong. I have an inner consistency that carries me through."

Nader had worked effectively with Congress before and felt certain he would again—it was simply a matter of identifying compelling new issues. For Nader, it was always about the issues. Between 1974 and 1976, he threw his considerable energy into two new ones: making government information more accessible and making nuclear power less acceptable.

BY THE MID-1970S, NO ONE had a better grasp of federal document-access rules than Nader. He had been on the scene for nearly a decade and had managed to poke into nearly every corner of the government. Invariably, Nader raids were accompanied by requests that a targeted agency hand over certain specified documents. The requests met with varied results. But over time, Nader developed a thorough understanding of the parameters of document access: what types of records were available, what was classified, and, importantly, what techniques agencies could use to stall or to avoid handing over information.

Guidelines for document access were originally spelled out in the Freedom of Information Act (FOIA). It was signed into law by President Johnson—amid much patriotic hubbub—on July 4, 1966. "This legislation springs from one of our most essential principles," stated LBJ. "A democracy works best when people have all the information that the security of the nation permits. No one should be able to pull curtains of secrecy around decisions which can be revealed without injury to the public interest."

From the outset, the law was designed to address competing tensions between openness and national security. Thus the original act featured nine exemptions. Documents that revealed sensitive information about the nation's defense capabilities were to remain classified. Ditto for documents that pertained to ongoing legal investigations. Under certain circumstances, even seemingly innocuous intraagency memos were protected. The idea was that government officials would clam up, and even casual communication would be hindered, if every last missive—spelling out an agency's vacation policy, say, or announcing a promotion—were open to public scrutiny.

Of course, the original act left agencies with broad latitude to withhold documents. Frequently Nader or his Raiders would request a document, only to be told that it fell under one of the nine exemptions. During the summer of 1969, for example, Nader dispatched a team of Raiders to investigate the Civil Aeronautics Board (CAB). Along the way, they learned about the existence of a CAB-commissioned survey that delved into consumer complaints about airline service. Supposedly the survey even named the airlines that were the worst offenders.

When the Raiders asked to see a copy, the request was denied. CAB claimed the survey might be relevant to a court case that was then under way. Therefore, it fell under FOIA's ongoing legal investigation exemption. Yet the same survey was made available to any airline that was interested. Here was a survey of consumer complaints, conducted using taxpayer dollars but available only to the airline industry.

Even when an information request was granted, Nader found that actually obtaining the documents could be a challenge. Sometimes an agency would stall for months or even years. Or it might tack on an exorbitant document-preparation fee. During a raid on the Agriculture Department, Naderites requested an internal report on the dangers of handling various pesticides. They were told they would first have to ante up a $91,840 administrative and copying fee. That put the documents out of reach, as surely as if the Agriculture Department had claimed a FOIA exemption.

It was not long before Nader had been exposed to the gamut, the variety of tactics employed by a host of government agencies. He responded in his standard fashion. He wrote articles such as one that appeared in the *Harvard Law Review* entitled "Freedom from Information." And he called press conferences, such as one on August 26, 1969, in which he asserted that the FOIA's nine exemptions are "so vast that to call them loopholes would be to indulge in the grossest kind of understatement." He concluded: "Thus the act, designed to provide citizens with tools of disclosure, has been forged into a shield against citizen access."

In 1972 Nader founded yet another of his organizations, the Freedom of Information Clearinghouse. It was under the aegis of Public Citizen's Litigation Group. The clearinghouse distributed information on the public's rights under FOIA. But job one was to litigate vigorously and often.

With an army of lawyers at his disposal, Nader was able to challenge narrow and often ridiculous interpretations of the act by various federal agencies. The Litigation Group lawyers took up a number of cases on behalf of journalists and academics who had been denied access to government records. Often these parties lacked the financial resources to wage a protracted legal battle. But if a case looked promising, Nader's lawyers would charge the client minimally, or not at all. The goal was to set precedents that would broaden the interpretation of FOIA, thereby increasing the flow of information to the public.

As Alan Morrison, head of the Litigation Group, recalls: "Ralph saw this as opening a wedge into government. He felt that information was power, that the law provided enormous access that you wouldn't otherwise have. But he also saw tremendous underuse by journalists and others. Ralph saw immediately how important the law was, and saw how important it was to litigate. Ralph understood that the more people use it [FOIA], the more gets done."

One of the most celebrated FOIA cases involved Carl Stern, a journalist for NBC, who wanted to do an investigative report on something called "Cointelpro-New Left." Allegedly this was an intelligence-gathering effort launched by FBI chief J. Edgar Hoover, designed to look into the activities of American "leftists." Allegedly it had been initiated in April 1968, in the wake of a student uprising that shut down Columbia University for several days. But this was all hearsay. The FBI was not in the habit of publicizing its initiatives.

Hungry to learn more, Stern submitted a document request to the FBI. The FBI rebuffed Stern, citing a variety of FOIA exemptions. Stern turned to his employer, NBC. But the network was unwilling to furnish the money necessary to wage a legal battle. So Stern approached Nader's sprawling advocacy empire, where he found lawyers ready to take up his case.

"People suspected there was a counterintelligence program," recalls Ronald Plesser, a one-time Nader attorney involved in the case. "But they did not know what it was or what it was supposed to do. Our position was, we don't care what you give us. We just want an organic document that establishes that the program has been set up. The FBI argued that this was classified information. How can the fact that a program exists be classified?"

Plesser and company eventually won the case—*Stern v. Richardson*—before a D.C. district court judge in 1973. "We wound up obtaining a document that was really quite extraordinary," says Plesser. "It was the first real evidence of the fact the FBI was doing these counterintelligence activities."

Stern's successful suit opened the floodgates. Other news organizations jumped on the story and made their own FOIA requests to the FBI. All manner of tawdry details emerged. Predictably, the FBI had looked into the activities of the Students for a Democratic Society and various civil rights organizations. But it had also investigated Sammy Davis Jr., Joan Baez, and labor organizer César Chávez. The revelations were extremely damaging to the FBI, and the Cointelpro-New Left program was dropped.

BY THE AUTUMN OF 1974, there was a movement afoot in Congress to amend the original Freedom of Information Act. This was partly due to the national mood. America had just gone through the wrenching experience of Watergate, and there was a sense that government secrecy was far from benign. Recently concluded congressional hearings on military surveillance of civilians and other intelligence abuses had succeeded in shaking public trust.

But congressional interest owed in no small part to Nader's efforts. "Ralph played an enormous role in evangelizing this subject," says Mark

Lynch, a former Litigation Group attorney who was heavily involved in FOIA. "Nobody knew more about it. It was a classic case of Nader synergy. Nader was on the outside, colliding with those inside Congress to create public momentum and to get legislation passed. Ralph lectured them, bullied them, and always said, 'You're not doing enough.'"

The plain fact was that government information was not flowing freely. As of 1974, the National Archive housed nearly a billion classified documents from the 1940s and 1950s, rather distant decades by then. Meanwhile, a memorandum that circulated in the Pentagon discussed the need to deem fewer documents as top secret. The only problem: The memo itself was stamped "top secret."

Senators Kennedy, Muskie, and Gary Hart (D–Colorado) pushed for amendments to FOIA. In the House the charge was led by Patsy Mink and Spark Matsunaga, Democrats from Hawaii. Mink and Matsunaga had been party to a FOIA lawsuit brought by several members of the House, seeking to obtain information about nuclear weapons tests. Congressional opponents included Strom Thurmond (R-South Carolina) and Jim Eastland, head of the Senate Judiciary Committee. They worried that relaxing rules for document access might hurt national security or law enforcement capabilities.

Nader testified frequently on FOIA and its abuses. And he kept the pressure on members of Congress, often using Lynch as his proxy. "I was the guy walking around, bugging people," recalls Lynch. "Ralph felt that if you didn't constantly stay on people they would get distracted. He would bug me and I would bug various Congressional staffers just to keep him off my back."

On October 7, 1974, Senate-House conferees put the finishing touches on a bill amending FOIA. It was submitted to President Gerald Ford, who promptly vetoed the measure. Ford shared Thurmond and Eastland's concerns about law enforcement and national security. He deemed the bill "unconstitutional and unworkable."

When Ford took over from Nixon, he promised a "good marriage" with Congress, but he was off to a rocky start. This was his thirteenth veto in just three and a half months in office. Congress was growing restive. Ultimately the veto was overridden, and the amendments became law.

FOIA in its new formulation included a number of changes. Time limits were set, granting government agencies a maximum of ten working days to respond to a request for information. There was also a prohibition against preposterous fees, such as $91,840 to obtain a report. Henceforth, agencies could only bill for actual clerical and photocopying costs. To make it easier to sue under FOIA, there was also an amendment regarding the disposition of legal fees. If a person seeking records sued a government agency and won, the agency would have to shoulder the entire cost of the lawsuit.

Of course, the bill that passed in 1974 merely contained amendments to the original—and often unworkable—1966 law. The new FOIA would still have shortcomings, as had the old FOIA. In years to come, Nader would continually fight to widen the wedge into government. Public Citizen's Litigation Group would take on a number of FOIA cases, and four—at latest count—went all the way to the Supreme Court.

LIKE DOCUMENT ACCESS, NUCLEAR energy was an issue on which Nader had already built a considerable track record by the mid-1970s. He had actually been quite early to take an interest. Back in the summer of 1970, he had sponsored a joint study with the University of Texas law review, peering into the inner workings of the Atomic Energy Commission (AEC). It is hard to imagine now, but this was during an era when the public was fairly complacent about nuclear energy. It was a confoundingly complex subject of interest and concern to only a handful of people. The near disaster at Three-Mile Island—a wake-up call for so many—was still nearly a decade in the future.

Nader did not initially approach nuclear energy from a safety standpoint. Rather, he was concerned about the way nuclear plants were regulated. The AEC had a dual mandate: to oversee nuclear plants and to promote the industry. This struck him as a clear conflict of interest. On the one hand, the AEC was supposed to monitor the activities of utilities as well as companies that built nuclear plants and equipment such as General Electric and Westinghouse. On the other hand, the AEC was supposed to tout nuclear energy at every opportunity as a clean and efficient source of electricity. In Nader's view, the AEC was parallel to the FTC, the ICC, and other targets of his investigations. It was a regulatory body that had been taken hostage by the very corporations it was supposed to police.

"You have to step back and look at Nader's worldview," says Joe Tom Easley, who as a recent graduate of University of Texas law was involved in the summer of 1970 project. "He is, shall we say, preoccupied with the issue of corporate power in this country and the lack of democracy. He is consumed by the fact that large corporations tend to have enormous power to distort the democratic process in every way. I don't think Ralph was so initially focused on safety as he was on this being another example where a handful of large corporations were perverting the democratic process by dominating a regulatory agency."

Michael Mariotte concurs. As executive director of the Nuclear Information and Resource Service, he has worked closely with Nader for many years. "One thing has held true throughout Nader's career," says Mariotte. "He has always been more interested in corporate power than in vague concepts like environmentalism, sexism, and racism. Nukes fit right in. He saw it initially as a corporate power issue. I'm not sure he saw it as an environmental issue per se."

Nuclear energy—or, more specifically, the way nuclear energy was regulated by the AEC—was simply part of Nader's evolving critique of the role of corporations in America. At least at the outset.

IN 1972 NADER WAS approached by two members of the Union of Concerned Scientists, Henry Kendall and Dan Ford. The Union of Concerned Scientists had been very early to address the issue of nuclear energy, but from a very different perspective than Nader. For them, the specifics of nuclear industry regulation were ancillary. Their big worry was the danger these plants potentially posed to humans and the environment.

Kendall and Ford were thoroughly grounded in topics such as ALAP, or "as low as practicable." This was a debate, in certain scientific circles, involving where to set a practical limit for routine radioactive emissions from nuclear plants. They were also versed in such minutiae as the exact temperature at which a plant's cooling core would experience a meltdown. These were worthy questions, but it was not easy material for the public to digest. Kendall and Ford hoped that Nader could give their message some flair, make it more accessible.

"We wanted Ralph to take the issue of nuclear power, and to colloquialize it," says Myron Cherry, then a lawyer for the Union of Concerned Scientists. "He could merely raise an issue and it would be instant news. For us to make instant news, we needed a seminal event. He could say nuclear power was bad and people believed it."

Originally, Nader had built his critique of auto safety on a foundation of work done by others—physicists, engineers, trial lawyers. Not one of them had figured out how to excite public interest, much less how to get the subject on Congress's radar. To do so was Nader's special genius. On the topic of nuclear energy, once again, he would act as a popularizer par excellence.

Always an avid reader, Nader dove into the subject's specialized literature. He steeped himself in nuclear energy as an environmental and safety issue. Over the next couple of years, he held a series of joint press conferences with the Union of Concerned Scientists. As they had hoped, Nader was able to lend his unique expository style to the highly technical nuclear debate. "This is the first time that this country has permitted development of an industry that can wipe this country out," said Nader during a press conference held on January 3, 1973. "We spend billions on defense while creating a basic vulnerability here."

BUT NADER'S MOST IMPORTANT effort was a conference called Critical Mass. It was held at the Statler Hotel in Washington, D.C., for three days beginning November 16, 1974.

Critical Mass brought together a number of notable figures including sociologist Margaret Mead, ecologist Barry Commoner, and George Wald, a Harvard biology professor and recipient in 1967 of a Nobel Prize. Robert Redford was in attendance. The conference also drew citizen groups from around the country who had been fighting against nuclear plants. In attendance were members of the New England Coalition on Nuclear Pollution, which had been taking on the Vermont Yankee power plant, among others. Also present were representatives of Northern Thunder, a group fighting plants in Wisconsin, and the Seacoast Anti-Pollution League, dedicated to challenging the Seabrook facility in New Hampshire.

Prior to the conference, these groups had communicated with one another in only the most limited fashion. The antinuclear movement, insofar as it even was a movement, was very localized and fragmentary. "There were little grassroots brush fires of concerned citizens," recalls Anthony Roisman, a lawyer involved in some seminal antinuclear battles and a Critical Mass attendee. "Many were near plants or proposed plants. But this was pre–e-mail, pre-fax. They all did their own thing, and there wasn't much networking."

The Critical Mass conference served as a kind of gathering of the antinuke tribes. As such, the focus was very much on practical matters. Workshops were held offering tips on organizing techniques. There was also discussion on how to deal with the press. David Comey, an antinuclear activist, urged the attendees to be unfailingly accurate, understating matters unless they had their facts down cold. Each attendee received a 161-page booklet assembled by Joan Claybrook and entitled *A Nuclear Catastrophe Is Too Big a Price to Pay for Our Electric Bill.*

In the interest of fair play, Nader also granted time to a couple of nuclear energy proponents. Ralph Lap, a physicist, stressed that nuclear waste should not be viewed as waste in the conventional sense. Rather, it should be thought of as a resource, as potential fuel. William Doub, a former member of the AEC, used his speech to take a direct shot at Nader. "He should confess his fallibility," said Doub, turning toward Nader who was sitting nearby on the dais. "He should admit that he is perhaps spread a bit too thin and try, by doing so, to restore public credibility in healthy technical criticism."

The nuclear industry proponents were not well received. Throughout their speeches, audience members groaned and booed. Afterward, Nader stated: "There. Now you've heard the very best they've got to offer."

As the conference progressed, one particular topic spread like wildfire among the attendees. Only a few days earlier—on November 13, 1974—Karen Silkwood had died under mysterious circumstances. It became the talk of the Critical Mass conference as attendees speculated about what might have happened.

Silkwood had worked for the Cimarron River plant near Crescent, Oklahoma. The facility, owned by Kerr-McGee Corporation, produced plutonium fuel rods for use in nuclear reactors. Silkwood was a technician in the metallography laboratory, and it was her job to provide quality control assurance. The job paid four dollars an hour.

Silkwood also served on the bargaining committee of the union that represents the nuclear industry rank and file—the Oil, Chemical and Atomic Workers International (OCAW). Kerr-McGee's recent dealings with the union had been fraught with tension.

In September 1974, Silkwood attended an OCAW meeting in Washington, D.C. One of the topics under discussion was the true dangers of plutonium. Exposure to even small amounts can cause cancer twenty or thirty years down the line. Silkwood was astounded. Kerr-McGee had been utterly negligent about setting up adequate safeguards or informing its employees about these dangers. In anticipation of an upcoming union contract negotiation, Silkwood began gathering evidence of lax plutonium handling at the Cimarron River plant.

On the night of November 13, 1974, Silkwood was on her way to meet with a reporter for the *New York Times*. She planned to share some documents regarding alleged radioactive materials safety violations on the part of Kerr-McGee. Silkwood's Honda Civic swerved off the road into a ditch and she was killed instantly. She was twenty-eight and left behind three small children.

Initially the Oklahoma Highway Patrol ruled that she had fallen asleep at the wheel. An autopsy found Quaaludes in her blood at twice the dosage necessary to produce extreme drowsiness. But then an accident reconstruction firm did an analysis showing that her car had been bumped from behind. Meanwhile, the documents she was on her way to deliver never turned up.

It was all very suspicious and left many people convinced of foul play on the part of Kerr-McGee. Silkwood's death would remain an enduring mystery and serve as the basis for a 1983 movie starring Meryl Streep and Cher.

Very few of these details were known during the 1974 Critical Mass conference. The events were simply too fresh.

Carrie Dickerson—a local activist who had been fighting the Black Fox plant in Oklahoma—was a conference attendee. Dickerson did not know Silkwood. But because Dickerson hailed from Oklahoma, same as Silkwood, she was able to call friends from home during the conference and gather scuttlebutt.

Dickerson, in turn, filled in Nader. "Ralph asked me about it," she recalls. "He was very interested that other people at the conference know as well. So he spoke to the whole conference about the Silkwood incident."

FOR BOTH NADER AND THE ANTINUCLEAR movement, Critical Mass was an extremely important event. Organizing a conference for local nuclear activists connects with other grassroots efforts by Nader, everything from his college speaking tours to the PIRGs to the prodigious amount of mail he received. Nader was getting a read on the pulse of the country and learning what issues were truly on people's minds. He was also building a constituency outside official Washington that was not subject to the whims of Congress or the major media.

As for the activist groups in attendance, Critical Mass laid down the rudiments of a network that would become galvanized during future antinuclear fights. Diana Sidebotham, a founder of the New England Coalition on Nuclear Pollution, was at the Critical Mass conference. "We were thrilled," she says. "We had all been working locally in our own backyards. Coming together like this was a clear boon to the movement. We were delighted that Ralph Nader jumped into the breach and began waging this fight."

Harvey Wasserman, another conference attendee, says, "A few grassroots groups were out there, fighting plants. But these organizations felt alone in the woods. Nobody questioned nuclear power, save for this small band. But there was no coherent national consciousness. Ralph really gave it coherence and a vision, by putting his name and prestige behind the issue and getting leaders together to learn who was fighting and where. It was absolutely essential to the antinuclear movement."

There would be another Critical Mass conference in 1975, held on the anniversary of Karen Silkwood's death. It featured a candlelight vigil, and her parents were in attendance.

The years between 1969 and 1976 can truly be called Nader's golden age. He achieved a fearsome ubiquity and managed to delve into a synapse-frazzling array of issues. In the battle against nukes, which was to be the final fight of this period, Nader employed many of the techniques that he had honed during the past decade. He had by this time developed a full-fledged system for waging consumer battles: lobbying Congress, enlisting whistle-blowers, obtaining government documents under FOIA, even bringing the PIRGs into the fray.

Nader started a lobbying group called Congress Watch in 1973 and tapped Joan Claybrook to head it up. The new organization took a lead role in a number of antinuclear fights. For example, Congress Watch's lobbying efforts were instrumental in helping abolish the Atomic Energy Commission in 1975. Two new agencies replaced the AEC, and each was handed a different piece of the commission's dual mandate. The Nuclear Regulatory Commission was formed to handle regulation, pure and simple, just as its name implies. Meanwhile, the task of promoting nuclear energy was given to a separate body, the Energy Research and Development Agency.

The AEC's original dual mandate had drawn Nader to the topic of nuclear energy in the first place. Now the functions of regulation and promotion had been split apart, and he had played a key role in the effort.

Nader and Claybrook were also early opponents of the metal fast breeder reactor. This was a new type of nuclear plant that was proposed in the mid-1970s. Rather than uranium, which degrades over time, it would use plutonium, a fuel source that can be recycled ad infinitum, at least in theory. It would be necessary from time to time to send out the plutonium to a reprocessing facility.

Even in an era long before September 11, this raised all kinds of nightmare scenarios about sabotage and terrorism. It meant that nuclear materials would be in periodic transit. And not just any nuclear materials: although the spent uranium from a nuclear reactor is radioactive and plenty dangerous, it cannot be fashioned into a working atom bomb. Not so plutonium. "The problem was plutonium could also be used to make a bona fide nuclear weapon," says James Cubie, then a lobbyist for Congress Watch. "The stuff would be traveling around, and theft was an issue. For a commercial industry to depend on materials used in bomb making was a big problem from a security point of view. We didn't want plutonium being a normal item in the utility business."

Congress Watch helped build an unusual bipartisan coalition opposing the metal fast breeder reactor. Conservatives opposed the project because it would be unduly expensive. Liberals cued into the manifold dangers posed by plutonium. It would be a long fight. Ultimately, development of a breeder reactor was shelved by the Humphrey-Bumpers amendment of 1983.

Whenever possible, Nader solicited the help of whistle-blowers. By the mid-1970s, the nuclear power industry was generating scores of Karen Silkwoods—insiders concerned for their own safety and troubled by the limits of the general public's knowledge. Plenty of them found their way to Nader. After all, he had worked hard to promote whistle-blowing as a civic duty, even an exalted role. John Darcy and Joseph Shapiro were guards at the Three Mile Island plant located near Harrisburg, Pennsylvania. They catalogued a number of safety violations at the facility: unmonitored security gates, malfunctioning electronic systems, and former and unauthorized personnel in possession of keys. In 1975 they approached Nader with their findings. Nader, in turn, publicized those findings far and wide.

The FOIA also proved an invaluable tool. Congress Watch managed to obtain government documents detailing 175 instances of threatened vandalism or terrorism against plants, dating back to 1969. Many were idle threats or hoaxes. But there were also some genuine arson attempts, botched break-ins, even bomb scares. Prior to Congress Watch's FOIA request, this information had been withheld from the public for the most part. The documents contained some chilling revelations, such as an August 1970 episode in which dynamite was found near the Point Beach reactor run by the Wisconsin-Michigan Power Company. On July 26, 1974, a bomb actually blew up near the Pilgrim plant run by Boston Edison. There was no damage. But the fact that such an event had occurred—and had been kept quiet—was disconcerting. Congress Watch's findings received considerable press play and generated public outcry in no small measure.

Even the PIRGs got involved in the fight against nuclear power—Nader's claims of independence notwithstanding, they looked to him for cues. Oregon's student PIRG was part of a successful effort in 1973 to stop the Cape Kiwanda plant from being built. In Vermont the PIRG joined a 1975 drive that resulted in the state becoming the first to require legislative approval for construction of a nuclear reactor. MassPIRG called for a moratorium on nuclear plant construction in its state. Not uncoincidentally, Nader testified on the same subject before a joint session of the Massachusetts legislature.

Nader's multipronged approach was both relentless and successful. The Palo Verde plant, which was ordered in October 1973 and became fully operational in 1988, is the last commercial plant in the United States to be ordered, built, and to actually go online. Other plants have been ordered and subsequently canceled. As of 2002, there were still some plants supposedly under construction, though they have been subject to interminable delays.

Unquestionably, economics played a large role in the decline of nuclear power in the United States. In the late 1960s, building a plant cost several hundred million dollars on average. Within a decade, the cost had risen to well over $1 billion. But Nader was a key factor, just as surely as the dwindling value of a dollar. Once again, he managed to spark public interest in an esoteric subject. His work at the grassroots level helped consolidate forces that would play a substantial role in the antinuclear debate for years to come.

WITH ELECTION SEASON HEATING UP, as America prepared for its usual quadrennial frenzy in 1976, there was Nader for president talk once again.

"Try saying it yourself," urged the *Nation*. "'Ralph Nader for President.' It's a phrase that sparks on the tongue; it peps you up, like a sudden shower on a muggy afternoon."

Columnist Mary McGrory averred: "If ever there was a public figure tailor-made to be the perfect post-Watergate presidential candidate it is Citizen Ralph Nader."

But this time around, the Democrats and assorted third parties knew better than to dangle high office in front of Nader. He had made his position quite clear: he was simply above politics. Instead, he was asked to play the role of kingmaker.

Early in the primary season, Birch Bayh of Indiana was a contender for the Democrats. In order to distinguish himself, it was suggested, he ought to promise that if elected president he would clear all cabinet appointments with Nader.

Georgia governor Jimmy Carter, who was weighing a presidential run, also took Nader's stature into consideration. He arranged to meet Nader in a suite at a hotel in Atlanta. Peter Petkas was present and recalls that Carter was extremely deferential toward Nader. "Carter indicated that he really respected Ralph," recalls Petkas. "He also said that he really agreed with much of what Nader had accomplished. Carter simply wanted some insights into the presidency, what a president ought to do and how he ought to conduct himself."

After the meeting, on the ride to the Atlanta airport, Nader was ecstatic. "Jimmy Carter is something special," he told Petkas. "You need to watch this guy. Something's going to happen. I've never met a politician quite like Carter, and I know a lot of them."

Nader was summoned once again in early August 1976. By this time, Carter had wrapped up the nomination and was the Democratic party's candidate for president. This second meeting was held in Plains, Georgia, in the den of Carter's home. It was a far-ranging discussion.

Carter lamented that as governor he had been unable to push through certain pieces of legislation. Nader requested that Carter give priority—in the event he was elected—to the establishment of a consumer protection agency, and quickly. Carter asked Nader to recommend some books he might read to be better prepared for the presidency. Among others, Nader suggested *America, Inc.*, cowritten by Morton Mintz, and *Taming the Giant Corporation* by one of his own teams of Raiders. "We talked about what he was going to confront in Washington," recalls Nader. "We talked about how he would be surrounded by people who were going to tell him what he wanted to hear."

The visit to Plains also featured a softball game—Jimmy Carter versus brother Billy. The two teams were filled out with assorted journalists, politicos, and townspeople. Fittingly, Nader was chosen to act as umpire. He wore a suit and tie, despite the stifling August heat.

It was the bottom of the sixth inning and Billy Carter's team was winning, 10 to 3. Suddenly, there was a loud explosion roughly two hundred yards from the ball field. A three-thousand-gallon fuel tanker had burst into flames, apparently ignited when the soda machine in front of Billy Carter's gas station had short-circuited, throwing a spark.

The softball players raced to the scene. As it turned out, no one was seriously hurt. But somebody had to restrain Billy Carter to keep him from rushing into his devastated gas station. There was nothing to be done. Everyone—Nader included—simply stood around gaping, watching as billows of thick black smoke rose into the air.

—14—

Carter, Not Camelot

THE HONEYMOON WITH CARTER was to be startlingly brief. During the post-election transition period, even before Carter formally took office, the relationship between the two men started to fray. For anyone who cared to watch closely, the tensions were manifestly clear during—of all things—an appearance by Nader on *Saturday Night Live.*

A few days shy of Carter's inauguration—on January 15, 1977—Nader hosted the show, then in its second season. George Benson was the musical guest. The show kicked off with Dan Aykroyd and Gilda Radner standing outside the elevator bank at NBC, worrying that host Nader might be late.

"He's the busiest man in the world," offers Aykroyd. "It doesn't matter. It's just such a coup to get him on the show. It's great."

"But don't you think he's too straight?" rejoins Radner. "He's kind of serious for the show."

The elevator doors open and out steps Nader, wearing a powder-blue cowboy suit, resplendent in fringe and lace. On his head is a white ten-gallon hat, and a kerchief is tied around his neck. The effect is jarring. It is clearly Nader, lanky and wan. Yet he is dressed in gaudy western wear, the kind that is the trademark of Nudie Cohn, tailor to Elvis and Hank Williams.

Aykroyd and Radner are stunned.

"I'm here to have fun tonight," Nader announces brightly. "Tonight, there will be no more of this defects and abuses I've managed to find twenty-four hours a day."

Aykroyd and Radner lead Nader backstage to his dressing room. Someone starts to apply makeup to his face and the jokes begin. "Wait a minute," says Nader, still in his cowboy costume. "Is that Eye-Chief makeup? Eye-Chief contains red dye No. 2. This makeup has the possibility of causing cancer."

Standing nearby is another cast member, taking dinner on the run. "Is that a hot dog you're eating?" asks Nader. "Do you enjoy eating rat excrement and rodent hairs?"

And so it goes. Nader appears in a number of skits, the point of each to ironically tweak his deadly serious image. In one sketch, Garrett Morris plays a reporter assigned to interview Nader. He arrives at Nader's hotel room, only to find the consumer advocate ministering to a pair of blowup dolls. Nader refers to them as Pam and Rita and continually interrupts the interview to reposition and reinflate them. Morris is puzzled. So Nader explains, "I hope to explore areas of consumer protection that have hitherto been ignored for reasons of taste or public indifference."

He even plans to issue a report, he says, *Party Dolls: Turn-On or Rip-Off?*

Nader in a cowboy getup, Nader with blowup dolls, yet still unable to break out of his stodgy mold—that is the show's main conceit. But there is also a subtler vein running through the evening's entertainment: tensions with Carter. In one skit, Nader plays Nader, while Aykroyd plays Carter, drawling deeply and dressed in Confederate army regalia complete with a saber. Sitting in the oval office, Nader works his way through a list of demands for the new president, such as: "How about a whistle-blower act to protect people like Ernie Fitzgerald, who blew the whistle on Pentagon waste."

The contrast between deeply serious Nader and kooky southern Carter is supposed to be hilarious. But as Nader issues his list of demands, there is scarcely a titter from the audience.

In another sketch, Nader moons: "Oh Carter! What a cabinet! I wonder if he cares what I think now that the election is over?"

When Nader delivers this, the way he delivers it, it simply hangs in the air. Again, it is not exactly a laugh line.

UNQUESTIONABLY, NADER'S UNIQUE BRAND of uncomedy—playing a straight man so straight as to make Ed McMahon look like Johnny Carson—fairly bristled with uncomfortable truths. The fact is, the tensions with Carter, hinted at on *Saturday Night Live,* were very, very real. They may have been little known by the public and they had received scant press play, but already the fissures were forming.

Carter felt that he had shown sufficient obeisance to Nader and his causes. He had met with him twice before the election and had consulted with him several times during the transition. But it was all a question of degree. Nader believed Carter had made lavish political promises during their meetings in Georgia, and he planned to hold the new president to them. There was a growing misunderstanding between the two—centering around Nader's access to and influence over the White House—that would only intensify in the years ahead.

Carter was the first president Nader had any hope of influencing from the outset. By the time Nader burst onto the scene in 1966, Johnson was already into his second term. Meanwhile, Nixon and Ford did not enter office exactly sympathetic to Nader's issues. One time, while Nixon was hosting a seventy-fifth birthday party for Mamie Eisenhower, a music box that was a gift to the former first lady failed to play. "Where's Ralph Nader," quipped Nixon. The answer: not welcome in the White House. During the previous eight years, Nader had managed to gain exactly one audience each with Nixon and Ford. Any of his victories during two straight Republican administrations were hard-won. With the 1976 elections, however, Democrats controlled the executive branch and both houses of Congress for the first time since 1968. Nader saw an opportunity to play a vastly expanded role in the political process.

One promising sign: Carter named a surprising number of Nader's current and former employees to posts in the government. Joan Claybrook, Nader's right-hand woman, was chosen to head up the National Highway Traffic Safety Administration. Where she had earned a modest $12,000 a year for heading up Public Citizen's Congress Watch, her salary now jumped to $52,000.

As his chief speech writer, Carter selected James Fallows, a one-time Raider. Harrison Wellford, former executive director of the Center for the Study of Responsive Law, was handed an equally unwieldy title: executive associate director at the Office of Management and Budget. Peter Petkas also joined the OMB.

In addition, Carter selected a number of people who, while not former Nader employees, might fairly be termed Nader sympathizers. The top job at the FTC was handed to Mike Pertschuk, a frequent Nader collaborator during his tenure as staff director of the Senate Commerce Committee. Carol Tucker Forman left the Consumer Federation of America to become assistant secretary at the Agriculture Department. As his consumer adviser, Carter picked Esther Peterson, an experienced hand from the Johnson administration. Peterson, in turn, chose as her assistant Nancy Chasen, formerly a lobbyist for Nader's Congress Watch. The combination of Peterson and Chasen looked particularly auspicious. Perhaps the Carter administration would finally push through a bill to establish a Consumer Protection Agency, although momentum on the bill was currently stalled. It was a pet legislative project of Nader's going back many years.

While the list of Naderites who joined the Carter government was really quite long, it was not long enough in Nader's estimation. True, Carter had drawn deeply from the consumer movement, filling numerous posts by raiding the Raiders quite literally. But Nader was quick to point out that Carter had been less progressive in his most senior appointments, particularly the various department heads. Carter and his staff had tapped plenty of Naderites, but not for the very highest echelons of government.

Around the time of his *Saturday Night Live* stint, Nader convened a group of consumer leaders for a conference. The topic at hand: how could those still fighting outside the government work effectively with the Carter administration? Mostly, Nader took the opportunity to criticize the way Carter's cabinet was taking shape. He lambasted the various candidates for Treasury secretary, saying, "There is not one who is not an old-line, money, establishment corporate type." He predicted that Carter's choice for agriculture secretary was certain to put "producer interests first, processors next, and consumers last." Nothing was going to change, lamented Nader: "The departments that have traditionally been in-house advocates for business interests will remain that way."

Nader's bitterest complaint was reserved for the fact that he had not even been consulted regarding certain high-level appointments, particularly in the cabinet. "I want access," he told the *New York Times*. "I want to be able to see him and talk to him. I expected to be consulted, and I was told that I would be, particularly on regulatory and consumer matters."

BY THE TIME CARTER ACTUALLY assumed the job of president, Nader already felt betrayed. With equal alacrity, Nader became frustrated with various former employees who had joined the government. During their meeting in Plains, Nader had cautioned Carter that he had a mere three-month grace period. After that, he was going to be besieged by special interests and it would become increasingly difficult to get anything done. Nader was on his usual hyperaccelerated time schedule. He had unbridled—unrealistic, some would say—hopes about what might be accomplished by a Democratic president, Democratic Congress, and a government stuffed full with his former charges. During the next four years, Nader would clash with former employees who failed to move at the speed he deemed appropriate. Woe be to ex-Raiders within the government who failed to see matters exactly as Nader did, from without.

Claybrook was the first to experience his wrath. The agency she headed, the National Highway Traffic Safety Administration (NHTSA), is part of the Department of Transportation. NHTSA had evolved from an agency that was established by the passage of the original auto safety bill, the one spurred on by the GM spy imbroglio and subsequent Ribicoff hearings. In a sense, then, NHTSA was Nader's baby. He had long kept very close tabs on its operations and had been very quick to criticize its administrators.

Back in 1966, William Haddon had been the first person selected to head up the new auto safety agency. Haddon was an auto safety pioneer whose work Nader had drawn on extensively in researching *Unsafe at Any Speed*. Nevertheless, the two had their share of skirmishes. "Bill, we've been friends and all," Nader once told him, "but it's my job to keep an eye on the bureau from my perspective."

Nader's criticism of Haddon tended to take the form of hectoring phone calls and letters meant for internal agency consumption. It was strictly intramural stuff. As such, it did not compare with the vociferous public assault Nader mounted against Claybrook, his former employee.

Claybrook assumed her new post in February 1977. The beginning of the Carter administration found NHTSA in the process of enacting auto industry regulations regarding so-called passive restraint systems, typically airbags. Transportation Secretary Brock Adams, Claybrook's boss, opted to slow down the phase-in period. Large automobiles would be required to have some kind of passive restraint system by 1982, small cars by 1984. To Nader, this was an intolerable delay.

Nader dashed off an open letter to Claybrook, dated November 30, 1977. It was eleven pages long, single-spaced, and fairly crackled with rage. He distributed it widely among the media. He did not even bother to send a copy to Claybrook.

In his letter, Nader complained about the phase-in period for airbag regulations, calling it "an unheard of lead time provision that not even the worst of the Nixon-Ford years produced." And he chastised Claybrook for not standing up to Transportation Secretary Adams. "Through a profound mismanagement of NHTSA's role in the decision," he wrote, "you undermined the regulatory integrity of your own agency."

Nader followed with a litany of complaints about Claybrook's performance. On her watch, NHTSA had failed to do sufficient seat-belt testing.

The agency had not done enough to deal with pedestrian deaths. The letter even accused Claybrook of being more beholden to the auto industry than to consumers. Never mind that until very recently Claybrook had worked for Nader as a consumer advocate.

Nader also criticized Claybrook for a failure to recruit "conscientious and experienced" personnel. Truth be told, Claybrook had inherited her eight-hundred-person staff from the previous administration. Civil service rules protected all but four of them. Claybrook was thus stuck with 796 employees whom she could not fire and could transfer to other government agencies only if a new job offered equal pay and responsibility. Claybrook's hands were tied by existing bureaucratic rules. Such considerations were not of interest to Nader. He wanted results, and he wanted them pronto.

Claybrook's tenure—all nine months of it—had fallen far short of his expectations. "This is more than a failure of leadership," he wrote in his infamous letter. "It is a failure of nerve." He concluded with a demand that she step down: "Resignation, accompanied by full explanation and revelation, is now your most constructive course of action."

To answer Nader's onslaught, Claybrook called a press conference. About fifteen minutes into it, Nader showed up. The two exchanged cool, monosyllabic greetings. A few minutes later, Nader tried to bait Claybrook by asking questions about her record at NHTSA. "I came here to talk to the press," she said, "not you."

Nader shot back, "But haven't you read my columns?" The point of his jibe: as someone who continued to write periodic op-eds and magazine articles, he was also a member of the media. Claybrook simply ignored the comment and proceeded with her press conference. No further words would pass between the two for the next couple of years.

The Nader-Claybrook clash wound up being very public and was even covered in a fledgling entertainment magazine called *People Weekly*. For many Nader admirers—average citizens who had followed his career with interest—it was their first exposure to a harder, meaner Nader. Numerous current and former employees were shocked and disheartened. True, NHTSA was his baby in a sense. But his tactics were so exceedingly blunt.

"There are no friends in government, only users and misusers of power," Nader explained at the time. "There is no animosity between Joan and me, but the stakes are too high for friendship and sentimentality."

Others did not exactly see it this way, including Claybrook. "Of course, I was very irritated about it," she recalls. "I didn't talk to him for a couple of years, although my mother said that I should forgive him. She understood that it was tactical. But it was also personal. I think he hurt himself by doing it. A lot of people have said, well, you shouldn't attack your former staff. They thought it was really lousy for him to do that."

The Claybrook flap received abundant press attention, but it was hardly a unique incident. A number of former Naderites, now in the government, felt the sting of Nader's reprisals. Take Harrison Wellford at OMB. Nader was highly critical of his new role, describing it to one reporter as mere "box shuffling."

Wellford was furious. A veteran of the civil rights movement, he had moved to Washington in 1969 to get more deeply involved in progressive causes. Initially that had meant working for Nader. But when Carter took office, Wellford leaped at the opportunity to join the government. Working on the inside for once was appealing. To Wellford, it represented professional growth and also a maturation of the consumer movement, now invested with genuine political clout.

"Most of us were advocates for a while," he recalls, "and then we went into the legislative branch or state governments or whatever. Ralph stayed out. He never had to face up to those issues. Therefore, he could engage in a kind of italicized public discourse that made for great sound bites. But it often greatly oversimplified the real issues."

Wellford adds: "There was no way you could please Ralph for any length of time. When you're on the inside, you have to deal with checks and balances in the system. Things were never as neat and clean as when you're on the outside."

Credit for coining the term "muckraker" goes to Theodore Roosevelt. During a speech in Washington in 1906, he made the following observation: "The men with the muck rakes are often indispensable to the well-being of society, but only if they know when to stop raking the muck."

The Carter government was crawling with Naderites. It could have been a blessing, and had Nader subscribed to a different moral code, it could have been an opportunity. Instead, ex-Raiders became the objects of his muckraking. The consumer movement still had the same constellation of enemies: rapacious businessmen, troglodytic senators, and agencies staffed with corporate patsies. Yet it sometimes seemed that Nader devoted more energy to the transgressions of his erstwhile employees.

All the while, Nader was not exactly working constructively with forces outside the government, such as assorted consumer groups and the like. It was during the Carter administration that Nader began to exhibit a quality that might best be described as "doesn't play well with others."

In 1978 Roger Hickey helped found a group called Consumers Opposed to Inflation in the Necessities, or COIN. Its goal was to push for alternative solutions to fighting inflation, a problem during three straight administrations. Rather than rely on conventional inflation-fighting methods such as interest-rate moves by the Federal Reserve, COIN proposed a series of reforms related to housing, energy, and agricultural policy. The group's members included Nader and noted liberal economist Gar Alperovitz, along with various union leaders and environmentalists.

With considerable effort, COIN managed to get an audience with Carter. In preparation, the various members agreed to divvy up areas of expertise. It was agreed that the Oval Office meeting should be very focused and carefully scripted. Each representative of COIN would be responsible for a different piece of the presentation. But Nader deviated from the script.

"When it was Nader's turn," recalls Hickey, "he launched into a personal pitch to Carter. It involved something totally unrelated to COIN. I'll tell you, most of us in the room were incredibly crestfallen. It was a symbol to me of Nader's unwillingness to be part of a coalition."

A similar observation is offered by Michael Harper, once a Nader employee who worked from 1975 to 1978 at the non-Nader-affiliated Center for Law and Social Policy: "At the center, we knew a lot of people in the government. We tried to use the contacts we had. That was not Nader's style. His top agenda was to show himself to be more righteous than people in the government. He feels, it seems, that because he doesn't compromise in life that anyone who does is as bad as everyone else. You don't work with Nader. He had to do it his own way, he wanted control."

The self-righteousness, the standoffishness, the fury, the caustic attacks: a standard rap on Nader is that all is fair as long as it gets the job done. It's always political, never personal. Once upon a time, this had been a useful distinction. When Nader placed late-night phone calls to Walter Mondale, for example, the senator found it personally irritating. But it was politically astute. The proof is in the fact that the Wholesale Meat Act passed and passed quickly. But sometime around the middle of the Carter administration, the question of whether Nader was motivated by secret personal animus or extreme political ardor became a moot one. His tactics were growing stale.

NADER'S WATERLOO WAS THE defeat in 1978 of legislation to establish a Consumer Protection Agency. The bill had been bouncing around for a long while, had already caused much contention, had already gone through convolutions aplenty. But its ultimate failure is a case study of Nader not at the top of his game.

Establishing a CPA had been a passion of Nader's going back many years. But the idea actually dates back even further, to Hubert Humphrey and Estes Kefauver (D–Tennessee), who introduced a bill in 1959 to create a Department of Consumer Affairs. It was roundly defeated. The torch then passed to Ben Rosenthal, a progressive and consumer-friendly Democrat from Queens, New York, who was elected to the House in 1962. A few years hence, when Nader became a force in Washington, he and Rosenthal became frequent legislative collaborators. Nader was taken by the idea of a Department of Consumer Affairs, but he convinced Rosenthal that a modification was necessary. There was a problem with a cabinet-level department: it would consolidate all the government's consumer programs under a single roof, an easy mark for lobbyists and other corporate interests. Better to create an independent agency, Nader argued, one that was mandated to argue cases from the consumer's perspective before the myriad of existing government bodies: FDA, FCC, SEC, Transportation Department, Treasury Department, on and on.

As Nader envisioned it, the CPA would be able to testify before the FDA to argue that more trials were needed before a drug was approved. Or it might challenge the laxness of the then Department of Health, Education and Welfare in enforcing federal fire safety regulations in nursing homes. The CPA could file petitions and appeal if an adverse ruling were handed down. It would also have so-called interrogatory powers: the ability to submit written questions to corporations that they had to answer under oath. The CPA would be staffed with lawyers, economists, and scientists.

Corporations have ample opportunity to argue their cases before government agencies. This would restore balance, in Nader's view, and provide consumers a needed voice at the federal level. He referred to the bill as "the most important piece of consumer legislation ever to come before Congress." By his own reckoning, Nader devoted more time throughout the 1970s to pushing the CPA legislation than to any other project. This is quite a tribute, given all the projects in which he was involved.

But when it came to the CPA, Nader would tolerate no tinkering.

Remember, it was a vote on the CPA bill in 1970 that produced the first public inkling that Nader played rough with friends and foes alike. The bill passed the Senate, only to have him denounce it as the victim of "intolerable erosions" and strike out at Ribicoff as the prime eroder. The bill died in committee soon thereafter.

Throughout the 1970s the bill was revived numerous times. On one occasion, there was a chance to pass the CPA bill if the interrogatory powers provision could be excised. Another time, a legislative compromise was proffered whereby the CPA would not be allowed to intervene in cases that involved fines or various other penalties. But Nader would accept no compromises. In these two cases—and several others as well—he withheld his support, crucially hampering the bill's momentum. All told, CPA legislation passed either the House or the Senate five times between 1970 and 1976. But it failed to build enough steam to become law. "Ralph could have had a consumer agency bill in any of three congresses," says Mike Pertschuk. "But he held out for the perfect bill."

With Carter's election, perfection at last seemed attainable. Carter assured Nader that passage of a CPA bill would be one of his very first priorities. Carter's consumer adviser, Esther Peterson, was a strong supporter of the measure. Before joining the government as Peterson's assistant, Nancy Chasen spent the bulk of her time at Congress Watch lobbying for a CPA. The executive branch was clearly onboard. Even so, getting the bill through Congress—particularly given its checkered past—was sure to be a challenge.

Beginning in June 1977, Nader mounted a ferocious push. The centerpiece was the notorious nickel campaign. In what he described as an orchestrated stab at "metallic irony," Nader urged the public to mail nickels to members of Congress who opposed the bill. The premise was that establishing an agency to protect consumers would cost a mere five cents per American. (The true amount was seven cents, but sending three coins was judged excessive.)

As it was, members of Congress found the ensuing hail of nickels irksome enough. Over the next two months, some forty-three thousand coins arrived at the offices of wavering senators and representatives. Predictably, there were mistakes. Norman D'Amours, a Democrat of New Hampshire, had always supported the bill. Nevertheless, he received five hundred nickels, including a wooden one. New York House Democrat Samuel Stratton claimed that the nickels represented a form of bribery. "If he can be bought for a nickel then he hasn't kept up with the rate of inflation," retorted Mark Green who, as head of Nader's Congress Watch, helped coordinate the campaign.

Nader put everything he had into winning converts to the CPA, a choice that he described as the "ultimate consumer litmus test." He even went to the extraordinary step of traveling into the districts of senators and representatives who opposed the bill. Once there, he would issue his own brand of color commentary, ripping members apart in their hometown newspapers, lambasting them on the local talk shows. He reserved special vehemence for wayward liberals on the theory that they could be swayed to his side, while conservatives were beyond redemption.

A case in point is Patricia Schroeder, a Democratic representative from Colorado. She had backed the CPA in both 1974 and 1975. But in 1977 she wrote Nader a letter posing questions about certain aspects of the bill. Nader's response was to write an op-ed for the *Denver Post* in which he branded Schroeder a "mushy liberal." Then he flew into Denver and held a press conference in which he accused Schroeder of opposing the bill in order to attract corporate campaign contributions. Meanwhile, he labeled Tom Foley "a broker for agribusiness raids on Treasury." A decade before, Nader had worked extremely effectively with Foley to deal a blow to agribusiness, passing a bill regulating intrastate meatpacking plants.

Frustrated, Esther Peterson told Nader at one point during his bill-storming tour: "Ralph, I shouldn't spend my energy picking up the pieces with the people you've offended."

On February 8, 1978, the CPA bill was put to a vote before the House. It lost 227–189. In casting a vote of "nay," one congressman reportedly hissed: "This one's for you, Ralph." Fully 101 Democrats voted against the bill. Among forty-nine freshman Dems, twenty-five voted for it, twenty-four against.

Nader was in Reno, Nevada, when the deciding vote was cast. He had flown out there to deliver an eleventh-hour attack against Republican representative James Santini. Mark Green broke the news to him during a phone call. The line crackled for five long seconds of silence. Then Nader said, "This is the world's greatest country, but it's being run by a bunch of pinheads."

Unbowed, he immediately set to strategizing about how the bill might be revived yet again. But the Senate had indicated that it would not even consider the measure unless it first got through the House. This time the moment had truly passed, the momentum was entirely lost. The CPA's long and tortuous legislative life had finally come to an end.

The postmortem would find that multiple culprits shared blame. But Nader was high on the list. House Speaker Tip O'Neill had been a staunch supporter of the bill. The day of the vote, he had taken to the floor to deliver a rousing speech in support. Asked about Nader's role in the defeat, he told the *Washington Post*: "Let's put it this way. It didn't help. I know of about eight guys who would have voted with us if it were not for Nader."

One was Robert Giamo, chairman of the House Budget Committee. Initially, he was undecided about the CPA, but converting him should have been a cinch. He was a Democrat, hailing from Nader's home state, Connecticut. But Nader chose to attack Giamo in his district during a radio interview. It was a move, Giamo later conceded, that steeled his opposition and convinced him to vote against the bill. One week after the CPA's defeat, WRC radio in Washington, D.C., conducted an informal poll, asking listeners whether Nader provided more help or hindrance on consumer issues. Hindrance was the verdict of twenty-four of thirty callers. Perceptions were hardening; Nader was starting to be seen as a spoiler of the very movement that he had created.

"He pissed off too many people," says Peter Barash, who was Ben Rosenthal's legislative assistant. "He just hit a critical mass. You can try to pick off a few senators or congressmen here or there. When attacking members becomes a pattern—the rule rather than the exception—the whole institution turns against you."

For his part, Nader parks blame for the CPA's demise squarely with Carter. They met twice in the Oval Office in January 1978, just weeks before the bill was slated to go to a vote. At Carter's urging, Nader provided a list of two dozen members who were on the fence and might respond to presidential arm-twisting. Apparently Carter called the first six—received six nays—and promptly gave up.

"He did not lift a finger to lobby," recalls Nader. "He let Esther Peterson do it all by herself. By this time, he was spending a huge amount of his time on matters such as trying to deregulate natural gas. He was getting ground under. He could not even convince his own congressmen from Georgia." (For the record, only one of the ten members of Congress from Georgia voted for the bill.)

But there is one other prime culprit. If the CPA provides a case study of Nader at his worst, it also offers a case study of business lobbying groups at their most effective. They took advantage of one of those subtle pendulum swings of public sentiment that become clear only much later. The fact was, many Americans were growing increasingly concerned with the ravages of a stagnant economy—jobs lost to foreign competition, whole industries in decline. Companies were even starting to look vulnerable in many cases. The idea of further regulation—particularly a consumer agency that would clash with corporations in multiple government venues—was no longer so appealing.

A variety of corporate groups joined forces to oppose the CPA: the U.S. Chamber of Commerce, Business Roundtable, National Association of Manufacturers, National Federation of Independent Business, and Grocery Manufacturers of America. This had hardly been a monolith before. In the past, this had been a fractured and fractious collection of business interests, unable to agree on much of anything. But they all agreed that the CPA was a bad idea. At a time when Nader was not exactly playing well with others, they formed a tight coalition. Nader's nickel campaign was merely an annoyance, but the coordinated efforts of the various business groups were extremely effective. While the Chamber of Commerce urged its members to write to Congress, the Business Roundtable launched a cartoon blitz, sending caricatures depicting Nader, the CPA, and the bloated federal bureaucracy to thirty-eight hundred newspapers. The result: thousands of letters poured into Congress, and two thousand newspapers around the country published the roundtable's canned cartoons.

The defeat of the CPA signaled a kind of business community resurgence, again in a way that would not be immediately clear. For a decade, Nader had held the ideological high ground. He had been the most visible and the most famous proponent of a worldview that pitted consumers against producers, government against corporations. Soon business would fight to regain moral authority. In the years ahead, Nader would find his efforts increasingly thwarted.

THE DEFEAT OF THE CPA WAS A watershed event. Its sting was doubly sharp for Nader due to the fact that he did not have a wealth of other projects to fall back on. Typically, Nader was a master of multitasking. But by 1978, he had worked his way through the alphabet and had raided just about every agency in government. Certainly he had plucked the low-hanging fruit, glaringly corrupt agencies such as the FTC and ICC. Going forward it would be tougher to find suitable targets. What's more, there were more groups out there working to ferret out corruption. This—in a bit of nonmetallic irony—was due in no small measure to Nader's own efforts and example.

The CPA battle consumed much of Nader's attention. Arguably, his most high-profile secondary project at the time was something called

F.A.N.S. (Fight to Advance the Nation's Sports). In something of a departure for Nader, it was a group aimed at neither a government agency nor a Fortune 500 company. Instead, F.A.N.S. was devoted to battling against cold hot dogs, warm beer, high ticket prices, lavish stadium subsidies, dangerous artificial turf, and a host of other iniquities large and small that hamper the enjoyment of sports lovers everywhere.

The new group was the brainchild of Nader and Peter Gruenstein, a veteran of the 1972 Congress Project. Nader remained a loyal Yankees fan; Gruenstein had grown up in Brooklyn, a Dodgers fan. Nader put up $10,000 of his own money to get the new group off and running.

F.A.N.S. was meant as a challenge to the sports establishment. Nader and Gruenstein planned to pursue a variety of avenues: legal action, consumer boycotts, congressional lobbying. In an article that appeared in *Playboy*'s March 1978 issue, Nader and Gruenstein outlined some of the most egregious ways in which sports fans get hoodwinked and proposed a ten-point fan's bill of rights that included "(1) participate in the formation of the rules and procedures that govern the play and operation of professional and amateur sports competition and (2) be informed about the operations and practices of professional and amateur sports."

Unlike so many previous Nader projects, however, F.A.N.S. failed to touch a nerve. Instead, it provoked derision. It was such an easy target. Sportswriters and consumer beat reporters alike took the opportunity to get off zingers, such as this one from the *Washington Post*: "Next thing, Nader will be demanding the replacement of shoulder pads with airbags." Or this one, from George Will, the columnist and baseball aficionado: "If Nader has his way about 'healthful' food, there may be spinach in the bleachers." But a few paragraphs later, Will cut to the heart of the matter: "Few sports fans care a patch for formulating sports rules. And they would prefer to be less, not more, informed about the 'operations' of their teams: Sports pages already read like financial and legal reports. Most fans only want the home team to win, and they are not particular about how that is accomplished."

F.A.N.S. staggered along for a couple years. It managed to attract perhaps twenty-five hundred members willing to pay the $9 annual membership fee. "A lot of people agreed that the issue of cold hot dogs in the stadium didn't require Ralph Nader," says Gruenstein. "Other than raising awareness some, offhand I can't remember anything directly attributable to F.A.N.S."

It was during the Carter administration that Congress tired of Nader. As Robert Eckhardt, Democrat from Texas, put it in 1978: "He is more attackable than he was ten years ago. House members say sarcastic things over lunch about Nader, joke about Nader."

Also during the Carter years, Nader lost favor with a constituency he had always handled with great adroitness, the press. Negative treatment of Nader and his projects, such as the coverage given to F.A.N.S., became far more commonplace. But even worse, far worse, he started to be ignored. The year 1971 had been a high-water mark for Nader, a year during which, to quote Phil Donahue: "Ralph was literally on every ten-most-admired list. He was right there around the Queen Mother and Billy Graham." In 1971 there were 148 articles about Nader in the *New York Times* and he was the subject of 38 feature stories in major magazines. In 1978, the number of *Times* articles plummeted to twenty-two and there were ten magazine features.

The reasons for the steep media falloff are various and have as much to do with a changing society as with a changed Ralph Nader. Sure, he had become churlish of late. But in some ways, the diminished attention owed just as much to what Walter Lippmann once termed the press's "bouncing spotlight." People had simply grown tired of Nader. What's truly extraordinary, in a way, is that a figure so thoroughly versed on such rarefied issues had commanded the public's attention for so long. "A person is a hero for a while, and then their star fades," offers Charles Peters, founding editor of the *Washington Monthly*. "Tune to another show. It's an immense factor in American life and it applied to Ralph Nader, no question."

Nader was also the victim of what might be termed Watergate syndrome. As already mentioned, Nader first became a public figure at a time when investigative reporting was a nascent endeavor. Many reporters investigated by proxy, simply calling Nader to get their scoops. Post-Watergate, newspapers beefed up their investigative staffs, and the new hires were expected to chase down their own stories.

As a corollary, after 1974 the press became generally more critical, more apt to scrutinize everyone from presidents to baseball stars. Nader had long held himself up as the purest in the land. Uncovering some real dirt—detailing a financial misdealing or hypocrisy on Nader's part—became a worthy challenge, kind of a Holy Grail in certain investigative circles. It is likely no coincidence that two unremitting attacks on Nader were published after Watergate, rather than before.

One is called *Me & Ralph: Is Nader Unsafe for America,* by David Sanford, an editor for the *New Republic*. The other is *Hit & Run: The Rise—and Fall?—of Ralph Nader,* by Ralph De Toledano, a conservative columnist. Both books are mean-spirited and impossibly picayune, dwelling endlessly on episodes of internecine strife within Nader's operations. For example, Ted Jacobs's tenure as executive director of the Center ended badly; he and Nader had a huge fight, and Nader went in one night, removed all of the files from his office, and basically drove him out. Sanford even devotes an entire chapter to the complaints of a single former Raider. Neither book exactly blew the lid off Ralph Nader.

But a pair of hatchet jobs was further evidence that Nader's media relations were souring. *Washington Post* reporter Morton Mintz had worked closely with Nader on a number of stories going back to 1966. Beginning in 1976, Mintz's editors reassigned him to a series of beats, such as covering the Supreme Court. Mintz left the *Post* in 1988, and during his final twelve years at the paper he did not use Nader as a source in a single story.

During this latter period, Mintz observed serious changes at his paper. He contends that Nader received substantially less coverage, in part, because the *Post*'s top brass became increasingly chummy with the business community. "There was a feeling radiating from the top down," recalls Mintz. "It wasn't a welcoming atmosphere to cover business misdealings and that meant it wasn't easy to cover Ralph Nader. The *Post*'s management was resistant to stories about Nader."

Nader himself has a similar assessment. "You start out with the *New York Times* being trendsetter. If the *Times* doesn't cover it, the *Post* won't cover it. Here, there's a two-word answer: Abe Rosenthal. When he took over the *New York Times* [in 1977], he literally told his reporters and Washington bureau chief that they should not cover me, unless there was a thorough response from corporations. The corporations knew this, they didn't respond, and there was no coverage. They'd give a 'no comment.'

"Rosenthal had a bias," continues Nader. "He may be anti-Communist, but he had a pro-corporate bias. He never really covered corporate abuses. I think he had a bias to me personally, judging from the feedback. Maybe there's an ethnic bias. That's come back to me. A lot of things happen at the *Times* that don't get back to me, but a lot of things happen that do. I don't know how to verify all this. He would never level with me in the few times I spoke with him."

Nader adds: "Rosenthal is probably one of the nastiest Canadians who has ever come to the United States."

Nader did not go quietly. In 1978 he questioned the integrity of Tom Snyder, host of NBC's *Tomorrow* show. The reason he had not been invited onto the show, Nader asserted, was that Snyder was beholden to his corporate sponsors. Snyder was simply afraid to air views that were controversial and antibusiness. "Nader is yesterday's news," Snyder shot back. "He's boring; he doesn't have a sense of humor . . . and I don't want him on the program."

In *The Sun Also Rises*, Ernest Hemingway describes the way in which a character goes financially bankrupt. "Two ways," he writes, "gradually and then suddenly." So it was with Ralph Nader. For years now he had been clashing with people who typically would have been allies, and he had gradually used up his political capital. And suddenly—snap, just like that—he was no longer such a formidable figure.

It was jarring experience. Looking back many years later, Nader expressed a certain amount of regret. "I didn't socialize much in Washington when I was well-known and heavily reported," he recalls. "I could have easily. I'm really sorry that I didn't do more of that. It was more like postponing it: 'I'm busy on this, I'm busy on that.' People loom much bigger now than they did when they were within a phone call. I felt I could always meet with them, so I put it off. That was a mistake."

NEAR THE END OF THE Carter administration Nader stepped down as president of Public Citizen. In years ahead, he would continue to work with people at the organization, frequently consulting with Sid Wolfe on consumer health care issues or talking legal strategy with Alan Morrison, head of the Litigation Group. As an interesting side note, Joan Claybrook and Nader eventually managed to reconcile and she returned to his orbit. Claybrook became president of Public Citizen in 1982. But never again would Nader play a formal role in the organization's day-to-day operations.

Nader had never enjoyed being an administrator. He simply had no patience for issues such as salary structures, vacation days, lines of authority. Nader's only skill in the administrative realm was hiring; he always had his pick of the brightest lights from the finest schools. In addition, he had a knack for sizing up people quickly by means of idiosyncratic methods such as asking, "What would you rather be, a spider or a butterfly?" (The right answer: spider, because it is the more aggressive insect.) As a result of Nader's canny hiring, Public Citizen had grown into a mature organization that was self-sustaining, capable of surviving without his help. "He does not have a proprietary interest in staying with organizations once he believes they're on their way," says Wolfe. "He's had extraordinary success in starting organizations. In an enormously large percentage of cases they've taken off and are still in existence today."

Leaving Public Citizen was a major move for Nader. Still, he did not choose to banish all bureaucracy from his life; he retained control of his initial organization, the Center for the Study of Responsive Law. But here, too, he changed his approach. Never again would he hire hundreds of students to descend on Washington. Going forward, he would conduct fewer projects and smaller projects. Though the people he hired at the Center were still Nader's Raiders, technically, no one would use that name anymore. It was kind of like being a member of one of the countless latter-day lineups of the Allman Brothers Band. There was a sense that the golden era lay in the past.

At the same time, Nader did succeed in transforming himself back into more of a lone operator, less tied to Washington. In a way, then, paring back can be seen as the first tentative step toward his eventual renewal as a force in American life. But that would not happen for a while. It was still a long way off—would require immense effort and hard work, even by Nader's standards.

NADER ENDED THE CARTER administration thoroughly disillusioned. In 1976 he had played kingmaker and relished a heightened role in a new presidential administration. Four years had passed and nothing had turned out as he expected. At a press conference—one much more sparely attended than Nader was accustomed to—he took shots at the president. "He has not spoken out," he said. "He does not appreciate the dimensions of national leadership." At around the same time, he told *Rolling Stone*: "In the last year we've seen the 'corporatization' of Jimmy Carter. Whereas he was impotent and kind of pathetic the first year and a half, he's now surrendered."

Nader added: "The two-party system, by all criteria, is bankrupt . . . they have nothing of any significance to offer the voters, so a lot of voters say why should they go and vote for Tweedledum and Tweedledee."

During the summer of 1980, Nader decided to develop a series of citizens' guides to the upcoming election. It was a kind of mini–Congress Project, a presidential-candidates project. His aim was to scour the records of Carter, Reagan, and third-party candidate John Anderson.

Jonathan Alter signed on for the project, a recent graduate of Harvard. He would later become a columnist for *Newsweek*. For the summer of 1980, he immersed himself in John Anderson's record. Nader had no great fondness for Anderson, a moderate Republican who had decided to fly the coop.

But what really struck Alter was Nader's total disgust with Carter. Alter knew Nader was not a registered Democrat, but he had expected that Nader would at least have a kind of pro-Democrat sympathy. "He felt that Carter was pretty worthless," recalls Alter. "There was no sense of, well, go hard on Reagan and a little easier on Carter. It was more like find as much fault as you can with both of them. He didn't seem overly distressed at the idea of Ronald Reagan becoming president."

In 1972 Nader had resisted offers to run on the ticket of the upstart New Party, in part fearing that he would hurt McGovern's chances and throw the election to Nixon. Come 1980 Nader had gone through a serious transition: he claimed no longer to see a difference between the two parties.

—15—

Back to Grass Roots

THE INAUGURATION OF RONALD REAGAN HAD more in common with a coronation. Previous presidents, Carter included, had chosen to be sworn in on the Capitol's east portico, which afforded a modest view out into a parking lot. By contrast, Reagan's ceremony was held on the Capitol's west side, with a spectacular panoramic view of the Mall, the Washington Monument spiking in the distance.

No one will ever forget the Hollywood-perfect moment that ushered the new president into office. As he was taking the oath of office—at the exact moment that he uttered the words "I, Ronald Wilson Reagan"—it was announced that the Ayatollah Khomeini had released the fifty-two American hostages held in Iran.

The new president then made the rounds of nine separate inaugural balls, held at such posh locations as Georgetown's Pisces Club. He moved with ease among entertainment world pals—notably Jimmy Stewart and Frank Sinatra—and corporate boosters such as broadcasting magnate Walter Annenberg and Earle Jorgensen, a California industrialist. The Beltway limo shortage was so severe that several New York City companies sent down parts of their fleets. All told, Reagan's assorted festivities cost $8 million, twice the cost of Carter's inaugural events in 1977.

On the day Reagan was sworn in, Public Citizen held a mock wake commemorating the "death of the consumer movement." The contrast is striking. Overworked and underpaid advocates stood around trading gallows humor and drinking fruit juice out of paper cups. Nader dropped by to visit with employees of the organization that he had so recently departed. Everyone was extremely down. But David Vladeck, a lawyer

Nader and Jimmy Carter—pictured here in Plains, Georgia, on August 7, 1976—did not remain in sync for long. CREDIT: AP/WIDE WORLD PHOTOS

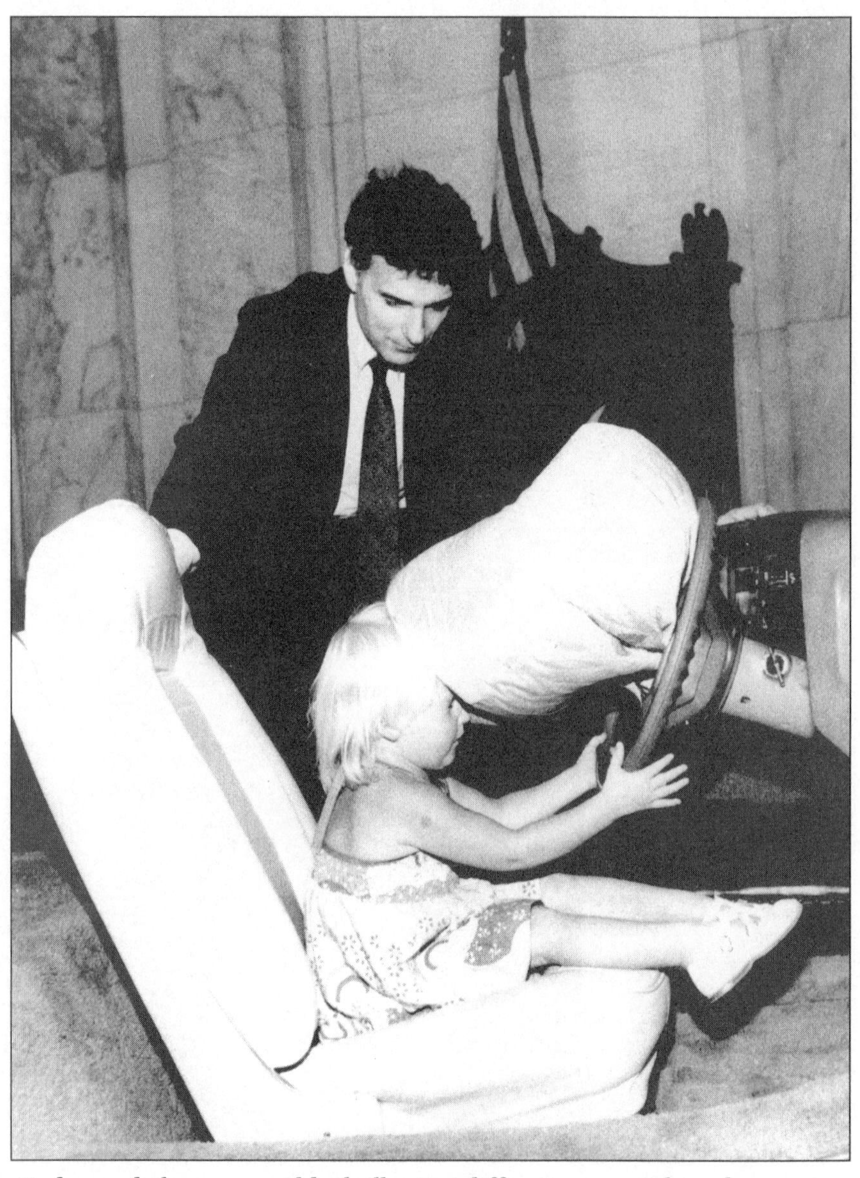

Nader and three-year-old Shelby Sutcliffe give an air-bag demonstration in 1977. CREDIT: AP/WIDE WORLD PHOTOS

Silent treatment: Nader had a very public clash in 1977 with Joan Claybrook, once a close associate. Here, she ignores him at a press conference. Afterwards, they would not speak for several years. CREDIT: AP/WIDE WORLD PHOTOS

Nader, a graduate of Harvard Law and frequent guest speaker at the school (the picture is from a 1981 appearance), has long maintained an ambivalence toward his alma mater. CREDIT: AP/WIDE WORLD PHOTOS

Repeatedly asked by Jay Leno what he likes to do for fun, Nader finally allowed, "I like to eat strawberries." CREDIT: AP/WIDE WORLD PHOTOS

In 1992, Nader made a first tentative run at the presidency. He received 6,311 votes in the New Hampshire primary. CREDIT: AP/WIDE WORLD PHOTOS

The super rally at New York's Madison Square Garden, which drew a sold-out crowd of 15,500, was a high-point of Nader's 2000 campaign.

CREDIT: NADER 2000

CREDIT: STEVE KELLEY, COPLEY NEWS SERVICE

Winona LaDuke, Nader's running mate in 1996 and 2000
CREDIT: NADER 2000

Still the Rage: Nader, 39 years after first moving to Washington, at an Enron-inspired corporate reform rally in April 2002.

CREDIT: AP/WIDE WORLD PHOTOS

with the Litigation Group, recalls that Nader was in the darkest mood of anyone.

"I know this guy," said Nader in Vladeck's recollection. "I had dealings with him when he was governor of California. He's the worst thing we've ever seen because people are going to like him. He's unbelievably conservative and completely disengaged. It's going to be very hard to get much done in the next four years. We're up a creek."

Here, Nader's stance seems thoroughly perverse. During the election, he had insisted that there was no difference between Carter and Reagan. But the instant Reagan became president, Nader began lamenting the damage that was likely to ensue. The fact is, there were substantial differences between Carter and Reagan. In the era ahead, the consumer movement would suffer drastic setbacks. And Nader would be virtually silenced until he lit upon some novel approaches for getting his message across.

Reagan's election signaled a sea change in attitudes about business and the role of the federal government. He swept into office calling for lower taxes coupled with the deregulation of a variety of industries. Carter had made some halting moves in this direction, but Reagan approached the issue with ideological fervor. Not for nothing was his ascension referred to—at least in some circles—as the "Reagan Revolution." He made it clear that he intended to dismantle a substantial portion of the federal regulatory mechanism. Many of these regulatory statutes were the ones Nader had played a role in getting on the books in the first place.

The ideas Reagan seized had been percolating for years, touted by conservative theorists such as Irving Kristol. Kristol is sometimes referred to as the "godfather of neoconservatism." In a way, he can be seen as an inverted Ralph Nader. Like Nader, Kristol helped build a formidable social movement in large part by encouraging and inspiring others. For example, Kristol was editor of an extremely influential journal called *The Public Interest*. He commissioned Jude Wanniski to write a series of articles popularizing the theories of Arthur Laffer, an economics professor at the University of Chicago.

One of those ideas—the Laffer Curve—holds that government revenues actually diminish when tax rates are set too high. Basically, people lose their incentive to work hard. They earn less money and therefore pay less in the way of taxes. The Laffer Curve provided the theoretical underpinning for Reaganomics: lower the tax rate, unleash people's entrepreneurial zeal, watch the government's tax receipts soar.

The name of Kristol's journal—*The Public Interest*—says it all. For many years, Nader had succeeded in making himself synonymous with the public interest. Through his actions, he defined where the public interest lay and identified who served as its champion, who was inimical to it. This identification was bolstered by the PIRGs—Public Interest Research Groups. To Nader's way of thinking, the interests of the public were served by pushing government agencies to keep tabs on corporations. Kristol sought to turn the idea on its head: working in the public interest could also entail fighting to scale back the role of government in American life.

Kristol was instrumental in founding the Institute for Educational Affairs. The organization was meant to help match corporate philanthropy with projects by conservative intellectuals. It endowed a number of fellowships and research projects at various right-leaning think tanks such as the Hoover Institution, the Heritage Foundation, and the American Enterprise Institute (AEI).

The AEI, where Kristol also served as a senior fellow, was a particularly effective voice on the issue of deregulation. It published a journal called *Regulation* that documented egregious examples of the government-as-nanny. AEI also sponsored research designed to prove that regulation was unwittingly harmful to the populace. One of AEI's most high-profile and controversial studies was conducted by Murray Weidenbaum, an assistant secretary of treasury during the Nixon administration. Where Nader and his cohorts argued that regulation benefited society, Weidenbaum put a price tag on regulation. He estimated that in 1976 such activity had cost the United States $66 billion in lost business opportunities, bloated federal payrolls, and so on.

All this think-tanking produced an intellectual framework for the business community to use in battling regulation. In the book *Fluctuating Fortunes: The Political Power of Business in America*, David Vogel provides the following insight: "But by the end of the 1970s, corporations and trade associations could draw upon an extensive body of literature—much of it professional and competent—that, in many important respects, buttressed their political positions. Thus for every horror story about corporate irresponsibility that had circulated at the beginning of the decade, by its end there was a matching horror story about the shortcomings of government regulation."

The public debate was shifting. In the past, the business community rarely had success gaining a sympathetic hearing in Washington. Research by the AEI and like-minded organizations provided much-needed ammo.

Emboldened, business began playing a growing role in the nation's capital. By the beginning of the Reagan administration there were nine thousand business lobbyists in Washington, along with twelve thousand corporate lawyers and fifty thousand representatives of trade associations. For the first time since the Hoover administration, the number of business advocates in Washington outnumbered federal employees.

CEOs in particular started getting more savvy about negotiating Washington. This was in large part due to the Business Roundtable—a unique organization with an ever shifting membership composed of two hundred CEOs from major corporations such as General Electric and Coca-Cola. The roundtable was originally formed in 1972 at the urging of Fed chairman Arthur Burns and John Connally, Nixon's treasury secretary. While meeting with a group of business leaders, the pair asserted that corporate America was losing the ideological battle. The problem—asserted Burns and Connally—was that business leaders were generally horrendous at public relations. "At congressional hearings, Nader would testify and all these cameras would be there," recalls John Post, one-time executive director of the Business Roundtable. "When he finished, if a businessperson was next to testify, all the cameras left. No question that a lot of CEOs were gruff."

The Business Roundtable set about doing a collective image overhaul. Many of its members signed up for media-training seminars. They learned how to dole out pithy sound bites and how not to appear so defensive when answering reporters' questions. By the late 1970s, many Fortune 500 CEOs were more like Irving Shapiro—head of DuPont and one-time president of the Business Roundtable. Shapiro actively courted the press, even providing his home phone number to select reporters. The two hundred CEOs of the Business Roundtable also began working together to develop common positions on issues such as corporate tax policy and international trade. The upshot: when members of Congress met with the CEOs of major corporations, the business leaders' positions were likely to be well-articulated and consistent.

There was a time when Nader felt that he could achieve anything. Between 1966 and 1973, Congress passed more than twenty-five pieces of consumer legislation, and Nader had a hand in most of them. But now business was fighting back.

"They're pretty brazen," says Nader. "I underestimated them. Here's the rule in retrospect: whenever you win a victory in government over corporations, immediately ask yourself what is going to be the reaction? How are they going to fight back? Instead of going off to some other foray, you have to figure it out."

Nader had allowed himself to get complacent. He had given insufficient attention to how the business community might regroup. The coalition that helped defeat the CPA in 1978 could be seen as a bellwether of a changing climate in Washington. During the Reagan administration, business would be truly resurgent.

"What happened was the free enterprise system adapted, as it always has," says Hank Cox, one-time communications director for the National Association of Manufacturers. "Nader was marginalized. He went back to spewing raspberries and hurling thunderbolts. Nader is a jeremiah, a bearded prophet who lives in the wilderness and wanders into town every now and then, condemning everyone, wanting to ban cars that go fast and food that tastes good."

REAGAN IMMEDIATELY LAUNCHED HIS promised regulatory rollback. On January 22, 1981, his second day in office, he announced the formation of the Task Force on Regulatory Relief. Vice President George Bush was appointed to head up the new effort. Reagan charged him with responsibility for "cutting away the thicket of irrational and senseless regulations."

One month later, Reagan issued Executive Order 12291. This spelled out that regulations could no longer be justified merely on the grounds of being useful, of eliminating certain hazards or saving lives. Instead, all significant existing regulations, and certainly any new ones, would need to be subjected to a cost-benefit analysis. OMB would oversee this process. Henceforth, the standard for regulations was that they must provide more benefit to society than cost, in strict dollar terms.

The new regulatory proceedings were highly secretive. Industry trade groups and individual corporations would go before Bush's task force to argue their cases. Consumer groups were not even informed about the proceedings, let alone invited to testify. Bush went so far as to solicit the views of various industries, asking which regulations they found particularly burdensome and wished to see stricken.

The auto industry was one of the first to step forward. GM and NHTSA jointly issued a claim that regulations were adding as much as $400 to the sticker price of a new car. As a result, Bush's regulatory task force agreed to delay or rescind thirty-four different environmental and safety standards. No new fuel efficiency standards would be issued, for example, and proposed regulations on odometer tampering were scrapped. Once again, airbags were delayed. Nader had been quick to take issue with NHTSA when it was run by Claybrook. NHTSA under Reagan would be Nader's worst nightmare.

Katherine Meyer was a lawyer at Public Citizen during the Reagan administration. She worked with Nader on several occasions trying to preserve regulations, always a steep challenge. It was a closed system, according to Meyer, with a process that went something like this: Industry goes before the Bush task force to complain about onerous regulation. OMB does cost-benefit analysis and determines that said regulation would carry a price tag of, say, $1.5 billion in lost economic opportunity. Proposed regulation is deep-sixed. Meyer contends that OMB could just as easily come up with a figure of $2 billion, $538 million, whatever. Regulations lived or died on the basis of OMB's cost-benefit calculations, and consumer groups were not privy to the math.

"Ralph was deeply concerned," she says. "Corporations were gaining secret access to those in power who make the decisions. We were not even invited to those meetings. This was a blatant institutionalization of the very thing Ralph had been battling against: regulated companies working hand in hand with the regulators."

Bush's task force was devastatingly effective. But it was not the only method for unspooling the regulatory apparatus. Reagan had the power to make appointments, and many of the people he selected to head up agencies were considerably more free market and laissez-faire in orientation than their predecessors. His choice to head up the EPA, for example, was Anne Gorsuch. As a Republican member of Colorado's state legislature, Gorsuch had been a frequent opponent of environmental laws. Reagan also pushed for deep budget cuts, particularly at agencies involved in consumer or environmental matters.

In terms of real dollars, the budgets of the various regulatory agencies had grown 400 percent from 1970 to 1980. But during Reagan's first year in office, they were flat. In 1982 the total budget for federal regulatory agencies was cut by 9 percent. Certain agencies faced especially deep cuts: NHTSA's budget fell 22 percent; the FTC dropped by 28 percent. The impact was nearly instantaneous: leaner agencies took on fewer projects. During Carter's four years in office, for example, the U.S. Fish and Wildlife Service had placed 150 animals on the endangered species list. In Reagan's first year, a single addition was made to the list.

Federal agencies were having difficulty getting anything accomplished. Many simply began to let existing regulations languish. Even if a statute was on the books, it was certainly possible to delay implementation, or simply to ignore it.

Nader was particularly pained by what he viewed as a do-nothing stance on the part of the Occupational Safety and Health Administration. Like NHTSA, OSHA was an organization in which Nader took a proprietary interest. He had been involved in pushing through the legislation that created OSHA. According to Public Law 91-956, passed on December 29, 1970, the agency's mission was "to assure safe and healthful working conditions for working men and women."

In the early days, OSHA set standards designed to limit workplace exposure to hazardous substances such as asbestos, arsenic, and assorted noxious emissions from coke ovens. During the Reagan administration, however, OSHA was completely defanged. To head up the agency, Reagan selected Thorne Auchter, a member of his 1980 campaign team who hailed from the construction industry. On Auchter's watch, OSHA simply refused to enforce regulations on a variety of substances such as ethylene oxide and grain dust.

Ethylene oxide is used frequently in hospital settings as a sterilant. Prolonged exposure can lead to leukemia, chromosomal damage, and, among pregnant women, an increased incidence of miscarriages. Grain dust is a substance that accumulates on the floor of silos and mills. Fine particles of grain are quite flammable, and in high concentrations they can explode with great force. Early in the Reagan administration, OSHA passed regulations on both substances, but the agency did nothing to enforce them.

Nader issued a report entitled *Reagan in the Workplace: Unraveling the Health and Safety Net*. According to the report, OSHA was dispatching fewer workplace inspectors than ever before and, by dint of that, was issuing fewer fines for violations. Fines were being reduced or dropped even in seemingly flagrant cases, such as a Wisconsin factory worker who lost his arm when he touched an exposed live wire. Initially, the factory was fined $640, but on review the violation was deemed "nonserious," and the fine was dropped.

Nader also worked with the Public Citizen Litigation Group to sue OSHA in an attempt to get various hazardous materials standards enforced. It would take until 1987 to prevail on OSHA to enforce its regulation regarding how much grain dust could accumulate on the floor of a silo. As for ethylene oxide, it would take until 1988 for Public Citizen to beat OSHA in court and finally get regulations on that substance enforced.

Working with Public Citizen, Nader was involved in dozens of these battles. They were drawn out and exhausting. Such legal wrangling brought none of the satisfactions of fighting to get a law passed. Rather, it involved trying to prevail on agencies to enforce existing statutes that had been allowed to lie fallow. It was necessary to rewin battles that, seemingly, had already been won. "All these fights took enormous time," says Nader. "It was not a good period, not good at all."

Nader sent Reagan a letter, dated January 18, 1982. It was lengthy, as Nader letters always are, and included the following: "Throughout our country, helpless people, children, the elderly, the disabled and millions of other innocent consumers are being denied the protection of their national government. From auto safety to antitrust to banking to food safety, your administration has joined with reckless business powers to strip away safeguards vital to consumers. By abandoning sound government regulation of companies you are permitting these companies to privately regulate consumers."

Reagan's response—penned by Mark Weinberg, the assistant White House press secretary—was terse: "The president believes that much federal regulation is wasteful and unnecessary and that the consumer's best protection is not a growing federal bureaucracy but a free and competitive economy."

Everything had changed. Nader may have been unhappy with Carter, but he could not get even a minute's face time with Reagan. He was reduced to writing letters that were answered by minor functionaries in the president's press office.

"They were trying to roll back the '60s and '70s," recalls Nader. "We had to fight on all these fronts. A whole culture of defense set in. You could really feel good if you saved a regulatory statute that had passed forty years ago. Once you slip and become on the defensive, it is almost impossible to get back on the offensive, unless you expend new political energies."

THAT IS PRECISELY WHAT Nader chose to do. The doors were shut in Washington, so Nader elected to direct his considerable political energy elsewhere. He decided to take his message out into the hinterlands.

This was an interesting transition that says a considerable amount about Nader's ability to handle adversity. In a weird way, the Carter administration can be seen as too much of a good thing for Nader. It is reminiscent of the old Speedy Gonzalez cartoon where Speedy and a mouse pal break into a cheese factory. They eat like mad and make themselves sick.

Likewise, the Carter years began as a big juicy promise of unchecked influence and unhindered legislative progress, or at least that's how Nader saw it. He became greedy and petulant with his demands, and managed to tick off Congress, former employees, the media, everyone.

In some ways, Nader was better suited to adversity. With the ascent of Reagan, adversity came his way by the barrelful. There was nary a glimmer of hope. To everything Nader stood for, Reagan was diametrically opposed. Nader found himself shut out to a far greater degree than he had ever before experienced. As a consequence, he was forced to unleash his restless creativity. Nader started looking for grassroots solutions, the very kinds his brother Shaf had long championed.

NADER BEGAN PEDDLING THE idea of a network of consumer organizations that would take on local utilities. They would battle for better service and would challenge rate hikes on gas and electric bills.

He called his idea residential utility consumer action groups, or RUCAGs. Along with the infelicitous name, RUCAGs had much in common with the student PIRGs, Nader's first grassroots endeavor. The concept is as follows. First, get consumers in a given community fired up about the prospect of fighting their local utilities. Next, get legislation passed—typically at the state level—forcing utilities operating in the community to include RUCAG solicitations with their bills. That is the key to the whole enterprise. When the utility bill arrives in the mail, it is accompanied by a solicitation letter. Interested consumers sign up, and an extra fifty cents or dollar is added to their monthly bill. That money is used to hire a professional staff of lawyers and accountants to act as watchdogs.

It's a favorite Nader concept: corporations being forced to participate in the hiring of their own ombudsmen. The RUCAGs would not even have to pay mailing costs. Thanks to a nifty legislative gambit, the group's materials got lumped in with the utility's mailings. It is kind of like a stowaway on an ocean liner.

Nader hired a couple of full-time organizers to travel around the country touting his idea. By the early 1980s, the concept had taken hold in Wisconsin, Oregon, and San Diego. Along the way, RUCAG morphed into the considerably more euphonious CUB, or consumer utility board. Nader's biggest CUB victory was getting one started in Illinois, a state in which consumers faced triple-digit rate hikes during the early 1980s.

During the autumn of 1983, the Illinois state legislature considered a bill to establish a CUB. Nader approached Springfield in the same manner that he had long approached Washington, lobbying key legislators, writing impassioned letters and placing his patented odd-hour phone calls. In a new venue, his techniques were fresh and communicated an unusually fervent dedication. The fact that he was now consumer advocate non grata in official Washington served only to heighten his appeal. He was unsullied, untainted, uncompromising. The CUB legislation passed with ease.

Nader traveled to Chicago to stir up publicity. Now that Illinois CUB was a legislative reality, it was important to inform consumers about the new organization. Nader appeared on WGN's *Wally Phillips Show,* a popular radio program in Chicago. He also held press conferences, attended town meetings, and spoke at Triton Community College. For his barnstorming tour, Nader was accompanied by Patrick Quinn, an Illinois politician, who was at that time running for lieutenant governor. "He gave credibility to the whole thing," recalls Quinn. "Here's the number-one consumer advocate coming to Chicago, telling people about this new law. Nader was the key to getting the membership to explode."

The CUB law included a sunset provision: if the new organization failed to attract ten thousand members in its first year, it would be disbanded. The initial CUB solicitation featured a cartoon image of a utility bill punching a customer in the mouth. The tag line: "Is this how you feel when you open your utility bill?" By law, the state's power providers were forced to slip this into their regular mailings. And it hit a nerve. Illinois CUB's membership swelled to 100,000 in year one, ten times what was necessary to stay alive. The enthusiastic response brought an unexpected windfall: a budget of more than $1 million during the first year of operation.

Illinois CUB hired a team of lawyers and assorted experts and set to work. The big issue: Illinois Power and Commonwealth Edison, the state's two major energy providers, had invested heavily in nuclear plants. Construction had begun in the early 1970s, before another seminal Nader grassroots effort helped check the growth of the nuclear energy industry in the United States. Come the 1980s, the Illinois plants had gone through a series of delays and design changes. The result was massive cost overruns, which the two utilities attempted to unload onto customers.

The hired experts of Illinois CUB battled the state's two major power companies. The average consumer may have appreciated the notion of not getting socked in the mouth by the utilities. But to get anything substantive accomplished required highly credentialed specialists, regulatory lawyers, and energy consultants. Before rate boards and utility commissions, they wrangled endlessly over issues that were almost mind-bendingly complex: amortization, depreciation, cost of capital. This was also quintessential Nader organization territory. "I've come to the conclusion that the most important things in life are boring," Nader once said. "That's why our problems persist."

After a protracted struggle, Illinois CUB defeated the two big utilities. It was ruled that consumers would not have to bear the entire cost of the long-delayed and way-over-budget nuclear plants. Illinois CUB also won a series of other cases that led in 1987 to a blanket settlement. Customers received a $1.3 billion rebate, still the largest ever provided by the utility industry. The average customer in Illinois got back $175, usually in the form of a 25 percent break on energy bills for an entire year. This was something the average consumer could understand, and it was headline news all over Illinois.

"Nader added heft and credibility to our issues," says Howard Learner, who served as the first chairman of Illinois CUB. "Public utility regulation involves a huge set of issues that truly affect people's daily lives. To his credit, Nader was perhaps less D.C.-centric than some other advocates. He recognized that many key consumer issues are decided at the state or local level."

GRASSROOTS TELEVISION WAS ANOTHER of Nader's favored projects. At various times, Nader had tried to prevail on Congress to legislate one hour per day of viewer-generated programming. It had long been his contention that the public legally owned the airwaves, and that the Federal Communications Commission (FCC) had merely divvied them up and assigned them to various media companies. He once described this as a "gross inequality of electronic access" that "forces the public to rely on a few corporations' perceptions of society, politics, the arts and the public itself."

During the Reagan administration, Nader started an organization called Citizens Television. He managed to obtain a 1,000-watt television station in Buffalo, New York. It held one of more than eight hundred low-power television (LPTV) licenses that the FCC made available in a lottery.

Under Nader's ownership, Buffalo's Channel 58 assembled an unusual slate of programming, including "Ethnic Showcase" that featured local Polish, Greek, and Italian folk dancing troupes. A show called "Best Chefs of Buffalo" surveyed restaurants such as the Anchor Bar, originator of the city's famous chicken wings. Nader's LPTV station was on the air twenty-four hours a day and filled the time with whatever programming it could find, including broadcasts of the Erie County Legislature and the local board of education.

The station was a nonprofit. It ran on a minuscule budget even by the standards of LPTV. Whereas most low-frequency channels operated on roughly $150,000 a year, Channel 58 got by on more like $50,000. It was staffed by a skeleton crew of harried and dramatically underpaid young people, a typical Nader organization.

Broadcasts of various civic meetings often featured a single camera panning from speaker to speaker. For a given event, one camera was all the station could spare. A primary revenue source for Channel 58 was advertisement slots sold for $10 each to local businesses that could not afford to advertise elsewhere.

"In some ways it demystified television," says Deborah Heisler. "I think that Ralph's vision was to create a real live television laboratory." Heisler was just twenty-three, fresh out of the University of Buffalo with a masters in communications, when she signed on to be the station manager. "It's crazy the stuff you can do when you have no money," she recalls.

Channel 58—Nader's noble and impecunious broadcasting experiment—managed to stay on the air until 1991.

NADER MAY HAVE GONE TO THE grass roots during the Reagan years. But among his detractors—and more than a few former Raiders—there was also a sense of diminished scope on his part. Once upon a time, he had slain entire industries. Now he was shuffling off to Buffalo to launch an edge-of-the-dial television station for the benefit of insomniacs and a smattering of political junkies. Even the victories of the various CUBs, while significant, were confined to individual states.

But this was an underestimation of Nader. It overlooked an almost bionic earnestness on his part. As a man consumed by notions about civic duty, he felt there was no battle too small. Almost as a point of pride, he often threw his energies behind tiny, unheralded causes. This was unusual in a man who had appeared on the cover of both *Time* and *Newsweek*, who had once been sought out by power brokers and presidents alike. It was also a quality that would help gradually pave his way back into prominence.

Jason Adkins was the first executive director of Buyers Up, a home heating oil purchasing collective, and yet another Nader grassroots effort of Reagan-era vintage. During 1983—its first year of existence—Buyers Up enrolled just 850 households, a truly tiny effort. Within a few years, however, membership had grown to fifteen thousand households with a combined buying power of nearly $10 million. Unlike Channel 58, Buyers Up is still in operation today.

"The idea is to plant seeds," says Adkins. "Nader was very cognizant that you need to first test an idea and prove its merit. He was always available, always getting people excited about their own power to get something started."

Of course, Nader's tremendous earnestness also made him a curious figure. There was something immutable about him. By the Reagan era, America had gone through so many changes that the 1960s were already a distant memory. But there was Nader still donning the same drab suits and same skinny ties that he wore to the GM hearings in 1966. He liked to brag that he was still working his way through the dozen pairs of shoes and four dozen pairs of socks that he had purchased at the army PX back in 1959.

There was also an increasing quality of solitude about Nader, not that he had ever been gregarious, at least in a conventional sense. In 1984 Nader turned fifty. He had built up a vast network of acquaintances and associates but had few genuine friends, people with whom it was possible to confide or discuss matters outside of work. Truly, there was no outside of work. During a 1984 interview, Claudia Dreifus of the *Progressive* asked if he regretted the fact that he had never gotten married or had a family. "Yeah sure," he said. But he quickly added: "Doing my kind of work, there was never enough time. . . . Millions of people can create kids. There have to be some people that help save them, protect them."

His image had solidified: a lone figure—saint or Savonarola depending on where one stood politically—ever vigilant, forever outraged, willing to sacrifice comfort and material gain to fight on behalf of the public. It was an image that he was happy to burnish when the opportunity arose.

The *New York Times* once asked various public figures to describe their typical Thanksgiving. The paper published responses from Mayor Ed Koch, actress Carol Channing, and writer Isaac Bashevis Singer, all extolling the pleasures of good eating in the company of friends and family. Nader's response: "I celebrate Thanksgiving by working to make our Constitution apply to our nation's policies. I eat by my work—one hand on the typewriter and the other on a piece of turkey. I work all Thanksgiving. That's the way I give thanks."

NADER CONTINUED TO DELIVER scores of speeches, yet another good way to build his beyond-the-Beltway reputation. This is something he had been doing seemingly forever. But during the Reagan years, he stepped up his schedule, adopted an almost inhuman pace.

Beginning in 1966, Nader had been represented by the American Program Bureau out of Newton, Massachusetts. The agency also arranged bookings for Bob Woodward, Gloria Steinem, and Julian Bond.

Ken Eisenstein handled Nader's engagements, and he recalls that Nader was the biggest trooper of anyone on the agency's roster. He would deign to go places that most speakers of his prominence would assiduously avoid. He was always up for any venue such as a tiny community college one hundred miles north of nowhere, and he was willing to brave a treacherous mountain pass to get to it. He still did not drive. His only rule was that the person who picked him up at the airport not show up in a Volkswagen, his personal candidate for most unsafe make of automobile. Based on research done by associates, he also preferred to avoid Fiats and Hondas if possible.

Circa the 1980s, Nader's standard opening line for a speech was: "How many of you are hungry to become fighters for justice in America?" He continued to electrify audiences with his own odd brand of anticharisma. As Eisenstein recalls: "When things were tough for him in Washington he was more popular than ever elsewhere in the country, particularly with college students. People were looking for a voice such as his, addressing issues that were being overlooked. I think people saw him as not a part of the system. In the '80s, he was not running for anything, and he was not asking for anything, save for participation by citizens."

Nader enjoyed speaking at law schools and always relished any opportunity to needle students at Harvard. On June 11, 1985, he delivered a speech at his alma mater entitled, "Harvard Lawyers: Nabobs of Narcissism Wallowing in Complacency?" He was also popular with medical groups such as the California Nurses Association. Whenever possible, he would hop into Canada, where his views about societal responsibility always played well.

Surprisingly, even corporate audiences were sometimes open to Nader. This was the era when "customer service" was a big buzzword, and consultants such as Tom Peters were busy spreading the gospel. Of course, nobody had offered more trenchant observations than Nader regarding the relationship between corporations and their customers. Certain companies and industry groups viewed booking a Nader speech as a way to learn from a critic. Such audiences tended to be receptive, if not exactly enthusiastic.

Other corporate venues proved impossible to crack. Randy Poe is communications director of the Conference Board, a business research group in New York City. During the 1980s, Poe remembers there would be periodic calls for staffers to suggest controversial speakers to appear at the organization's events. Repeatedly, he put Nader's name into the hopper. "I could never get him through," recalls Poe. "We had hoodlum union organizers, the pope one year: we had all kinds of strange and horrible people. But nobody wanted him. I've never seen such fear among mainstream executives as was provoked by that one name, Ralph Nader."

There is an axiom in the speech-booking business that the more you pay the less you get. The most sought-after speakers—ex-presidents, folk-hero CEOs, sports stars—often confine their appearance to one hour. Nader's trademark was the three-hour speech followed by the extended Q&A, taking questions until not a single raised hand was left in an auditorium. After that, he might meet with stragglers to discuss starting a PIRG or a CUB or whatever he was currently touting.

One time Nader was in Hawaii to deliver a speech and found himself with several hours of unstructured time. He called Eisenstein to see if it was possible to make any kind of last-minute arrangement.

"How about taking a walk on the beach," offered Eisenstein.

This was met with silence on the other end of the line.

NADER WOULD CONTINUE TO tour the country tirelessly. He would also continue to explore a variety of populist approaches and grassroots endeavors. But first Nader would have to get through 1986, the worst year of his life.

That year, he developed a condition called Bell's Palsy. It affects the nerves in a person's face. Common symptoms include various ticks and twitches, and even partial paralysis of facial muscles. The condition is often unilateral, affecting only one side of a person's face. Bell's Palsy takes its name from Charles Bell, a Scottish doctor who in 1882 was first to document the condition. The cause is still unknown, although it is suspected to be a virus. Nader was sure that he had contracted the condition from recirculating air while traveling on a plane.

In his case, Bell's Palsy initially froze the left side of his face, although that gradually abated. But he had continued difficulty controlling the muscles on that side. His left eyelid also began to droop. For some, Bell's Palsy lasts only a few weeks, but in Nader's case it would linger. He took to wearing dark sunglasses and began to joke with audiences that he could no longer be accused of talking out of both sides of his mouth.

Then, in August 1986, Shafeek died of prostate cancer. Nader was devastated by the death of his older brother.

A memorial service was held for Shaf at a church in the Georgetown section of Washington, D.C. Nader delivered a eulogy in which he described how his brother had been an inspiration. He reminisced about growing up together, recalled how Shaf had helped him learn to read. As Nader spoke, he wept openly.

Mike Pertschuk was in attendance and after the service he approached Nader to offer his condolences. Nader threw his arms around Pertschuk and held him in a tight embrace.

"I only wish you could have known him," said Nader.

"It was just not a Ralph you had ever seen before," says Pertschuk. "It was a really vulnerable, open, loving Ralph."

Shaf's death was the first really significant loss Nader experienced. Both parents were still alive, though his father was now in his nineties.

Nader had been on the go for years. He had raided Congress, published a best-seller, umpired a presidential softball game; he had taken down the FTC, met Upton Sinclair, been spied on, pissed off, parodied by *Mad*; he had been involved in the passage of two dozen federal consumer laws; Nader had launched PIRGs, CUBs, and all manner of acronymous organizations; he had hired thousands, fired off angry missives, been lauded and lambasted in articles beyond counting; he had been high, low, up, down, in and out of favor.

Following Shaf's death, Nader returned to his boyhood home in Winsted, Connecticut. For three months, he did absolutely nothing.

—16—

In Torts We Trust

WHEN SHAF FIRST BECAME ILL, NADER WAS in California fighting a proposal to place limits on civil suits. During the Reagan era, this was perhaps Nader's most dedicated and controversial grassroots effort: he was willing to travel anywhere, anytime, to battle efforts to modify the tort system. After his hiatus in Winsted, he resumed the fight with a vengeance.

Nader had an abiding faith in lawyers and in the capacity of the law to solve ordinary people's problems. This stance owes a considerable debt to Roscoe Pound, father of sociological jurisprudence and Nader's mentor during Harvard days. Pound's views had launched a revolution in legal thinking during the first part of the twentieth century. The crux of his argument: instead of merely being a code of abstract principles, the law should attend to actual problems in society.

In a nod to Pound, Nader's breakthrough book, *Unsafe at Any Speed*, offered a blueprint for a legal action that would address a societal ill. It rigorously documented the design defects of a single model, the Chevrolet Corvair. Of course, it had been crucial during the Ribicoff hearings to establish that Nader was not litigating by day and castigating by night. That would have violated one of the American Bar Association's professional canons. But nothing prevented other lawyers from using the information Nader had culled. GM was slapped with countless Corvair suits, and *Unsafe at Any Speed* was like a *Cliff Notes* for lawyers in search of evidence, strategies, and potential friendly witnesses.

It is fair to say that *Unsafe*—along with Nader's subsequent attacks on various corporations—made him a hero among trial lawyers. From 1966 on,

Nader was a celebrated speaker at venues such as the annual meeting of the American Trial Lawyers Association. Nader raids and reports issued by Nader organizations continued to provide blueprints for subsequent actions by plaintiffs' attorneys. For instance, Public Citizen's Health Group might issue a report documenting the adverse effects of a particular pharmaceutical product. Such a report was a boon to lawyers involved in suits against the manufacturer, just as *Unsafe* had aided the lawyers who took on GM.

The relationship between Nader and the trial lawyers would be a lasting one. It was also one that made even some of Nader's most ardent supporters uneasy. It was seen by some as a kind of marriage of convenience. From the outset, Nader had fought ceaselessly against corporate power and all its myriad abuses. Trial lawyers also take on corporations, suing them on behalf of their clients. In the process, many of them also get very, very rich.

Therein lies the heart of a common criticism of Nader. Sure, trial lawyers battle corporations, goes the argument, but they do so in part to line their own pockets. The sleaziest of them are mere ambulance chasers. Many people—even people who agreed with Nader on most things—felt his faith in trial lawyers was misguided. Others questioned his motives. But Nader was unequivocal in his support.

For their part, the plaintiffs' lawyers loved being associated with America's number one consumer advocate. It gave them a social mandate. It elevated them from hired-gun status, transformed them into champions of the little guy versus marauding corporate interests.

In 1982, Nader helped found an organization called Trial Lawyers for Public Justice (TLPJ). It was another of his nonprofits, this one predicated on the notion that plaintiffs' attorneys are geographically dispersed across the United States. Many are sole practitioners with limited experience. TLPJ was designed as a networking organization. If a lawyer in Fayetteville, Arkansas, took on his first case involving defective tires, there might be another lawyer in Ames, Iowa, who had handled a variety of similar cases. Match the two up—via TLPJ—and the more experienced lawyer could offer needed guidance.

One of TLPJ's first cases involved lending expertise to Jan Schlichtmann, who needed help preparing a so-called toxic tort case against W. R. Grace. The company's facility in Woburn, Massachusetts, had improperly disposed of the chemical trichlorethylene. It wound up contaminating the town's water supply. Ultimately, Schlichtmann won a large settlement for eight families whose children had died of leukemia. The case was the basis of the best-selling book *A Civil Action*. "The way to get people to stop doing bad things is to make them pay through the nose," says Arthur Bryant, the executive director of TLPJ.

On this, both Nader and the trial lawyers were in total agreement. As a consequence, Nader could be counted on as a vocal opponent of any restriction on the use of tort law.

During the mid-1980s, Nader viewed torts as a kind of last bastion for consumer protection. By this time, two entire branches of the federal government were hostile to his agenda: the executive branch under Reagan and the legislative branch, which was moving increasingly to the right. But Nader retained a faith in the judicial branch, which he once described as "the least corruptible of the three branches of government." He hoped that lawyers, juries, and judges would continue to uphold the interests of consumers.

"He wanted to keep the courthouse door open," says J. D. Lee, a Knoxville trial lawyer who has worked closely with Nader over the years. "He hoped actions of the courts would help make products safer and make society safer. You could not depend on the federal regulatory bodies. The only thing left was the civil justice system."

Even on this front, Nader began to face significant opposition. In the mid–1980s, a large-scale push began for tort reform, or as Nader liked to call it, "tort deform." The main proponents were business interests such as trade associations and insurance companies. But unlike so many business-generated proposals, tort reform had a broad, almost populist appeal. Then as now, there were abundant news stories about modestly injured parties suing corporations and winning multimillion-dollar judgments. Such activities contributed to an impression that the court system was more like a lottery. During the 1980s, in particular, there were concerns that huge verdicts were harming the competitive standing of entire industries vis-à-vis Japan. Advocates of tort reform also argued that companies were withholding useful products due to liability concerns.

Tort reform is typically a state matter. The most common proposals of 1980s vintage involved placing caps on the size of damage awards. But there were also more specialized proposals on the table, involving issues such as joint-and-several liability, statutes of repose, and forum shopping. Nader resisted them all, categorically.

Joint-and-several liability is the practice of shifting damages from one defendant to another. Say a drunk driver slams into a car, causing an explosion that seriously injures the occupants. Any sensible plaintiff's attorney will name as defendants both the drunk driver and the manufacturer of the car that exploded. One possible outcome: a $10 million award in which the driver is found 90 percent responsible for the accident and the automaker is handed 10 percent of the blame. In all likelihood, the driver cannot come up with that much money. Recovery of damages then shifts to the automaker, which can wind up stuck with the entire cost even though it was found only 10 percent liable.

During the 1980s, joint-and-several liability reform was pushed in particular by municipalities. In almost any accident, it is possible to claim that road conditions played a role. A common legal strategy is to sue the driver, the automaker, and the city in which the accident took place. "There's always a question of whether a stop sign is visible or whether a road's center line is clear. It has a tremendously distorting effect on litigation," says Marty Connor.

Connor—former public affairs counsel for General Electric and a frequent opponent of Nader's perspective on civil litigation—was one of the founders in 1986 of the American Tort Reform Association.

Statutes of repose are similar to statutes of limitation. This reform was pushed in particular by the machine tool industry. As of the 1980s, it was facing fierce competition from overseas. Domestic machine tool makers were having trouble moving their products. Meanwhile, the industry's legal costs were piling up. The reason: even many years after a sale, the manufacturer of a piece of industrial equipment can often still be sued. Consider, for example, an accident in which a factory worker is injured while using a lathe. Standard legal strategy is to go after the lathe's manufacturer, even if the tool is old and in poor working condition. Tort reforms involving statutes of repose were designed to shift liability away from industrial equipment makers after a given time period, typically ten or fifteen years. The argument: a twenty-year-old lathe is the responsibility of the factory where it is operated or the employees who maintain it, and the tool's original manufacturer should not still be liable.

Forum shopping is the practice of searching around for a court that will be especially sympathetic to the plaintiff's perspective. In a class action suit, there can sometimes be thousands of litigants spread across the United States. It is often possible to select a favorable venue. For example, the state court in Holmes County, Mississippi, is notorious for handing down pro-plaintiff rulings, often in the multimillion-dollar range.

Nader fought tort reform at every turn. It was his practice to parachute into a state that was considering a measure and testify before the legislature. Victor Schwartz is a former professor at the University of Cincinnati law school, where he taught a course on torts. During the 1980s, he was a lobbyist for the Product Liability Alliance, a group that represented the interests of manufacturers and insurance companies. He frequently squared off against Nader. "He was extremely effective," says Schwartz. "When he was introduced in front of state legislatures, it would be as 'consumer advocate Ralph Nader.' Before I had even said a word, I would be behind the eight ball."

Schwartz adds: "The trial lawyers would never testify themselves. They ran the risk of appearing partisan. I would never even see them at hearings. Instead, I would see Ralph Nader. He was their poster boy. They would treat him the way Catholics treat the pope. It was something to behold."

Nader's record on the tort issue is impossible to tally in simple wins and losses. During the mid-1980s, a number of measures passed that placed caps on damage awards. In 1986, for example, Maryland capped punitive damages at $350,000 despite Nader's opposition. Nearly forty states passed laws regarding joint-and-several liability. Meanwhile, Nader deserves at least partial credit for virtually every proposed modification to the tort system that did not pass. There were plenty of examples of this, too. "We won a preponderance of the battles," says Nader, "and we lost a significant number of them."

But one thing is certain: whenever any kind of tort reform was being considered anywhere, it was always against Nader's objection. On this heated and divisive issue, he finally seemed capable of being in two places at once.

Nader even fought reforms that sought to merely clarify the tort system. Fifty states, each with varied statutes regarding tort law, formed a crazy quilt. Some states proposed legislation during the mid-1980s designed to better spell out their particular tort laws. But Nader feared that if corporations knew the rules, they might start making calculations: "so much for a hand, so much for a leg, almost like a workers' comp system," as he puts it. Better to keep them in a state of uncertainty and unease. If a company fears that it might face a fat multimillion-dollar verdict, it is likely to be extra cautious. In a 1988 article in the *Denver University Law Review*, Nader wrote: "The prospect of tort liability deters those manufacturers, builders, doctors and other tort-feasors from repeating their negligent behavior; it provides them with a proper economic incentive to curb their damaging practices and to make their endeavors more safe."

On the topic of tort reform Nader is an absolutist. His view is the equivalent of how certain civil liberties advocates approach free speech. *If Americans truly value free speech, they must be willing to tolerate speech they find objectionable*—it's a hallowed First Amendment defense, trumpeted by everyone from William Kunstler to *Hustler* publisher Larry Flynt. Nader held similar notions regarding torts. The system has to be left unfettered, even to the point of the occasional preposterous $10 million for a hangnail verdict. A society that starts limiting the system, goes Nader's argument, runs the risk of heading down a slippery slope. Invariably, it is individual consumers who suffer and corporations that get off the hook.

NADER'S IMPLACABLE POSITION ON tort reform left even his critics puzzled. "It is so inconsistent with the rest of his message," says Mike Hotra, a spokesman for the American Tort Reform Association. "This is a man who wants to regulate virtually every aspect of American life. But that whole perspective disappears when he talks about civil justice reform. He simply doesn't want anything done, ever. He's the most laissez-faire out there."

One compelling scenario—taken up over the years by a series of investigative reporters—is that Nader was simply in bed with the trial lawyers financially. There have even been suggestions that members of the plaintiffs' bar tithe, giving a portion of each verdict to Nader in exchange for his continued and vocal opposition to tort reform. In an article entitled "Ralph Nader Inc.," *Forbes* magazine tried to establish a link. But the two authors resorted to fairly shoddy investigative techniques. For example, the assertion that Nader was financially beholden to the plaintiffs' attorneys was based largely on anecdotal evidence: quotes from a handful of lawyers admitting that they donated money to Nader and his various organizations. Not a single source volunteered an amount. Sources were invariably identified as follows: "Miami's J. B. Spence (1988 income, $2.5 million)." The implication was obvious: this trial lawyer made a mint, he admitted giving money to Nader, so he must be contributing a considerable sum. As for the cumulative amount of donations Nader had received from trial lawyers since 1966, the best *Forbes* could do was "minimum $1 million, maximum?"

Over the years, Gary Sellers worked on a variety of projects involving Nader and the trial lawyers. "That's ridiculous," he says of the money-for-influence charges made by *Forbes* and others. "Sure he received some money from the trial lawyers. And he could have made many millions out of them, though I doubt he even tried. You have to remember, during this period he could get all the money he desired from a variety of other sources."

In the mid-1980s, Nader made hundreds of thousands of dollars per year from speeches and book royalties. His Center for the Study of

Responsive Law continued to receive substantial grants from wealthy benefactors such as the Rockefeller Family Fund.

Here, once again, the conventional explanation does not seem to hold when it comes to Nader. It seems unlikely that a person as obsessively principled as Nader would allow himself to be bought. This seems doubly so, when one considers that he had all kinds of other sources of income. The more likely explanation is that Nader and the trial lawyers simply shared a viewpoint, albeit a strongly held one. Both parties wanted an unfettered civil justice system that maximized the potential verdicts against corporations. The plaintiffs' attorneys objected to any efforts to alter tort law, in part because it would hurt their substantial income stream. Nader was in total agreement thanks to philosophical convictions all his own . . . or somewhat his own.

Nader's views—it is worth noting—were shaped in part by the work in anthropology done by his sister Laura. At Berkeley, victims' rights had long been one of her areas of expertise. By the time Ralph began his tort reform battle, she had already conducted extensive research on victims' rights, including a 1978 book called *The Disputing Process*. This work examines systems of redress in ten different societies, ranging from Sardinia to Lebanon to Mexico to New Guinea.

In the Naders' ancestral Lebanon, for example, a grievant goes to the muhtar—or town mayor—who makes a ruling. By contrast, Laura Nader found that the practice among certain tribal societies in New Guinea is for the parties in a dispute to take to the streets and yell out their troubles. People start lining up behind the party with whom they agree. The disputant with the longer line wins. "This is where my work and my brother's work dovetailed," says Laura Nader.

Ralph Nader was especially taken with his sister's contention that there is a paucity of litigation in the United States, rather than too much. Her anthropological research suggested that in less developed societies, disputants often were on fairly equal ground. But in an advanced industrial society, large and entrenched interests simply find ways to tilt the balance. Tort reform—in the eyes of both Naders—was simply a sneaky way for corporations to duck the kind of verdicts judges and juries were likely to dole out. It was a way to deny victims their rights.

"Compensation is what most people in the world expect," she says. "It's nothing new, and it's not something that comes with civilization. It's something that humankind has built. If you don't get compensation or some kind of recognition, you just build resentment. So what happens when there's no access to law and no compensation and no alleviation? What do you do? That was my question as an anthropologist. Ralph picks it up on the other side as a legal-policy matter."

Nader conferred regularly with his sister on the tort system. He even quoted from her scholarly work in some of his own prepared materials on the issue.

IN 1988 NADER RETURNED to California to wage a pitched tort battle. Two years earlier, he had failed to defeat a proposal on the issue of joint-and-several liability. Known as the "deep pockets" initiative, it curbed a plaintiff's ability to draw damages disproportionately from the wealthiest defendant in a lawsuit. Back then, Nader had been in the first throes of Bell's Palsy. It was also during this period that he had first learned that Shaf was gravely ill.

But the autumn of 1988 found Nader back in California, lending his support to Proposition 103. Prop 103 called for an immediate 20 percent cut on auto insurance rates, paring them back to 1987 levels. It also called for an insurance commissioner who was elected rather than appointed. If the ballot initiative passed, a great deal more disclosure would be required of the insurance industry.

Prop 103 was authored by Harvey Rosenfield, a graduate of Georgetown law school who once earned $600 as a summer Nader Raider and later headed out to California to work with the state's student PIRG. For his Prop 103 fight, Rosenfield started an organization called Voter Revolt and set up offices in a dingy warehouse in Santa Monica. He assembled a group of volunteers to canvass door-to-door, gathering signatures so that Prop 103 could appear on the ballot.

Rosenfield was known as a master of the publicity gimmick. One of Voter Revolt's early stunts involved trying to dump a truckload of cow chips in front of State Farm's headquarters in Los Angeles. Ultimately, Rosenfield would get vastly more publicity for Prop 103 through far simpler means: enlisting the support of his one-time boss, Ralph Nader.

In 1988 Californians were contending with exorbitant auto insurance rates, third highest in the nation behind Alaska and New Jersey. Over the previous several years, premiums had been climbing at a 20 percent annual clip. It was the contention of Rosenfield, Nader, and other supporters of Voter Revolt that the high rates were the result of sloppy policy writing and poor financial controls on the part of the auto insurers. Prop 103 was a bid to regulate the industry.

There were three other competing ballot initiatives, including Prop 104, sponsored by the insurance industry. Where Nader and company blamed high rates on the insurers' own financial mismanagement, it was the industry's contention that premium inflation was caused by lawsuits that were too frequent and were sometimes even fraudulent. As such, Prop 104 was essentially a tort-reform proposal. It called for an innovation known as no-fault auto insurance.

Under such a system, drivers involved in accidents recover damages only from their own insurance companies. Drivers who were injured would be able to collect money for car repairs and medical bills. But because no party is assigned blame for the accident, lawsuits seeking to recover damages for pain and suffering would be eliminated. According to the insurance industry, no-fault would put a stop to such bogus practices as someone getting in a car accident, complaining of whiplash, showing up at court in a neck brace, and walking away with $1 million for pain and suffering. If insurers could avoid such unreasonable costs, argued the industry, then premiums would stop spiking.

Prop 104 was anathema to Nader. To him, it was simply a thinly veiled effort by the insurance industry to limit the ability of consumers to seek redress. Nader launched a blitz in support of rival Prop 103, which sought to bring down rates through regulation.

He traveled all over California. During one six-day stretch, he stumped for Prop 103 in Los Angeles's Grand Central Market, aboard a cable car in San Francisco, in an Oakland firehouse, at a San Diego day care center, and on the steps of the capitol building in Sacramento, accompanied by Gray Davis, then the state controller. Along the way, he made a memorable late-night appearance at a truck stop in Santa Nella, a town along Interstate 5.

A couple of Voter Revolt staffers got on the loudspeaker system and announced that Nader would begin speaking in fifteen minutes. A crowd of truckers began to gather, intrigued that a noted consumer advocate was going to talk about why insurance rates were so high. At the appointed time, Nader took up a position in the parking lot. But it was too dark to see him very well. So several of the trucks trained their headlights on him. Thus illuminated, Nader worked himself into a fine outrage, stating at one point that the insurance industry was "high on the narcotic of its own gluttonous profits."

This was pure Nader. Insurance was an important topic, yet deadly dull. The fact that there were four competing ballot initiatives served only to up the yawn quotient and increase confusion. As in his early battles in Washington, Nader showed himself once again to be a master at extracting the essence of a complex and technical issue. He even crafted a little jingle that he would repeat at his various stops: "103 is the one for me . . . you pay more with 104 . . . the one to nix is 106."

As the battle of the ballot initiatives heated up, an opinion poll taken in California produced the following finding: Among state residents who admitted knowing absolutely nothing about the four rival proposals, 67 percent said they would vote for Prop 103 simply because it was associated with Ralph Nader. That compares to 13 percent who said they would vote for Prop 104 because it was being pushed by the insurance industry.

Nader may have possessed a Q rating to die for, but the insurers had an advantage of their own. They had money, lots of it. In the final days before the November 8 election, they saturated the airwaves with pro–Prop 104 messages. Voter Revolt supporters responded with grassroots guerrilla tactics, such as spraying "Prop 103" on overpasses above the Santa Monica freeway. Over the weekend prior to the election, L.A.'s famous hillside Hollywood sign was draped with a banner that read, "Yes on 103."

Nader's proposal won in the end, garnering 51 percent of the vote. It would mark a substantial victory for California's consumers going forward. Between 1989 and 1998, insurance premiums in the state declined by 4 percent, while they went up by nearly 40 percent on average across the rest of the country. This, according to a study by the Consumer Federation of America. As for the larger issue—tort reform—nothing was really resolved. It would continue to be a state-by-state, case-by-case matter with only one constant—Nader's opposition was guaranteed.

For Nader personally, the passage of Prop 103 was a huge victory. He had won in California, virtually on name recognition alone. There was a David-versus-Goliath element resonant of his first victory against GM. Voter Revolt had spent a paltry $2.9 million pushing Prop 103, while the insurance industry had sunk $65 million on its rival proposal. It was Nader's most high-profile activity since the defeat of the Consumer Protection Agency, a full ten years before. It grabbed headlines far outside of California and led to a spate of Nader-is-back stories.

Even more significant: stumping on behalf of Prop 103 marked the closest Nader had ever gotten to outright political campaigning. After all, he had crisscrossed a single state, California, delivering speeches in support of a proposal that ultimately had to win favor not with senators or Washington political columnists but with ordinary citizens in the voting booth. For Nader, this was a revelation that would profoundly affect how he expended his energies in the decade ahead.

—17—

Mars Invades

ONCE UPON A TIME, NADER SAID he would only enter politics if there was an "invasion from Mars." So what made Ralph run–and run three times, no less—between 1992 and 2000? "There was an invasion from Wall Street," he quips. "I never thought the government would crumble so thoroughly."

Nader may have been disillusioned by Carter. He may have found himself shut out during the Reagan-Bush era. But these were mere grumbles compared with the heaping resentment he would build during two terms of Bill Clinton. For the first time in his experience, Nader found himself ignored as thoroughly by a Democratic administration as ever he had been by a Republican one. It was a situation that he summed up by referring to the president as "George Ronald Clinton."

Nader and Clinton did not meet a single time in the course of eight years. At one point, when Clinton was preparing to sign legislation eliminating the fifty-five miles per hour speed limit on interstate highways, Nader requested a five-minute sit-down. Raising the speed to sixty-five, he feared, would lead to an increase in accidents. Clinton did not even respond.

Al Gore also turned a cold shoulder. During the Reagan years, Gore had actually been something of an ally, or at least he was as close to an ally as one could be with Nader. At a time when Nader was welcome in precious few congressional offices, he found Gore to be receptive on issues such as broadcast licensing and biotechnology. "He was in the top ten of the hundred senators," Nader grudgingly recalls. "On the environment, he was okay. On torts, he was especially good."

Vice President Gore was a different matter. Stiffed by Clinton, Nader also failed to gain an audience with Gore. At one point, his assistant received a letter: "The vice president has no time to meet with Mr. Nader." Puzzled and distressed, Nader placed a phone call to Gore. The vice president was noncommittal about setting up a meeting, closing the phone call with a terse "Well, I'll see." Those were the last words Nader and Gore would exchange.

As for the Clinton-era Congress, Nader found that he was a pariah, even among the most liberal members. In 1997 Peter DeFazio and Bernard Sanders invited Nader to speak before the House Progressive Caucus. For someone who had once addressed Congress on an almost daily basis, this now counted as a rare appearance. Although the House Progressive Caucus seemed as if it might be an ideal venue for Nader, only five of the fifty caucus members even bothered to show up.

From Nader's standpoint, the icy reception in Washington was proof of serious drift among Democrats. They had simply pilfered the Republican political agenda, shuffled it around, rechristened a few elements, and called it their own—a process he termed "protective imitation." He was fond of pointing out that Clinton and Gore would not have qualified as liberal Republicans in 1970.

The doors were all shut, tighter than ever. As he did during the Reagan years, Nader went to the grass roots, attending to issues on the local level. But he was finding that there were limits to what could be accomplished with CUBs and PIRGs. Nader wanted to have a say on weighty national issues such as the various Clinton-era free trade treaties, which he vehemently opposed. More than ever before, he found it hard to get any political traction. Nader was now a bit like the proverbial tree falling in the woods: he talked plenty about GATT and NAFTA, but no one in official Washington heard a sound.

Nader did not relent. As an undergrad at Princeton, he had read Schopenhauer and other philosophers in an effort to understand the nature of pessimism. He came to the conclusion that it served no practical purpose in life. Four decades later—facing widespread opposition and indifference—Nader simply refused to allow himself to fall into despair.

Instead, Nader began to hone his anticorporate critique. Always before, Nader had looked at corporate abuses on a case-by-case basis. He had scrutinized the activities of DuPont or Citibank, had raided the ICC and the FDA. However, his growing status as a true political outsider forced him to reevaluate his ideas. *Why was it next to impossible to get a hearing with a member of Congress, even a Democrat?* Nader's answer: because the party was increasingly beholden to corporate campaign contributions. *If the press is free, why was it so difficult to air alternative viewpoints?* His answer: major media outlets are owned by large corporations. Nader developed a kind of single-gunman theory: democracy itself was in crisis because of the pervasive influence of corporations.

Such an observation was hardly grist for a Raider report. He did not hire a fresh armada of eager young Ivy League grads to dash off *Sold Out: How American Democracy Has Been Perverted by Corporations*. Instead, Nader's observations added up to something more like a theory, a political theory. Nader became increasingly convinced that if he were ever again going to make a genuine difference, he was going to have to find yet another outlet. This time he decided to go directly to the root of the problem. So it was that the perennial outsider chose to enter politics. He did not necessarily expect to win elective office; few third-party candidates do. Rather, it was another way to get his message out, about the only one he had not yet tried. Maybe, in a nod to Norman Thomas, he could even persuade the Democrats to steal some parts of his agenda.

Of course, this was no overnight transformation. It required years of contemplation and ample discussion with various friends and colleagues. Marcus Raskin, who approached Nader about running on the New Party ticket in 1972, was also privy to Nader's evolving views about the political realm.

"What he saw happening was that everything he stood for was being taken away piece by piece," says Raskin. "Whether it was health and welfare, social legislation, consumer protection—it was all going down the tubes. I think there were public policy reasons to go the way he did. There may have been personal reasons, too."

Gary Sellers, who also spoke extensively with Nader during this period, stresses the personal reasons: "He felt that his star was being eclipsed. In the 1960s, he had terrified people. He figured that getting involved in electoral politics might open doors once again. People would take him seriously and return his phone calls. There was a sense of lost opportunity. It was very poignant, and it was based on reality."

Nevertheless, Nader took his time. Entering into politics was a gradual process, akin to lowering oneself into a pool of cold water. Barnstorming across California in support of Prop 103 can be seen as the first tentative toe dip. He followed up with a pair of presidential runs in 1992 and 1996, the first placing him ankle deep in politics, the second taking him up to about his knees.

In 1992 Nader participated only in the New Hampshire primary. Insisting "I'm not a politician, I'm a citizen advocate," he stumped on behalf of what he called a toolbox for democracy, a collection of issues such as campaign finance reform and public ownership of the broadcast airwaves. His big issue was adding a none-of-the-above line to ballots. Potentially, the none-of-the-above option could defeat the other candidates in an election. If this happened, there would need to be a fresh election. Nader appreciated the intimacy of the New Hampshire primary and relished speaking before small groups. He spent three weeks in the state, declaring himself a proxy for the idea of none-of-the-above. He urged people to write in his name if they were uninspired by the other Democratic contenders: Tom Harkin, John Kerry, Paul Tsongas, and Bill Clinton. He received 6,311 votes.

In 1996 Nader decided to be a bona fide presidential candidate, sort of. Around the time Clinton snubbed him on the speed limit issue, the California Green Party approached him about participating in the state primary as the Green candidate. He accepted. In rapid succession, Nader was also approached by Greens in other states, including Alaska, Colorado, and Oregon. He wound up on the ballot in twenty-one states. When asked about his candidacy, however, he offered answers such as: "You remember when I said I wasn't running for elective office? You remember when I said it several times? Some people have heard me say it two hundred times. I don't break that."

Ever the lawyer, Nader attempted in 1996 to run and not run at the same time. He approached this latest political flirtation with a whole set of hesitations, qualifications, and disclaimers. He did not register as a Green, nor did he adopt the party's platform. His campaign purchased no ads and took no contributions. He promised not to spend more than $5,000 of his own money, thereby avoiding federal regulations regarding disclosure of his personal finances. And he traveled virtually nowhere. In Nader's parlance, he "stood for president" in 1996 as opposed to actually running.

Nevertheless, the Clinton reelection team worried that Nader might tip the election. During the summer of 1996, he was polling 8 percent in California, where his Prop 103 victory was still a fresh memory. Whenever he was asked about his possible role as spoiler, Nader's stock response was: "Nobody but Clinton can beat Clinton."

Nader received 580,627 votes in 1996, good for 0.6 percent of the electorate. He came in fourth behind Reform Party candidate Ross Perot (8.5 percent) and just ahead of Harry Browne of the Libertarian Party (0.5 percent). Considering that Nader had merely "stood" for president, it was an impressive outcome. He began to wonder what would happen if he ever ran in earnest. So, too, did the Green Party. The stage was set for 2000.

THE FASCINATING THING ABOUT Nader's 2000 run is that he was such a known quantity. He had been on the national stage for thirty-five years. By this time he was the public personality equivalent of lead, a fairly immutable atomic element. Even his contradictions had hardened; he simply was who he was.

As such, his campaign style—when he finally decided to run for real—was quintessential Nader. He maintained a maniacal travel schedule, delivered triathlon speeches, guarded his privacy fiercely, concentrated on the grass roots, adopted a vast array of issues, favored the statistical absolutism of body rights over the messy emotionalism of civil rights, clashed with former employees, relied on lawyers to sue numerous parties, and demonstrated a boundless faith in young people. It was all there, a kind of compendium of all his years of work. He even recycled old phrases such as comparing the two rival candidates to "Tweedledum and Tweedledee"—a line Nader first used during an interview with *Rolling Stone* in 1979.

Present, too, was an intense animus for politics-as-usual, but one that was directed more at Gore—the prodigal Democrat—than at Bush, the hopeless and hapless Republican. And the result was similar to Nader's Consumer Protection Agency battle from the Carter era: he incurred the wrath of countless liberals, seemingly his most natural constituency.

About the only thing that set Nader's 2000 run apart from his earlier career was the degree to which he had become marginalized. He had been shut out of establishment Washington for twenty years, through three successive administrations. As such, Nader 2000 was a far cry from the classic raids, featuring clean-cut young lawyers rifling through the files of obscure government agencies. Rather, Nader's candidacy drew its share of the pink-haired and the multipierced, who brought with them a melange of issues: legalize drugs, illegalize sport utility vehicles, free Mumia Abu-Jamal. Candidate Nader did not endorse all these various views. But the fact that many of his supporters advocated such positions drew criticism, especially from former Raiders who wondered how their old boss—once a sober Washington insider—could tolerate being surrounded by such fringe-politik loopiness.

It would be a momentous, tumultuous campaign. This time Nader would stay the course, emerging as a central figure in an election that was nail bitingly close and wildly controversial.

NADER FORMALLY ANNOUNCED HIS candidacy on February 21, 2000, at the Madison Hotel in Washington, D.C. By political campaign standards this was extremely late. Incumbents often begin planning their next campaign the moment they win an election. Even third-party candidates often devote years to preparation. Then again, Nader is someone who once investigated the entire Congress in the course of a summer. He was better prepared than most for the hypercondensed time frame of a presidential run.

The first order of business was assembling a campaign staff. This proved a challenge for Nader. A huge number of talented people had worked at his assorted outfits over the years: Joan Claybrook, Sid Wolfe, Bob Fellmeth, Donald Ross, Davitt McAteer, Harrison Wellford, the list goes on and on, literally stretching into the thousands. But virtually none of them was willing to join Nader's effort. The reasons varied, everything from professional commitments to philosophical disagreement with Nader's candidacy. Some ex-Raiders were Democrats, after all, and some were even registered Republicans. Nader also had a history of clashing with his former employees, and many had parted ways unamicably. Given all these factors, the pool was actually quite small. Phil Donahue, who signed on as cochair, was one of the few campaign staffers with whom Nader shared any history. In the course of six thousand episodes of the *Donahue Show,* Nader appeared thirty-three times, the most of any guest. Even Donahue was initially hesitant, given Nader's tepid showings in 1992 and 1996.

"You've got to be serious this time," said Donahue when Nader called him about joining the campaign.

Nader assured him, saying, "I'm going all-out."

Mostly Nader was forced to recruit young people with limited experience. As campaign manager, Nader chose Theresa Amato, a thirty-five-year-old NYU law grad whom he had first met when she was working at Public Citizen's Litigation Group. The last campain she had run was in high school. But Nader turned this into a plus. During their interview, when Amato admitted how little experience she had, Nader assured her this was no problem, saying his was going to be a "different kind of campaign." Ultimately Nader would pull together a campaign staff more than 100 strong, along with thousands of volunteers, who were on average in their early twenties.

Nader also had to start raising money, and quickly. As a long-time advocate of campaign finance reform, Nader opted to take no PAC money and no corporate contributions. Instead, he limited his campaign to individual donations. Here again, his fund-raising proved a challenge. Because he was committed to smaller donations, he needed vastly more donors than the average candidate.

Of course, Nader knew a huge number of people. It made sense for him to place many of the calls personally, working his way down a long list of potential contributors. Often the same people who would not join his campaign were not inclined to give money either.

"I told him I wasn't supporting him," says Roger Hickey, codirector of the Campaign for America's Future. "I told him that I respected what he was doing but could not get behind it."

David Halberstam, Nader's boyhood friend, simply wished him good luck. As quickly as Nader could punch up phone numbers, the brush-offs rolled in. He tried to make the best of it, chatting with various old acquaintances, seeking to get a handle on problems and issues that faced various parts of the country.

Later, when the Nader campaign gathered some momentum, there was a flurry of contributions, typically in amounts of less than $100. The truly amazing thing is that Nader 2000 raised more than $8 million in this fashion, quite respectable for a third-party effort. But during the early going, Nader found fund-raising a disheartening experience.

Meanwhile, field volunteers were busy circulating petitions in an effort to get Nader on various state ballots. This was yet another fight on another front. Many states have ballot-access barriers that serve to discourage third-party candidacies. North Carolina, for example, required that 51,324 signatures be gathered by May 17, 2000. Texas asked for 37,713 signatures, to be collected during a window of just seventy-five days. Pennsylvania simply required that the petition be a very specific shade of orange. "Every state has different deadlines, different arcane procedures," recalls campaign manager Amato. "Some states put up the kind of obstacles that would make a foreign dictator blush."

Whenever Nader was unable to meet a given state's ballot-access requirements, he mounted a legal challenge. Here, the campaign worked with the Brennan Center for Justice at New York University, which helped Senator John McCain get on the ballot for the New York Republican primary. Lawyers at the Brennan Center won a number of these cases, and Nader wound up on the ballot in forty-three states plus the District of

Columbia. The states where he was not on the ballot: Georgia, Idaho, Indiana, Oklahoma, North Carolina, South Dakota, and Wyoming.

Ross Perot—it is worth noting—is one of the only third-party candidates in recent memory to get on the ballot in all fifty states. But he spent $10 million in 1996 to pursue ballot-access by paying petitioners and various other means. "It's an incredible burden for third-party candidates," says Elizabeth Daniel, one of Nader's Brennan Center lawyers. "Instead of getting their message out with rallies and press, campaigns end up expending considerable resources to deal with ballot access."

During the campaign's earliest days, Nader confronted one other major issue: breaking into the presidential debates. This was crucial. If recent elections served as any guide, as many as 90 million people could be expected to tune in to the debates in 2000. Nader knew that he could barnstorm, stump, speechify, kiss babies until he was blue in the face. But there was a limit to how much impact he could have. In terms of reaching voters, in terms of sheer blanket coverage, nothing compares to the debates.

But the Commission on Presidential Debates had set a very high hurdle for inclusion in the 2000 events: candidates were required, as of September, to have attained 15 percent voter support averaged across five national opinion polls. Many suspected that the commission was trying to prevent another wild card from entering the debates à la Ross Perot in 1992. But Nader cut right to the heart of the matter, questioning the legitimacy of the commission itself. He was struck by the arbitrariness of the 15 percent hurdle. After all, candidates need to win only 5 percent of the vote in order to qualify their party for federal matching funds in the next election. Furthermore, the commission had a totally different formula during the 1996 election, requiring candidates to meet twelve criteria before they could participate in the debates.

For many years, presidential debates were run by the League of Women Voters. But for the 1988 election, the Commission on Presidential Debates took over. Though the name suggests some kind of official government organ, the commission is actually a private corporation. It is headed by Paul Kirk Jr. and Frank Fahrenkopf Jr., former Democratic and Republican party chairmen respectively. Of course, putting on debates costs money. In 1992 and 1996, the commission sold sponsorships to a variety of corporations, including AT&T, IBM, Philip Morris, and Sara Lee.

Nader—never at a loss for vitriol—summoned special fury for the commission. Here was a private entity, funded by corporate contributions, headed by a Democrat and a Republican, making decisions about who to include in the debates. Nader filed a lawsuit in federal court, charging that corporate contributions in connection with presidential debates violate the Federal Election Campaign Act. But the lawsuit dragged out. Nader had no choice but to push forward, hoping to hit 15 percent in the polls or else strike a blow against the debate commission. “It was on our map from the beginning,” says Amato. “Either meet the criteria or expose the criteria. We wanted to get a discussion going about who really controls this entity, and how it creates this duopolic system.”

ON MARCH 1, 2000, Nader embarked on a campaign tour that was ambitious even by his exhausting standards. He decided to visit all fifty states in advance of the Green Party convention, scheduled for June in Denver. He hoped that traveling around the country would up his polling numbers and help him break into the debates. In 1996 he visited just a dozen states, and only one in seven people even knew he was running for president, according to one survey. The fifty-state tour was also a deliberate effort to prove to the Greens that he was serious this time around.

Nader tore across the country, visiting places like Modesto, California, Toledo, Ohio, and Durango, Colorado. In Boston he spoke out against a proposal to build a new stadium for the Red Sox, heavily financed with taxpayer dollars—shades of his defunct F.A.N.S. initiative. In Birmingham, Alabama, he met with the local Green Party and learned that in order to get on the ballot five thousand signatures were needed by August 31. That would be a breeze in most states, but the Greens are not exactly entrenched in the Deep South.

Nader visited Alaska and Hawaii, states that the average candidate ignores. He held a press conference at Cyrano’s Bookstore in Anchorage, where he discussed a range of indigenous Alaska issues such as proposed oil drilling in the state’s national wildlife refuge. In Hawaii Nader talked industrial hemp with Woody Harrelson, an outspoken activist for hemp in both its practical and smokeable forms. Fiber and oil from the plant are used in everything from paper to textiles to cosmetics. U.S. farmers are forbidden from growing it, though importing it from China, Canada, and elsewhere is allowed.

As a memento of the visit, Harrelson gave Nader a shirt made out of hemp. Industrial hemp became a major issue during the campaign. Nader’s civics buttons were pushed by the fact that it was grown by both George Washington and Thomas Jefferson. As for plain old pot—a cause célèbre among many Nader supporters—Nader failed to see the draw. "Do you think I'd turn my brain against my body," he asked at one point.

Whatever the topic, whether industrial hemp or industrial waste, Nader always worked his way back around to his central thesis: both major parties—equally besotted by corporate money—were now too similar to offer fresh solutions. To stress their interchangeability, he referred to the candidates as "Gush and Bore."

Whenever possible, throughout the tour, Nader stayed in Hampton Inns because he liked the free breakfast. And he always paid by check or cash. As a consumer advocate, Nader has long opposed the tricky practices of credit card companies. He once owned a Studebaker, but he has never had a credit card. When Nader flew, he invariably purchased tickets in coach. But he also traveled in rented cars over long stretches, often accompanied by Tarek Milleron, a member of his "kitchen cabinet." Milleron is Laura Nader's son.

For Nader, being an automobile passenger was not a passive endeavor. He was often accompanied by reporters and would try to work in an interview on route between campaign stops. Or else he would devour a stack of newspapers and magazines, marking them up in preparation for a future speech. Sometimes he rode along in silence, thinking intently. "He's got so many things going," says Milleron. "He really pushes himself hard in terms of staying on top of a variety of issues. The pressure of being prepared is intense. Anyone who knows my uncle has seen a familiar pose, bent over, kind of looking at his nails, and you just know he's cranking through a lot of information in his brain."

Late in June, Nader crossed the Missouri River into Kansas, state number fifty. He spoke at a community college, careful as always to tailor his remarks to local concerns. In this case, he discussed the dangers that giant agribusiness companies pose to small family farms. Then it was on to Colorado.

THE GREEN PARTY CONFAB was held at the Renaissance Hotel in Denver on June 24–25, 2000. The hotel was chosen in part because it agreed to prepare certain organic dishes. The Republican National Convention this was not: people beat tom-tom drums to call meetings to order and indulged in a custom called "twinkling," which involves silently wiggling one's fingers in lieu of applause.

The Green movement in America has a loose lineage that traces back to political parties that were founded in Europe and New Zealand during the early 1970s. But there is no formal affiliation. By their very nature, Green parties are decentralized. As such, they are kind of like the PIRGs. They share certain issues—environmental protection, opposition to nukes—but there is little coordination across national borders. During the brief history of Greens in America, there has been little coordination, even across state borders.

The Green movement began in the United States in 1984 as a state and local phenomenon. Political gains were made locally, as when in 1990, for example, Alaska became the first state in which Greens were given ballot status. As Greens gained ground in America, a philosophical schism developed between those who wanted to stick to local activism and those who wanted to delve into presidential politics. By 2000 these two schools had formally split.

The Denver convention was held by the group that coveted national elective office, known as the Association of State Green Parties. The rival faction—known as Green Party USA—remained focused on grassroots activism. To confuse matters, it held a convention anyway, in Chicago, where it endorsed Nader. The issues on its platform included abolition of the U.S. Senate and 100 percent taxation for the portion of a person's income above $100,000. Nader refused to accept the rival Green party's endorsement. But throughout his campaign, many voters and journalists were justifiably confused.

To clarify the record: Nader ran in 2000 as the candidate for the Association of State Green Parties. He ran in support of universal health care, D.C. statehood, legalization of industrial hemp, limits on genetic engineering, and a welter of other issues. He did not support abolition of the Senate or a maximum-income tax, nor did he adopt a number of other positions advocated by Green Party USA.

Greens are a contentious lot. They met their match in Nader, who lent new meaning to the term "independent candidate." Even something as simple as whether to have balloons at the Denver convention was hotly contested. The Greens (the party for which Nader ran in 2000—the Association of State Green Parties—will henceforth be referred to as the Greens or Green Party) worried about the environmental impact. The Nader camp argued that it was a fittingly presidential touch. Final decision: yes to balloons.

Nader's fifty-state tour may have convinced people that he was serious. But the marriage between Nader and the Greens continued to be uneasy. In 2000, once again, Nader refused to register as a member of the party, saying that he had promised his father that he would always remain independent. This quite naturally heightened the impression that Nader was running under the Green umbrella but pushing his own agenda. The Greens have taken up a veritable bouillabaisse of social and environmental causes: alternative energy sources, protection of endangered timber wolves, abolition of the death penalty, preservation of the ozone layer. What Nader brought to the party was a refined critique of the dangers of corporate power. Often Nader and the Greens were like a Venn diagram, converging only at certain points.

At the Denver convention, Nader made a show of endorsing the party's platform. Among many Greens, there were still bitter recollections of 1996, when Nader not only refused to endorse the platform but was downright dismissive of certain elements. One of the party's planks at that time endorsed same-sex marriage. When *New York Times* columnist William Safire inquired about the issue during a 1996 interview, Nader quipped, "I'm not into gonadal politics." The comment cast a long shadow that would creep across Nader's 2000 run as well.

NADER WAS THE PRESUMPTIVE nominee at Denver, but he had challengers, including Jello Biafra and Stephen Gaskin. This was—after all—a nominating convention.

Biafra is former lead singer of the Dead Kennedys, known for such seminal punk fare as the album *Frankenchrist* and the song "California über Alles." He may have been a strange candidate, but Biafra was no stranger to politics, having run for mayor of San Francisco in 1979. One of his proposals: businessmen must wear clown suits during working hours. He came in fourth with 3.5 percent of the vote.

During the Denver convention, to much applause and some twinkling, Biafra announced that if elected president he would nominate Madonna as secretary of education and Marilyn Manson as head of the National Endowment for the Arts. Among his other proposals: lower the voting age to five and convert sports stadiums into homeless shelters. As for a running mate, Biafra selected Mumia Abu-Jamal, currently on death row, convicted of the 1981 murder of a Philadelphia police officer.

Stephen Gaskin ran on a narrower platform. As founder of the Farm, a commune in Tennessee, his primary issue was the legalization of pot.

Nader received 295 votes from the Denver delegates, while Biafra and Gaskin got ten apiece. Clearly the Greens needed Nader, if for no other reason than because he brought legitimacy and experience. And Nader needed the Greens because they were an established political party (well, somewhat) with a national organization and infrastructure in place (well, sort of).

Nader's choice of running mate was Winona LaDuke, a writer, farmer, activist, graduate of Harvard with a degree in native economic development, and a member of the Mississippi band of the Anishinaabeg Indians. In 1997 LaDuke was deemed Woman of the Year by *Ms.* magazine, and *Time* magazine named her one of fifty leaders of the future. She was also Nader's running mate in 1996, or rather "standing" mate.

Convincing LaDuke to sign on for the 2000 effort was somewhat difficult, though. When Nader first approached her in November 1999, she was six months pregnant. But Nader was insistent. "He told me that if need be, he would get on his knees," recalls LaDuke. "The image of Ralph on his knees was almost too much for me."

Nader assured LaDuke that she would only be involved in a limited number of campaign events. She lives on the White Earth Indian Reservation in Minnesota, thirty-five miles from the nearest small town. When Nader asked LaDuke to run, she was already caring for four children—two of her own, a niece, and a nephew—with another on the way. LaDuke is not the first American Indian to run for vice president. LaDonna Harris, a member of the Comanche Nation, was on the Citizens Party ticket in 1980 alongside Barry Commoner. With the birth of Gwekaanimad ("when the wind shifts") in February 2000, LaDuke did become the first nursing vice presidential candidate in U.S. history.

For LaDuke, apparently, one of the draws to joining Nader was that she was handed a rare opportunity to run for high office while balancing work/family issues. She felt it would add some diversity to the race. "Ralph asked me knowing my circumstances," she says. "And I know that I represent millions of people. Of the candidates who ran for office, I was the only one who was not a millionaire. I'm actually a working mother. So I could not go everywhere because I had to work and I had to do laundry. I'm sure those guys [Gore, Bush] don't do laundry."

Unlike Nader, LaDuke is a member of the Green Party. Nader's vehement pursuit stemmed in part from the fact that she complements him in the way of a classic presidential ticket. Often a candidate from the North picks a southerner (Kennedy, Johnson) or a Washington "outsider" picks an insider (Bush, Cheney). Nader and LaDuke were a similar type of pairing. "He is far more urban, Washington-based, and national-policy oriented," says LaDuke. "I am far more rural. He is far better at analyzing the mechanics of corporations. I'm far better at seeing how public policy actually affects a community."

She adds: "I have a lot more experience parenting than he does. But he is an excellent uncle."

There was one other interesting way in which Nader and LaDuke formed a balanced ticket. More about that later.

For Nader, selecting LaDuke was an attempt to align himself with all those soft Green issues. For example, LaDuke is an adherent of the so-called seventh-generation principle once practiced by the Iroquois Nation. When weighing the ramifications of a decision, tribal leaders attempted to look seven generations distant. LaDuke advocates adding a seventh-generation amendment to the U.S. Constitution. It would require the government to think hundreds of years into the future when making decisions about the use of land, air, and water.

Nader and LaDuke made quite a team. In Denver, LaDuke talked about the benefits of wind power and the sacredness of the land, and promised that "any descendant of a slave who built the White House can stay in the Lincoln Bedroom." Meanwhile, Nader delivered a hard-issue-laden acceptance speech that clocked in at one hour and fifty minutes.

—18—

"Let Ralph Debate"

NOMINATING CONVENTIONS USUALLY FURNISH CANDIDATES WITH a popularity bounce, and the Green Party convention was no exception. In the days after Denver, Nader jumped as high as 8 percent in certain national polls. His candidacy was starting to generate interest and, withal, criticism.

On June 30, 2000, the Nader campaign received its first significant barb in the form of an unsigned *New York Times* editorial. The *Times* labeled Nader a potential "spoiler" and sounded an alarm that he might tilt the balance in key states such as California. The piece chastised Nader for his claim that there was no difference between candidates George W. Bush and Al Gore. And it urged him to step aside, deeming his campaign a "self-indulgent exercise that will distract voters from the clear-cut choice represented by the major-party candidates."

Around the same time, syndicated columnist Molly Ivins laid out a strategy for voters who were attracted to Nader's candidacy but troubled by the spoiler issue. She suggested that the residents of safe states—places where either Bush or Gore held a commanding lead—could afford to vote their "hearts." But in swing states, she urged people to vote their "brains." This came to be known as the "Ivins Rule."

Taken together, the *Times* editorial and Ivins Rule set the standard for the way the media would cover Nader's campaign. Personally, Nader did not appreciate either approach. Certainly he did not relish being slapped with the "spoiler" tag. Neither did he approve of the Ivins Rule, with its suggestion that people vote strategically instead of "voting their conscience," as he frequently termed it.

Throughout the 2000 election, and afterward, Nader would complain frequently and bitterly about his coverage—and lack of coverage—by the media. His own account of the election, *Crashing the Party*, contains many pages of grousing. Often he takes a kind of Manichaean view. Tim Russert (good): During the election, Nader was a guest on his program *Meet the Press* five times. Oprah (bad): She did not have him on her show.

Throughout the campaign, Nader also stuck to his single-gunman theory: the major media were owned by major corporations, and therefore disinclined to cover a corporate critic. Yet he regularly appeared on shows such as *Hardball with Chris Matthews*, broadcast on MSNBC. MSNBC is a collaboration between Microsoft and NBC's parent, General Electric—it is hard to get more corporate. Nader was on *Hardball* three times during the campaign. He also was a guest on *Crossfire, Face the Nation,* and *Politically Incorrect,* and he made a fresh appearance on *Saturday Night Live,* his fourth since 1977. If anything, Nader received far more coverage than the average presidential candidate.

He likely would have received even more had he not made mistakes in his own media-outreach efforts. In June 2000, for example, Nader released a document laying out his personal finances. Due to privacy concerns—his old bugaboo—Nader refused to make his tax returns public, a step taken by most candidates. As a compromise, the Federal Election Commission accepted a financial-disclosure document prepared by Nader himself. Nader's campaign promised the document as an exclusive to the *Washington Post*. But the *Baltimore Sun* wound up running the story first. "I hate to say it, but we screwed the *Post* early in the campaign," says Tom Adkins, Nader's assistant press secretary. "We promised them an exclusive on Nader's financial disclosure. But the *Sun* broke the story. That might well be the underlying reason why the *Post* coverage was so limited. They very well may have been punishing us."

Nader never would have made this kind of mistake in the 1960s or 1970s. Back then, Nader had superb media relations and prided himself on maintaining an intimate knowledge of the needs and deadlines and competitive pressures of his various contacts.

By the way, Nader's net worth was $3.8 million as of June 2000. He owned $1.2 million in Cisco Systems stock and more than $100,000 worth of shares in Fidelity's Magellan Fund. The Magellan Fund, in turn, holds considerable stakes in both Raytheon and Occidental Petroleum, respectively a defense contractor and a company with business interests in South

American rain forests. This, from a man who once urged GM's shareholders to revolt in an effort to force the company to be more socially responsible. Then again, Nader estimated during his presidential run that he had made around $14 million since 1967. He gave the bulk of that money away, financing his own causes and numerous others. As always, Nader is full of contradictions inside of contradictions, like Chinese boxes.

Throughout his election run, Nader would keep the media at arm's length regarding his personal life. In his earliest days as a consumer advocate, this had been an immensely effective strategy. It served to shroud Nader in a sense of mystery. The media was not nearly as enamored of a furtive presidential candidate. During the campaign, Nader complained loudly about a *Washington Post* story covering a Gore family vacation in North Carolina. Meanwhile, candidate Nader refused to even reveal where he lived. He was willing only to narrow it down to the general vicinity of DuPont Circle. Some reporters continued to believe that Nader lived in his original rooming house, was still paying $80 a month in rent. During an appearance on the *Tonight Show,* Jay Leno asked Nader what he did for fun. Nader hesitated. So Leno worked his way down a list of possibilities: did Nader go to movies, did he date? To each, Nader demurred. Finally, Nader said, "I eat strawberries."

NADER CONTINUED TO WREAK havoc in his inimitable way. At one point, he slipped onto the floor of a rival party's convention. Meanwhile, he was sued by a major corporation and a group of his former colleagues organized against his candidacy. It was going to be a short, hot summer.

On August 2, 2000, Nader crashed the floor of the Republican National Convention in Philadelphia. He was accompanied by Amy Goodman, a reporter for Pacifica Radio. He arrived while Dick Cheney was delivering a speech to the delegates. The crowd was chanting, "Go Bush go. Go Bush go. Go Bush go . . . "

Goodman interviewed Nader while he interacted with delegates who were variously provoked, bemused, and annoyed.

"What do you hope to accomplish in coming here?" a delegate asked.

"Well, I wanted to observe the thing in action," said Nader. "It's hard to believe when you see it recorded. You have to see it to believe it. I mean, this is the most spectacular display of cash-register politics with corporate fat cats in the history of the country. And it's always good to see the state of the art, shamelessly paraded on national TV."

Then Goodman asked, "What's your message for the delegates here?"

"My message is to go home and rethink what they're doing to the country when they sell politics to corporate fat cats in return for political favors. And that's what I say to the Democrats as well. My democracy's being hijacked by large commercial interests against the interests of everyday people."

A delegate then weighed in with a question: "Sir, some stations are saying 7 or 8 percent, would you be the spoiler if this race is close?"

"You can't spoil a system that is spoiled to the core."

Nader's appearance at the Philadelphia convention was akin to street theater, with Goodman asking questions and delegates chiming in. This was hostile territory, too, and Nader was frequently baited. "Do you know we're from New Jersey and you're going to lose big time," said one delegate. "But good luck."

"What party do you think I represent?" inquired Nader.

"You represent the party of your own twisted ideas."

For a while, Nader and Goodman took up near the Florida delegation until the leader ran them off. So they moved over near the Michigan group. At one point, Nader and Goodman tried to enter the US Airways hospitality suite. They were barred by a guard who informed them that no press was allowed.

"I'm a customer of US Airways," insisted Nader.

"This is a private party," said the guard.

"That's not a good way to treat their frequent flyer customers," concluded Nader.

DURING THE LULL BETWEEN the Republican and Democratic national conventions, the Nader campaign chose to run its first television ad. Historically, this has been a slow news period. That makes it a perfect time for a third-party candidate to get the message out. The campaign had budgeted a small sum for advertising. Nader hoped to steal a little thunder from the two major parties. But even he could not have anticipated the sonic boom that would be set off by his ad.

The spot was created by Bill Hillsman of North Woods Advertising, a boutique outfit located in Minneapolis. Hillsman is the image doctor behind Jesse Ventura's successful run for governor of Minnesota in 1998. For Nader, Hillsman created a parody of MasterCard's well-known "priceless" campaign. Hillsman figured that making reference to an existing ad was the best approach, given Nader's limited budget. Together, the Bush and Gore campaigns earmarked $150 million for advertising. In crafting their images, both candidates could afford to start from scratch. But Nader could hardly match that sum, and he was not exactly a big fan of advertising besides. With this in mind, Hillman's strategy was, as he puts it, "to hitchhike on the notion of an already established campaign."

Nader's "priceless" ad starts off with assorted photos of Bush and Gore, accompanied by the song "Hail to the Chief." This is followed by a montage of images of Nader over the years. A voice-over intones: "Grilled tenderloin for fund-raiser: $1,000 a plate. Campaign ads filled with half-truths: $10 million. Promises to special interest groups: over $10 billion. Finding out the truth: priceless." And the kicker: "Without Ralph Nader in the presidential debates, the truth will come in last."

The thirty-second spot aired in a variety of markets including Los Angeles, San Francisco, Seattle, and New York. It certainly caught the attention of MasterCard CEO Robert Selander, who called Nader directly while vacationing in the tropics. He demanded that the campaign pull the ad immediately or face a lawsuit. One of the company's complaints was that the spots had the potential to mislead viewers into believing there was some association between Nader and MasterCard.

In response to Selander's threat, Nader issued a statement: "Let me assure MasterCard's executives that the last thing I want consumers to believe is that my campaign is in the business of selling credit cards." He added: "Our advertisement is a parody and fair political speech. . . . They should lighten up. They're taking their name 'Master' too seriously. This is America."

Back came MasterCard with a lawsuit, claiming trademark and copyright infringement. The company demanded $15 million in damages. The Nader campaign pulled the ad, pending the outcome of the lawsuit. But it was remarkable how much mileage Nader got out of a single ad. Countless articles about the debacle appeared in places such as *Slate* and *George*. Nader campaign headquarters received hundreds of cut-up MasterCards.

The great irony is that while Nader accused MasterCard of failing to appreciate a parody, he was also on shaky ground. "You're talking about a guy who doesn't really watch TV," says Hillsman. "Sure, Nader understood the concept of parody, on a kind of theoretical level. But at the outset—when we first met to discuss doing the ad—he wasn't actually familiar with MasterCard's 'priceless' ads. He had never even seen one."

ON AUGUST 5, 2000, NADER held a fund-raising luncheon at Nora Pouillon's restaurant in Washington, D.C. There were about fifty people in attendance, including Victor Navasky, publisher of the *Nation*, and John Anderson, third-party presidential candidate in 1980. Nader delivered a speech and took questions afterward. Among those present was Gary Sellers, one of Nader's closest associates during the 1970s. Sellers took the floor and challenged his former boss.

"You cannot claim there's no difference between the parties," he said. "Why is it that 95 percent of the time, we used to work with Democrats? We used to celebrate if a Republican signed on to one of your crusades."

Sellers added: "Ralph, this is shaping up to be Ross Perot all over again. You'll be the Perot of the left. It's likely to be very destructive."

A hush settled over the room.

Ralph replied, "Oh, Gary, I wish I could be as clairvoyant as you."

Nader assured Sellers that the election was unlikely to be the nail-biter pundits were predicting. "Don't you worry," he said. "George Bush is so dumb, Gore will beat him by twenty points."

Sellers remained unconvinced. Once upon a time, he and Nader had worked in tandem, bearing down on Ribicoff's staffers about reopening the Corvair case. Sellers knew how stubborn his old boss could be.

Immediately following the Nora's fund-raiser, Sellers registered a web site under the name "Nader's Raiders for Gore" (NRFG). Sellers then recruited a group of former Naderites including Joe Tom Easley, James Fallows, Peter Petkas, and Harrison Wellford—some of Nader's closest associates from the old days.

This clash between Nader and former employees had a distinctly intergenerational flavor, but with an odd twist. The ex-Nader's Raiders had all gotten older. Some had become involved in politics; some had taken corporate jobs to support families. Meanwhile, Nader had remained the same—unmarried, unburdened, untainted. "The only true aging is the erosion of one's ideals," he once said. A supporter in 2000 described him in the following florid terms: "the sea-green incorruptible, the truest, purest, best, smartest, longest-standing, hardest-working, never-sold-out Good Guy in the whole country."

One man's idealist is another man's case of arrested development. Or at least that is how the members of NRFG tended to see their former boss. Nader had always resisted the pull of politics. Now that he had finally entered the fray, Sellers and company felt that he was feeding his eager young supporters a steady diet of gross oversimplification.

The members of NRFG wrote a collective letter to Nader. They lauded their former boss for teaching them the value of hard work and rigorous analysis. But they also pointed out that Nader's central claim—that the two parties were virtually identical—would not have withstood his own truth tests, at least in an earlier era. "No Raider report would support that assertion," argued the letter. "Here we saw a situation where Ralph, for a reason we deeply disagreed with, was endangering the future of the country," says Easley. "We got very very angry about it. I'm sure we would not have done this if we did not have this intense personal relationship and this feeling, for many of us, that Ralph is kind of a savior of democracy. There was a deep sense of disillusionment."

Nader simply ignored NRFG. In response to the insurrection among a group of former associates, Nader issued a simple statement: "There are always a few who lose their zest and will to fight for progressive ideas and settle for moderate conservatives like Al Gore."

The attacks on Nader's campaign continued to mount. Some of the harshest criticism came from political liberals who had a stake in various civil rights causes: gay rights, women's rights, rights for the disabled. During his early years as a consumer advocate, Nader had been disciplined in selecting certain issues while leaving civil rights and Vietnam to others. Recast as a politician, Nader often appeared impassive about so-called identity politics. He made an effort, but he always appeared more comfortable and knowledgeable talking about the Taft-Hartley Act, a law that limits the ability of unions to organize. It was one of the primary issues in Nader's 2000 campaign.

He even made occasional stabs at connecting corporate power and identity politics to form a kind of grand theory of everything. "Whatever your issue is," he said at one point, "whether it's racism or homophobia or policy issues or taxes or urban decay or health care, you're not going to go anywhere with it if we don't focus on the concentration of power." Such notions struck his critics as vague. To many, it seemed that Nader was seeking to avoid having to delve into individual civil rights issues with all their attendant messiness.

In mid-August, the National Stonewall Democrats adopted a resolution warning gays and lesbians about the dangers of supporting Nader. His "gonadal politics" comment continued to haunt him. Around the same time, Patricia Ireland of the National Organization for Women circulated a letter denouncing Nader for showing no real appreciation of women's issues. Ireland noted that in the course of his ten-page candidacy announcement, Nader "did not mention any explicitly feminist issues, not birth control or abortion . . . and not violence against women." The Democrats and Republicans had each attended to the issue of abortion in their party platforms, and in ways that were diametrically opposed. Bush and Gore—Ireland pointed out—were likely to appoint Supreme Court justices with vastly different views about *Roe v. Wade.* Signatories of Ireland's letter included the National Black Business Council, the National Asian Pacific Publishers Association, the Latino Business Association, and the Greenlining Institute. John Gamboa, head of the Greenlining Institute, added: "He's stuck in a time warp. He still thinks consumer issues are middle-class white issues."

Here was yet another criticism. The Green Party may have been colorful, but it was not exactly a rainbow coalition. The crowds drawn to Nader's political events, detractors were quick to point out, were mostly white, and their concerns—environmentalism, drug decriminalization—were decidedly middle class. Of course, Nader's running mate was Winona LaDuke, an American Indian. Then again, Nader selected her in part to try to gain more credibility on social issues.

CONVENTIONAL WISDOM HOLDS THAT third-party runs tend to flame out around Labor Day. Even getting that far was looking questionable given the rising chorus of acrimony, from women's groups, black business associations, gay and lesbian organizations, former employees. To those unschooled in the fine points of Naderism, any and all of these would appear to be his natural supporters. His candidacy was in danger of being quashed; Gush and Bore might not even have to raise a finger. But salvation came in the form of a novel political idea that would vitalize Nader's campaign. The idea was born in Oregon, the state where Nader had often gone for support throughout his long career, the place where he had started the first PIRG.

Nader planned to be in Portland in late August. He called his old friend, Greg Kafoury, and said, "I want you to put on an exquisite event."

Kafoury is a trial lawyer who has known Nader since 1973. He is also an advance man par excellence, one of four brothers whose number also includes a former state senator and a wrestling promoter who is also a radio personality. Kafoury and his law partner, Mark McDougal, tossed around the idea of how to craft an "exquisite event" for Nader. They lit on the idea of having him appear at Portland's Memorial Coliseum, a ten-thousand-seat arena that typically plays host to rock concerts and sporting events.

It was a wildly ambitious plan. Kafoury and McDougal put their law practice on ice and threw themselves full-time into organizing the event. They pursued grassroots promotional techniques, hiring volunteers to fan out around Portland, selling tickets at popular bars such as Goose Hollow and the Lucky Lab. They referred to this as their "beer hall putsch." Tickets were $7 apiece—unusual, given that most political events are free. But in their promotional efforts, Kafoury and McDougal attempted to turn this into a positive. "People have to pay for politics," explains McDougal. "Somebody has to pay for a politician to run. It's either going to be corporations or us. That's just the reality."

Simply renting Memorial Coliseum for a single night was going to cost $20,000. And that price covered just an empty arena space, providing only for what McDougal termed "hippies in a concrete box." The two lawyers realized that they needed some frills. They teamed up with Lowell McGregor, a concert promoter who has worked with acts such as REM, Bob Dylan, and Alanis Morissette. McGregor suggested adding some rock-star-worthy touches, including a two-truss lighting system, Big Shot brand confetti cannon, and EAW KF850 speakers, the standard for acts ranging from Pearl Jam to the Pointer Sisters. All of this added another $50,000.

The escalating price tag made Nader's D.C. campaign staff extremely nervous. They estimated that Nader would only sell around three thousand tickets. Nader's staffers feared the media response to a two-thirds empty arena. Along with the financial blow, it would also be seen as a political death knell. "All we needed was a bust in Portland," says Amato, "and it would have sunk the campaign."

Nader stuck by the two Portland lawyers. At one point, he called Kafoury and said, "You know, I had this vision. It was a newspaper headline, 'Greg comes through.'"

This was pure Nader—when it comes to people currently working for him, he has always favored a no-threats, no-tantrums style. As he had with the Raiders of yore, he pushed the pair by calmly communicating that only success was tenable. "There was so much adrenaline going over the prospect of failure," says McDougal. "We did not want to be the guys who talked Nader into doing something that made him look like an idiot. We were just maniacs trying to sell tickets."

But in the days leading up to Nader's Portland appearance, things looked bleak. The event was scheduled for August 25, a Friday night. By the day of the show, only six thousand tickets had been sold. Kafoury and McDougal were nearly sick with anxiety. It looked as if all their efforts would result in an arena that was nearly half empty. Then the walk-ups began. In the hours before the event, another four thousand tickets were bought. Nader sold out Portland Memorial Coliseum. People even had to be turned away.

The event kicked off with speeches by local activists and politicians such as Lloyd Marbet and Tre Arrow. Marbet was the Green Party candidate for Oregon secretary of state. Arrow had gained notoriety by sitting for eleven days on a ledge of the U.S. Forest Service building in Portland as a protest against timber cutting. He was running for state congress. Kafoury emceed the event and LaDuke—Nader's nursing running mate—made a rare appearance on behalf of the campaign. She had grown up in nearby Ashland, Oregon. Finally it was time for the evening's big draw.

Enter Nader, to a burst of confetti from the Big Shot cannon. As he paused to survey the crowd, he was illuminated according to the standards of a Michael Jackson show rather than a political whistle-stop. To the audience looking on, Nader was not merely a tiny figure, lost on a vast expanse of concert stage. He was buttressed by giant inflatable tubes, colored red, white, and green. The podium was surrounded by potted plants, a touch meant to evoke both ecology and the Green Party. The crowd went crazy.

"Wow, what a rousing Oregon welcome," said Nader. Then he launched into his speech, amplified and clarified by the EAW KF850s. He talked about reforming the educational system so that kids would learn to be citizens rather than consumers. He talked about lessening the average American's tax burden, slapping fines on corporate polluters as a way to lower the taxes on necessities such as food and medicine. As always he was full of ideas, but careful always to circle back to his overarching theme: no progress can be made in a corrupt political system. He described the Republicans and Democrats as "one corporate party with two heads wearing different makeup."

Same message, different packaging. Nader received ovation after ovation from the sold-out crowd of 10,571. Nader was buoyed by the audience reaction and the adulation. A few days later, he called Kafoury and said, "I want you to do these all over the country."

Meanwhile, up in Seattle, Eddie Vedder happened to catch a taped broadcast of Nader's Portland performance on cable-access. Vedder is the lead singer of the band Pearl Jam. He liked what he saw.

PORTLAND WAS THE FIRST super rally. In the weeks to come, Nader's campaign put on roughly a dozen of them at places such as the Target Center in Minneapolis and Kaiser Auditorium in Oakland. It was always the same drill: a crazed rush to procure an arena followed by a mad dash to publicize the event. It was also the most original and visible aspect of Nader's campaign. The ambience was one part William Jennings Bryan stump speech, one part Vermont organic food collective, one part arena rock show. The audience demographic tilted into WB-network territory. Nader took pride in the fact that his campaign drew a large number of disenfranchised voters into the political process. The rallies are the reason.

Nader managed to draw sellout crowds to a whole series of big-city arenas. As the super rally concept gained momentum, the campaign was able to add various high-profile speakers to its roster. Portland was the only event that featured strictly local politicians and activists, as well as the only one that lacked musical acts. Going forward, Nader's campaign recruited what might be termed political celebrities, people such as Michael Moore and Jim Hightower. They were more than happy to participate.

Moore is a gonzo journalist, a kind of blue-collar Hunter Thompson. Nader helped bankroll his 1989 breakthrough film, *Roger & Me.* Ostensibly the film is about Moore's futile efforts to land an interview with Roger Smith, CEO of GM. But in the process of chasing Smith, Moore unearths all kinds of tragicomic details about the devastation the company has caused to his hometown—Flint, Michigan. Hightower is a popular and populist radio commentator, former Texas agricultural commissioner, and author of *If the Gods Had Meant Us to Vote They Would Have Given Us Candidates.*

Hightower and Moore became a kind of political vaudeville act opening for Nader. Hightower showed a flair for folksy one-liners: "5-watt bulbs sitting in 100-watt sockets" is what he called typical politicians, for example. Moore was given to a more madcap style. He regularly urged audiences to vote for one of the campaign's ubiquitous onstage potted plants over Gore and Bush. Plants generated oxygen, Moore pointed out, so at least they did something. Phil Donahue took on the role of master of ceremonies. At most events, the core team was joined by various special guests: actor Danny Glover, oral historian Studs Terkel, or Doris Haddock a.k.a. Granny D, famed for walking across America at the age of eighty-nine in support of campaign finance reform.

A key to the super rallies coming together was Eddie Vedder. Shortly after Portland, he got in touch with Nader's campaign. He signed on to play solo at a super rally at the Key Arena in Seattle on September 23. He was also instrumental in obtaining other music acts such as Ben Harper. The super rally concept had now congealed: politically slanted comedy, socially conscious music, activists waving banners for "Free Tibet" and other causes, tables set up by organizations such as Compassionate Action for

Animals. To cap the evening, Nader would come on and speak at great length.

NADER WAS CLEARLY THE ISSUES candidate. While he may have been tone deaf regarding identity politics, he staked out a number of issues that resonated with voters. For example, Nader continued to tout his none-of-the-above ballot option, the centerpiece of his New Hampshire primary run in 1992. To increase turnout at the polls, Nader also believed that the United States should institute voting on weekends or maybe designate a national voters holiday.

Going back to the days of the Congress Project, Nader had been an advocate of campaign finance reform. He favored public financing of elections by means of a nominal checkoff ($3 or so) on individual tax returns. Such a funding mechanism is similar to the one often used by CUBs and PIRGs.

He also came down as a resolute opponent of trade treaties such as GATT and NAFTA. Congress passed these treaties under fast-track authority, and Nader's concern was that there had been insufficient public debate. What many people do not know—what Nader worked hard to publicize during his campaign—was that NAFTA and GATT were written in such a way that they have the potential to supersede the laws of the participating countries. In other words, rules governing free trade can undercut domestic laws designed to protect consumers and the environment.

One real-life example: the Canadian company Methenex produces a gasoline additive called MTBE, meant to cut down on auto emissions. Meanwhile, an executive order in California prohibited MTBE, citing the substance as a possible carcinogen. Methenex is currently suing the United States for $970 million, claiming California's executive order constitutes a barrier to free trade as spelled out by NAFTA. The final decision will be rendered not by a California court, nor by a U.S. federal court, but by a NAFTA tribunal.

This is akin to Reagan's regulatory task force, only on a grand international scale. Not surprisingly, trade treaties were a major issue for Nader even before the election. In fact, he was present in Seattle for the WTO protests in November 1999. He played no role in the violence and looting, as has sometimes been mistakenly reported. Rigorously documenting the so-called democracy gap is Nader's style, not inciting people to throw bricks through the windows of Gap stores.

During the 2000 election, Nader was a vast repository of factoids and statistics. There is a 20 percent rate of child poverty in the United States, union membership has fallen to 10 percent of the workforce, 450,000 people died in 1999 from smoking cigarettes. He regularly recited a plan for funding universal health care—aiding 45 million uninsured Americans—by means of a 3.5 percent payroll levy on employers combined with a tax on stock transactions that would generate $120 billion annually. By contrast, Bush could not even pronounce the word "subliminal."

The fact that Nader had a grasp of the details on such a broad range of issues begged the question: why was he excluded from the presidential debates? Of course, this too was one of his campaign's major issues. Unable to meet the 15-percent-by-September hurdle, Nader kept an early campaign promise and "exposed the criteria" instead. Throughout the campaign, he offered withering criticism of the Commission on Presidential Debates. "They have the keys," he said at one point. "This debate commission is a private company created by the two parties."

During interviews, in speeches, at any opportunity, Nader laid out the Catch-22 faced by his third-party candidacy. In order to participate in the debates, he needed to poll high. But it was difficult to achieve the necessary numbers without appearing in the debates. Ross Perot (in 1992) had been included in the debates, and afterward he shot up above 20 percent in the polls. Third-party challengers who do not receive this crucial exposure typically sink like stones.

A poll by Fox News conducted in July 2000 found that 64 percent of respondents wanted both Nader and Reform Party candidate Pat Buchanan included in the debates, while 25 percent opposed the idea. Nearly three-quarters of the same respondents agreed that the debates would be "more interesting" if Nader and Buchanan participated.

Super rallies regularly erupted with chants of "Let Ralph Debate." The Nader 2000 web site posted various suggestions on what people could do to protest their candidate's exclusion. Holding a "death of democracy vigil" was one of the most popular. At colleges all around the country, groups of students dressed in black and held mock funerals. Other protesters donned chicken suits and crashed the rallies of the two major-party candidates: "Al Gore, you're a chicken debater. You'll debate George Bush, but not Ralph Nader." Or vice versa: "George Bush, you're a chicken debater . . . "

Nader also took a stab at formulating foreign policy positions in 2000, though critics were quick to point out his lack of international experience. He suggested that the U.S. military could be cut by $62 billion without unduly harming national security. The $62 billion figure was based on an estimate made by Lawrence Korb, a former assistant defense secretary who had served in the Reagan administration. "An effort to cut waste, fraud, and redundancy from the military budget is long overdue," said Nader at one point during the campaign. "Instead Al Gore and George W. Bush are competing to curry favor of the defense contractors, each arguing that they will commit more dollars to the military than the other."

Nader also weighed in on the Middle East situation, particularly the escalating tensions between the Israelis and Palestinians. Due to his Lebanese ancestry, Nader has been dogged by occasional charges of anti-Semitism throughout his career. These were revived during the campaign and there were some whispers that Nader had an innate Arab bias. Never mind that his forbears were Lebanese Christians, a group historically persecuted by Muslims. Furthermore, Nader's campaign position on the Israeli-Palestinian issue was thoroughly plain vanilla. "It's very simple," he says. "Palestinian statehood and security for Israel. Those are the two pivots."

But the truly bizarre twist was that during the campaign not one article mentioned the fact that Nader's running mate happened to be half Jewish. It is impossible to say whether this was a willful oversight or a desire on the part of reporters to play up LaDuke's exotic Indian-ness. While her father is Anishinaabeg, her mother is Jewish. Her maternal grandparents lived in the Bronx, where one worked as a house painter, the other in a purse factory.

Chalk this up as another way in which Nader and LaDuke formed a balanced ticket. Together, they had as much right to discuss the Israeli-Palestinian question as Gore/Lieberman. But who knew?

Nader weighed in on matters about which he likely knew more than any living human. Political considerations prompted him to weigh in on other subjects about which he had little feel. And sometimes he broached an issue—such as the Middle East—for which he had more authority than he was given credit.

Throughout the campaign, no matter what, he was rarely more than a few sentences away from bashing Bush and Gore for being indistinguishable. This topic was to 2000 what GM was to an earlier era. It was Nader's be-all, catch-all, number-one priority. It was his obsession.

However, no matter how hard he tried to be evenhanded in doling out criticism of Bush and Gore, Nader did show a bias. It was reminiscent of the famous dictum in George Orwell's *Animal Farm*: "All animals are equal, but some are more equal than others." Close observers of Nader's campaign could not help but notice that he was rougher on Gore. *All major-party candidates are equally compromised, but some are more equally compromised than others.*

Nader regularly referred to Gore as a "political coward" or an "environmental poseur," which he would carefully balance with a dig against Bush, like calling him "a major corporation disguised as a human being." But during the Portland super rally, Nader also said something quite revealing. He described Gore as "more reprehensible" than Bush and added: "He knows so much and refuses to act on his knowledge. George W. Bush can plead ignorant, but Al Gore cannot."

Nader's old friend Mike Pertschuk has a theory about the tougher-on-Gore stance. "I keep returning to the metaphor of Nader as an Old Testament prophet," says Pertschuk. "Prophets don't make good presidents. They attack and attack and attack. But to be the public scold, to call people to account for not living up to moral codes, that's the role Ralph performs best. His genuine contempt for Gore came out during the election. Maybe prophets are hardest on those who are lapsed. Ralph showed a real disillusionment with Gore's move away from public-interest advocate and environmentalist, his move to the right to become more and more a creature of corporate Washington and lobbyists."

During the campaign, it was even reported that Nader had said, if forced to choose, he would vote for Bush. Nader insists this was a misquotation. He wound up getting a lot of mileage out of pointing out that he never said he would vote for Bush over Gore.

But the question of whether he was misquoted distracted from the real issue. It was clear to many—especially those who knew him personally—that he truly despised Gore, while he was merely dismissive of Bush.

Gary Sellers, organizer of Nader's Raiders for Gore, had extensive discussion with his old boss during the autumn of 1999. He recalls that leading up to the election, at least, Nader seemed virtually consumed by his feelings toward the vice president. "He had a personal animus toward Gore," says Sellers. "Gore had moved to the center and that enraged Ralph. Gore also did not return his phone calls. It was clear that Ralph's feelings were hurt. This was the kind of thing you'd expect from an adolescent. It was embarrassing. He was furious and he was going to teach Gore a lesson."

THE FIRST PRESIDENTIAL DEBATE of the 2000 season was held in Boston on October 3. Throughout the week leading up to the event, the city was the scene of various pro-Nader protests. For example, a group of people wearing three-pointed hats boarded a replica of a colonial-era tea schooner that was docked in the harbor. To protest Nader's exclusion from the debates, they held a "Boston TV party," tossing a dozen or so television sets overboard. Of course, ropes were attached to the sets, and, being eco-conscious and all, the protesters hauled them right back up. On October 1—two days before the debate—Nader held a super rally at the Fleet Center, which drew a sellout crowd of twelve thousand people. The words "Let Ralph Debate" were projected by lights against the arena's walls.

Though Nader was not a participant, he managed to obtain a ticket to the October 3 presidential debate from a college student. The debate was being held at the University of Massachusetts's Clark Athletic Center. But the ticket in question was actually for an adjacent auditorium, where an overflow crowd would have the opportunity to watch the debate on closed-circuit TV. Nader held a press conference at Harvard in which the student handed over the ticket, which said nothing about being nontransferable. Then Nader and a group of his campaign staffers hopped on the T and rode from Harvard Square to the UMass stop. "The mood was pretty electric," recalls Laura Jones, the campaign's deputy press secretary. "We knew a big protest was going on. We didn't know what was going to happen."

Because only he had a ticket, Nader separated from everyone in his party except Tarek Milleron, his nephew. The two got on a special bus that was shuttling audience members directly to the debate site. As soon as the bus hit the UMass campus, it was surrounded by a sea of protesters. The driver slowed way down. Because the lights were on inside the bus, people on the outside could clearly see that it was Nader slowly traveling by. People yelled and waved and raised their fists in solidarity. A chant went up of: "Hey, hey, corporate state. Let Ralph Nader debate."

Nader got off the bus and headed for the auditorium. Immediately he was met by John Vezeris, a representative of the Commission on Presidential Debates (CPD). Vezeris was accompanied by three police officers.

Nader explained that he had a valid ticket to the event. To which Vezeris responded: "It's already been decided that, whether or not you have a ticket, you are not invited."

Nader was stunned. "Deep down inside, do you agree?" he asked.

"Sir, it's irrelevant," answered Vezeris.

Hoping to defuse the tensions, Nader—who has always shown a facility for languages—addressed Vezeris in Greek. "Ti Kanis," inquired Nader. (Translation: "How are you?") "Kala," was Vezeris's reply ("fine").

Following this brief exchange, Vezeris quickly reverted to English and intransigence. Meanwhile, one of the officers stepped forward and asked, "Mr. Nader, is it your intention to be arrested here?"

Nader shot back, "I always prefer to be a plaintiff rather than a defendant."

After asking Vezeris for a business card, and committing one of the officer's names to memory, Nader turned on his heels and left. But then he remembered that he had a scheduled interview with the Fox network to be conducted on the debate premises. He tried to enter the auditorium a second time and once again was rebuffed. Nader wound up doing his interview—and watching the debates on TV—at the Fox studios in downtown Boston.

Meanwhile, back at UMass, things were getting ugly. The debate protesters, estimated at nine hundred strong, were a loose aggregation of Nader supporters, WTO opponents, free-Mumia heads, and those who were simply pissed and looking to break things. People locked arms and sat in the street, barring the shuttle buses from leaving for forty-five minutes after the debate. There was also some rock throwing, spitting on police cars, and various acts of petty vandalism, leading to sixteen arrests.

Still later that evening, David Letterman declared Nader the winner in absentia of the debate, which was widely considered a snoozefest, at least inside the auditorium. Nader's poll numbers, which had flagged in recent weeks, jumped back up to around 7 percent.

Two days later, Nader issued a statement demanding a full apology from the CPD. He also requested that it donate $25,000 to a Harvard law school project on electoral reform. He gave the commission until October 10 to reply.

The deadline came and went. So on October 17, Nader filed a lawsuit in U.S. district court in Boston alleging that his First Amendment rights of free speech and free association had been violated. Naturally, he was the plaintiff—per his preference—and named as defendants Vezeris along with CPD commissioners Kirk and Fahrenkopf. He also named the police officer whose name he still remembered.

A few weeks later, the second debate was held at Washington University in St. Louis. For Nader, it was a reprise of the first: once again he obtained a ticket and once again he was denied entry. But this time the people who barred him had a Nader plan. Fearing legal action, they refused to utter their names or hand over business cards.

—19—

A Contact Sport

THE HIGH POINT OF THE CAMPAIGN was a super rally in New York City on October 13. Arranging the event involved the usual eleventh-hour giga-frenzy. After signing a contract with Madison Square Garden, Jason Kafoury, the son of Portland rally organizer Greg Kafoury, had exactly ten days to pull everything together. Volunteers handed out 175,000 "Nader Rocks the Garden" fliers and slathered posters on every available surface in Manhattan. Once again, Eddie Vedder played a key role, promoting the event at concerts and during an interview with VH-1. Publicists for Vedder's record company, as well as other acts on the same label, also worked to get the word out.

Still, only nine thousand of the fifteen thousand-plus seats had sold by the day of the show. Admission this time was $20. There was talk of closing off a tier or so to make the arena look less empty. Again, salvation came from a surge of walk-up ticket buyers. A few minutes into the rally, Phil Donahue took the stage to announce that Nader had sold out Madison Square Garden. There was a thunderous three-minute ovation that gradually subsided into a chant of "Let Ralph Debate."

For the Garden super rally, Nader's campaign managed to assemble an impressive celebrity lineup. Regulars such as Moore and Vedder were joined by Ben Harper, Bill Murray, Ani DiFranco, Susan Sarandon, and her husband, Tim Robbins. Taking the stage, Moore made reference to a recent *Rolling Stone* interview in which Bush boasted that he remembered the names of all fifty-five of his Yale frat brothers. "What I want to know," Moore asked, "is could you name for us the last fifty-five people you executed?"

Susan Sarandon, wearing black leather pants and a "Babes for Nader" button, introduced singer Ani DiFranco, calling her the "female Ralph Nader." DiFranco took a moment to survey the audience before saying: "How surreal is this? We have a huge American flag, we have a bunch of guys in suits, and it's good. It's good." She then launched into a song she described as "a little ditty about the drug war."

Tim Robbins rolled out in a wheelchair, an American flag draped over his legs. The actor was in the guise of Bob Roberts, a conservative politician left paralyzed by an assassination attempt. Robbins made a mockumentary about Roberts in 1992. "It's an honor to be here at this rally to support George W. Bush," said Robbins/Roberts. Hisses from the crowd. He picked up an acoustic guitar and strummed a couple of songs dedicated to his "brethren on Wall Street." Bill Murray delivered what he jokingly termed "the biggest political speech of my life."

When Eddie Vedder came on, he apologized for not having penned a song specifically for Nader. Instead, he launched into Dylan's "The Times They Are A-Changin.'" It was one of the rally's highlights. The song was a hit in 1964, the year after Nader came to Washington.

At last it was time for the man himself. Throughout the opening acts, Nader had been sitting backstage, scribbling last-minute notes for his speech. When he walked on, he was overwhelmed. Even Nader—deliverer of thousands of speeches in thousands of places—was stunned by the size and sheer electricity of the crowd. "It was extra-dimensional," he recalls. "To have that many people under one roof: seems like there's a real difference between 10,000 and 15,500. They seemed even more excited than at a Knicks game. It was one of those reasons for running that keeps the flame alive."

Nader's opening line was, "Welcome to the politics of joy and justice." The crowd erupted. Over the years, Nader says, he has developed a geiger-fine gauge of audience moods. That night at the Garden he felt buoyed by the crowd and delivered what he considers one of the best speeches of his career. "We are building a historic, progressive political movement in America," he continued. This he followed with an hour-long speech that delved into a variety of his campaign issues: election reform, land conservation, public ownership of the airwaves, and of course, Bush and Gore as "Tweedledum and Tweedledee." The speech was pure Nader, technical yet accessible, lacking in traditional structure or buildup (example of wrongdoing followed by example of wrongdoing followed by example of wrongdoing) yet oddly affecting. He ended with a plea to disenfranchised voters:

"To the 51 percent of nonvoters who sat out: Don't drop out of democracy. We need you. We even need your skepticism."

The Garden rally ended with all the celebrities joining Nader on stage. They formed a kind of socially conscious chorus line. Patti Smith played a rousing version of her anthem, "People Have the Power." Moore and Murray, Donahue and DiFranco, and all the rest swayed back and forth and sang along. "I think Ralph even did something that may have been dancing," says campaign staffer Laura Jones. "But none of us was sure." Throughout the evening, boxes had been passed around the audience to distribute and collect voter registration cards. Midnight was the deadline in New York state. After the rally, Sarandon led a march to the post office near Madison Square Garden to drop off the registration cards. From there, a loose band of revelers continued up Seventh Avenue into Times Square, chanting "let Ralph debate."

The Madison Square Garden rally was the Nader campaign's most triumphant moment. But behind the scenes, considerable stresses were building. The super rallies were something of a devil's bargain. They were the most dynamic aspect of the campaign, yet they required Nader to throw in his lot with celebrities, many of whom were nearly his equal at being headstrong, some of whom were just plain flaky.

At the Garden rally, during the "biggest political speech" of his life, Murray mentioned that he was currently starring in the movie *Charlie's Angels.* This annoyed Nader, who viewed it as a shameless plug. Nader also had his tensions with Michael Moore, who was not always willing to stay on message: Bush and Gore, Gush and Bore. Moore clearly found more comic potential in the marble-mouthedness of the Texas governor, and razzed him far harder than he did Gore. Then there was Ben Harper, who chose to play a version of Marvin Gaye's "Sexual Healing" at the New York event. Given the candidate, given his history, the campaign staff was bemused by the sheer inappropriateness of this choice.

But there were issues far more substantial than celebrity hijinks, such as the fact that the rallies were a considerable drain on Nader's resources. Over and over, in rapid succession, his staffers had to do this scramble-to-find-and-fill-a-stadium drill. The rallies tied up large amounts of money, too. Putting on the Madison Square Garden event cost $250,000, for example. It managed to break even. But there was always a fear that if a rally was underattended, the campaign would take a major financial hit.

To protect against this possibility, abundant effort was put into drawing local Green Party members to events in various cities. Rallies may have been an effective tool for Nader to reach out to disenfranchised voters. But most rallies also had a substantial Green Party presence. This meant that Nader was preaching to the converted. Among many of his advisers, there was a feeling that it would be better to place less reliance on super rallies, more on techniques that might win over undecided voters who were not being reached. But the campaign placed very little emphasis on methods such as cold calling.

Yet another issue: for all their energy, there was something ephemeral about the rallies. They rolled into a town, generated hoopla, then quickly moved on and were soon forgotten. It was kind of like a traveling circus. This is an issue faced by most political candidates as they jump from campaign stop to campaign stop. Many opt to combat the problem by purchasing advertising. It is a time-tested way to reinforce messages—commercial, political, and otherwise.

Nader raised $8 million, much more than anticipated. Given a war chest that size, says campaign media strategist Bill Hillsman, Nader should have allotted from $3 million to $5 million for advertising. After all, the campaign got huge play out of its MasterCard ad. In what Hillsman calls "a dirty little secret," Nader spent only $300,000 on advertising after Labor Day. That is when the campaign gained momentum, and according to Hillsman, placing some ads would have built on that. Hillsman developed a parody of Anheuser-Busch's "Whazzup" commercial that was never even produced.

"I think he was relatively naive about the use of advertising," says Hillsman. "Ralph has this blind spot. He knows TV stations are owned by corporations and he hates them. But it's the most effective way to reach people. He needed 5 percent. Spending $5 million would have been the easiest route."

As always, Nader chose to do things his own way. He ignored the counsel of Hillsman, whom he had hired because of his track record as media strategist for Jesse Ventura, Senator Paul Wellstone, and others. Following the Garden rally, the campaign entered a final mad dash toward November 7.

Five percent or not 5 percent—that was the question.

LESS THAN A MONTH remained until the election. The campaign had been a frantic exercise from the outset. Now things kicked into warp speed. There were new developments almost moment by moment. The criticism directed at Nader's run—a steady drumbeat from early in the campaign—literally exploded.

Nader had stayed in the race much longer than anyone expected. Polls were starting to indicate that the race between Gore and Bush was likely to be much closer than anyone had imagined. The political left took aim at Nader with a renewed fury, criticizing his campaign's central message and demanding that he withdraw.

Americans for Democratic Action—an organization cofounded in 1947 by Eleanor Roosevelt—placed op-eds in college newspapers in strongholds of Nader support such as Wisconsin and Oregon. "Nader's campaign was arguing that the Democrats and Republicans were the same," says spokesman Mike Alpern. "We tried to communicate to young people that this was the most important election since 1968. America was at a crossroads on important issues such as a the environment and a woman's right to choose. We tried to say to these college students, 'Hey, you're young, you may not have such a sense of history. But here's what will happen on a whole range of issues if Bush is elected.'"

Meanwhile, the Democratic Party dispatched so-called surrogates. Bearing pro-Gore/anti-Nader messages a bevy of people, including Bill Bradley, Jesse Jackson, Martin Sheen, and Robert Redford, fanned out into the various swing states.

Against this backdrop, Nader made another gaffe, the equal of his "gonadal politics" comment. On October 29, while appearing on ABC's *This Week,* Nader questioned all the concern being voiced by liberals about abortion rights. "Even if *Roe v. Wade* is reversed, that doesn't end it," he said. "It just reverts back to the states."

If his opponents were livid before, this pushed people to the brink of apoplexy. Nader responded that he was simply offering clarification: if *Roe v. Wade* is struck down, decisions about abortion rights would be made by individual states. As a fine point of judicial procedure, this was undoubtedly true. Each of the fifty states would still be able to make an individual decision about abortion. But for many, this did not seem like the kind of point that would be made by someone who cared a whit about the issue. It registered as further confirmation of what Representative Barney Frank (D–Massachusetts) had once described as "Nader's lifelong lack of interest in major social causes like civil rights, women's rights, gay rights, and poverty."

Nader's disinterest was no big deal—opponents contended—so long as Nader remained a consumer advocate. But now he was a presidential candidate, peddling a message of major-party indistinguishability. What's more, it appeared that his real agenda was to punish Gore and teach the

Democrats a lesson. Gloria Steinem posted a list on the Internet: "Top Ten Reasons Why I'm Not Voting for Nader." She was joined by the Sierra Club, the United Auto Workers, and a number of Democratic members of Congress. The entire left establishment, it seemed, was calling on Nader to drop out of the race.

But Nader was pretty much impervious to criticism. Here, after all, was someone who had once cited his number-one criterion for a good public interest advocate as "no anxiety to be loved." His long years as a public figure had served to thicken his skin. Nader has often said that he much prefers the honesty that comes with open hostility to the patent phoniness that attends most polite discussions. If anything, Nader thrived on the conflict his candidacy generated.

"Frightened liberals," is how he described his critics during interviews, or "well-intentioned cowards." Nader gave as good as he got. "The only way they could elevate Gore was to depress me," he recalls. "There wasn't much to say about Gore, even after eight years. Instead of going after Bush, or trying to elevate Gore, they decided they had to scare away my voters. It was an impoverished strategy."

Back and forth went the recriminations. As his critics grew increasingly agitated, Nader only became more resolute.

A potential compromise appeared. The Ivins Rule had suggested that people vote their hearts in safe states, their brains in swing states. Thanks to the Internet, it was possible to do a twist on Ivins's notion. In the final days before the election, a number of web sites appeared that made it possible for people to trade their votes.

Say someone wanted to vote for Nader but lived in Michigan, a swing state, where the race between Bush and Gore was very close. The web site would match up the Michigan voter with someone in a safe state such as Texas, where the electoral outcome was not in question. The two people would agree to swap votes. The person in Michigan would vote for Gore, while the person in Texas would vote for Nader. This was a potentially elegant solution, making it possible for voters to support Nader while diminishing the risk that the election would be thrown to Bush. A vote-swapping site called win-wincampaign.org described the goal succinctly: "Five percent of the popular vote for Ralph Nader; four years in the White House for Al Gore. We can have it all."

As to who dreamed up the idea of vote swapping, no one is exactly sure. It appears to be one of those spontaneous shared eurekas for which the Internet is famous. Certainly, vote swapping got a big boost from an article posted on October 24 in the online magazine *Slate*. It was written by Jamin Raskin, a professor at American University who happens to be the son of Marcus Raskin, Nader's old friend and adviser.

Vote swapping was a compelling idea with perfect timing. During the final weeks of the race, a number of vote swapping sites appeared, including NaderTrader.org, VoteExchange.com, and VoteSwap2000.com. Interestingly, Nader did not approve of the idea. "We opposed it," says campaign manager Amato. "Our campaign theme was vote your conscience, not your fears. Ralph Nader's position was that people should vote for who they want and not engage in elaborate schemes."

It was a moot point anyway. About the time vote swapping started to gain momentum, various state attorney generals took notice. They started shutting the sites down on the grounds that they violated various election laws. According to one estimate, fifteen thousand people agreed to trade votes during the brief life span of online vote trading.

The race was down to its final days. Nader had to make some key decisions about which states to visit. His campaign advisers drew up a matrix, weighing various considerations. One option—favored by certain members of his staff—was for Nader to concentrate on safe states. For example, he could campaign actively in New York, a solidly Gore state. Conversely, Nader could also visit states that were unassailably in the Bush camp, such as Texas. Nader could focus his efforts on Austin and other pockets of support. Because they did not have to worry about tilting the election, people in safe states could be expected to feel more comfortable voting for Nader. Such an approach might help him get 5 percent.

Buchanan—it is worth noting—chose the safe-state option. During the final days of his campaign, Buchanan concentrated on Connecticut, Massachusetts, and Minnesota. Essentially, his message was: *Gore has this state wrapped up so there is no sense voting for Bush. Vote for me.*

Nader decided to travel to the hotly contested swing states. His reasoning was simple: swing states are where the action is. Gore and Bush were concentrating their efforts on Michigan, Wisconsin, Florida, and the like. As a consequence, the media was flocking to these states as well. Nader had not exactly run on an accommodationist platform. All along he had argued that Gore and Bush were the same, so why not go right to the election's front lines to deliver the message one last time? Certainly, it was a way for Nader to get ample attention. This, too, was a possible route to 5 percent.

To truly understand Nader's decision, one has to remember his unique views about political messages. When it comes to making an impact, many candidates draw little distinction between press coverage and advertising. In fact, image consultants often treat the two forms of publicity as equal, referring to them as "earned media" and "purchased media" respectively. By contrast, Nader was a longtime consumer advocate who hated advertising. He was also a sometime journalist who had seen his career rise and fall in accordance with his press profile.

Because his campaign ran virtually no ads, it was necessary for Nader to rely on media attention more than most candidates did. He realized that the swing states were where he would find the media. Of course, this was another devil's bargain. Candidates can control their message in a political advertisement. Relying on the whims of assorted reporters is a bit more dicey. "Nader went into the swing states thinking that's where the press was, that's where he would get publicity," says Hillsman. "But I warned him, 'Only if you want more stories about being a spoiler.'"

During his campaign's home stretch, Nader visited a number of non-swing states. He also visited Michigan and Pennsylvania and, most controversially, made a stop in Florida on November 4, just three days before the election. Per Nader's instincts, he received abundant earned-media attention. In keeping with Hillsman's warning, many of the stories were also of the Nader-as-spoiler variety.

Meanwhile, the Gore campaign was growing desperate. For months, they had mostly tried to ignore Nader, not wanting to draw attention to him, hoping he would just go away. They had left the dirty work of trying to discredit him to surrogates like Bill Bradley. Now, time was running out. Because the Green Party was so amorphous, Gore's handlers had trouble even figuring out whom to contact. It was difficult to make sense of the party hierarchy or even discern if there was a party hierarchy, and they had no idea who might be able to exercise pull with Nader. Earlier in the campaign Gore himself had called Phil Donahue from aboard Air Force 2. That had been to no avail.

It so happened that Myron Cherry, a high-ranking staffer in Gore's campaign, had worked with Nader back in the 1970s fighting against nuclear power. He gave Nader a call directly and requested that he bow out of the race. In exchange, Cherry suggested that Gore would be receptive to Nader's ideas about certain key appointments, such as head of the EPA. Cherry may not have realized it, but he was offering Nader a reprise of the Carter years, at best. The request was not well received. "He responded like I'd joined the devil," recalls Cherry. "He would not talk to me and indicated we had nothing to offer him. It was like we were pariahs."

The Democrats had once last wild card. Toby Moffett, a one-time Nader Raider and former congressman from Connecticut, approached Joan Claybrook in hopes that she might have some sway with Nader. Claybrook just laughed. "It would be a waste of my time," she told the *New York Times*. "He's one of the most stubborn people in the United States."

Election night at last: Nader held a party for his campaign staff in a rented ballroom at the National Press Club. The mood was surface-jovial; staffers hugged and congratulated one another on making it to the end of a difficult campaign. But there was an undercurrent of immense anxiety. Jake Lewis, Nader's media director, had prepared four different press releases. Each attended to a different contingency: Nader gets 5 percent, Nader fails to get 5 percent, Gore wins, Bush wins.

A placard set up in the ballroom featured a quotation from Brandeis, subject of Nader's abiding ambivalence: "We can have democracy or we can have the concentration of wealth in the hands of the few. We cannot have both." Winona LaDuke was piped in via satellite from her home on the reservation in Minnesota. She thanked the staffers for their hard work. Then Nader took the stage for the first of several speeches he would deliver in the course of the evening. He was flanked by an ex-secret service agent. The agent had just been hired, a concession to the fact that it had been a very controversial run. "The Green Party is now the third largest party in the United States after only eight months of campaigning," he said. "It's the fastest-growing party, and it's the most spirited party—even up against the enormous odds of an entrenched two-party system and a media obsessed with the horse-race aspects, instead of the issue aspects, of the presidential campaign."

Nader's staff applauded wildly. But many in attendance also felt that he was skirting more pressing matters. Exit polls were indicating that Nader was not getting anything close to 5 percent of the vote. The early results also showed that Bush and Gore were headed for a photo finish.

Halfway across the country, at a Sheraton hotel in Nashville, Gore was throwing a tense election eve bash of his own. Throughout the campaign, Gore had refused to utter Nader's name. Privately, Gore's campaign staff had referred to him simply as the "grim reaper" or "that bastard." On November 7, whenever Nader popped up on the bank of TVs at the Sheraton, Gore staffers simply turned down the volume.

Shortly after 8:00 P.M. EST, on television screens across the country, Florida switched from being blue. The networks had been premature in assigning the state to the Gore column. Suddenly one of Lewis's four scenarios emerged as the most likely: Nader fails to get 5 percent and Bush wins. At Nader's campaign headquarters, the gasps were clearly audible.

Still, Nader appeared unfazed. In the wake of the Florida flip-flop, he conducted a series of interviews with Peter Jennings, Tom Brokaw, and Larry King. The spoiler issue was becoming increasingly clear and present. But Nader remained defiant, saying things to the general effect of *it does not matter whether we get an arbitrary 5 percent, the campaign was about building a third party. It does not matter whether Bush or Gore wins; America deserves better than either of them.* Staffers dutifully booed and hissed at the impertinence of the various interview questions. "Screw the corporate media," yelled one young woman while Nader was being interviewed by Tom Brokaw.

Nader's staffers did their best to put on a brave face. But few of them had the steely nerves of their leader. He had been at this for thirty-five years, not a few of which were spent wandering in the policy wonk desert; when it came to public sentiment he was truly an independent. Corey Eastwood was a nineteen-year-old freshman at New York University when he signed on to work for Nader 2000. He remembers that during the previous week, hundreds of calls had come into campaign headquarters from people cursing Nader, calling him a traitor, saying that he was downright evil. But the calls served only to strengthen Eastwood's convictions. On election night—facing the eminent possibility of a sub–5 percent showing by Nader and the election of Bush—Eastwood finally let his own doubts come flooding in. "It was a tough night," says Eastwood. "I myself was in a confused daze. Nothing made sense."

Carolyn Danckaert, the campaign's volunteer coordinator, has a similar impression: "As it got closer between Bush and Gore, every time there was a new return, it got a little tenser. Some people appeared unconcerned, but quite a few were very concerned."

Around 10:00 P.M., Nader took the stage for another speech, this time accompanied by various relatives including his sisters and his mother. "I'd like to introduce the person who really was the cause for this entire movement and this entire mobilization, and she started a long time ago: my mother, Rose Nader. When I was a schoolboy, once I came home, we were having dinner table conversations about all the things that go on in the world and she looked at me and she said, 'Ralph, do you really love your country?' And I said, 'Of course, Mother,' thinking, what's going to come next? And she said, 'Well, I hope you will grow up and work hard to make your country more lovable.'"

After midnight, with Florida still unresolved, the tension at Nader's party became nearly unbearable. Some staffers abandoned message entirely and took to cheering when it was announced that Gore had won various states such as California and Pennsylvania. A CNN broadcaster declared that Florida was still too close to call and someone yelled, "Come on, Florida!" Nader came on one last time to address his charges. Among other things, he said: "I'll tell you who's squirming now. There are a lot of people in the Democratic Party who are squirming."

Then people began to trickle out of the National Press Club. Sometime after 1:00 A.M., Nader returned to his home in an undisclosed location in Washington. He flicked on a small black-and-white television, one of the very few indulgences he has allowed himself over the years. Then he stayed up until 3:30 watching the returns.

On November 8, Americans awoke to a novel concept: a presidential election that remained unresolved. Gore held a slim lead in the popular vote, 48.4 percent to 47.9 percent. In a projected tally of Electoral College votes, Gore also held the lead, 260 to 246. But 270 votes are required to win the Electoral College. Florida—with twenty-five outstanding votes—was the giant missing puzzle piece. Whichever candidate won Florida would win the election.

Nader came in third with 2,658,281 votes. That was roughly 3 percent of the popular vote. He had failed by a considerable margin to gain the 5 percent that would be worth about $13 million in federal matching funds during the 2004 election. Buchanan came in a distant fourth with 443,135 votes.

Nader held a press conference in which he officially conceded. Throughout, members of the media kept asking him about the 96,915 votes he had received in Florida. Clearly this was more than Gore required to win the state, though that number would shift in the days to come. The question of whether Nader was truly a spoiler was also not so clear-cut, and Nader would come up with a number of defenses in the months and years ahead, some of them convincing, some not.

But on November 8—in answer to reporters' questions—he was simply defiant. "I've always said that it was Al Gore's election to lose, that only Al Gore could beat Al Gore," said Nader. "In the end, the Democratic Party must face the fact that it has become very good at electing very bad Republicans. Apparently, it can't even win in Tennessee and Arkansas."

Nader added: "Democrats must now either find their progressive roots or watch the party gradually wither away, or basically become a crypto-Republican Party, bidding for the same money and, increasingly, for the same voters. America can do better, much better."

Nader concluded with one last twist of the knife: "By the way, I do think that Al Gore cost me the election, especially in Florida."

To the uninitiated, Nader's stance was shocking; he clearly relished his role in disrupting Gore's chances. But there was another thread running through his comments that was hard to place for people who were not familiar with him or his history. What they may not have realized was that they were hearing the faint echoes of a Connecticut mill town boyhood, now half a century distant. Growing up, Nader had been taught that democracy was a contact sport. His family had always been the most active, the most vocal, to the point that even at Winsted's town meetings people found something alien and off-putting in the Naders' manner. And so it was that on the day after one of the most tumultuous events in U.S. electoral history, instead of being contrite or fittingly subdued, Nader was still playing hard at democracy, and with the contrarian glee that is his hallmark.

Of course, the Democrats knew only to be outraged. The wonder of it was that they were able to summon still more anger for Nader. Seemingly, the campaign would have exhausted their supply. As frustrations mounted over the election impasse, Nader was the target of a fresh onslaught from the Left. For the first time in his career Nader was not simply a controversial figure. He was downright vilified. The Democrats rushed to outdo themselves in their criticism. "I will not speak his name," said Democratic strategist James Carville. "I'm going to shun him, and any good Democrat, any good progressive, ought to do the same thing."

"Ralph Nader is not going to be welcome anywhere near the corridors," said Senator Joe Biden, a Democrat from Delaware. "He cost us the election." For good measure, Biden added: "God spare me the purists."

If anyone was psychologically prepared for this kind of upbraiding, it was Nader. He has a favorite phrase for people who cannot take the heat; he describes them as having "skin so thin they can be blistered by moonbeams." Clearly Nader had skin so thick he could not even be bruised by brickbats. Whenever members of the press asked him about the venom directed at him, he gave answers that were the equivalent of verbal shrugs. To *Time* magazine, he described his critics as "otherwise good people. They just don't have the courage of their forebears." Nevertheless, it is hard to imagine that anyone could be so unmoved by so much anger.

In late November, Nader had a conversation with Ed Levin, his roommate during his first year at Harvard law. "He was clearly affected and unhappy about so many comments that he had cost Gore the election," recalls Levin. "He certainly was not going to make a public statement that it was getting to him. But it was clear that he was disturbed by it."

The election impasse continued for thirty-five days. America learned about "chads" and "butterfly ballots"; found a new demi-celebrity in Katherine Harris; and then, at the end of it all, Florida flashed red and Bush was declared the winner. In mid-December, the press came looking for fresh comments—surely Nader would have some choice words now that Bush was president. But he was nowhere to be found. Nader had been called to jury duty.

—20—

Next for Nader

NOW TO SOME LARGE AND LINGERING QUESTIONS about Nader: Is he truly a spoiler? How best to assess his overall legacy? What is next on his agenda and do his plans include another run in 2004?

The spoiler question is particularly slippery; the answer lies somewhere near the intersection of political perceptions and first-grade math. Following the Election Day deadlock, a recount was launched in Florida. But the U.S. Supreme Court put an end to further tallying, the state's result was certified, and Bush defeated Gore by a mere 537 votes. Nader received 96,915 votes in Florida.

Since the election Nader has gone on record with a number of different—oft contradictory—positions. For example, his most frequent assertion has been a simple but elegant *Gore beat Gore*. Sure, Nader took votes from Gore in Florida, but had the vice president made a better showing the outcome would have been different. "Let's put it this way," he told the *National Journal*. "Al Gore slipped on 15 banana peels, and they're picking one." Nader has frequently pointed out that Gore lost his home state (Tennessee), Bill Clinton's home state (Arkansas), and a longtime Democratic stronghold (West Virginia). Florida, he points out, is simply the crowning bumble in Gore's poorly run campaign.

Often he has amplified the Gore-beat-Gore theme by reminding people of the value of competition. Nader likes to point out that competition is a venerated business principle, especially in America, most certainly during the Clinton boom years. No one would expect a high-tech start-up to back down, he argues, simply because it is taking profits from a larger established corporation. So why are presidential candidates held to a different standard? "No political system can regenerate without outside competition," he said during a speech in New York City on January 31, 2002. "Agendas throughout history have been pushed by third parties. Yet somehow the two political parties have expected to reform themselves without external jolts."

Sometimes—when backed into a corner or wearying of the spoiler issue—Nader has taken yet another tack. *If you are going to blame me for a Republican White House, you have to give me credit for the Democratic Senate.* It requires a few somersaults to explain this one, but here goes: Nader received 103,000 votes in Washington state from Greens. Election Day also featured a senatorial race in Washington between Democrat Maria Cantwell and Republican Slate Gordon. Cantwell won by nineteen hundred votes. Because there was no Green Party challenger in the race, one can safely assume that many of the Greens who turned out to vote Nader for president also voted for Cantwell in the Senate. This helped produce a Senate split fifty-fifty between Democrats and Republicans. The switch of Vermont's Jim Jeffords from Republican to Independent tipped the balance, giving the Democrats the majority. "I haven't gotten one letter of thank-you," quips Nader.

To complicate matters, Nader has given signals indicating that he relishes the fact that Bush is now in office. His reason: a so-called intensify-the-contradictions theory. Remember, Nader had some of his most conspicuous successes with President Nixon in office, and by contrast he felt stymied under Carter and Clinton. Often he has benefited from the stark relief provided by Republican politics. Unquestionably, a Bush presidency threatens Nader's agenda on everything from antitrust to torts. But Nader has actually suggested that the threat might help galvanize progressives. "Both parties do the same thing, one covertly, one overtly," he said during a 2001 Green Party fund-raiser. "Which one is going to get more people mad? Which one is going to get more people organized?"

In December 2001, Nader called up his old friend Frederick Condon to complain about Attorney General John Ashcroft. "He's trying to take all our freedoms away," said Nader. "Have you been reading about this?" Throughout the conversation, he seemed to be oblivious to the irony: Ashcroft would not be there had Gore been elected. Or maybe he was simply thrilling at the intensified contradictions.

The wild card in all of this is September 11. Some liberals have stopped complaining about Nader because of their doubts concerning how Gore as president would have handled terrorism.

One can go round and round. Sometimes it seems easiest to return to simple math. Nader got 96,915 votes in Florida; Gore needed 538. Even here, Nader introduces a wrinkle. He brought legions of new, disenfranchised voters into the political process. This is not a matter of mere addition and subtraction, then. Often Nader argues that much of his Florida base would not have voted at all, and thus he cannot be held responsible for actually taking votes from Gore.

Exit polls in Florida showed that about one-third of those who voted for Nader were in fact disenfranchised; otherwise he took votes from both Gore and Bush, by a margin of two to one. That means he siphoned off roughly forty thousand votes from Gore. Libertarian candidate Harry Browne, Howard Phillips of the Constitution Party, and John Hagelin of the Natural Law Party garnered 18,856, 4,280, and 2,287 votes respectively. Some of their voters were most certainly disenfranchised, but no doubt they each snatched a minimum of 538 votes from Gore. So why aren't they considered spoilers?

The answer involves a jump from math into the realm of perceptions. During the election, Nader trotted out the classic George Wallace third-party lament that there is not "a dime's worth of difference" between the two majority parties. Nevertheless, he was not viewed as a typical out-on-the-fringes third-party candidate. As a former Beltway insider, he had a long history of accomplishments, many achieved while working closely with Democrats. He was held to a different standard by critics, one that might best be described as "Nader should know better." With this in mind, the more nuanced Nader-as-spoiler arguments sidestep the whole question of whether he was a mathematical spoiler. Instead, they cast Nader more as an ideological spoiler, bedazzling young people with a self-serving and overly simplified political message.

Roger Hickey, cochair of the Campaign for America's Future, offers this criticism: "I felt that Ralph Nader was projecting the wrong strategy for mature political action to the younger voters he was energizing. It was a message of purity, of retiring to the strongholds, rather than engaging in a battle to build a political majority. I lived through the '60s. Some of the political strategies we pursued helped split the Democratic Party and led to Nixon, Ford, and Reagan. A lot of us have been working for a long time to overcome those divisions. That Nader was going back to that polarizing mode aggravated a lot of us."

OBVIOUSLY, WHETHER NADER IS a spoiler is in the eye of the beholder. For the legions of Nader supporters, his intractability, his defiance, the fact that he refused to drop out despite intense pressure from the Democrats, is a symbol of his enduring integrity. For detractors, many of whom appreciated Nader's earlier incarnation as a kind of shadow congressional whip, his role in the 2000 election is a troubling late-career chapter that can be neither overlooked nor forgotten.

But Nader has been on the scene for a long time, long enough for various positive and negative associations to coexist. Certainly, he has a vast legacy of accomplishments. Even his very first crusade continues to pay dividends. By some estimates, as many as a million lives have been saved since Nader's original auto safety law went into effect. In 1966, the fatality rate for automobiles was 5.6 deaths per million vehicle miles traveled, a number that has slid steadily to 1.6 as of 2000.

Under the Freedom of Information Act, the government now processes 2 million requests per year with varying degrees of efficiency. Public Citizen continues to fight to broaden the window. In 1996, Nader's old organization pushed for the passage of a series of amendments that created the so-called eFOIA, which covers the storage and retrieval of electronic records. Public Citizen has also been involved in cases seeking to set guidelines for the disposition of presidential e-mails. Under legal pressure, Ronald Reagan agreed not to destroy his e-mails upon leaving office, turning the bulk of them over to his presidential library. Clinton agreed to do the same.

Nader has been involved in issues large and small, vital and trivial. "Ralph travels at seventy ideas an hour," says an old friend. That is an unsafe speed, of course, and plenty of his notions have simply crashed and burned. During the late 1960s, for example, he dispatched a Raider to attend rock concerts in order to measure the decibel levels. Nader figured that he might be able to stir up concern for a pervasive societal ill that he termed "rock 'n roll deafness." For every aborted crusade, he has launched another that has been right on target. Many of them are not as well remembered as auto safety or nukes, but they had significant benefits nonetheless. It is Nader who took the lead, during the late 1960s, in getting baby food manufacturers to stop adding MSG as a taste enhancer. It is Nader, during the early 1970s, who pushed for a ban on holiday candles with lead in their wicks, a possible health hazard.

For someone who has frequently been viewed as a lone operator, Nader has also proved a master organization builder. In 1989 he founded a group called Princeton Project 55. His idea was startlingly simple and consonant with "Princeton in the world's service," a notion about the university that had appealed to him in the first place. Basically Nader observed that many of his classmates had achieved a level of prominence in various fields such as law, business, and medicine. They were at that time in life—their mid-fifties—when people often start thinking about giving back to society. Nader wanted to launch something more substantial than the standard alumni fund-raising drive. He envisioned an organization that would provide people the opportunity to volunteer their time, often lending expertise in their chosen fields.

Nader showed up at a class reunion and did what he does best, get people fired up. He delivered a rousing speech, passed around a yellow legal pad to collect names and numbers, and the organization was off and running. "All things start with a sign-up sheet," he said. As of 2002, Princeton Project 55 had a permanent office and a full-time staff of six. True to Nader's vision, a number of his fellow '55ers—the same group he once dismissed as Silent Generation dropouts—have joined the organization. For example, the project's membership includes several doctors and pharmaceutical company executives. They have started an initiative to push for increased awareness and better treatments for tuberculosis, a disease that does not get much attention in the United States. Worldwide, it is the second largest killer among infectious diseases behind HIV/AIDS. Nader founded an organization similar to Princeton Project 55 at Harvard law, called the Appleseed Foundation.

The key to his success has been to set up organizations with strong mandates but loose reins. As of 2002, roughly one hundred college campuses in twenty-four states have PIRG chapters, and nearly twenty thousand students actively participate. Then there are all those other organizations—not nearly as well-known as Public Citizen or the PIRGs—that are still in existence today, including the CUBs, Center for Auto Safety, Aviation Consumer Action Project, Consumer Project on Technology, and Buyers Up.

Maybe the most telling measure of Nader's reach is the legion of former Raiders, now scattered about, working in a variety of different fields. All have been exposed in varying degrees to the Nader approach: work harder, sleep less, be endlessly creative, never give up. Many of them have gone on to do advocacy work of their own. Eric Glitzenstein and Katherine Meyer, a husband-and-wife team, worked with Nader during the 1980s. Currently they run a Washington, D.C., law firm that specializes in wildlife and conservation issues. They have handled cases involving California gray whales, Mount Graham red squirrels, pygmy owls, ocelots, manatees, and a huge variety of other species. "We feel that our lives and careers were overwhelmingly influenced by Ralph," says Glitzenstein. "I think after working with him, we both felt it was important to devote our lives to public purpose. Once you come in contact with him, it just kind of stays with you."

Lawyers make up the largest proportion of Nader alums, but there is also generous representation among the ranks of the media. Michael Kinsley, a Raider of early 1970s vintage, has gone on to be a cohost of CNN's *Crossfire* and editor in chief at three different magazines, the *New Republic*, *Harper's*, and *Slate*. A former Carter speech writer, James Fallows has served as editor of *U.S. News & World Report* and is a correspondent for the *Atlantic*. Bill Taylor became a founder and co-editor of *Fast Company*, a magazine that acted as a kind of start-up firm cheerleader during the booming 1990s. Back in the 1980s, Taylor worked with Nader in producing a book called *The Big Boys*, which offered a rather more critical appraisal of corporations and chief executives. There are also plenty of ex-Naderites in academia. Judy Areen, one of the original seven Raiders, is dean of Georgetown University's law school. Joel Seligman is dean of the law school at Washington University in St. Louis.

Professionally speaking, Nader alums are truly a diverse and dispersed lot. This allows for a multiplier effect far beyond anything Nader could possibly have accomplished on his own. Many ex-Raiders are working in areas where even Nader, in the course of traveling seventy ideas an hour for nearly forty years, may not have dreamed of delving on his own. Ralf Hotchkiss, a Raider from 1968 to 1979, has a second thoracic paraplegia—he has the use of his arms and hands but not his legs—as the result of a motorcycle accident in 1966. Ever since, Hotchkiss has been on a quest to design better wheelchairs. In 1989 he was awarded a MacArthur genius grant to help him with his life's work.

Currently Hotchkiss is partnered with Physicians Against Landmines and is working on the Whirlwind, a rough-terrain wheelchair specially designed for people injured during wartime in places such as Afghanistan. "I'm trying to make them go where normal wheelchairs won't," says Hotchkiss. "We're trying to get further and further off the main road. Most people in the world live at the end of an unpaved pathway."

As for Nader's influence on his work, Hotchkiss says: "He showed me how to be persistent in getting down to the root problems. He taught me not just to work on the technical puzzle, but to look at the whole picture."

Nader's positive legacy is vast and assured. But he is not exactly the type to wax valedictory. "I'm more future oriented," he said in a recent interview. The period since the 2000 election has been as busy as any other time for Nader, as he has attempted to seize fresh issues. For example, he urged the NBA to conduct a thorough investigation of the officiating during game six of the 2002 playoffs between the Sacramento Kings and the L.A. Lakers. He has also started a couple of new organizations, tried to obtain funding for a museum, waged several lawsuits, worked to build the Green Party, and grappled with the question of whether to make a fourth run at the presidency.

Being sixty-eight in human years is not the same as being sixty-eight in Nader years: he continues to maintain a frenetic pace, having traveled recenty to Geneva, New York, Lawrence, Kansas, Stockholm, and Berlin. In July 2002, Nader visited Cuba for the first time since 1959. He and Castro met for six hours over dinner, a special vegetarian feast prepared in Nader's honor. "We discussed global infectious disease problems," says Nader. "We discussed a lot of the history of U.S.–Cuba relations as well as the usual stuff, lifting travel restrictions, ending the embargo. We talked about all kinds of issues, auto safety for one—they don't have many seat belts because their cars are so old. Castro is a great conversationalist and he's got an enormous recall of historical events and details."

If ever there were an issue tailor-made for Nader, it is Enron: a massive business scandal with tentacles that reach into the accounting profession, various regulatory agencies, and both the Democratic and Republican parties. Nader has worked to make it his own, but so far with limited results. On the issue of corporate crime, unquestionably, no one has better credentials than Nader. He also appears prescient, having made campaign finance reform one of his primary issues during the 2000 election. Because he did not take a cent of Enron money, he is that rare clean politician.

Shortly after the scandal broke, Nader made the rounds of talk shows to discuss Enron, among them NBC's *Meet the Press*, PBS's *Firing Line*, and Fox News's *O'Reilly Factor.* On January 21, 2002, he called a press conference—one that was packed with TV cameras and members of the media, unlike some of his 1980s clunkers. "Crime in the suites damages more people's health, safety, and economic resources by far than crime in the streets," he asserted. Then he laid out his plan for preventing future Enrons: more stringent oversight of the accounting profession, greater protection for whistle-blowers, a threefold increase in funding for the SEC, and a spate of corporate decency acts on the state level, spelling out when it is permissible to dispose of documents. On another occasion, Nader was involved in a bit of anti-Enron performance art; as he spoke, people fed pieces of wood marked "democracy, "families," and "truth" into a large wood chipper, which proceeded to shred these cherished values.

Still, Nader has had difficulty getting much traction on Enron. The scandal is widely covered, with journalists, politicians, and regulators swarming all over it. Furthermore, in order for Nader to get anything substantive accomplished, he would need to be able to work with Congress, as he did in the old days. But he is not about to swallow his pride, and members of Congress are unlikely to be receptive even if he did. Very few of them even return his phone calls. That has left Nader—who likes to describe his work as "playing fifty chess games simultaneously"—scrambling for a different approach. He is currently trying to build a citizen coalition to push for "authentic legislation rather than the window dressing being offered by the Democrats and Republicans, both of whom have their hands sticky with Enron money."

Recently, there seem to be fresh business scandals on an almost daily basis, with WorldCom, Merrill Lynch, and Johnson & Johnson to name just a few. Members of Congress scrambled to pass a bill that would make it possible to put executives in jail if found guilty of certain transgressions. Of course, it is an idea Nader has been hammering on since 1966. On the topic of corporate crime, don't be surprised if Nader finds a way to insert himself back into the center of the public debate.

Besides Enron and assorted business scandals, the other big issue that Nader has addressed—or has been forced to address—is the threat of terrorism. The world has changed drastically since November 2000, and Nader could not escape this issue if he tried. Whenever he speaks, invariably he gets questions about September 11. *How is Bush handling the war on terrorism? What would Nader do differently were he president?* It has forced Nader to formulate positions on an issue that is well outside his expertise and comfort level. He made a bold pronouncement during an interview with the *Chicago Tribune* that appeared in the February 17, 2002, issue. Had he been president, he asserted, September 11 would not have happened because he would have enacted various airline safety measures that he has been pushing for years. Yet it seems manifestly unlikely that one of his first acts as president, during peace time, would have been to push for reinforced cockpit doors on airplanes. Certainly it was not among the myriad issues he raised during his campaign. To compound matters, Nader's *Tribune* comment was widely reprinted in truncated, snippet form: "This war would never have happened had I been president."

Recently Nader has worked to develop a more acceptable position, centering around international law and the doctrine of hot pursuit. Taking issue with the war in Afghanistan, Nader has said, "Bush burned down a haystack to try to find a couple of needles. He didn't find the needles, but there have been thousands of innocent civilian deaths."

Instead, Nader says he would have organized a modest multinational force and sent them into Afghanistan to arrest Osama bin Laden, a kind of police raid. Then he would have tried him at The Hague, Milosevic style. "It [September 11] was an international crime, a massacre," Nader said during a February 1, 2002, speech in Philadelphia. "We should have gone forward with international law. If we don't go forward with some basis in law—domestic or international—what do we stand for?"

RECENTLY NADER FOUNDED A couple of new organizations. Democracy Rising is intended to keep the super-rally concept alive. Since the election, Nader has continued to hold stadium rallies in a number of cities including Boston, Cleveland, Phoenix, and Portland, Maine. Once again, he has been joined by an expanding cast of musicians and celebrities: Danny Glover, Michael Moore, Patti Smith, Jackson Browne, and Michelle Shocked. Because Nader is not officially running for office (just yet), he chooses to address the broader theme of civic involvement. At a typical Democracy Rising rally, there are tables set up for various advocacy groups. When Nader finishes speaking, audience members have the opportunity to sign up for assorted causes such as cleaning up a local toxic dump. "You have a very short time where you can capture people's attention. We're trying to take the energy and excitement of the super rallies and channel it directly into action," says Jason Kafoury, who heads up Democracy Rising.

Citizen Works, Nader's other recent start-up, is essentially an Internet-age networking organization. For a person who sometimes borders on Ludditism, it is a surprising choice. Nader wrote his latest book, *Crashing the Party*, the same way he wrote *Unsafe at Any Speed*—on an Underwood 5. "You can't get carpal tunnel syndrome with an Underwood," he says. "It has a spring to it." Nevertheless, Nader views the PC revolution with a pragmatist's eye, seeing its potential even though he has not become a convert. During his 2000 run, he brought some hot-shot young web masters into the campaign and had a better Internet presence than either Bush or Gore. Nader is that unique person who does not own a computer, does not surf the Net, and does not exchange e-mail—but still reads *Computer World* magazine.

The Citizen Works web site—maintained by others, of course—serves as a kind of portal for advocacy groups, providing links to other organizations involved in progressive causes. Say a visitor to the site is interested in fighting the death penalty; the site would connect the person to various groups involved in the issue. Citizen Works also provides venues for some old-fashioned networking, regularly hosting Washington, D.C., mixers that throw together people from the Sierra Club, the Student Peace Action Network, and other organizations. "We allow people to make connections, to know what other people in the citizen movement are doing," says Theresa Amato, campaign manager for Nader 2000 and now president of Citizen Works. "I'm taking the long view. I want to build bonds for ten years from now."

NADER HAS ALSO BEEN trying to start a museum. It has been a dream of his, going way back, to open the American Museum of Tort Law, and he even has a suitable building—an old factory in Winsted, on the banks of the Mad River. During the town's industrial glory days, the building housed the Strong Manufacturing Company, a coffin-trimmings maker that produced the silver handles used on Ulysses Grant's casket. The building sits mostly empty now and belongs to the Nader family. It seems that Nader is actually getting a touch nostalgic, though in his own inimitable way, as recent years have found him seeking to reconnect—civically at least—with Winsted, Princeton, and Harvard.

For his museum, Nader envisions various exhibits devoted to the history of tort law, such as Joe Camel cigarette ads and blown-out Firestone tires. There might be a medical devices room featuring silicone breast implants and the Dalkon Shield, a dangerous birth control device that was removed from the market. Certainly there would be a gift shop, perhaps offering scale models of the Corvair and other tchochkes. Not surprisingly, the idea—the mere idea—of a tort museum is a magnet for jokes. *What if someone slips and falls while visiting the museum*, ask wags in Winsted, which has always had an uneasy relationship with its most famous son. *What happens if someone gets scalded by the coffee served in the cafeteria?*

Plans for the museum are currently in limbo because Nader has managed to raise only $1.5 million of the $5 million he needs. Originally, a number of trial lawyers were behind this project, but following Nader's role in the 2000 election the promised financial support has evaporated. Among the groups that turned on Nader, the trial lawyers have done so with a special vehemence. James Carville was the speaker at the 2001 annual meeting of the American Trial Lawyers Association, a gathering that Nader has often addressed in the past. "The biggest lie in politics is that there's no difference between Gore and Bush," offered Carville, to thunderous applause.

More than most groups, the trial lawyers perceived vast differences between the two candidates. As governor of Texas, Bush was a major proponent of tort reform and as president, he will appoint numerous judges—and likely several Supreme Court justices—who share his perspective. Gore, meanwhile, saw his sister die of lung cancer related to smoking and has often opposed efforts to rein in the abilities of individuals to sue. For years, there have been rumors that Nader was bought by the trial lawyers; were this so, they might have succeeded in influencing his actions in 2000. As matters stand, the election caused a serious rift between Nader and a group that has long been a source of support philosophically, and, in some measure, financially.

As for Nader's recent slate of lawsuits—he typically has a few going at any given time—the verdicts have been mixed. At the beginning of his 2000 run, Nader filed a lawsuit claiming that the use of corporate money in financing presidential debates violates the Federal Election Campaign Act. This suit was appealed to the Supreme Court, which refused to hear it. Meanwhile, Nader settled his case against the debate commission and security guard John Vezeris, the one related to being barred from the Boston debate on October 3, 2000. Nader received a letter of apology, as requested, along with $51,000, which went to pay his attorneys. He plans a Raider-style report, to be released in the autumn of 2002, which he says will "expose the debate commission so that its reputation is worse than a used car salesman." At press time, MasterCard's $15 million trademark and copyright infringement lawsuit—centering on Nader's "Priceless" campaign commercial—was still unresolved.

Over the past couple of years, probably the bulk of Nader's time has been devoted to building the Greens. Since the election, Nader has been involved in roughly forty Green Party fund-raisers around the country. He says that his goal for upcoming elections is for the Greens to field a thousand candidates, quadruple the number in 2000. Many of these would be at the state and local level, where the Greens have made some inroads. But Nader is also pushing for increased participation in national elections.

In 2000, fifty-six Green candidates ran for Congress from nineteen different states, none successfully. At least one played a spoiler role. In the election for a House seat in Michigan's Eighth District, Republican Mike Rogers beat Democrat Dianne Byrum by eighty-eight votes. That race featured a Green Party candidate, Bonnie Bucqueroux, who received 3,484 votes.

Nader says he has no problem with Greens picking off a Democrat here or there. In fact, he appears to savor the prospect of Dems facing the wrath of the "Green hammer," as he terms it. "The Greens will run against whoever they want to run against," he says. "I'm not going to discourage them. You can't pick and choose like that. Once you do, you perform like a fusion party. And whenever there's a good Democrat you find yourself saying, 'We're not going to grow our party in this district for this office, because he's okay.' Certainly they would never show us that kind of solicitude."

He adds: "The Democrats are going to lose more and more elections unless they become more progressive."

As to whether he will ever again run for president, Nader is noncommital. In this one way at least, he has become a typical politician. It is worth noting that most everyone who has ever known him predicts that he will run again. It is also worth noting that Nader is quick to warm to hypothetical questions regarding things he would do differently, in the event that he runs. "Just about everything," he says. But Nader insists that he is saving the official decision until the timing is just right.

Recently Nader was in Philadelphia to make a speech. A woman recognized him on the street and stopped to ask him if he planned another run at the presidency. "It is too early to say," responded Nader. With that, he turned and continued on, a familiar figure in an old gray suit—moving, always moving.

SELECTED BIBLIOGRAPHY

Acton, Jay, and Alan LeMond. *Ralph Nader: A Man and a Movement*. New York: Warner, 1972.

Cox, Edward, et al. *Nader's Raiders*. New York: Grove, 1970.

De Toledano, Ralph. *Hit & Run: The Rise—and Fall?—of Ralph Nader*. New Rochelle, N.Y.: Arlington House, 1975.

Dickerson, Carrie Barefoot. *Aunt Carrie's War Against Black Fox Nuclear Power Plant*. Tulsa, Okla.: Council Oak, 1995.

Esposito, John, et al. *Vanishing Air: The Report on Air Pollution*. New York: Grossman, 1970.

Gorey, Hays. *Nader and the Power of Everyman*. New York: Grosset & Dunlap, 1975.

Green, Mark, et al. *Who Runs Congress?* New York: Bantam, 1972.

Hodgson, Godfrey. *The Gentleman from New York: Daniel Patrick Moynihan*. Boston: Houghton Mifflin, 2000.

McCarry, Charles. *Citizen Nader*. New York: Saturday Review Press, 1972.

Meyer, Katherine, et al. *Risking America's Health and Safety: George Bush and the Task Force on Regulatory Relief*. Washington, D.C.: Public Citizen, 1988.

Nader, Ralph. *Crashing the Party*. New York: St. Martin's, 2002.

______. *The Ralph Nader Reader*. New York: Seven Stories, 2000.

______. *Unsafe at Any Speed*. New York: Grossman, 1965.

Nader, Ralph, and Donald Ross. *Action for a Change*. New York: Grossman, 1971.

Nader, Ralph, et al. *Whistle Blowing*. New York: Grossman, 1972.

Nader, Rose, and Nathra Nader. *It Happened in the Kitchen: Recipes for Food and Thought*. Washington, D.C.: Center for the Study of Responsive Law, 1991.

Pertschuk, Michael. *Revolt Against Regulation*. Berkeley: University of California Press, 1982.

Sanford, David. *Me & Ralph*. Washington, D.C.: New Republic Book Company, 1976.

Townsend, Claire, et al. *Old Age: The Last Segregation*. New York: Grossman, 1971.

Vogel, David. *Fluctuating Fortunes: The Political Power of Business in America*. New York: Basic, 1989.

Wathen, Thomas. *Winsted, Connecticut: The Promise of a Small Town*. Washington, D.C.: Public Interest Research Group, 1989.

Whiteside, Thomas. *The Investigation of Ralph Nader*. New York: Arbor House, 1972.

For Young Adults

Bowen, Nancy. *Ralph Nader: Man with a Mission*. Brookfield, Conn.: Twenty-First Century Books, 2002.

Celsi, Teresa. *Ralph Nader: The Consumer Revolution*. Brookfield, Conn.: Millbrook, 1991.

Graham, Kevin. *Ralph Nader: Battling for Democracy*. Denver: Windom, 2000.

NOTES

Preface

Page xiv "offered a guided tour," *Washington Post*, May 27, 1974
Page xiv "bumped from a plane," *Washington Post*, January 11, 1978
Page xv "'He gave me," James Cubie to JM, interview on December 18, 2001

Chapter 1

Page 1 "His three older," Claire Nader to JM, interview on March 1, 2002
Page 1 "Nathra Nader," Ralph Nader to JM, interview on February 1, 2002
Page 1 "Rose Bouziane," Rose and Nathra Nader, *It Happened in the Kitchen*, p. 13
Page 2 "Rose married Nathra," *New York Times*, June 27, 1977
Page 2 "old industrial town," Joseph O'Brien to JM, interview on April 22, 2002
Page 2 "the Iron Age," Thomas Wathen, *Winsted, Connecticut: The Promise of a Small Town*, p. 10
Page 2 "upon moving to Winsted," Joseph O'Brien to JM, interview on April 22, 2002
Page 2 "song in Arabic," Claire Nader to JM, interview on March 1, 2002
Page 2 "checked the clock," Hays Gorey, *Nader and the Power of Everyman*, p. 181
Page 2 "'He simply absorbed," Claire Nader to JM, interview on March 1, 2002
Page 3 "boat trip," Laura Nader to JM, interview on February 22, 2002
Page 4 "'Who knows what," Ralph Nader to JM, interview on February 1, 2002
Page 4 "Upon returning from Lebanon," Charles McCarry, *Citizen Nader*, p. 34
Page 4 "Blanche Root Perol," Hays Gorey, *Nader and the Power of Everyman*, p. 180
Page 4 "Nancy Morgan," Nancy Morgan to JM, interview on September 27, 2001
Page 5 "'Statue of Liberty," Rose and Nathra Nader, *It Happened in the Kitchen*, p. 151
Page 5 "cows mooing," Thomas Wathen, *Winsted, Connecticut: The Promise of a Small Town*, p. 5
Page 5 "'The library was," Ralph Nader to JM, interview on February 1, 2002
Page 5 "county courthouse," Kevin Graham, *Ralph Nader: Battling for Democracy*, p. 24
Page 5 "town meetings," Claire Nader to JM, interview on March 1, 2002
Page 5 "Winsted's charter," Thomas Wathen, *Winsted, Connecticut: The Promise of a Small Town*, p. 19
Page 5 "'Value that person," Claire Nader to JM, interview on March 1, 2002
Page 6 "the Highland Arms," composite based on interviews with Ralph Nader, his two sisters, and Joseph O'Brien
Page 6 "'He joshed them," Claire Nader to JM, interview on March 1, 2002
Page 7 "'I hate you," Robert Buckhorn, *Nader: The People's Lawyer*, pp. 39–40
Page 7 "much of a gadfly," Joseph O'Brien to JM, interview on April 22, 2002
Page 7 "'We weren't raised," Laura Nader to JM, interview on February 22, 2002
Page 7 "social divisions," composite based on interviews by JM with long-time Winsted residents including Dennis Nalette on September 17, 2001
Page 7 "a Methodist church," Claire Nader to JM, interview on April 22, 2002
Page 7 "Naders were freestanding," John Bushnell to JM, interview on November 5, 2001
Page 7 "Fred Silverio," Fred Silverio to JM, interview on November 1, 2001
Page 8 "Jeha stories," Laura Nader to JM, interview on February 22, 2002
Page 8 "'Father was basically," Ralph Nader to JM, interview on February 1, 2002
Page 8 "very health conscious," Claire Nader to JM, interview on March 1, 2002
Page 9 "Dinnertime discussions," composite based on interviews with Ralph Nader and his sisters
Page 9 "Maxwell Auto Works," composite based on articles including *Cobblestone* magazine, July 1987
Page 10 "'He always wanted," Ralph Nader to JM, interview on February 1, 2002

Page 10 "As Claire recalls," Claire Nader to JM, interview on March 1, 2002
Page 10 "And as Laura," Laura Nader to JM, interview on February 22, 2002
Page 10 "'He wanted Ralph," Claire Nader to JM, interview on March 1, 2002
Page 11 "Helen Keller's autobiography," Ralph Nader to JM, interview on February 1, 2002
Page 12 "Lou Gehrig," *Mother Jones*, July-August 1996
Page 12 "'Well, it seemed. . . ," David Halberstam to JM, interview on June 21, 2002
Page 12 "Igor Stravinsky," Ralph Nader to JM, interview on February 1, 2002
Page 13 "The Gilbert School," composite drawn from interviews with Winsted residents and Thomas Wathen, *Winsted, Connecticut: The Promise of a Small Town*
Page 13 "Who is Eck?" Saul Miller to JM, interview on November 20, 2001
Page 13 "Meanwhile, Bushnell recalls," John Bushnell to JM, interview on November 5, 2001
Page 13 "hard-studying kids," Fred Silverio to JM, interview on November 1, 2001
Page 13 "class discussion," John Bushnell to JM, interview on November 5, 2001
Page 13 "As Silverio recalls," Fred Silverio to JM, interview on November 1, 2001
Page 14 "Mary Nix," Mary Nix to JM, interview on September 18, 2001
Page 14 "playing chess," Fred Silverio to JM, interview on November 1, 2001
Page 14 "disinterested in dating," John Bushnell to JM, interview on November 5, 2001
Page 14 "The motto under Nader's picture," *Miracle* yearbook, 1951
Page 15 "the Class Will," Charles McCarry, *Citizen Nader*, p. 39
Page 15 "'I chose Princeton," Ralph Nader to JM, interview on February 1, 2002

Chapter 2

Page 16 "'What a way," Jay Acton and Alan LeMond, *Ralph Nader: A Man and a Movement*, p. 31
Page 16 "a gentleman's C," Ralph Nader to JM, interview on February 1, 2002
Page 17 "He regularly crept," *Time*, December 12, 1969
Page 17 "Princeton's unofficial dress code," composite drawn from interviews by JM with Ralph Nader and classmates including Kenly Webster on December 28, 2001
Page 17 "Bill Shafer is," Bill Shafer to JM, interview on February 4, 2002
Page 18 "'Prospect was different," Chet Safian to JM, interview on December 17, 2001
Page 18 Discussion of Princeton, Woodrow Wilson School, and the Dodge family, composite drawn from a variety of sources including JM interview with Nader's classmate, Mike Robbins, on February 4, 2002
Page 19 "Harper Hubert Wilson," Jay Acton and Alan LeMond, *Ralph Nader: A Man and a Movement*, pp. 28–29
Page 19 "Eric Goldman," Roger Lloyd, Princeton classmate of Nader's, to JM, interview on February 13, 2002
Page 19 "DDT was sprayed," *New York Times*, March 3, 1996
Page 20 Norman Thomas description a composite drawn from sources including *Encyclopedia of World Biography*, 1998
Page 20 "a great debater," Ralph Nader to JM, interview on February 1, 2002
Page 21 "Albert Einstein," ibid.
Page 21 "Nader ended his," Rose Nader to JM, interview on April 22, 2002
Page 21 "pursue a Ph.D.," Charles McCarry, *Citizen Nader*, p. 46
Page 21 "summer of 1955," Ralph Nader to JM, interview on February 1, 2002
Page 23 "build a dry dam," Rose and Nathra Nader, *It Happened in the Kitchen*, p. 36
Page 23 "home or your business?" Claire Nader to JM, interview on April 22, 2002
Page 23 "entry exam," Teresa Celsi, *Ralph Nader: The Consumer Revolution*, p. 29
Page 23 "'I was contemptuous," Ralph Nader to JM, interview on February 1, 2002
Page 24 "Nader's roommate," Ed Levin to JM, interview on November 20, 2001
Page 24 "part-time jobs," Ralph Nader to JM, interview on February 1, 2002
Page 25 "a distinct memory," Joe Tom Easley to JM, interview on April 1, 2002
Page 25 "'high-priced tool factory.'" For example, *Newsweek*, January 22, 1968
Page 25 "landlord-tenant law," Joe Page to JM, interview on November 17, 2001
Page 25 "good at cramming," Frederick Condon to JM, interview on December 3, 2001
Page 25 "'He didn't see," Ed Levin to JM, interview on November 20, 2001
Page 26 "Friends would receive postcards," Frederick Condon to JM, interview on December 3, 2001
Page 26 "ill with malaria," Laura Nader to JM, interview on February 22, 2002
Page 26 "'He didn't talk," Joe Page to JM, interview on November 17, 2001
Page 26 "yen for privacy," Ralph Nader to JM, interview on February 1, 2002
Page 27 "Alpheus Thomas Mason," ibid.
Page 27 Roscoe Pound description a composite drawn from sources including David Wigdor, *Roscoe Pound: Philosopher of Law* (Greenwood Press, 1974)

Page 28 "'He was almost," Ralph Nader to JM, interview on February 1, 2002
Page 28 "An editorial arguing," *Harvard Law School Record*, October 27, 1955
Page 28 Nader's article on American Indians appeared in the *Harvard Law School Record*, April 5, 1956
Page 28 "Clyde Kluckhohn," Laura Nader to JM, interview on February 22, 2002
Page 29 "Nader became president," announcement in *Harvard Law School Record*, November 15, 1956
Page 29 Nader's article on Puerto Rico appeared in the *Harvard Law School Record*, December 13, 1956
Page 29 "'He wanted the," Robert Oliver to JM, interview on November 15, 2001
Page 29 "his 1949 Studebaker," Robert Buckhorn, *Nader: The People's Lawyer*, p. 45
Page 29 "'You met all," ibid., p. 41
Page 30 "a glove compartment," Kevin Graham, *Ralph Nader: Battling for Democracy*, pp. 44–45
Page 30 "'I got a," Harold Katz to JM, interview on December 13, 2001
Page 30 "medical/legal seminar," Joe Page to JM, interview on November 17, 2001
Page 30 "received an A," Ralph De Toledano, *Hit & Run*, p. 32

Chapter 3

Page 31 "off to Alaska," Ralph Nader to JM, interview on February 1, 2002
Page 32 "Fidel Castro," David Binder to JM, interview on November 7, 2001
Page 32 "by Charles Porter," David Binder to JM, interview on November 15, 2001
Page 32 "the Havana Hilton," David Binder to JM, interview on November 7, 2001
Page 32 "'Castro was," Ralph Nader to JM, interview on February 1, 2002
Page 33 "54 Church Street," courtesy of Harvard Business School's Baker Library historical collection; detective report, dated January 28, 1966, part of Vincent Gillen Collection, "Correspondence (C1)"
Page 33 "'bumming corners," Joseph O'Brien to JM, interview on April 22, 2002
Page 33 "an eccentric genius," Andrew Grinvalsky to JM, interview on September 18, 2001
Page 33 Description of George Athanson, a composite drawn from interviews including Frederick Condon to JM on December 3, 2001
Page 33 "'I thought it," Chet Safian to JM, interview on December 17, 2001
Page 33 "profile of Roscoe Pound," *Reader's Digest*, February 1961
Page 33 "'The Safe Car," *Nation*, April 11, 1959
Page 33 "testified on auto safety," *Playboy*, October 1968
Page 34 "Meanwhile, Ed Levin," Ed Levin to JM, interview on November 20, 2001
Page 34 "So Joan Levin," Joan Levin to JM, interview on December 5, 2001
Page 34 "trip to Scandinavia," Charles McCarry, *Citizen Nader*, pp. 60–61
Page 34 "traveled to Moscow," Harold Berman to JM, interview on November 13, 2001
Page 34 "The letter appeared," *Harvard Law School Record*, May 1, 1958
Page 34 "'Ralph Nader was," Harold Berman to JM, interview on November 13, 2001
Page 35 "establish an ombudsman," Charles McCarry, *Citizen Nader*, pp. 60–61
Page 35 "through Latin America," Joe Page to JM, interview on November 17, 2001
Page 35 "'I've always been," Ralph Nader to JM, interview on February 1, 2002
Page 35 "Page and Nader," Joe Page to JM, interview on November 17, 2001
Page 37 Meetings between David Halberstam and Ralph Nader and Nathra Nader; Kevin Graham, *Ralph Nader: Battling for Democracy*, p. 51 and Charles McCarry, *Citizen Nader*, p. 60
Page 37 "move to Alaska," Frederick Condon to JM, interview on December 3, 2001

Chapter 4

Page 38 "Harry Barr, General Motor's," *New York Times*, January 28, 1965
Page 38 "Around the same," Ralph Nader, *Unsafe at Any Speed*, p. 219
Page 38 "Fatal auto accidents," *Atlantic*, October 1966
Page 38 "H. H. Bliss," Ralph Nader, *Unsafe at Any Speed*, p. 240
Page 39 "One cutting-edge," ibid., p. 144
Page 39 "'body rights," Ralph Nader to JM, interview on February 1, 2002
Page 39 "He hitchhiked down," *Atlantic*, October 1966
Page 39 "'I had watched," *New York Times*, October 29, 1967
Page 40 "Daniel Patrick Moynihan," Thomas Whiteside, *Investigation of Ralph Nader*, p. 5
Page 40 "During his stint," Charles McCarry, *Citizen Nader*, p. 70
Page 40 "$50 a day," Godfrey Hodgson, *Gentleman from New York*, p. 62
Page 40 "'Ralph was a," Charles McCarry, *Citizen Nader*, p. 74
Page 40 "While at Labor," Godfrey Hodgson, *Gentleman from New York*, p. 63

Page 40 "Meanwhile, Elizabeth Moynihan," Charles McCarry, *Citizen Nader*, p. 6
Page 40 "summer of 1964," Thomas Whiteside, *Investigation of Ralph Nader*, p. 7
Page 41 "Grossman Publishers was," Jill Kneerim, Richard Grossman's former wife, to JM, interview on April 17, 2001
Page 41 "Grossman had first," Richard Grossman to JM, interview on April 20, 2001
Page 41 "1719 19th Street, NW," address given by numerous close associates, including Andrew Egendorf, to JM, interview on April 23, 2001
Page 41 "When Grossman finally," Richard Grossman to JM, interview on April 20, 2001
Page 41 "already amassed," Jerome Sonosky to JM, interview on May 2, 2001
Page 41 "For example, Nader," Federal Role in Traffic Safety, Hearings before the Subcommittee on Executive Reorganization of the Committee on Government on Government Operations of the United States Senate, March 22, 1966, p. 1507
Page 41 "California Highway Department," Ralph Nader, *Unsafe at Any Speed*, p. 3
Page 41 "disillusioned auto-industry," Ralf Hotchkiss to JM, interview on April 17, 2001
Page 42 "Once source told," *Nation*, April 11, 1959
Page 42 Hugh DeHaven description a composite drawn from sources including "Nova," no. 2605 "Escape: Because Accidents Happen," broadcast on PBS, February 16, 1999
Page 42 William Haddon Jr. description a composite drawn from sources including Johns Hopkins University web site (jhsph.edu)
Page 43 "organize a protest," Saint Barnabas Hospital web site (stbarnabashospital.org)
Page 43 "Rose Nader carried," Hays Gorey, *Nader and the Power of Everyman*, p. 182
Page 43 Abraham Ribicoff description a composite drawn from sources including *Manchester Guardian*, February 24, 1998
Page 44 "Early 1965 found," Jerome Sonosky to JM, interview on May 2, 2001
Page 44 "Ribicoff officially announced," *Atlantic*, October 1966
Page 44 "The original plan," *Saturday Review*, October 7, 1972
Page 44 "Finally, Grossman simply," Richard Grossman to JM, interview on April 20, 2001
Page 45 "official publication date," *Saturday Review*, October 7, 1972
Page 45 "The next day," Richard Grossman to JM, interview on April 20, 2001
Page 45 "the Chevrolet Corvair," Ralph Nader, *Unsafe at Any Speed*, pp. 1–32
Page 46 "fatally gored," ibid., p. 17
Page 46 "bitch-goddess," ibid., p. 28
Page 46 "Grossman felt certain," Richard Grossman to JM, interview on April 20, 2001
Page 46 "'a searing document," *San Francisco Chronicle*, October 8, 1965
Page 46 "*Scientific American* praised," *New Republic*, June 4, 1966
Page 46 "*Book Week* called," *Book Week*, January 23, 1966
Page 46 "veteran Broadway flack," Richard Grossman to JM, interview on April 20, 2001
Page 46 "The press conference," Thomas Whiteside, *Investigation of Ralph Nader*, p. 11
Page 47 "'That day, Ralph," Richard Grossman to JM, interview on April 20, 2001
Page 47 "gone to Iowa," Lawrence Scalise to JM, interview on June 12, 2001
Page 47 "Kirkwood Hotel," *New Republic*, March 12, 1966
Page 47 "'I began to," Ralph Nader to JM, interview on February 1, 2002
Page 47 "'I can't believe," Richard Grossman to JM, interview on April 20, 2001
Page 47 "'C'mon Ralph," Jerome Sonosky to JM, interview on May 2, 2001
Page 47 "'Why don't you," Thomas Whiteside, *Investigation of Ralph Nader*, p. 18
Page 47 "By Nader's count," *New York Times*, March 6, 1966
Page 47 "'Mr. Nader, please," Thomas Whiteside, *Investigation of Ralph Nader*, p. 18
Page 48 "'The annual model," Federal Role in Traffic Safety, Hearings before the Subcommittee on Executive Reorganization of the Committee on Government Operations of the United States Senate, February 10, 1966, p. 1267
Page 48 "Onlookers from that day," general impression of varied sources including Robert Wager to JM, interview on May 29, 2001
Page 48 "'He was powerful," Jerome Sonosky to JM, interview on May 2, 2001
Page 48 "Dirksen Senate Office," *New Republic*, March 12, 1966
Page 48 "on an elevator," Kevin Graham, *Ralph Nader: Battling for Democracy*, p. 11
Page 48 "named Marshall Speake," *Washington Post*, February 13, 1966
Page 49 "Bryce Nelson," Bryce Nelson to JM, interview on May 31, 2001
Page 49 "Morton Mintz," Morton Mintz to JM, interview on May 22, 2001
Page 49 "'Car Safety Critic," *Washington Post*, February 13, 1966

Page 50 "Thomas Lambert Jr.," *New Republic*, March 12, 1966
Page 50 "'I knew something," Ralph Nader to JM, interview on May 23, 2002
Page 50 "This was followed," *New York Times*, March 6, 1966
Page 50 "'Pardon me," *New Republic*, March 12, 1966
Page 50 "Then, on February 22, 1966," Senate hearing on March 22, 1966, p. 1533
Page 51 "'I think Ralph," Laura Nader to JM, interview on February 22, 2002
Page 51 "The mysterious Mr. Warren," Senate hearing on March 22, 1966, pp. 1533–1536
Page 51 "'This guy calls," Frederick Condon to JM, interview on December 18, 2001
Page 51 "On arriving at," Senate hearing on March 22, 1966, pp. 1533–1536
Page 52 "Digging by Ridgeway," *New Republic*, March 12, 1966
Page 53 "Ridgeway's story appeared," Thomas Whiteside, *Investigation of Ralph Nader*, p. 33
Page 53 "The media firestorm," ibid., p. 34
Page 53 "A *New York Times*," *New York Times*, March 6, 1966
Page 53 "Yet GM had remained," Thomas Whiteside, *Investigation of Ralph Nader*, p. 34
Page 53 "Late on the," Senate hearing on March 22, 1966, p. 1389
Page 53 "Ribicoff was livid," Jerome Sonosky to JM, interview on May 2, 2001
Page 53 "maximum penalty," *New Republic*, March 19, 1966
Page 53 "Prior to," Jerome Sonosky to JM, interview on May 2, 2001

Chapter 5

Page 54 "A capacity crowd," *Washington Post*, March 23, 1966
Page 54 "Arrayed along," Robert Buckhorn, *Nader: The People's Lawyer*, p. 28
Page 54 "Ted Sorenson," Jerome Sonosky to JM, interview on May 2, 2001
Page 55 James Roche description a composite drawn from sources including *New York Times Magazine*, September 12, 1971
Page 55 "'To the extent," Senate hearing on March 22, 1966, p. 1381
Page 55 "Canon 20," Thomas Whiteside, *Investigation of Ralph Nader*, p. 53
Page 55 "'It is impermissible," Senate hearing on March 22, 1966, p. 1382
Page 56 "William O'Neill," Robert Buckhorn, *Nader: The People's Lawyer*, p. 11
Page 56 "Eileen Murphy," Thomas Whiteside, *Investigation of Ralph Nader*, p. 55
Page 56 "Danner subcontracted," *New York Times*, November 17, 1966
Page 56 "the detective report," Senate hearing on March 22, 1966, p. 1464
Page 57 "Gillen's instructions," ibid., p. 1506
Page 57 "spectacularly buffoonish," impression of various participants in Senate hearing including Jerome Sonosky to JM, interview on May 2, 2001
Page 57 "opened his testimony," Senate hearing on March 22, 1966, p. 1523–4
Page 57 "miniature spy camera," Thomas Whiteside, *Investigation of Ralph Nader*, p. 77
Page 57 "'If you wish," Senate hearing on March 22, 1966, p. 1537
Page 58 "'fairness to Ralph," ibid., p. 1549
Page 58 "'Mr. Chairman, members," ibid., p. 1465
Page 58 "'General Motors executives," ibid., p. 1469
Page 59 "Nader also sought," ibid., p. 1511
Page 59 "devote any royalties," ibid., p. 1501
Page 59 "'While you have," ibid., p. 1506
Page 59 "lasted six hours," *Washington Post*, March 23, 1966
Page 59 "by chauffeured limo," Hays Gorey, *Nader and the Power of Everyman*, p. 17
Page 60 "'We can hardly," *New York Times*, April 23, 1966
Page 60 "Auto executives descended," *Atlantic*, October 1966
Page 60 "Henry Ford II," *New York Times*, May 14, 1966
Page 60 "'We saw him," Robert Wager to JM, interview on May 29, 2001
Page 60 "Nader delivered," Jerome Sonosky to JM, interview on May 2, 2001
Page 60 "Ribicoff sent telegrams," *New York Times*, April 8, 1966
Page 60 "Ribicoff held a," *New York Times*, May 7, 1966
Page 61 "Lloyd Cutler," *Atlantic*, October 1966
Page 61 "Clinton wound up," *Business Week*, November 11, 1996
Page 61 "in one anteroom," Jerome Sonosky to JM, interview on May 2, 2001
Page 61 "Nader would leak," *Litigation*, Fall 1996
Page 61 "auto safety bill," *New York Times*, August 26, 1966
Page 61 "Nevertheless Nader pronounced," *Atlantic*, October 1966

Page 61 "President Johnson signed," *New York Times*, September 10, 1966
Page 62 "A television ad," *New York Times*, September 25, 1966
Page 62 "University of Michigan," *Consumer Reports*, April 1970
Page 62 "reached number five," Kevin Graham, *Ralph Nader: Battling for Democracy*, p. 8
Page 62 "half a million copies," *Saturday Review*, October 7, 1972
Page 62 "Nader earned $53,000," *Playboy*, October 1968
Page 62 "discontinued the model," *New York Times*, May 13, 1968
Page 62 "So Nader filed," Thomas Whiteside, *Investigation of Ralph Nader*, p. 96
Page 62 "Ironically, this tort," *Litigation*, Fall 1996
Page 63 "Nader sued Gillen," *New York Times*, November 16, 1966
Page 63 "a serendipitous move," *Litigation*, Fall 1996

Chapter 6

Page 64 "Enter Neal Smith," Edward Mezvinsky to JM, interview on June 8, 2001
Page 64 "The law on," *New Republic*, July 15, 1967
Page 65 "trying since 1960," *New York Times*, December 16, 1967
Page 65 "But his efforts," Nick Kotz to JM, interview on May 5, 2001
Page 65 "'The process doesn't," Edward Mezvinsky to JM, interview on June 8, 2001
Page 65 "The foyer," Robert Buckhorn, *Nader: The People's Lawyer*, pp. vii–viii
Page 65 "Nader paid $80," Ralph Nader to JM, interview on May 23, 2002
Page 66 "'room was antiseptic," Edward Mezvinsky to JM, interview on June 8, 2001
Page 66 "Every time I," Charles McCarry, *Citizen Nader*, p. 6
Page 66 *New Republic* articles on tainted meat, July 15, 1967 and August 19, 1967
Page 67 "'I broke the," Nick Kotz to JM, interview on May 5, 2001
Page 67 "Nader took raw," *Time*, December 12, 1969
Page 67 "This resulted in," Meat Inspection, Hearings before a Subcommittee of the Senate Committee on Agriculture and Forestry, November 14, 1967
Page 67 "Nader also set," *Newsweek*, January 22, 1968
Page 67 "most enduring observations," widely held impression including Joe Tom Easley to JM, interview on June 2, 2001
Page 68 "a tractor-beam," Richard Falknor to JM, interview on May 23, 2001
Page 68 "'Thanks to all," Nick Kotz to JM, interview on May 5, 2001
Page 68 "Nevertheless, the House," *Newsweek*, January 22, 1968
Page 68 "Instead, the House," *New York Times*, December 3, 1967
Page 69 "Kotz broke a," Nick Kotz to JM, interview on May 5, 2001
Page 69 "Johnson made a plea," *New York Times*, November 27, 1967
Page 69 "Mondale had been," *New Republic*, August 19, 1967
Page 69 "ungodly hour, Mondale," Hays Gorey, *Nader and the Power of Everyman*, p. 53
Page 69 "Mondale's bill was," *New York Times*, December 19, 1967
Page 69 "The bill passed," Charles McCarry, *Citizen Nader*, p. 152
Page 69 "repugnant passages," *Newsweek*, January 22, 1968
Page 70 "Upton Sinclair," Ralph Nader to JM, interview on February 1, 2002
Page 70 "There's no formula," *Newsweek*, January 22, 1968
Page 71 "Alan Morrison," Alan Morrison to JM, interview on August 13, 2001
Page 71 "During the period," Charles McCarry, *Citizen Nader*, p. 155
Page 71 "Nader was introduced," Claire Nader to JM, interview on April 22, 2002
Page 71 "Nader proceeded to," *New Republic*, September 2, 1967
Page 71 "He also drummed," *New York Times Magazine*, October 29, 1967,
Page 71 "Testifying before the," *New York Times*, May 16, 1968
Page 71 "Nader enlisted the," Morton Mintz to JM, interview on May 3, 2001
Page 72 "Technicians who took," *Playboy*, October 1968
Page 72 "American Dental Association," *New Republic*, September 2, 1967
Page 72 "color television," *Time*, December 12, 1969
Page 72 Discussion of Johnson and consumerism drawn from a variety of sources including Bob Dallek, LBJ biographer, to JM, interview on May 31, 2001
Page 73 "'That goddamned Nader," *Time*, December 12, 1969
Page 73 "Upton Sinclair, Ida Tarbell," Richard Current, *American History: A Survey Since 1865*, p. 557
Page 73 "Nader even became," *New York Times*, October 13, 1968
Page 74 "$20,000 in seed money," Robert Sherrill to JM, interview on May 31, 2001
Page 74 "Around this time," Anthony Mazzochi to JM, interview on July 9, 2001

Chapter 7

Page 75 "They happened to," Andrew Egendorf to JM, interview on April 23, 2001
Page 75 "a joint letter," Letter, dated January 29, 1968, furnished to JM by Andrew Egendorf
Page 75 "A few days," Andrew Egendorf to JM, interview on March 18, 2002
Page 75 "'It was an," Andrew Egendorf to JM, interview on April 23, 2001
Page 76 "William Howard Taft IV," *Time*, September 13, 1968
Page 76 "Edward Finch Cox," Robert Buckhorn, *Nader: The People's Lawyer*, p. 78
Page 76 "Peter Bradford," Edward Cox et al., *Nader's Raiders*, p. 2
Page 76 "'It's a matter," *Wall Street Journal*, July 10, 1968
Page 76 "John Schulz," *Time*, September 13, 1968
Page 76 "'None of us," Andrew Egendorf to JM, interview on April 23, 2001
Page 77 "Or as Fellmeth," Robert Fellmeth to JM, interview on September 13, 2001
Page 77 "Early in 1968," William Taft IV to JM, interview on June 4, 2001
Page 77 "This was supposed," Edward Cox et al., *Nader's Raiders*, p. vii
Page 77 "a previous investigation," *New York Times*, January 6, 1969
Page 77 "Regarding the agency's," Andrew Egendorf to JM, interview on April 23, 2001
Page 78 "Nader's initial instructions," Source to JM, interview on background
Page 78 "The FTC's own," Edward Cox et al., *Nader's Raiders*, p. ix
Page 78 "Nader's team determined," ibid., p. 59
Page 78 "On average, it," ibid., p. 78
Page 78 "About the only," ibid., p. ix
Page 78 "Carter's Little Liver Pills," Hays Gorey, *Nader and the Power of Everyman*, p. 277
Page 78 "The FTC's case," Edward Cox et al., *Nader's Raiders*, p. 57
Page 78 "When it came," ibid., p. 43
Page 78 "Little had changed," ibid., p. 142
Page 78 "a field office," ibid., p. 137
Page 79 "Of five hundred lawyers," ibid., p. 132
Page 79 "The students identified," ibid., p. 147
Page 79 "On arriving to," ibid., p. 148
Page 79 "'When Dixon threw," Edward Cox to JM, interview on July 9, 2001
Page 79 Discussion of the year 1968 composite drawn from sources including freespeech.com
Page 80 "'Nader's neophytes," *Time*, September 13, 1968
Page 80 "'Nader's Raiders," William Greider to JM, interview on November 28, 2001
Page 80 "The report describes," Edward Cox et al., *Nader's Raiders*, p. vii
Page 80 "Another barb," ibid., p. 170
Page 80 "an ego trip," William Taft IV to JM, interview on June 4, 2001
Page 80 "'Here you are," Robert Fellmeth to JM, interview on November 16, 2001
Page 81 "Richard Nixon," *New Yorker*, October 8, 1973
Page 81 "The ABA deemed," *New York Times*, September 16, 1969
Page 81 "Caspar Weinberger," *New York Times*, October 26, 1969
Page 81 "reorganized the FTC," *New York Times*, June 9, 1970
Page 81 "It began undertaking," Charles McCarry, *Citizen Nader*, p. 191
Page 81 "'I don't work," Alan Morrison to JM, interview on August 13, 2001
Page 81 "the industrial revolution," *Newsweek*, January 22, 1968
Page 82 "one hundred interns," *Time*, December 12, 1969
Page 82 "a small stipend," Robert Buckhorn, *Nader: The People's Lawyer*, p. 88
Page 82 "Nader rented it," Joe Tom Easley to JM, interview on May 13, 2002
Page 82 "handful of grants," Robert Buckhorn, *Nader: The People's Lawyer*, pp. 147–150
Page 82 "He lived frugally," ibid., p. 225
Page 82 "A hand-lettered," Jay Acton and Alan LeMond, *Ralph Nader: A Man and a Movement*, p. 90
Page 82 "'There was a," Harrison Wellford to JM, interview on April 24, 2001
Page 83 "Nader did not," Joe Tom Easley to JM, interview on May 30, 2001
Page 83 "He paid $97," *Life*, October 3, 1969
Page 83 "An interesting side note," Joan Levin to JM, interview on December 5, 2001
Page 83 "working at Oak Ridge," Claire Nader to JM, interview on April 22, 2002
Page 83 "Shaf had returned," Claire Nader to JM, interview on March 1, 2002
Page 83 "'He was to," Ralph Nader to JM, interview on February 1, 2002
Page 84 "'Ralph has this," Joe Tom Easley to JM, interview on May 30, 2001
Page 84 "Applications in 1970," Jay Acton and Alan LeMond, *Ralph Nader: A Man and a Movement*, pp. 89–90

Page 84 "'We were hard-working," Michael Charney to JM, interview on April 19, 2001
Page 84 "Nader's hiring methods," widely held impression including Peter Petkas to JM, interview on April 26, 2001
Page 84 "102 of them," *Time*, December 12, 1969
Page 85 "He had limited," Marcus Raskin to JM, interview on July 11, 2001
Page 85 "In a *Playboy* interview," *Playboy*, October 1968
Page 85 "'You should not," Robert Buckhorn, *Nader: The People's Lawyer*, p. 35
Page 86 "His own work," widely held impression including Jim Turner to JM, interview on April 18, 2001
Page 86 "he had smoked," Charles McCarry, *Citizen Nader*, p. 133
Page 86 "'Relaxing is a," *Playboy*, October 1968
Page 86 "As a young lawyer," Mark Green to JM, interview on June 6, 2001
Page 86 "Nader generally paid," *Science*, November 21, 1969
Page 86 "'Ralph wants to," Alan Morrison to JM, interview on August 13, 2001
Page 86 "'We were fanatics," Beverly Moore to JM, interview on April 19, 2001
Page 87 "'laborious leisure," *Playboy*, October 1968
Page 87 "'I'll bet Jeneen," Michael Pertschuk to JM, interview on August 20, 2001
Page 87 "'I can remember," Peter Petkas to JM, interview on April 26, 2001
Page 87 "Per the martial analogy," *Parade*, April 21, 1974
Page 87 "'Ralph was notorious," Joe Tom Easley to JM, interview on June 2, 2001
Page 88 "'He said that," Ed Levin to JM, interview on November 20, 2001
Page 88 "demands of family life," Harrison Wellford to JM, interview on April 24, 2001
Page 88 "As one Raider," Jim Turner to JM, interview on April 18, 2001
Page 88 "A report, Nader style," There is a list of Nader reports in Hays Gorey, *Nader and the Power of Everyman*, pp. 312–315
Page 89 "The best of," Richard Grossman to JM, interview on April 20, 2001
Page 89 "Michael Kinsley," *Seventeen*, September 1971

Chapter 8

Page 90 "When Nader first," *Reader's Digest*, June 1973
Page 90 "*Rochester Times Union*," Robert Buckhorn, *Nader: The People's Lawyer*, p. 56
Page 91 List of journalists with whom Nader worked closely drawn from variety of sources including Morton Mintz to JM, interview on May 3, 2001
Page 91 "(Nader had far," Joe Tom Easley to JM, interview on June 2, 2001
Page 91 "'His story ideas," Morton Mintz to JM, interview on May 3, 2001
Page 91 Discussion of state of investigative reporting circa the 1960s drawn from variety of sources including Nick Kotz to JM, interview on May 5, 2001
Page 92 "a science reporter," Joe Tom Easley to JM, interview on May 30, 2001
Page 92 "'I learned one," Robert Buckhorn, *Nader: The People's Lawyer*, p. 65
Page 92 "Rivers and Harbors," Alan Saeks, one-time Minnesota PIRG lawyer, to JM, interview on July 11, 2001
Page 93 "In the estimation," Daniel Guttman to JM, interview on May 21, 2001
Page 93 "The memorable terms," *Time,* July 25, 1969
Page 93 Discussion of Nader projects that were low-hanging fruit drawn from a variety of sources including Harrison Wellford to JM, interview on April 24, 2001
Page 93 Discussion of small errors in Nader reports: Both *Time*, April 3, 1972, and *Reader's Digest*, June 1973, took retrospective looks at some reports that contained errors.
Page 93 "'I can't make," *New York Times Magazine*, March 21, 1971
Page 93 "'He had the facts," Nick Kotz to JM, interview on May 5, 2001
Page 93 Phillip Burton description a composite drawn from sources including John Jacobs, *A Rage for Justice: The Passion and Politics of Phillip Burton*
Page 93 Warren Magnuson description a composite drawn from sources including Michael Pertschuk, *Revolt Against Regulation*
Page 95 "'Nader was able," Michael Pertschuk to JM, interview on August 20, 2001
Page 95 "talent is mimicry," Joe Tom Easley to JM, interview on June 2, 2001
Page 95 Discussion of Nader's facility with congressional staffs drawn especially from interviews with Joe Tom Easley and Michael Pertschuk
Page 96 "Tom Susman is," Tom Susman to JM, May 31, 2001
Page 96 "'Ralph Nader, Washington, D.C.'," Harrison Wellford to JM, interview on April 24, 2001
Page 96 "'Read this, Ralph!'" Robert Buckhorn, *Nader: The People's Lawyer*, pp. 245–246
Page 97 "own idiosyncratic method," Joe Tom Easley to JM, interview on June 2, 2001
Page 97 "A Milwaukee landlord," Robert Buckhorn, *Nader: The People's Lawyer*, p. 251

Page 97 "got a Popsicle," ibid., p. 248
Page 97 "'It's come off," *New York Times Magazine*, October 29, 1967
Page 98 "Unruly stacks of," Robert Buckhorn, *Nader: The People's Lawyer*, p. 250
Page 98 "In 1971 a," Ralf Hotchkiss to JM, interview on April 17, 2001
Page 98 "'I remember him," Phil Donahue to JM, interview on November 15, 2001
Page 98 "'One day while," *New York Times Magazine*, March 14, 1971
Page 98 "On November 20," *Princeton Alumni Weekly*, February 23, 1971
Page 99 Miss Porter's School description a composite drawn from sources including usnews.com
Page 99 "Robert Townsend," *New York Times Magazine*, March 14, 1971
Page 99 "through tremendous upheaval," Lallie Lloyd to JM, interview on June 15, 2001
Page 99 "230 girls present," *Princeton Alumni Weekly*, February 23, 1971
Page 99 "'He's a very passionate," Lallie Lloyd to JM, interview on June 15, 2001
Page 99 "filled her diary," Claire Townsend diary entries reprinted in *Princeton Alumni Weekly*, February 23, 1971
Page 100 "Nader selected five girls," *New York Times Magazine*, March 14, 1971
Page 100 "Lallie Lloyd was," Lallie Lloyd to JM, interview on June 15, 2001
Page 100 "A bemused press," *New York Times Magazine*, March 14, 1971
Page 101 "a mongrel dog," Lallie Lloyd to JM, interview on June 15, 2001
Page 101 "'The nurse I," *Princeton Alumni Weekly*, February 23, 1971
Page 101 "'This guy knew," Lallie Lloyd to JM, interview on June 15, 2001
Page 102 "'I have a," *Princeton Alumni Weekly*, February 23, 1971
Page 102 "What truly worked," Lallie Lloyd to JM, interview on June 15, 2001
Page 102 "Dr. Robert Butler," *New York Times Magazine*, March 14, 1971
Page 102 "Nader told the girls," *Princeton Alumni Weekly*, February 23, 1971
Page 103 "Reviews were overwhelmingly," *New York Times Magazine*, March 14, 1971 and *Reader's Digest*, June 73
Page 104 "'Above all,' he," *New York Times Magazine*, March 14, 1971

Chapter 9

Page 105 "In the year," Robert Buckhorn, *Nader: The People's Lawyer*, pp. 301–303
Page 105 "Cowan and Moore," Geoffrey Cowan to JM, via email dated May 8, 2002
Page 106 "Nader met Cowan," Charles McCarry, *Citizen Nader*, p. 233
Page 106 "Over tea, the," *New Yorker*, June 20, 1970
Page 106 "Among other things," Geoffrey Cowan to JM, interview on May 30, 2001
Page 106 "Their proposed slate," Charles McCarry, *Citizen Nader*, p. 22
Page 106 "Nader demurred, explaining," Geoffrey Cowan to JM, interview on May 30, 2001
Page 106 "(This was not," *New York Times*, May 22, 1966
Page 106 "'Ralph said he," Geoffrey Cowan to JM, interview on May 30, 2001
Page 107 "Each team member," *New Yorker*, June 20, 1970
Page 107 "To formally launch," *New York Times*, February 8, 1970
Page 107 "286 million shares," *New Yorker*, June 20, 1970
Page 107 "During the press," *New York Times*, February 8, 1970
Page 107 "Step one for," *New York Times*, February 22, 1970
Page 108 "Not surprisingly, GM," *New York Times*, March 20, 1970
Page 108 "As for the," *New York Times*, April 10, 1970
Page 108 "One Campaign GM," *New York Times*, February 8, 1970
Page 108 "Campaign GM faced," *New York Times*, March 8, 1970
Page 108 "Because of Nader's," examples of press attention for Campaign GM include *New Yorker*, June 20, 1970; *Time*, June 1, 1970; *Business Week*, January 9, 1971
Page 108 "Under pressure, Penn's," *Newsweek*, April 27, 1970
Page 108 "GM launched a," *New York Times*, April 10, 1970
Page 109 "Along with Penn," *Newsweek*, April 27, 1970
Page 109 "By far the," *New York Times*, May 20, 1970
Page 109 "Dreyfus Fund," Robert Buckhorn, *Nader: The People's Lawyer*, p. 118
Page 109 "Stewart Rawlings Mott," *New Yorker*, June 20, 1970
Page 110 "John Esposito," *New York Times*, February 8, 1970
Page 110 "Campaign GM's 'guru,'" *New Yorker*, June 20, 1970
Page 111 "a strategic masterstroke," Geoffrey Cowan to JM, interview on May 30, 2001
Page 111 "'Why are there," *New Yorker*, June 20, 1970
Page 111 "The measure of," *Multinational Monitor*, December 1988

Page 112 "'My impression was," Geoffrey Cowan to JM, interview on May 30, 2001
Page 112 "In some sense," *Business Week*, January 9, 1971
Page 112 "Sullivan had once," *Time*, January 18, 1971
Page 112 "'I know General," Robert Buckhorn, *Nader: The People's Lawyer*, p. 117
Page 112 "On August 13," *Litigation*, Fall 1996
Page 112 "Better to take," *New York Times*, August 14, 1970
Page 112 "a $425,000 settlement," Charles McCarry, *Citizen Nader*, p. 204
Page 113 "At the outset," *Litigation*, Fall 1996
Page 113 "It turned out," *New Republic*, February 18, 1967
Page 113 "investigated Danny Kaye," *New York Times*, February 5, 1967
Page 113 "Gillen's tape collection," Robert Buckhorn, *Nader: The People's Lawyer*, p. 14
Page 113 "Gillen also had," *New Republic*, February 18, 1967
Page 114 "Under questioning from," *Litigation*, Fall 1996
Page 114 "alleged sex lures," Thomas Whiteside, *Investigation of Ralph Nader*, pp. 157, 167
Page 114 "Years later, one," Source to JM, interview on background
Page 115 "Nader had long," Charles McCarry, *Citizen Nader*, pp. 170–172
Page 115 "Some indicated the," examples in *Unsafe at Any Speed* and *Reader's Digest*, June 1973
Page 115 "In 1970, Nader," Robert Buckhorn, *Nader: The People's Lawyer*, p. 76
Page 115 "Nixon-Lodge campaign," Charles McCarry, *Citizen Nader*, p. 207
Page 115 "Nader hired a," Harrison Wellford to JM, interview on April 24, 2001
Page 115 "At the new," Neil McBride, one-time Nader Raider, to JM, interview on June 4, 2001
Page 115 "The door featured," Robert Buckhorn, *Nader: The People's Lawyer*, p. 76
Page 115 "'I file by," Jim Turner to JM, interview on April 18, 2001
Page 115 "'People often ask," *Time*, May 10, 1971
Page 116 "'That fact alone," John Esposito and Larry Silverman, *Vanishing Air*, p. 290
Page 116 "Nader signed off," Charles McCarry, *Citizen Nader*, pp. 199–200
Page 116 "In a news," ibid., p. 202
Page 116 "'It certainly surprised," Michael Pertschuk to JM, interview on August 20, 2001
Page 117 "Harrison Wellford," Harrison Wellford to JM, interview on April 24, 2001
Page 117 "Nader put enormous," Ralph Nader to JM, interview on February 1, 2002
Page 117 "During a 1970," *New York Times*, December 2, 1970
Page 117 "'Ribicoff was very," Robert Wager to JM, interview on May 29, 2001
Page 118 "died in committee," Charles McCarry, *Citizen Nader*, p. 234

Chapter 10

Page 119 "Nader took the," Christian White to JM, interview on May 22, 2001
Page 119 "'The best lawyers," *Time*, December 12, 1969
Page 120 "the mirror image," Thomas Stanton to JM, interview on May 30, 2001
Page 120 "very Brandeisian," discussion of Brandeis's battles with big business drawn from sources including Howard Zinn, *A People's History of the United States*, p. 577
Page 120 "'The leading lawyers," Robert Buckhorn, *Nader: The People's Lawyer*, p. 125
Page 121 "Nader dismissed Brandeis," Charles McCarry, *Citizen Nader*, p. 50
Page 121 "In 1970, the," ibid., p. 52
Page 121 "'How many of," ibid., p. 50
Page 121 "Nader managed to," Christian White to JM, interview on May 22, 2001
Page 121 "to Gary Sellers," Gary Sellers to JM, interview on November 6, 2001
Page 122 "He once described," Charles McCarry, *Citizen Nader*, p. 229
Page 122 "the truest believer," widely held impression including Harrison Wellford to JM, interview on April 24, 2001
Page 122 "Another key Nader associate," Joan Claybrook to JM, interview on January 22, 2002
Page 122 "'John Wilkes," *Progressive*, March 1999
Page 123 "To launch the," Thomas Stanton to JM, interview on May 30, 2000
Page 123 "'Ralph told us," Karen Ferguson to JM, interview on June 19, 2001
Page 123 "The firm petitioned," *Business Week*, November 28, 1970
Page 123 "Advertisements touted Excedrin," Karen Ferguson to JM, interview on June 19, 2001
Page 123 "Nader cracked down," Christian White to JM, interview on May 22, 2001
Page 123 "'What do you," Thomas Stanton to JM, interview on May 30, 2001
Page 124 "curious Nader observation," Joe Highland, one-time PIRG organizer, to JM, interview on June 26, 2001
Page 125 My Lai massacre description composite drawn from sources including "My Lai Massacre," pbs.org

Page 126 "Nader envisioned the," Donald Ross to JM, interview on July 9, 2001
Page 126 "negative checkoff option," Janet Niver of MassPIRG to JM, interview on June 4, 2001
Page 126 "American Program Bureau," Ken Eisenstein to JM, interview on February 7, 2002
Page 127 "'The average student," *Redbook*, November 1971
Page 127 "Nader concentrated his efforts," Donald Ross to JM, interview on July 9, 2001
Page 127 "During the fall," *New York Times*, November 22, 1970
Page 127 "eight different colleges," Robert Buckhorn, *Nader: The People's Lawyer*, p. 169
Page 127 "Nader also did," Karim Ahmed to JM, interview on June 13, 2001
Page 128 "Petition drives were," Steve McCarthy to JM, interview on June 25, 2001
Page 129 "For example, PIRG," Thomas Stanton to JM, interview on May 30, 2000,
Page 130 "Not everyone met," Christian White to JM, interview on May 22, 2001
Page 130 "To supplement their," Donald Ross to JM, interview on July 9, 2001
Page 130 "By 1974 PIRGs," *New York Times*, November 24, 1975
Page 130 Discussion of various PIRG projects drawn from sources including *New York Times*, September 5, 1973
Page 131 "'Ralph is a," Steve McCarthy to JM, interview on June 25, 2001
Page 132 "An amusing side note," *Washington Post*, September 2, 1975
Page 132 "Consequently, OSPIRG," Steve McCarthy to JM, interview on June 25, 2001
Page 132 "Students at Pennsylvania," *Chronicle of Higher Education*, July 7, 1975
Page 132 "Today, many PIRGs," Janet Niver to JM, interview on June 4, 2001
Page 133 "'The price of liberty," *Reader's Digest*, June 1973
Page 133 "While researching *Unsafe*," Ralph Nader, Peter Petkas, and Kate Blackwell, *Whistleblowing*, p. vii
Page 133 "As erstwhile Raider," Peter Petkas to JM, interview on April 26, 2001
Page 133 "Late in the autumn," Ernest Fitzgerald to JM, interview on June 5, 2001
Page 134 Ernest Fitzgerald description drawn from sources including Ralph Nader et al., *Whistleblowing*
Page 134 "'Ralph was sympathetic," Ernest Fitzgerald to JM, interview on June 5, 2001
Page 134 "On January 30," Ralph Nader et al., *Whistleblowing*, p. vii
Page 135 "Jacqueline Verret," ibid., p. 90
Page 135 "Ralph Stein," ibid., p. 126
Page 135 "A. Dale Console," ibid., p. 119
Page 135 "'The key question," ibid., p. 5
Page 135 "Nader suggested that," *Time*, April 17, 1972
Page 135 "Nader spelled out," Ralph Nader et al., *Whistleblowing*, p. 241
Page 135 "chose Peter Petkas," *Harper's Bazaar*, September 1972
Page 135 "The clearinghouse received," Peter Petkas to JM, interview on May 1, 2001
Page 136 "a mere $24," *Harper's Bazaar*, September 1972
Page 136 "'The idea was," Peter Petkas to JM, interview on July 10, 2001
Page 136 "Soon the clearinghouse," *Harper's Bazaar*, September 1972
Page 136 "A major thrust," *New York Times*, January 27, 1971
Page 136 "The Occupational Safety," Peter Petkas to JM, interview on July 10, 2001
Page 137 "Critics nicknamed Nader's," Robert Buckhorn, *Nader: The People's Lawyer*, p. 186
Page 137 "'Some of the," *New York Times*, March 26, 1971

Chapter 11

Page 138 "'No movement in," *New York Times Magazine*, January 18, 1976
Page 138 "*Webster's Third International*," *New York Times*, January 27, 1972
Page 138 "nonpartisan, cutting across," *New York Times*, June 30, 1969
Page 138 "States including New York," *New York Times*, August 9, 1970
Page 138 "Harris poll," *Reader's Digest*, June 1973
Page 139 "lampooned in *Mad*," Ralph De Toledano, *Hit & Run*, p. 20
Page 139 "recreational fishermen," Robert Buckhorn, *Nader: The People's Lawyer*, p. 121
Page 139 "required $250,000," *New York Times Magazine*, March 21, 1971
Page 139 "'I candidly told," *Business Week*, February 14, 1970
Page 140 "roughly $250,000, annually," Hays Gorey, *Nader and the Power of Everyman*, p. 152
Page 140 "raised $1.1 million," *New York Times*, November 24, 1975
Page 140 "Dr. Sidney Wolfe," Sidney Wolfe to JM, interview on February 27, 2002
Page 140 "the Litigation Group," Alan Morrison to JM, interview on August 13, 2001
Page 140 "Beyond the organizations," *Newsweek*, April 17, 1972
Page 141 "'Nothing is possible," Kenly Webster to JM, interview on December 28, 2001

Page 141 That Nader is not a talented administrator a widely held impression including John Sims, one-time Nader employee, to JM, interview on December 20, 2001
Page 141 "personally sign the paychecks," Gary Sellers to JM, interview on March 6, 2002
Page 141 "Walter Wriston," Robert Buckhorn, *Nader: The People's Lawyer*, p. 89
Page 141 "James Kemper Jr.," *Human Events*, January 13, 1973
Page 141 "'bitter gypsies of dissent,'" Robert Buckhorn, *Nader: The People's Lawyer*, p. 53
Page 141 "To the end," *New York Times Magazine*, September 12, 1971
Page 141 "A Harris poll," *Fortune*, January 1972
Page 142 "David Sarnoff," Robert Buckhorn, *Nader: The People's Lawyer*, p. 235
Page 142 "Chrysler and Pan," Hays Gorey, *Nader and the Power of Everyman*, p. 283
Page 142 "Jeffrey O'Connell," *New York Times*, January 3, 1972
Page 142 "John Banzhaf III," *New York Times*, December 18, 1969
Page 143 "Representative Benjamin Rosenthal," *New York Times*, April 26, 1971
Page 143 Jerry Brown description composite drawn from sources including governor.ca.gov
Page 143 "traveled to Japan," *Time*, February 1, 1971
Page 143 "Speaking before capacity," *New York Times*, July 17, 1971
Page 143 "He faced off," *Time*, February 1, 1971
Page 143 "challenged Japanese automakers," *New York Times*, July 17, 1971
Page 143 "'Nader's arrival here," *Esquire*, June 1972
Page 144 "also visited Australia," Alan Morrison to JM, interview on August 13, 2001
Page 144 "'konsumentombudsman,'" *New York Times*, April 14, 1970
Page 144 "*Nagyito* (Magnifying Glass)," *New York Times*, September 6, 1970
Page 144 "a French wanna-be," *Washington Post*, August 29, 1973
Page 145 "shaking hands," widely held impression including Hays Gorey, *Nader and the Power of Everyman*, p. 52
Page 145 "autograph seekers," *Parade*, April 21, 1974
Page 145 "Nader asked Fischer," Hays Gorey, *Nader and the Power of Everyman*, p. 35
Page 145 "Tammy Wynette," Anne Zill to JM, interview on June 14, 2001
Page 145 "Marx Brothers movie," James Fallows to JM, interview on June 14, 2001
Page 145 "'Oh, I like," *Newsweek*, January 22, 1968
Page 146 "'Even something as," Charles McCarry, *Citizen Nader*, p. 14
Page 146 "A profile in," *New York Times*, January 10, 1971
Page 146 "A *Reader's Digest*," *Reader's Digest*, June 1973
Page 146 "Then a woman," David Sanford, *Me & Ralph*, pp. 24–25
Page 146 "'I never got," Morton Mintz to JM, interview on May 22, 2001
Page 146 "Finally, the rumor," David Sanford, *Me & Ralph*, pp. 24–25
Page 147 "David Sanford," ibid., p. 26
Page 147 Nader lived in a townhouse on Bancroft Place a widely held impression including Lowell Dodge to JM, interview on April 30, 2001
Page 147 "'Ralph has a," Jim Turner to JM, interview on April 18, 2001
Page 147 "'I am sure," James Oglesby to JM, interview on February 25, 2002
Page 148 "It was noted," Anne Zill to JM, interview on June 14, 2001
Page 148 "'We always thought," Beverly Moore to JM, interview on April 19, 2001
Page 149 "'Close as I was," Lowell Dodge to JM, interview on April 30, 2001
Page 149 "'Here's a man," Peter Petkas to JM, interview on May 1, 2001
Page 149 "'He had very," Anne Zill to JM, interview on June 14, 2001
Page 149 "run for the Senate," Mark Green to JM, interview on June 6, 2001
Page 149 "'At various times," Harrison Wellford to JM, interview on April 24, 2001
Page 149 "Mike Royko," *Esquire*, June 1972
Page 150 "lay the groundwork," Robert Buckhorn, *Nader: The People's Lawyer*, p. 260
Page 150 "Over July 4," *New York Times*, July 6, 1971
Page 150 "DuPont Circle headquarters," Robert Buckhorn, *Nader: The People's Lawyer*, p. 260
Page 150 "lame campaign song," Ralph De Toledano, *Hit & Run*, p. 143
Page 151 "Julius Hobson," *New York Times*, November 28, 1971
Page 151 "'People frequently urged," Mark Green to JM, interview on June 6, 2001
Page 151 "throw the election to Nixon," Marcus Raskin to JM, interview on July 11, 2001

Chapter 12

Page 152 "The time was right," Marcus Raskin to JM, interview on July 11, 2001
Page 152 "By declaring the," Hays Gorey, *Nader and the Power of Everyman*, p. 254

Page 153 "more private gripes," widely held impression including Marcus Raskin to JM, interview on July 11, 2001
Page 153 "Others thought this," *New York Times Magazine*, January 18, 1976
Page 153 "'no-law laws,'" Harrison Wellford to JM, interview on April 24, 2001
Page 153 "campaign financing," Joan Claybrook to JM, interview on January 22, 2002
Page 153 "'You know, when," Jim Turner to JM, interview on April 18, 2001
Page 153 "On November 2," *New York Times*, November 3, 1971
Page 153 "484 of the 535," *New York Times*, October 22, 1972
Page 153 "To allay any," Ralph Nader to JM, interview on February 1, 2002
Page 153 "a whole year," *New York Times*, November 3, 1971
Page 154 "Nader planned to hire," Robert Fellmeth to JM, interview on November 16, 2001
Page 154 "To accommodate this," Ted McConnell, who worked on the Congress Project, to JM, interview on June 12, 2001
Page 154 "'Children's Crusade,'" Ralph De Toledano, *Hit & Run*, p. 57
Page 154 "Meanwhile, Fellmeth put," Congress Project questionnaire, courtesy of Daniel Taubman
Page 154 "'I had absolutely," Robert Fellmeth to JM, interview on November 16, 2001
Page 154 "Grossman Publishers," *Saturday Review*, October 7, 1972
Page 154 "For the most," Robert Fellmeth to JM, interview on November 16, 2001
Page 155 "Sarah Glazer, newly," Sarah Glazer to JM, interview on May 29, 2001
Page 155 "Because this was," Ted Siff, who worked on the Congress Project, to JM, interview on May 3, 2001
Page 155 "room and board," Sarah Glazer to JM, interview on May 29, 2001
Page 155 "On June 3, 1972," *Harvard Law School Record*, October 20, 1972
Page 155 "'Many of you," entry in Daniel Taubman's diary dated June 3, 1972, courtesy of Daniel Taubman
Page 155 "Nader warned against," *Harvard Law School Record*, October 20, 1972
Page 155 "'If it's not," Entry in Daniel Taubman's diary dated June 3, 1972, courtesy of Daniel Taubman
Page 155 "'I was 24," John Immerwahr to JM, interview on May 4, 2001
Page 156 "A case in," *Time*, July 31, 1972
Page 156 "'I'm not going," *New Republic*, July 22, 1972
Page 156 "'The conservative members," Fred Khedouri to JM, interview on May 21, 2001
Page 156 "It took about," *New Republic*, July 22, 1972
Page 156 "'Do you believe," Congress Project questionnaire, courtesy of Daniel Taubman
Page 156 "Joel Broyhill," *New Republic*, July 22, 1972
Page 157 "a great imposition," *Time*, July 31, 1972
Page 157 "All told, 63," *New York Times*, October 22, 1972
Page 157 "'You had so," Sarah Glazer to JM, interview on May 29, 2001
Page 157 "writing nine profiles," *Harvard Law School Record*, October 20, 1972
Page 157 "Joan Claybrook took," Joan Claybrook to JM, interview on January 22, 2002
Page 157 "docked $50," Ralph De Toledano, *Hit & Run*, p. 86
Page 157 "And she began," Sarah Glazer to JM, interview on May 29, 2001
Page 157 "'It was apparent," Anne Zill to JM, intervew on June 14, 2001
Page 158 "'It was a massive," Peter Schuck to JM, interview on April 25, 2001
Page 158 "Frustrated, the profile," entry in Daniel Taubman's diary dated July 16, 1972, courtesy of Daniel Taubman
Page 158 "To address their concerns," entry in Daniel Taubman's diary dated July 19, 1972, courtesy of Daniel Taubman
Page 158 "Nader did, however," *Harvard Law School Record*, October 20, 1972
Page 159 "Around midnight," entry in Daniel Taubman's diary dated August 5, 1972, courtesy of Daniel Taubman
Page 159 "Nader declined McGovern's," Joan Claybrook to JM, interview on January 22, 2002
Page 159 "It was meant," *Harvard Law School Record*, November 17, 1972
Page 159 "This infuriated," widely held impression including Ted Siff to JM, interview on May 3, 2001
Page 160 "'These were people," Robert Fellmeth to JM, interview on November 16, 2001
Page 160 "A number of them," entry in Daniel Taubman's diary dated August 3, 1972, courtesy of Daniel Taubman
Page 160 "'A lot of people," Daniel Taubman to JM, interview on May 29, 2001
Page 160 "On August 8," Entry in Daniel Taubman's diary dated August 8, 1972, courtesy of Daniel Taubman
Page 160 "Fallows, Green," James Fallows to JM, interview on June 14, 2001
Page 160 "Reputedly, it was edited," *Harvard Law School Record*, October 20, 1972
Page 161 "exercise in uncontrolled chaos," widely held impression including Arthur Magida to JM, interview on May 3, 2001
Page 161 "'We knew we," Anne Zill to JM, interview on June 14, 2001

Page 161 "The first printing," *Harvard Law School Record*, October 20, 1972
Page 161 "*Time* magazine slammed," *Time*, October 16, 1972
Page 161 "Another review, syndicated," *Human Events*, January 13, 1973
Page 161 "totaled 13,720 pages," *Saturday Review*, October 7, 1972
Page 161 "'It was a," Joan Claybrook to JM, interview on January 22, 2002
Page 161 "Unfortunately, the profiles," Daniel Taubman to JM, interview on May 29, 2001
Page 161 "'To the surprise," *New York Times*, October 22, 1972
Page 161 "*The Denver Post*," *Human Events*, January 13, 1973
Page 162 "Jonathan Bingham," *New York Times*, October 22, 1972
Page 162 "Representative William Minshall," *Human Events*, January 13, 1973
Page 162 "'We expected them," Ralph Nader to JM, interview on February 1, 2002
Page 163 "$500,000," ibid.
Page 163 "'My C–5A,'" for example, *New York Times Magazine*, January 18, 1976
Page 163 "There is one," Anne Zill to JM, interview on June 14, 2001
Page 164 "It had long," *Congressional Record*, Senate, March 27, 1973, p. 9775
Page 164 "Nader claimed there," ibid., p. 9750
Page 164 "From the instant," sampling of letters contained in *Congressional Record*, Senate, March 27, 1973
Page 164 "At one point," Charles McCarry, *Citizen Nader*, p. 171
Page 164 "Ribicoff was not," Robert Wager to JM, interview on July 26, 2001
Page 164 "'Mr. Auto Safety,'" Charles McCarry, *Citizen Nader*, p. 171
Page 164 "In the years following," Jerome Sonosky to JM, interview on May 3, 2001
Page 164 "But Nader kept," Robert Wager to JM, interview on July 26, 2001
Page 164 "'Now comes decisive," letter from Ralph Nader to John Volpe, secretary of transportation, dated September 4, 1970. Copy also sent to Ribicoff. Entered in *Congressional Record*, Senate, March 27, 1973, p. 9775
Page 164 "What finally grabbed," Robert Wager to JM, interview on July 26, 2001
Page 165 "For example, Sellers," *Congressional Record*, Senate, March 27, 1973, p. 9760
Page 165 "In fact, they grew," Robert Wager to JM, interview on May 8, 2002
Page 165 "Predictably, this conclusion," Robert Wager to JM, interview on July 26, 2001
Page 165 "Soon the investigation," *Congressional Record*, Senate, March 27, 1973, p. 9755
Page 165 "'He could not," Robert Wager to JM, interview on July 26, 2001

Chapter 13

Page 167 "'For about a," Donald Etra to JM, interview on May 22, 2001
Page 167 "'I have a," Robert Buckhorn, *Nader: The People's Lawyer*, p. 289
Page 168 "'This legislation springs," Edward Cox et al., *Nader's Raiders*, p. 106
Page 168 "featured nine exemptions," *New York Times*, August 27, 1969
Page 168 "During the summer," *New York Times*, November 26, 1969
Page 169 "$91,840," *U.S. News & World Report*, February 5, 1973
Page 169 "'Freedom from Information,'" *Harvard Law Review*, January 1970
Page 169 "called press conferences," *New York Times*, August 27, 1969
Page 169 "In 1972," Ronald Plesser to JM, interview on May 29, 2001
Page 169 "The Litigation Group," Alan Morrison to JM, interview on August 13, 2001
Page 169 "involved Carl Stern," Ronald Plesser to JM, interview on May 29, 2001
Page 169 Discussion of "Cointelpro-New Left," drawn from sources including "The Cointelpro Papers," at members.partisan.net
Page 170 "'People suspected there," Ronald Plesser to JM, interview on May 29, 2001
Page 170 "*Stern v. Richardson*," Stern v. Richardson, 367 F. Supp. 1316 (D.D.C. 1973)
Page 170 "'We wound up," Ron Plesser to JM, interview on May 29, 2001
Page 170 "Congressional hearings on," Tom Susman to JM, interview on May 31, 2001
Page 170 "'Ralph played an," Mark Lynch to JM, interview on June 6, 2001
Page 171 "As of 1974," *U.S. News & World Report*, February 5, 1973
Page 171 "In the House," *New York Times*, March 15, 1974
Page 171 "Congressional opponents included," Tom Susman to JM, interview on May 31, 2001
Page 171 "'I was the guy," Mark Lynch to JM, interview on June 6, 2001
Page 171 "On October 7," *New York Times*, October 8, 1974
Page 171 "his thirteenth veto," *New York Times*, November 22, 1974
Page 171 "FOIA in its," *Time*, December 2, 1974
Page 172 "Like document access," Joe Tom Easley to JM, interview on May 30, 2001
Page 173 "Michael Mariotte concurs," Michael Mariotte to JM, interview on July 26, 2001

Page 173 "In 1972, Nader," *New York Times*, November 24, 1975
Page 173 "Kendall and Ford," Diana Sidebotham to JM, interview on December 7, 2001
Page 173 "'We wanted Ralph," Myron Cherry to JM, interview on July 11, 2001
Page 174 "'This is the," *New York Times*, January 4, 1973
Page 174 "Critical Mass," *New York Times*, November 17, 1974
Page 174 Critical Mass attendees drawn from recollection of sources including Carrie Dickerson to JM, interview on August 20, 2001
Page 174 Various antinuclear coalitions present at Critical Mass drawn from recollections of sources including Diana Sidebotham to JM, interview on December 7, 2001
Page 174 "'There were little," Anthony Roisman to JM, interview on July 26, 2001
Page 174 "David Comey," James Cubie to JM, interview on December 18, 2001
Page 175 "In the interest," Robert Backus to JM, interview on November 28, 2001
Page 175 Karen Silkwood description and information drawn from a variety of sources including *Dictionary of American Biography, Supplement 9, 1971–1975*
Page 176 "'Ralph asked me," Carrie Dickerson to JM, interview on August 20, 2001
Page 176 "'We were thrilled," Diana Sidebotham to JM, interview on December 7, 2001
Page 176 "'A few grassroots," Harvey Wasserman to JM, interview on August 20, 2001
Page 177 "anniversary of Karen Silkwood's," Diana Sidebotham to JM, interview on December 7, 2001
Page 177 "abolish the Atomic," James Cubie to JM, interview on December 18, 2001
Page 177 "Two new agencies," Michael Mariotte to JM, interview on July 26, 2001
Page 177 "Nader and Claybrook," James Cubie to JM, interview on December 18, 2001
Page 178 "John Darcy and," *Washington Post*, June 12, 1975
Page 178 "Congress Watch managed," *New York Times*, March 30, 1976
Page 179 "Oregon's student PIRG," Steve McCarthy to JM, interview on June 25, 2001
Page 179 "MassPIRG called for," *MassPIRG Retrospective, 25 Years*
Page 179 "The Palo Verde," Kay Drey, anti-nuclear activist, to JM, interview on December 3, 2001
Page 179 "Unquestionably, economics plays," Michael Marriott to JM, interview on July 26, 2001
Page 179 "'Try saying it," *Nation*, August 30, 1975
Page 179 "Columnist Mary McGrory," David Sanford, *Me & Ralph*, p. 2
Page 180 "'Carter indicated that," Peter Petkas to JM, interview on May 1, 2001
Page 180 "'We talked about," Ralph Nader to JM, interview on February 1, 2002
Page 180 "softball game," *Washington Post*, August 8, 1976

Chapter 14

Page 181 *Saturday Night Live* details taken from viewing by JM of show, originally broadcast January 15, 1977, courtesy of the Museum of Television and Radio, New York City
Page 182 "He had met," *New York Times*, December 1, 1976
Page 183 "Nader believed Carter," Peter Petkas to JM, interview on May 1, 2001
Page 183 "a growing misunderstanding," Joe Tom Easley to JM, interview on June 2, 2001
Page 183 "Mamie Eisenhower," *Esquire*, December 1983
Page 183 "During the previous," *New York Times*, December 1, 1976
Page 183 "Joan Claybrook," Joan Claybrook to JM, interview on January 22, 2002
Page 183 "jumped to $52,000," *Fortune*, October 1977
Page 183 "As his chief speech writer," James Fallows to JM, interview on June 14, 2001
Page 183 "Harrison Wellford, former," *New York Times*, April 20, 1977
Page 183 "'Peter Petkas," Peter Petkas to JM, interview on May 1, 2001
Page 183 "The top job," Mike Pertschuk to JM, interview on May 14, 2002
Page 183 "Carol Tucker Foreman," *New York Times*, April 20, 1977
Page 183 "Esther Peterson," Nancy Chasen to JM, interview on December 10, 2001
Page 184 "But Nader was," *New York Times*, December 8, 1976
Page 184 "'I want access," *New York Times*, December 1, 1976
Page 184 "During their meeting," Laura Nader to JM, interview on February 22, 2002
Page 185 "'Bill, we've been," Charles McCarry, *Citizen Nader*, p. 106
Page 185 "Claybrook assumed her," *New York Times*, February 14, 1977
Page 185 "passive restraint systems," *Consumer Reports*, April 1978
Page 185 "He did not even," Joan Claybrook to JM, interview on January 22, 2002
Page 185 portions of Ralph Nader's letter to Joan Claybrook, dated November 30, 1977, appear in the *Washington Post*, December 1, 1977, and *Consumer Reports*, April 1978
Page 186 "To answer Nader's," *New York Times*, December 1, 1977
Page 186 "No further words," Joan Claybrook to JM, interview on January 22, 2002

Page 186 "The Nader-Claybrook clash," *People Weekly*, January 16, 1978
Page 186 "Others did not," Joan Claybrook to JM, interview on January 22, 2002
Page 187 "'box shuffling,'" *U.S. News & World Report*, December 19, 1977
Page 187 "'Most of us," Harrison Wellford to JM, interview on April 24, 2001
Page 187 "'The men with," *New York Times*, December 8, 1977
Page 188 "In 1978 Roger," Roger Hickey to JM, interview on November 8, 2001
Page 188 "A similar observation," Michael Harper to JM, interview on May 21, 2001
Page 188 "standard rap," widely held impression including Jim Turner to JM, interview on April 18, 2001
Page 189 The notion that the defeat of the CPA in 1978 was Nader's Waterloo is a widely held impression including Thomas Stanton to JM, interview on May 30, 2001
Page 189 "But the idea," *New Times*, April 3, 78
Page 189 "The torch then," Peter Barash to JM, interview on December 4, 2001
Page 189 "As Nader envisioned," Richard Wegman, who, during the 1970s, was counsel and staff director of the Senate Governmental Affairs Committee, to JM, interview on November 28, 2001
Page 189 "'the most important," Robert Buckhorn, *Nader: The People's Lawyer*, p. 283
Page 190 "On one occasion," Francis Cwenig, one-time Congress Watch lobbyist for CPA bill, to JM, interview on December 18, 2001
Page 190 "All told, CPA," *Washington Post*, February 26, 1978
Page 190 "'Ralph could have," Mike Pertschuk to JM, interview on August 20, 2001
Page 190 "Carter assured Nader," *New Times*, April 3, 1978
Page 190 "Before joining the," Nancy Chasen to JM, interview on December 10, 2001
Page 190 "notorious nickel campaign," *New York Times*, June 30, 1977
Page 190 "(The true amount," *New Times*, April 3, 1978
Page 191 "'ultimate consumer litmus," *New York Times*, June 30, 1977
Page 191 "He even went," *New Times*, April 3, 1978
Page 191 "Patricia Schroeder," *Washington Post*, February 19, 1978
Page 191 "Frustrated, Esther Peterson," *Money*, June 1978
Page 191 "On February 8," *Washington Post*, February 9, 1978
Page 191 "'This one's for," *New Times*, April 3, 1978
Page 191 "Fully 101 Democrats," *Washington Post*, February 26, 1978
Page 191 "Nader was in Reno," *New Times*, April 3, 1978
Page 191 "But the Senate," *New York Times*, June 30, 1977
Page 192 "a rousing speech," *New Times*, April 3, 1978
Page 192 "'Let's put it," *Washington Post*, February 10, 1978
Page 192 "Robert Giamo," *New Times*, April 3, 1978
Page 192 "WRC radio," *Money*, June 1978
Page 192 "'He pissed off," Peter Barash to JM, interview on December 4, 2001
Page 192 "'He did not," Ralph Nader to JM, interview on February 1, 2002
Page 192 "(For the record," *New Times*, April 3, 1978
Page 192 "If the CPA," Jeffrey Joseph to JM, interview on December 12, 2001
Page 193 "A variety of," David Vogel, *Fluctuating Fortunes: The Political Power of Business in America*, p. 161
Page 193 "This had hardly," John Post to JM, interview on February 11, 2002
Page 193 "While the Chamber," David Vogel, *Fluctuating Fortunes: The Political Power of Business in America*, p. 161
Page 193 "The defeat of," ibid., p. 162
Page 193 "Arguably, his most," Peter Gruenstein to JM, interview on December 18, 2001
Page 194 "1. Participate," *Playboy*, March 1978
Page 194 "'Next thing Nader," *Washington* Post, November 10, 1977
Page 194 "'If Nader has," *Washington Post*, October 2, 1977
Page 194 "'A lot of," Peter Gruenstein to JM, interview on December 18, 2001
Page 195 "'Ralph was literally," Phil Donahue to JM, interview on November 15, 2001
Page 195 "In 1971 there," numbers based on JM's count of Nader stories in *New York Times* index and periodicals index
Page 195 "People had simply," widely held impression including Curtis Wilkey, former *Boston Globe* reporter, to JM, interview on December 3, 2001
Page 195 "'A person is," Charles Peters to JM, interview on February 13, 2002
Page 195 "As a corollary," widely held impression including Eleanor Randoph, *New York Times* editor, to JM, interview on November 27, 2001
Page 196 "Sanford even devotes," David Sanford, *Me & Ralph*, chapter entitled "Lowell Dodge Blows the Whistle," pp. 33–49

Page 196 "Beginning in 1976," Morton Mintz to JM, interview on February 7, 2002
Page 196 "Nader himself has," Ralph Nader to JM, interview on February 1, 2002
Page 196 "Tom Snyder," *Esquire*, July 4, 1978
Page 197 "'Two ways, he," Ernest Hemingway, *The Sun Also Rises*
Page 197 "'I didn't socialize," Ralph Nader to JM, interview on February 1, 2002
Page 197 "Near the end," *Washington Post*, October 28, 1980
Page 197 "frequently consulting," Sidney Wolfe to JM, interview on February 27, 2002; Alan Morrison to JM, interview on August 13, 2001
Page 197 "As an interesting," Joan Claybrook to JM, interview on January 22, 2002
Page 197 "'What would you," Katherine Meyer to JM, interview on February 21, 2002
Page 197 "'He does not," Sidney Wolfe to JM, interview on February 27, 2002
Page 198 "Nader ended the," widely held impression including Joe Tom Easley to JM, interview on May 13, 2002
Page 198 "'He has not," *Washington Post*, May 8, 1979
Page 198 "'In the last," *Rolling Stone*, August 23, 1979
Page 199 "'He felt that," Jonathan Alter to JM, interview on December 13, 2001

Chapter 15

Page 200 Details of Ronald Reagan's inauguration drawn from a variety of sources including *New York Times*, January 26, 1981
Page 200 "a mock wake," David Vladeck to JM, interview on February 6, 2002
Page 201 "Kristol is sometimes," *Esquire*, February 13, 1979
Page 201 "the Laffer Curve," Martin Anderson, *Revolution*, p. 147
Page 202 "Kristol sought to," *Esquire*, February 13, 1979
Page 202 "Kristol was instrumental," David Vogel, *Fluctuating Fortunes*, p. 222
Page 202 "The AEI, where," Michael Pertschuk to JM, interview on August 20, 2001
Page 202 "It published a," David Vogel, *Fluctuating Fortunes,* p. 224
Page 202 "One of AEI's," *New York Times*, October 10, 1979
Page 202 "'But by the," David Vogel, *Fluctuating Fortunes,* p. 225
Page 203 "For the first," ibid., pp. 197–198
Page 203 "CEOs in particular," John Post to JM, interview on February 11, 2002
Page 203 "Between 1966 and," *Esquire*, December 1983
Page 203 "'They're pretty brazen," Ralph Nader to JM, interview on February 1, 2002
Page 204 "'What happened was," Hank Cox to JM, interview on December 11, 2001
Page 204 "On January 22," *Risking America's Health and Safety: George Bush and the Task Force on Regulatory Relief*, publication of Public Citizen, p. 3
Page 204 "The new regulatory," Eric Glitzenstein, former attorney with Public Citizen's Litigation Group, to JM, interview on December 12, 2001
Page 204 "The auto industry," *Washington Post*, April 8, 1981
Page 205 "Katherine Meyer," Katherine Meyer to JM, interview on February 21, 2002
Page 205 "Anne Gorsuch.," David Vogel, *Fluctuating Fortunes,* p. 248
Page 205 "In terms of," ibid., pp. 248–249
Page 205 "During Carter's four," ibid., p. 250
Page 205 "Even if a statute," John Sims to JM, interview on December 20, 2001
Page 206 "Nader was particularly," Ralph Nader to JM, interview on February 1, 2002
Page 206 "In the early," osha.gov
Page 206 "To head up," David Vogel, *Fluctuating Fortunes,* p. 248
Page 206 "On Auchter's watch," David Vladeck to JM, interview on February 6, 2002
Page 206 "Ethylene oxide," *Risking America's Health and Safety*, p. 20
Page 206 "Grain dust," ibid., p. 22
Page 206 "Nader issued a," *New York Times*, September 5, 1983
Page 206 "Nader also worked," David Vladeck to JM, interview on February 6, 2002
Page 206 "It would take," *Risking America's Health and Safety*, p. 23
Page 206 "As for ethylene," ibid., p. 21
Page 207 "'All these fights," Ralph Nader to JM, interview on February 1, 2002
Page 207 "Nader sent Reagan," *Washington Post*, January 20, 1982
Page 207 "'They were trying," Ralph Nader to JM, interview on February 1, 2002
Page 207 Discussion of reasons for Nader returning to grass roots based on impression of multiple sources including Eric Glitzenstein to JM, interview on December 12, 2001
Page 208 "RUCAGs," Howard Learner to JM, interview on February 13, 2002

Page 208 "The concept is," Martin Cohen of Illinois CUB to JM, interview on February 8, 2002
Page 208 "Nader hired a couple," Patrick Quinn to JM, interview on December 10, 2001
Page 208 "By the early," Rich Starck of Wisconsin CUB to JM, interview on December 10, 2001
Page 208 "Nader's biggest CUB," Howard Learner to JM, interview on February 13, 2002
Page 208 "During the autumn," Patrick Quinn to JM, interview on December 10, 2001
Page 209 "The fact that," Howard Learner to JM, interview on February 13, 2002
Page 209 "Nader traveled to," Patrick Quinn to JM, interview on December 10, 2001
Page 209 "The CUB law," Martin Cohen to JM, interview on February 8, 2002
Page 209 "Illinois CUB hired," Seamus Glenn of Illinois CUB to JM, interview on December 10, 2001
Page 209 "Before rate board," Martin Cohen to JM, interview on February 8, 2002
Page 210 "'Nader added heft," Howard Learner to JM, interview on February 13, 2002
Page 210 "At various times," *Washington Post Magazine*, May 23, 1982
Page 210 "'gross inequality of," *Ralph Nader Reader*, p. 438
Page 210 "During the Reagan," *New York Times*, July 30, 1990
Page 210 "Under Nader's ownership," Deborah Heisler to JM, interview on June 13, 2002
Page 210 "Nader's LPTV," *New York Times*, July 30, 1990
Page 211 "It was staffed," Deborah Heisler to JM, interview on February 21, 2002
Page 211 "Jason Adkins was," Jason Adkins to JM, interview on February 7, 2002
Page 212 "During a 1984," *The Progressive*, July 1984
Page 212 "'I celebrate Thanksgiving," *New York Times*, November 18, 1981
Page 213 "Beginning in 1966," Ken Eisenstein to JM, interview on February 7, 2002
Page 213 "avoid Fiats and Hondas," *Washington Post Magazine*, May 23, 1982
Page 213 "'How many of," *Esquire*, December 1983
Page 213 "'When things were," Ken Eisenstein to JM, interview on February 6, 2002
Page 213 "On June 11," *New York Times*, June 2, 1985
Page 213 "He was also," Ken Eisenstein to JM, interview on February 7, 2002
Page 213 "Other corporate venues," Randy Poe to JM, interview on February 8, 2002
Page 214 "One time Nader," Ken Eisenstein to JM, interview on February 7, 2002
Page 214 "Bell's Palsy," *Washington Post*, November 19, 1988
Page 214 Details about Bell's Palsy drawn from multiple sources including mayohealth.com
Page 214 "In his case," *Washington Post Magazine*, July 23, 1989
Page 214 "He took to," *Fortune*, May 22, 1989
Page 214 "A memorial service," Michael Pertschuk to JM, interview on August 20, 2001
Page 215 "Shaf's death was," widely held impression, including Joe Tom Easley to JM, interview on June 2, 2001
Page 215 "For three months," Teresa Celsi, *Ralph Nader: The Consumer Revolution*, p. 88

Chapter 16

Page 216 "When Shaf first," *Fortune*, May 22, 1989
Page 216 "It is fair," widely held impression including Fred Baron, trial lawyer, to JM, interview on November 19, 2001
Page 216 "From 1996 on," Carlton Carl, spokesman for ATLA, to JM, interview on November 5, 2001
Page 217 "ardent supporters uneasy," For example, James Fallows to JM, interview on June 14, 2001
Page 217 "In 1982, Nader," Anthony Roisman to JM, interview on December 5, 2001
Page 217 "One of TLPJ's," Arthur Bryant to JM, interview on January 10, 2002
Page 218 "During the mid-1980s," Joanne Doroshow, who, during the 1980s was a staff attorney with the Center for the Study of Responsive Law, to JM, interview on November 10, 2001
Page 218 "'the least corruptible," *New York Times*, September 21, 1990
Page 218 "'He wanted to keep," J. D. Lee to JM, interview on November 19, 2001
Page 218 "'tort deform," Victor Schwartz to JM, interview on September 18, 2001
Page 218 Characterization of tort reform as a business-driven but populist movement drawn from multiple sources including Mike Hotra to JM, interview on November 5, 2001
Page 218 "Advocates of tort," Philip Howard, lawyer and tort reform advocate, to JM, interview on February 8, 2002
Page 218 "Tort reform is," Mike Hotra to JM, interview on November 5, 2001
Page 218 "Joint-and-several," Marty Connor to JM, interview on February 19, 2002
Page 219 "Forum shopping," Mike Hotra to JM, interview on November 5, 2001
Page 219 "It was his practice," Joanne Doroshow to JM, interview on November 10, 2001
Page 219 "Victor Schwartz," *American Spectator*, September 1990
Page 220 "'He was extremely," Victor Schwartz to JM, interview on September 18, 2001
Page 220 "Maryland capped punitive," *Washington Post*, February 18, 1987

Page 220 "Nearly forty states," Marty Connor to JM, interview on February 19, 2002
Page 220 "'We won a," Ralph Nader to JM, interview on February 1, 2002
Page 220 "always against Nader's objection," Bill Fry, trial lawyer, to JM, interview on November 5, 2001
Page 220 "Nader even fought," Victor Schwartz to JM, interview on September 18, 2001
Page 220 "'so much for a hand," Ralph Nader to JM, interview on February 1, 2002
Page 220 "In a 1988 article," Reprinted in the *Ralph Nader Reader*, p. 283–300
Page 221 "'It is so inconsistent," Mike Hotra to JM, interview on November 5, 2001
Page 221 "plaintiff's bar tithe," *American Spectator*, September 1990
Page 221 "*Forbes* magazine tried," *Forbes*, October 29, 1990
Page 221 "Over the years," Gary Sellers to JM, interview on March 6, 2002
Page 222 "At Berkeley, victims'," Laura Nader to JM, interview on February 22, 2002
Page 223 "He even quoted," Joanne Doroshow to JM, interview on November 10, 2001
Page 223 "'deep pockets' initiative," *San Francisco Chronicle*, August 8, 1988
Page 223 "Prop 103 called," Robert Hunter, who worked with Nader on Prop 103, to JM, interview on November 26, 2001
Page 223 Harvey Rosenfield description from *Los Angeles Times*, December 3, 1988
Page 223 " exorbitant auto insurance," *San Francisco Chronicle*, August 8, 1988
Page 224 "Prop 104 was anathema," Joanne Doroshow to JM, interview on November 10, 2001
Page 224 "He traveled all," *Los Angeles Times*, November 2, 1988
Page 224 "truck stop," Harvey Rosenfield to JM, interview on December 18, 2001
Page 224 "'high on the narcotic," *Los Angeles Times*, November 2, 1988
Page 225 "As the battle," *Washington Post Magazine*, July 23, 1989
Page 225 "Voter Revolt supporters," Harvey Rosenfield to JM, interview on December 18, 2001
Page 225 "Nader's proposal won," *Washington Post Magazine*, July 23, 1989
Page 225 "Between 1989 and," *Denver Post*, June 15, 2001
Page 225 "a paltry $2.9 million," Harvey Rosenfeld to JM, interview on December 18, 2001
Page 225 "Nader-is-back stories," for example, *Fortune*, May 22, 1989

Chapter 17

Page 226 "'invasion from Mars,'" *New York Times Magazine*, January 18, 1976
Page 226 "'There was an," Ralph Nader to JM, interview on February 1, 2002
Page 226 "'George Ronald Clinton," *New York Times Magazine*, October 20, 1996
Page 226 "'He was in," Ralph Nader to JM, interview on February 1, 2002
Page 227 "'The vice president," Ralph Nader, *Crashing the Party*, p. 52
Page 227 "In 1997 Peter DeFazio," ibid., p. 33
Page 227 "'protective imitation,'" ibid., p. 44
Page 227 "He was fond," *Detroit News*, July 4, 1996
Page 227 "As an undergrad," Ralph Nader during Green Party fund-raiser in New York City on January 31, 2002
Page 228 "Nader became increasingly convinced," widely held impression including Michael Pertschuk to JM, interview on August 20, 2001
Page 228 "did not necessarily expect to win," Ralph Nader to JM, interview on February 1, 2002
Page 228 "'What he saw," Marcus Raskin to JM, interview on July 11, 2001
Page 228 "'He felt that," Gary Sellers to JM, interview on November 6, 2001
Page 229 "'I'm not a politician," *Nation*, December 23, 1991
Page 229 "toolbox for Democracy," *Washington Post*, February 16, 1992
Page 229 "none-of-the-above line," Anthony Roisman to JM, interview on July 26, 2001
Page 229 "Nader appreciated the," Ralph Nader, *Crashing the Party*, p. 39
Page 229 "He received 6,311 votes," ibid., p. 43
Page 229 "Around the time," ibid., p. 45
Page 229 "ballot in twenty-one states," *New York Times Magazine*, October 20, 1996
Page 229 "'You remember when," *Nation*, January 8–15, 1996
Page 229 "register as a Green," *Nation* , July 8, 1996
Page 229 "'stood for president,'" Winona LaDuke to JM, interview on March 6, 2002
Page 229 "polling 8 percent," *Nation*, July 8, 1996
Page 230 "Nader received 580,627," *New York Times*, November 9, 1996
Page 230 "He even recycled," *Rolling Stone*, August 23, 1979
Page 231 "Nader formally announced," *Content*, February 21, 2001
Page 231 "extremely late," Carolyn Danckaert to JM, interview on December 11, 2001
Page 231 Impression that few former employees were willing to join Nader's 2231, campaign based on multiple interviews including Joan Claybrook to JM, interview on January 22, 2002

Page 231 "'You've got to be," Phil Donahue to JM, interview on November 15, 2001
Page 231 Theresa Amato description based on Theresa Amato to JM, interview on November 29, 2001
Page 232 "It made sense," Ralph Nader to JM, interview on February 1, 2002
Page 232 "'I told him," Roger Hickey to JM, interview on November 27, 2001
Page 232 "David Halberstam," Ralph Nader, *Crashing the Party*, p. 72
Page 232 "raised more than $8 million," Theresa Amato to JM, interview on November 29, 2001
Page 232 "North Carolina, for," greens.org
Page 232 "'Every state has," Theresa Amato to JM, interview on November 29, 2001
Page 232 "Brennan Center," Elizabeth Daniel to JM, interview on May 8, 2002
Page 233 "The five states," Todd Main, field director of Nader 2000, to JM, interview on December 11, 2001
Page 233 "'Ross Perot," Elizabeth Daniel to JM, interview on May 8, 2002
Page 233 "'It's an incredible," Elizabeth Daniel to JM, interview on December 18, 2001
Page 233 "In terms of reaching," widely held impression including Theresa Amato to JM, interview on November 29, 2001
Page 233 "Candidates were required," Ralph Nader, *Crashing the Party*, p. 59
Page 233 "Many suspected that," widely held impression including Jamin Raskin to JM, interview on January 10, 2002
Page 233 "But for the 1988," Ralph Nader, *Crashing the Party*, p. 223
Page 233 "Paul Kirk and Frank Fahrenkopf," George Farah, advance man for Nader 2000, to JM, interview on February 1, 2002
Page 234 "Nader filed a lawsuit," Jamin Raskin to JM, interview on January 10, 2002
Page 234 "'It was on," Theresa Amato to JM, interview on November 29, 2001
Page 234 "a dozen states," Ralph Nader to JM, interview on July 11, 2002
Page 234 "one in seven," *Nation*, December 20, 1999
Page 234 "The fifty-state tour," widely held impression including Dean Myerson to JM, interview on December 19, 2001
Page 234 "In Boston he," Ralph Nader, *Crashing the Party*, p. 80
Page 234 "In Birmingham, Alabama," ibid., p. 93
Page 234 "Nader visited Alaska," ibid., p. 130
Page 234 "In Hawaii, Nader," Tarek Milleron to JM, interview on March 2, 2002
Page 234 "Nader's civics buttons," Nader 2000, campaign press release, September 8, 2000
Page 235 "'Do you think," *People*, November 27, 2000
Page 235 "Hampton Inns," Theresa Amato to JM, interview on November 29, 2001
Page 235 "'He's got so," Tarek Milleron to JM, interview on March 2, 2002
Page 235 "Late in June," Ralph Nader to JM, interview on February 1, 2002
Page 235 "The Green Party confab," *Progressive*, August 2000
Page 235 "The hotel was chosen," Dean Myerson to JM, interview on December 19, 2001
Page 235 "beat tom-tom," *Progressive*, August 2000
Page 235 "'twinkling,'" Nancy Allen, Green Party spokesperson, to JM, interview on December 17, 2001
Page 235 Description of Green movement drawn from a variety of sources including nebraskagreens.org
Page 236 "abolition of the U.S. Senate," *National Journal*, January 6, 2001
Page 236 "Nader refused," Dean Myerson to JM, interview on December 19, 2001
Page 236 "In 2000, once again," Nancy Allen to JM, interview on December 17, 2001
Page 237 "This quite naturally," widely held impression including Tom Adkins to JM, interview on December 7, 2001
Page 237 "At the Denver," Nancy Allen to JM, interview on December 17, 2001
Page 237 "gonadal politics,'" *New York Times*, March 21, 1996
Page 237 Jello Biafra description a composite based on sources including angelfire.com
Page 237 "Stephen Gaskin ran," usatoday.com
Page 238 Winona LaDuke description a composite based on sources including *A Report to the People of the Red Lake Band of the Chippewa Indians*, August 11, 2000,
Page 238 "'He told me," Winona LaDuke to JM, interview on March 6, 2002
Page 238 "LaDonna Harris," *News from Indian Country*, mid-October 2000
Page 238 "'Ralph asked me," Winona LaDuke to JM, interview on March 6, 2002

Chapter 18

Page 240 "On June 30, 2000," *New York Times*, June 30, 2000
Page 240 "Molly Ivins," Ivins's syndicated column, July 15, 2000
Page 240 "Neither did he," Theresa Amato to JM, interview on December 4, 2001

Page 241 "Tim Russert," Ralph Nader, *Crashing the Party*, p. 147
Page 241 "Oprah (bad)," ibid., pp. 175–176
Page 241 "'Hardball with Chris Matthews'," *Content*, February 2001
Page 241 "*Saturday Night Live,*" Ralph Nader, *Crashing the Party*, p. 175
Page 241 "In June 2000," *Ethics in Government Act Report on Behalf of Ralph Nader*, June 14, 2000
Page 241 "Due to privacy," Theresa Amato to JM, interview on November 29, 2001
Page 241 "'I hate to," Tom Adkins to JM, interview on December 7, 2001
Page 241 "worth $3.8 million," *Ethics in Government Act Report on Behalf of Ralph Nader*, June 14, 2000
Page 241 "in both Raytheon," *Salon*, October 18, 2000
Page 242 "$14 million," *Washington Post*, June 18, 2000
Page 242 "Gore family vacation," *Content*, February 2001
Page 242 "He was willing," *Washington Post*, June 18, 2000
Page 242 "'I eat strawberries," *People*, November 27, 2000
Page 242 "On August 2," transcript, Amy Goodman interview of Ralph Nader for Pacifica Radio
Page 243 "For a while," Ralph Nader, *Crashing the Party*, p. 4
Page 243 "'I'm a customer,'" transcript, Amy Goodman interview of Ralph Nader for Pacifica Radio
Page 243 Bill Hillsman description based on Bill Hillsman to JM, interview on November 7, 2001
Page 244 "Nader's 'priceless' ad," Nader 2000, campaign press release, August 15, 2000,
Page 244 "The thirty-second," *George*, August 2000
Page 244 "It certainly caught," Bill Hillsman to JM, interview on November 7, 2001
Page 244 "In response to Selander's," Nader 2000, campaign press release, August 17, 2000
Page 244 "Back came MasterCard," Sharon Gamsin, MasterCard spokesperson, to JM, interview on November 7, 2001
Page 244 "Nader campaign headquarters," *Working for Change*, September 23, 2000
Page 244 "'You're talking about," Bill Hillsman to JM, interview on November 7, 2001
Page 244 "As of press time," Sharon Gamsin to JM, interview on June 25, 2002
Page 244 "On August 5," Gary Sellers to JM, interview on April 24, 2001
Page 244 "'You cannot claim," Gary Sellers to JM, interview on November 6, 2001
Page 245 "Immediately following the," Gary Sellers to JM, interview on April 24, 2001
Page 245 "'The only true," he has said this at least twice, in slightly different formulations; *Playboy*, October 1968 and *Village Voice*, December 20, 2000
Page 245 "A supporter in," Ivins's syndicated column, July 15, 2000,
Page 245 "Or at least," widely held impression including Harrison Wellford to JM, interview on April 24, 2001
Page 245 "The members of NRFG," "An Open Letter to Ralph Nader," from NRFG web site
Page 246 "'Here we saw," Joe Tom Easley to JM, interview on June 2, 2001
Page 246 "'There are always," *St. Louis Post Dispatch*, October 21, 2000,
Page 246 "Recast as a politician," widely held impression including Anne Zill to JM, interview on June 14, 2001
Page 246 "But he always," Tom Adkins to JM, interview on December 7, 2001
Page 246 "'Whatever your issue," *Mother Jones*, July-August 2000
Page 246 "National Stonewall Democrats," National Stonewall Democrats press release, August 15, 2000
Page 246 "Patricia Ireland," *Working for Change*, September 14, 2000
Page 247 "Signatories of Ireland's," *San Francisco Chronicle*, September 18, 2000,
Page 247 "'He's stuck in," *Working for Change*, September 14, 2000
Page 247 "Greg Kafoury," Greg Kafoury to JM, interview on October 6, 2001
Page 248 "'People have to," Mark McDougal to JM, interview on November 2, 2001
Page 248 "McGregor suggested adding," Lowell McGregor to JM, interview on November 26, 2001
Page 248 "The escalating price tag," widely held impression including Theresa Amato to JM, interview on November 29, 2001
Page 248 "around 3,000 tickets," Greg Kafoury to JM, interview on October 6, 2001
Page 248 "'All we needed," Theresa Amato to JM, interview on November 29, 2001
Page 248 "'You know, I," Greg Kafoury to JM, interview on October 6, 2001
Page 248 "'There was so," Mark McDougal to JM, interview on November 2, 2001
Page 248 "By the day," Greg Kafoury to JM, interview on October 6, 2001
Page 249 "People even had," *Working for Change*, November 7, 2000
Page 249 "The event kicked," *Willamette Week*, August 30, 2000
Page 249 "He talked about lessening," Ralph Nader, *Crashing the Party*, p. 190
Page 249 "'one corporate party," *Eugene Register-Guard*, August 26, 2000
Page 249 "crowd of 10,571," votenader.com
Page 249 "'I want you," Greg Kafoury to JM, interview on October 6, 2001
Page 249 "Eddie Vedder," Jason Kafoury to JM, interview on December 4, 2001

Page 250 "Nader helped bankroll," *New York Times*, January 19, 1990
Page 250 "5-watt bulbs," *Working for Change*, June 25, 2000
Page 250 "Shortly after Portland," Tarek Milleron to JM, interview on March 2, 2002
Page 250 "He was also instrumental," Mark McDougal to JM, interview on November 2, 2001
Page 251 "To increase turnout," Theresa Amato to JM, interview on November 29, 2001
Page 251 "GATT and NAFTA," Patrick Woodall of Public Citizen to JM, interview on February 21, 2002
Page 252 "a 20 percent rate," *Working for Change*, October 14, 2000
Page 252 "union membership," Nader 2000, campaign press release, September 8, 2000
Page 252 "$120 billion annually," Nader 2000, campaign press release, October 13, 2000
Page 252 "'They have the keys," NewsMax.com, October 4, 2000
Page 252 "A poll by Fox," votenader.com
Page 252 "Holding a 'death," Corey Eastwood to JM, interview on November 29, 2001
Page 252 "cut by $62 billion," Nader 2000, campaign press release, November 3, 2000,
Page 253 "'It's very simple," Ralph Nader to JM, interview on February 1, 2002
Page 253 "mother is Jewish," Winona LaDuke to JM, interview on March 6, 2002
Page 254 "'political coward,'" *Atlanta Journal Constitution*, November 2, 2000
Page 254 "'environmental poseur,'" open letter from Ralph Nader to Carl Pope, president of the Sierra Club, October 20, 2000
Page 254 "'a major corporation," *Los Angeles Times*, October 31, 2000,
Page 254 "'He knows so much," *Eugene Register Guard*, August 26, 2000
Page 254 "'I keep returning," Michael Pertschuk to JM, interview on August 20, 2001
Page 254 "Gary Sellers, organizer," Gary Sellers to JM, interview on November 6, 2001
Page 255 "To protest Nader's exclusion," Jamin Raskin to JM, interview on January 10, 2002
Page 255 "On October 1," votenader.org
Page 255 "obtain a ticket," Jason Kafoury to JM, interview on December 4, 2001
Page 255 "The debate was," Ralph Nader, *Crashing the Party*, p. 220
Page 255 "Nader held a press," Laura Jones to JM, interview on January 10, 2002
Page 255 "John Vezeris," *Boston Globe*, October 18, 2000
Page 255 "addressed Vezeris in Greek," Ralph Nader to JM, interview on May 23, 2002
Page 255 "'I always prefer," Tarek Milleron to JM, interview on March 2, 2002
Page 256 "After asking Vezeris," Ralph Nader to JM, interview on July 11, 2002
Page 256 "But then he," Laura Jones to JM, interview on January 10, 2002
Page 256 "Meanwhile, back at UMass," Reuters, October 4, 2002
Page 256 "David Letterman," *Newsweek*, October 23, 2000
Page 256 "Two days later," Nader 2000, campaign press release, October 5, 2000
Page 256 "So on October 17," Nader 2000, campaign press release, October 18, 2000
Page 256 "Fearing legal action," Tom Adkins to JM, interview on December 7, 2001

Chapter 19

Page 257 "The highpoint," widely held impression including Phil Donahue to JM, interview on November 15, 2001
Page 257 "Arranging the event," Jason Kafoury to JM, interview on December 4, 2001
Page 257 "Eddie Vedder," Lowell McGregor to JM, interview on November 26, 2001
Page 257 "Still, only nine thousand," Jason Kafoury to JM, interview on December 4, 2001
Page 257 "'What I want," *Salon*, October 14, 2000,
Page 258 "'How surreal is," *Working for Change*, October 14, 2000
Page 258 "Tim Robbins," *Salon*, October 14, 2000
Page 258 "Bill Murray," *Working for Change*, October 14, 2000
Page 258 "When Eddie Vedder," Jason Kafoury to JM, interview on December 4, 2001
Page 258 "'It was extra-dimensional," Ralph Nader to JM, interview on February 1, 2002
Page 258 "Nader's opening line," *Working for Change*, October 14, 2000
Page 258 "audience moods," Ralph Nader to JM, interview on February 1, 2002
Page 259 "'To the 51 percent," *Salon*, October 14, 2000
Page 259 "The Garden rally," Laura Jones to JM, interview on January 10, 2002
Page 259 "a loose band of revelers," Corey Eastwood to JM, interview on November 29, 2001
Page 259 "This annoyed Nader," Tom Adkins to JM, interview on December 7, 2001
Page 259 "'Sexual Healing,'" Laura Jones to JM, interview on January 10, 2002
Page 259 "$250,000," Theresa Amato to JM, interview on December 4, 2001
Page 260 "preaching to the converted," widely held impression including Tom Adkins to JM, interview on December 7, 2001

Page 260 "Given a war chest," Bill Hillsman to JM, interview on November 7, 2001
Page 261 "Americans for Democratic," Mike Alpern to JM, interview on November 1, 2001
Page 261 "surrogates," *U.S. News & World Report*, November 6, 2000
Page 261 "Against this backdrop," *New York Times*, October 31, 2000
Page 261 "'Nader's lifelong lack," *Boston Globe*, July 17, 2000
Page 262 "Gloria Steinem," Ralph Nader, *Crashing the Party*, p. 102
Page 262 "'The only way," Ralph Nader to JM, interview on February 1, 2002
Page 262 "'Five percent of," *Insight on the News*, December 4, 2000
Page 262 "vote swapping," *Slate*, October 24, 2000
Page 263 "'We opposed it," Theresa Amato to JM, interview on November 29, 2001
Page 263 "shutting the sites," Jamin Raskin to JM, interview on January 10, 2002
Page 263 "fifteen thousand people," *National Journal*, January 6, 2001
Page 263 "concentrate on safe states," Bill Hillsman to JM, interview on November 7, 2001
Page 263 "Buchanan concentrated on Connecticut," *New Republic*, October 30, 2000
Page 263 "His reasoning was," Bill Hillsman to JM, interview on November 7, 2001
Page 264 "stop in Florida," Nader 2000, campaign press release, November 4, 2000
Page 264 "Because the Green Party," Myron Cherry to JM, interview on July 11, 2001
Page 264 "Air Force 2," Phil Donahue to JM, interview on November 15, 2001
Page 264 "Myron Cherry," Myron Cherry to JM, interview on July 11, 2001
Page 265 "Toby Moffett," *New York Times*, October 31, 2000
Page 265 "The mood was," widely held impression including Corey Eastwood to JM, interview on November 29, 2001
Page 265 "Jake Lewis, Nader's," Tom Adkins to JM, interview on December 7, 2001
Page 265 "Winona LaDuke," Winona LaDuke to JM, interview on March 6, 2002
Pate 265 "ex-secret service agent," *Progressive*, December 2000,
Page 265 "Exit polls were," Jason Kafoury to JM, interview on December 10, 2001
Page 265 "Halfway across the," *People*, November 27, 2000
Page 265 "Privately, Gore's campaign," *Manchester Guardian*, November 10, 2000
Page 265 "turned down the volume," *People*, November 27, 2000,
Page 265 "Shortly after 8:00 P.M.," *Working for Change*, November 7, 2000
Page 266 "In the wake," *Progressive*, December 2000
Page 266 "Staffers dutifully booed," *New Republic*, November 20, 2000,
Page 266 "'Screw the corporate," *Progressive*, December 2000,
Page 266 "'It was a tough," Corey Eastwood to JM, interview on November 29, 2001
Page 266 "Carolyn Danckaert," Carolyn Danckaert to JM, interview on December 11, 2001
Page 266 "Around 10:00 P.M.," *Working for Change*, November 7, 2000
Page 267 "'Come on Florida!'" *New Republic*, November 20, 2000,
Page 267 "Then people began," Corey Eastwood to JM, interview on November 29, 2001
Page 267 "He flicked on," Ralph Nader to JM, interview on May 23, 2002
Page 267 "On November 8," CNN.com, November 8, 2000
Page 267 "'In the end," *Wall Street Journal*, November 9, 2000
Page 268 "'I will not speak," *Nation*, December 4, 2000
Page 268 "'God spare me," *Manchester Guardian*, November 10, 2002
Page 268 "'otherwise good people," *Time*, November 20, 2000
Page 268 "'He was clearly," Ed Levin to JM, interview on November 20, 2001
Page 269 "called to jury duty," *National Journal*, January 6, 2001

Chapter 20

Page 270 "Following the election-day," news.bbc.co.uk, December 14, 2000
Page 270 "'Let's put it," *National Journal*, January 6, 2001
Page 271 "'No political system," Nader speech attended by JM at the 92nd Street Y, New York City, on January 31, 2002
Page 271 "Nader received 103,000," Ralph Nader, *Crashing the Party*, p. 207
Page 271 "'I haven't gotten," Nader speech attended by JM at Free Library in Philadelphia on February 1, 2002
Page 271 "intensify the contradicitions," widely held impression, including James Fallows to JM, interview on June 14, 2001
Page 271 "'Both parties do," Nader Green Party fund-raiser attended by JM at Angel Orensanz Gallery in New York City on May 16, 2001
Page 271 "'He's trying to," Frederick Condon to JM, interview on December 18, 2001
Page 272 "Exit polls in Florida," *National Journal*, January 6, 2001

Page 272 "Then again, Libertarian," *Boston Globe*, November 12, 2000
Page 272 "he was not viewed," widely held impression, including James Fallows to JM, interview on June 14, 2001
Page 272 "Roger Hickey," Roger Hickey to JM, interview on November 27, 2001
Page 273 "By some estimates," Ralph Nader, *Crashing the Party*, p. 19
Page 273 "Under the Freedom," Michael Tankersly, lawyer with Public Citizen's Litigation Group, to JM, interview on February 1, 2002
Page 273 "'Ralph travels at," Fred Baron to JM, interview on November 19, 2001
Page 273 "decibel levels," Ralf Hotchkiss to JM, interview on April 17, 2001
Page 273 "stop adding MSG," *Time*, December 12, 1969
Page 273 "holiday candles," *New York Times*, December 7, 1973
Page 274 "Basically, Nader observed," Princeton Project 55 details based on multiple sources including Kenly Webster on December 28, 2001
Page 274 "100 college campuses," Wendy Wendlandt, political director, National Association of State PIRGs, e-mail to JM on February 8, 2002
Page 275 "'We feel that," Eric Glitzenstein to JM, interview on December 12, 2001
Page 275 "Bill Taylor," See Ralph Nader and William Taylor, *The Big Boys* (New York: Pantheon, 1986)
Page 275 Joel Seligman to JM, interview on May 21, 2001
Page 275 "'I'm trying to," Ralph Hotchkiss to JM, February 7, 2002
Page 275 "'I'm more future oriented," Ralph Nader to JM, interview on February 1, 2002
Page 276 "'We discussed global," Ralph Nader to JM, interview on July 11, 2002
Page 276 "Shortly after the," *Nation*, February 25, 2002
Page 276 "On January 21, 2002," Ralph Nader press release, January 21, 2002
Page 276 "On another occasion," CNNfn.com, April 7, 2002
Page 277 "difficulty getting much traction," Ralph Nader to JM, interview on May 23, 2002
Page 277 "He made a bold," *Chicago Tribune*, February 17, 2002
Page 278 "'Bush burned down," Nader speech attended by JM at the 92nd Street Y, New York City, on January 31, 2002
Page 278 "'You have a," Jason Kafoury to JM, interview on December 10, 2001
Page 278 "carpal tunnel syndrome," Ralph Nader to JM, interview on May 23, 2002
Page 279 "'We allow people," Theresa Amato to JM, interview on January 22, 2002
Page 279 "start a museum," Ralph Nader to JM, interview on February 1, 2002
Page 279 "Ulysses Grant's casket," Thomas Wathen, *Winsted, Connecticut: The Promise of a Small Town*, p. 10
Page 279 "The building sits," observation of JM, visit to Winsted, Connecticut, on April 22, 2002
Page 279 "For his museum," details about tort museum drawn from a variety of sources, including J. D. Lee, a lawyer involved in planning the museum, to JM, interview on November 19, 2001
Page 279 "Plans for the," Ralph Nader to JM, interview on February 1, 2002
Page 280 "'The biggest lie," Carlton Carl, spokesman for ATLA, to JM, interview on November 5, 2001
Page 280 "appealed to the Supreme Court," Associated Press Online, April 30, 2001
Page 280 "Meanwhile, Nader settled," Ralph Nader to JM, interview on May 23, 2002
Page 280 "'expose the debate commission," Nader speech attended by JM, at Free Library in Philadelphia on February 1, 2002
Page 280 "MasterCard's $15 million," Sharon Gamsin to JM, interview on June 25, 2002
Page 280 "goal for the 2002 midterm," Ralph Nader to JM, interview on May 23, 2002
Page 280 "In 2000, 56," *National Journal*, January 6, 2001
Page 281 "'Green Hammer'" *USA Today*, October 2, 2000
Page 281 "'The Greens will run," Ralph Nader to JM, interview on May 23, 2002
Page 281 "Recently Nader was," Observation of JM, while accompanying Ralph Nader in Philadelphia on February 1, 2002

INDEX

ABOUT THE AUTHOR

Justin Martin is author of the best-selling *Greenspan: The Man Behind Money*. The paperback edition was selected as a notable book for 2001 by the *New York Times Book Review*. He has written work published in *Fortune*, *New York Newsday*, *Newsweek*, *Poets & Writers*, and *Worth*. Martin is a 1987 graduate of Rice University in Houston, Texas. He lives in New York City with his wife and twin sons.